The Journals of the Lewis and Clark Expedition, Volume 5

July 28–November 1, 1805

Sponsored by the Center for
Great Plains Studies,
University of Nebraska-Lincoln
and the American
Philosophical Society, Philadelphia

A Project of the Center for
Great Plains Studies,
University of Nebraska-Lincoln
Gary E. Moulton, Editor
Thomas W. Dunlay, Assistant Editor

The Journals of the Lewis & Clark Expedition

July 28–November 1, 1805

University of Nebraska Press

Lincoln and London

The preparation of this volume was assisted by
grants from the National Endowment for the
Humanities.

The paper in this book meets the minimum
requirements of American National Standard for
Information Sciences–Permanence of Paper for
Printed Library Materials, ANSI z39.48-1984.

Library of Congress Cataloging-in-Publication Data
(Revised for volume 5)

The Journals of the Lewis and Clark Expedition.

Vol. 2-   : Gary E. Moulton, editor; Thomas W.
Dunlay, assistant editor.
Vol.2-   has title: The Journals of the Lewis & Clark
Expedition.
"Sponsored by the Center for Great Plains Studies,
University of Nebraska–Lincoln, and the American
Philosophical Society, Philadelphia"–Vol. 1, t.p.
Includes bibliographies and indexes.
Contents: v. 1. Atlas of the Lewis & Clark
Expedition–v. 2. August 30, 1803-August 24, 1804–
v. 3. August 25, 1804-April 6, 1805–v. 5 July 28-
November 1, 1805.

1. Lewis and Clark Expedition–(1804-1806)–Collected works. 2. West (U.S.)–Description and
travel–To 1848–Collected works. 3. United
States–Exploring expeditions–Collected works.
4. Lewis, Meriwether, 1774-1809. 5. Clark, William,
1770-1838. I. Lewis, Meriwether, 1774-1809.
II. Clark, William, 1770-1838. III. Moulton, Gary E.
IV. Dunlay, Thomas W., 1944- V. University of
Nebraska–Lincoln. Center for Great Plains Studies.
VI. American Philosophical Society. VII. Journals
of the Lewis & Clark Expedition.

F592.4   1983   917.8'042   82-8510
ISBN 0-8032-2861-9 (v. 1)

Contents

Preface

Annotation in this volume again makes use of United States Geological Survey (USGS) maps and other maps not specifically cited in the sources. We continued to use Robert N. Bergantino's set of USGS maps (1° x 2°, 1 : 250,000) on which he has plotted Lewis and Clark's route, camps, and points of astronomical observation through Montana and part of Idaho (from Lemhi Pass to Lost Trail Pass). Bergantino was also kind enough to read the portion of this volume dealing with Montana. We used his maps in checking Lewis and Clark's locale and for obtaining modern place names but did not cite them in notes. For more detail we also used other USGS maps (30° x 60°, 1 : 100,000); these are cited in notes where used and are also listed in "Sources Cited."

Other special maps were also used but not cited in the sources. For the Bitterroot Mountains portion of the expedition we turned to the Salmon National Forest map (Lemhi Pass to Lost Trail Pass), the Bitterroot National Forest map (North Fork, Idaho, to Missoula, Montana), and the Clearwater National Forest map (Lolo Trail). Beyond the Lolo Trail, as the party entered modern Washington and Oregon, we returned to the USGS maps. As the notes indicate, we used extensively the works of Ralph Space and John J. Peebles about the Lolo Trail. Space was also generous enough to read the portion of the volume dealing with the trail and to provide us with useful comments. We have cited the articles Peebles published in *Idaho Yesterdays* in the 1960s. Not specifically cited but carefully consulted was his map of the Lolo Trail, which was published with his article about the crossing. The Idaho Historical Society later published Peebles's three articles (the third being about the expedition's return trip on the Lolo Trail) together as *Lewis and Clark in Idaho*, Idaho Historical Series Number 16 (December 1966). With these essays and map, Space's magnificent book, and the Clearwater National Forest map, one is fully prepared to follow the Corps of Discovery along the Lolo Trail.

Persons who have shown us kindnesses and courtesies in numerous ways deserve our gratitude for their help in carrying this project forward and they have our heartfelt thanks as friends and colleagues. John L. Allen, Donald Jackson,

James P. Ronda, and W. Raymond Wood not only wrote books and essays which serve this endeavor well but also added personal encouragement and professional assistance in many ways. Robert E. Lange of Portland, Oregon, has done leg work for the project at the Oregon Historical Society and answered questions about the Columbia River portion of Lewis and Clark's trip, while Bob Saindon of Helena, Montana, has happily responded to some difficult questions about Montana nomenclature. Michael E. Dotson of Crest Hill, Illinois, reminded us not to overlook clothing as a Lewis and Clark topic. Advice for tracing the Lewis and Clark trail in their locales or places of interest came from Duane Annis (Orofino, Idaho), Stephen D. Beckham (Portland, Oregon), Fred Crandall (Nevada City, California), Ralph H. Rudeen (Olympia, Washington), and James R. Wolf (Bethesda, Maryland).

At the two principal repositories of Lewis and Clark expedition materials we have had the gracious assistance of able curators, librarians, and administrators: Beth Carroll-Horrocks, Edward C. Carter II, Roy E. Goodman, Randolph S. Klein, and Murphy D. Smith (all of the American Philosophical Society, Philadelphia); and Duane R. Sneddeker (Missouri Historical Society, St. Louis). At the project's office we have benefited from the work of a dedicated staff and research assistants: Jennifer Frost, Virginia J. Maca, Vernon Volpe, and Thomas Wakeley. Persons from the Center for Great Plains Studies, University of Nebraska-Lincoln, provided much-appreciated administrative help: Rosalind Carr, Georgia Lowenberg, Frederick C. Luebke, and Mary Lee Yetter. The Lewis and Clark Trail Heritage Foundation has continued to support the project financially as have individual contributors, Robert B. Betts (New York City), Gladys Levis (Alton, Illinois), William P. Sherman (Portland, Oregon), and Lyle S. Woodcock (St. Louis, Missouri). Their gifts lifted our spirits as much as they filled our coffers.

Scholars have been generous in their help in explaining Lewis's and Clark's references to their areas of expertise. The depth of the scientific annotation in this and other volumes owes its existence to such unselfish labors.

ARCHAEOLOGY: Kenneth M. Ames, Portland State University; Warren Caldwell, Orofino, Idaho; R. Lee Lyman, University of Missouri-Columbia. BOTANY: A. T. Harrison, Sandy, Utah. GEOLOGY: Robert N. Bergantino, Montana Bureau of Mines and Geology, Butte. LINGUISTICS: American Indian linguistic data in the notes were collected by Raymond J. DeMallie, Indiana University, and were provided by the following individuals: *Shoshone.* Sven Liljeblad, University of Nevada-Reno. All forms are given in the Numic orthography used by Catherine S. Fowler and Sven Liljeblad, "Northern Paiute," in *Handbook of North American Indians,* vol. 11, *Great Basin,* edited by Warren L. D'Azevado (Washington, D.C.: Smithsonian Institution, 1986). Additional and corroborative Shoshone data were provided by Wick R. Miller, University of Utah, and David Shaul, Indiana University-Purdue University, Fort Wayne. *Flathead.* Sarah G. Thomason, University of Pittsburgh. *Nez Perce/Shahaptian (Sahaptin).* Haruo Aoki, University of California-Berkeley, and Bruce Rigsby, University of Queensland, Australia. For Nez Perce orthography, see Haruo Aoki, *Nez Perce Grammar* (Berkeley: University of California Press, 1970). *Chinook/Chinookan.* Michael Silverstein, with additional data from Robert Moore, both of the University of Chicago. For Chinookan orthography, see Michael Silverstein, "Chinookans of the Lower Columbia," in *Handbook of North American Indians,* vol. 7, *Northwest Coast,* edited by Wayne Suttles (Washington, D.C.: Smithsonian Institution, forthcoming). METEOROLOGY: Jay S. Hobgood, University of Nebraska-Lincoln; ZOOLOGY: Royce E. Ballenger, University of Nebraska-Lincoln (frogs); Thomas O. Holtzer, University of Nebraska-Lincoln (insects); Paul A. Johnsgard, University of Nebraska-Lincoln (birds); John D. Lynch, University of Nebraska-Lincoln (fish).

Custom prescribes and honesty dictates that we state that none of these persons is responsible for any errors that might appear in this edition.

EDITORIAL SYMBOLS AND ABBREVIATIONS

[roman]   Word or phrase supplied or corrected.

[roman?]   Conjectural reading of the original.

[*italics*]   Editor's remarks within a document.

[*Ed: italics*]   Editor's remarks that might be confused with *EC, ML, NB, WC,* or *X*.

[*EC: italics*]   Elliott Coues's emendations or interlineations.

[*ML: italics*]   Meriwether Lewis's emendations or interlineations.

[*NB: italics*]   Nicholas Biddle's emendations or interlineations.

[*WC: italics*]   William Clark's emendations or interlineations.

[*X: italics*]   Emendations or interlineations of the unknown or an unidentified person.

⟨roman⟩   Word or phrase deleted by the writer and restored by the editor.

SPECIAL SYMBOLS OF LEWIS AND CLARK

α ALPHA

$\angle$ Angle

☽   Moon symbol

☞   Pointing hand

★   Star

☉   Sun symbol

♍   Virgo

COMMON ABBREVIATIONS OF LEWIS AND CLARK

Altd., alds.	altitude, altitudes
Apt. T.	apparent time
d.	degree
do.	ditto
h.	hour
id., isd.	island
L. L.	lower limb
L., Larb., Lard., Lbd., or Ld. S.	larboard (or left) side
Lad., Latd.	latitude
Longtd.	longitude
m., mts.	minute, minutes
M. T.	mean time
mes., mls., ms.	miles
obstn.	observation
opsd.	opposite
pd., psd.	passed
pt.	point
qde., quadt., qudt.	quadrant
qtr., qutr.	quarter
s.	second
S., St., Star., Starbd., Stb., or Stbd. S.	starboard (or right) side
sext., sextn., sextt.	sextant
U. L.	upper limb

Note: abbreviations in weather entries are explained at the presentation of the first weather data, following the entry of January 31, 1804.

Meriwether Lewis in Indian tippet (see August 20,
1805). Portrait by Charles B. J. F. de Saint-Mémin, 1807,
courtesy of the New-York Historical Society.

Introduction to Volume 5

Three Forks of Missouri River, Montana, to the Cascades of Columbia River, Washington-Oregon

July 28–November 1, 1805

Lewis and Clark had reached the Three Forks of the Missouri, which they named the Jefferson, the Madison, and the Gallatin, on July 27, 1805. Beyond lay the major obstacle in their journey to the Pacific, the passage over the Rocky Mountains to some navigable tributary of the Columbia River. To make this trip they needed the assistance of the Shoshone Indians, Sacagawea's people, and although they had seen signs indicating the presence of these people, none of them had yet appeared.

What Lewis and Clark hoped to find was the "pyramidal height of land," the point from which, geographical theorists believed, the great rivers of the West flowed toward the Pacific, the Gulf of Mexico, and the Gulf of California. It would be, in 1805, the closest thing still possible to the Northwest Passage that so many mariners had yearned and searched for, that James Cook had sought less than thirty years before, and that Alexander Mackenzie had failed to find in the previous decade but had thought might exist somewhere in the continent. The information supplied by the Mandans and Hidatsas suggested there might yet be an easy portage to the Columbia headwaters.

The captains decided to proceed up the Jefferson, the westernmost fork, with Lewis going ahead with a few men to search for the Shoshones. Clark, unable to do much walking because of illness and a bad boil on his ankle, would command the main party in the canoes. The passage of the canoes became increasingly difficult as the streams became more shallow and unnavigable because of rapids. Much of the time the men had to draw the canoes along by hand, wading in the water. The party moved on up the Jefferson and then its main tributary, the Beaverhead. Lewis proceeded ahead, past the forks of the Jefferson and such landmarks as Beaverhead Rock. He left a message for Clark to take the Beaverhead River instead of the west fork, which they named Wisdom River (today's Big Hole River), but a beaver chewed down the pole on which he left the message and Clark took the wrong fork, causing another day's delay.

Lewis was amazed that the rivers penetrated so far into the mountains while still being navigable, but he knew that this situation would not long continue. On August 10 he reached the forks of the Beaverhead River and followed the western fork into the valley the captains later called "Shoshone Cove." The next day, following an Indian trail, the advance party came upon a Shoshone on horseback. Lewis tried to convince him by signs that they were friendly, but the Indian evidently feared they were Blackfeet raiders and fled.

On August 12 Lewis and his three men continued following Indian paths up later Trail Creek. At the head of that stream they reached what they considered the source of the "heretofore deemed endless Missouri." A short distance beyond was the ridge of the Continental Divide. From this vantage point Lewis could look west and and see further ranges of mountains—proof that the portage to the waters of the Columbia would not be as easy as he had hoped. His immediate problem, however, remained that of making friendly contact with the Shoshones.

Lewis's party had crossed Lemhi Pass into Idaho, the first U.S. citizens to traverse the Continental Divide. On August 13 they continued down into the valley of the Lemhi River, still following the Indian trail. Once again they encountered some Indians, who fled at their approach. Finally they found a woman and two girls who did not see them until they were quite close. One of the girls fled, but the woman and the other girl apparently thought it was too late to run and sat waiting for the strangers to kill them. Lewis took the woman's hand, repeating the word "*ta-ba-bone*," which he evidently obtained from Sacagawea and which he thought meant "white man." He rolled up his sleeve to show his white skin and gave the two Shoshones presents. Somehow he calmed them and, through George Drouillard's sign language, persuaded them to call back the girl who had fled before she could raise an alarm in the main Shoshone camp.

Through these three Shoshones Lewis was able to make contact with their people who were camped on the Lemhi River. The chief, Cameahwait, seemed friendly, but his people were still afraid that the strangers were in league with the Blackfeet and would betray them into the hands of their enemies. Lewis, try-ing to persuade them to go with him to meet Clark's party on the Beaverhead River, feared that they would take alarm and disperse into the mountains, where he knew that he would never find them, and that his command would be left stranded in the mountains with winter coming on. To prevent this he used every form of persuasion he could think of, including promises that white traders would follow him and would provide the Shoshones with trade goods, such as guns to use against their enemies. He gave the chief his own gun, saying that Cameahwait could shoot him if he proved unfaithful. Recovering a message he himself had left at the forks of the Beaverhead for Clark, he stalled for time, saying it was a message from Clark that the main party would soon be there. These means, along with stories about a man with black skin and another with red hair—wonders that greatly intrigued the Indians—persuaded them to wait at the forks until Clark's party arrived on August 17. Such was the captains' relief that they called the campsite at the forks of the Beaverhead "Camp Fortunate."

Geographical information obtained from the Shoshones was not encouraging. A reconnaissance by Clark confirmed that the principal streams in the vicinity, though they did flow toward the Columbia, were unnavigable because of rapids. The only alternative was to obtain horses from the Shoshones and cross the mountains by land. Fortunately, they secured the services of an Indian they called "Old Toby," who knew of a route over the ranges. The latter part of August and much of September would be consumed by the overland trek, which would take them back into Montana, then back to Idaho, and would include a journey over the rugged Lolo Trail. Along the way they met the Flathead Indians, another tribe who had never seen white men.

The trip over the Bitterroot Mountains via the Lolo Trail was perhaps the severest test of the whole expedition. Winter was already beginning in the high country in September, and the party would struggle through deepening snow. Lack of game forced them to kill and eat some of their horses. Pack animals slipped and fell down steep mountainsides. Old Toby misled them at one point, costing even more time. Finally the captains decided to adopt their old procedure of sending one of the officers ahead with a small party to find open country and make contact with friendly Indians. Accordingly, Clark set out with six men on September 18 and two days later reached Weippe Prairie, an open area in west-central Idaho, where he was the first white man to meet the Nez Perce Indians. The long and difficult trip from mountain pass to meadows dashed all hope of a short portage across the Rocky Mountains and ended dreams of an easy passage to the Orient.

The Indians offered the party roots to eat, but the food proved a mixed blessing, for it caused indigestion and diarrhea among most of the Corps' men. In spite of their suffering they established a camp on the Clearwater River and began building dugout canoes for the trip to the Pacific. On October 7 they were ready to start out, leaving their horses with the Nez Perces to await their return.

The Clearwater flows into the Snake and the Snake into the Columbia. Following these streams, the Corps passed out of the mountains down to the Great Columbian Plain. The party had traveled through a variety of ecosystems previously unknown to Anglo-Americans. From the Great Plains, semi-arid and largely treeless yet teeming with game, they had entered the Rocky Mountains, the first English-speaking whites to do so with the exception of Alexander Mackenzie's Canadian party to the north of a few years earlier. In the mountains they found a region heavily wooded in many places, where the game necessary for sustenance was scarce and the natives often lived on the edge of starvation. Even so, they encountered unfamiliar species at every turn. They saw the birds that would bear the captains' names, Lewis's woodpecker and Clark's nutcracker. They were the first whites on record to examine the hide and horns of the mountain goat, and Clark caught a distant sight of one, although the party would never obtain a full specimen. In traversing the mountains they saw new trees such as grand fir and lodgepole pine. On the western side of the mountains they found the camas root, a vital element in the diet of tribes like the Nez Perces. Their own diet shifted drastically as they passed from the abundance of buffalo and elk on the plains to the scarcity of the mountains. They supplemented the increasingly scarce deer with roots and with the flesh of their own horses. The changes sometimes had drastic effects on their health.

Coming down to the Columbian Plain, they again entered a new world, barren of trees like the Great Plains but also barren of game. They shifted from an area inhabited by horseback tribes who hunted on the plains east of the mountains to tribes who traveled by canoe and subsisted on salmon and roots. They were able to observe the end of the great salmon run on the Columbia, the numbers of which Clark found "incrediable to say." The steelhead trout appeared near the falls of the Columbia. Clark thought he saw a sea otter, but this mammal never leaves salt water and the creature sighted was probably the harbor seal, another species new to Anglo-Americans.

The captains had expected to find rapids and falls on the Columbia, and they did. They reached the Celilo, or Great, Falls on October 22, and beyond them lay the Cascades, passing through the mountain range of the same name. They portaged some of these obstacles and, to save time, ran through some others, lowering the canoes with elkskin ropes. Beyond the Cascades lay the final run to the Pacific Coast, which they had come so far to reach.

The Journals of the Lewis and Clark Expedition, Volume 5

July 28–November 1, 1805

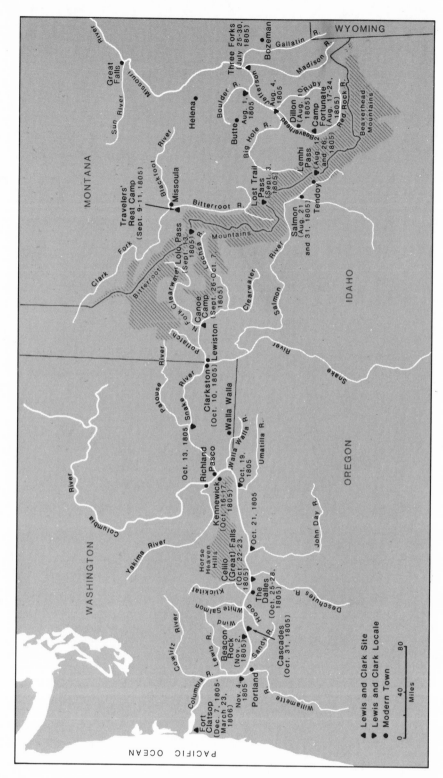

The Expedition's Route, July 28–November 1, 1805

Chapter Eighteen

From Three Forks to Beaverhead Rock

July 28–August 10, 1805

[Lewis]   *Sunday July 28th 1805.*

My friend Capt. Clark was very sick all last night but feels himself somewhat better this morning since his medicine has opperated.[1] I dispatched two men early this morning up the S. E. Fork to examine the river; and permitted sundry others to hunt in the neighbourhood of this place. Both Capt. C. and myself corrisponded in opinon with rispect to the impropriety of calling either of these streams the Missouri and accordingly agreed to name them after the President of the United States and the Secretaries of the Treasury and state having previously named one river in honour of the Secretaries of War and Navy. In pursuance of this resolution we called the S. W. fork, that which we meant to ascend, Jefferson's River in honor of ⟨that illustrious personage⟩ Thomas Jefferson. [*NB?: the author of our enterprise.*][2]   the Middle fork we called Madison's River in honor of James Madison, and the S. E. Fork we called Gallitin's River in honor of Albert Gallitin.[3]   the two first are 90 yards wide and the last is 70 yards.   all of them run with great valocity and thow out large bodies of water. Gallitin's River is reather more rapid than either of the others, is not quite as deep but from all appearances may be navigated to a considerable distance. Capt. C. who came down Madison's river yesterday and has also seen Jefferson's some distance thinks Madison's reather the most do much walking because of illness and a bad boil on his ankle, would command rapid, but it is not as much so by any means as Gallitin's. the beds of all these streams are formed of smooth pebble and gravel,[4] and their waters perfectly transparent; in short they are three noble streams. there is timber enough here to support an establishment,[5] provided it be erected with brick or stone either of which would be much cheaper than wood as all the materials for such a work are immediately at the spot. there are several small sand-bars along the shores at no great distance of very pure sand and the earth appears as if it would make good brick.[6] I had all our baggage spread out to dry this morning; and the day proving warm, I had a small bower or booth erected for the comfort of Capt. C. our leather lodge when exposed to the sun is excessively hot. I observe large quantities of the sand rush in these bottoms which grow in many places as high as a man's breast and stand as thick as the stalks of wheat usually do. this affords one of the best winter pastures on earth for horses or cows, and of course will be much in favour of an establishment should it ever be thought necessary to fix one at this place. the grass is also luxouriant and would afford a fine swarth of hay at this time in parsels of ma[n]y acres together.[7] all those who are not hunting altho' much fatiegued are busily engaged in dressing their skins, making mockersons lexing [leg-gings] &c to make themselves comfortable. the Musquetoes are more than usually troublesome, the knats are not as much so.[8] in the evening about 4 O'Ck the wind blew hard from South West and after some little time brought on a Cloud attended with thunder and Lightning from which we had a fine refreshing shower which cooled the air considerably; the showers continued with short intervals untill after dark. in the eve-ning the hunters all returned they had killed 8 deer and 2 Elk. some of the deer wer in excellent order. those whome I had sent up Gallitin's river reported that after it passed the point to which I had seen it yester-day that it turned more to the East to a considerable distance or as far as they could discover the opening of the Mountains formed by it's valley which was many miles. the bottoms were tolerably wide but not as much so as at or near it's mouth. it's current is rappid and the stream much divided with islands but is sufficiently deep for canoe navigation. Our present camp is precisely on the spot that the Snake Indians were encamped at the time the Minnetares of the Knife R. first came in sight of them five years since. from hence they retreated about three miles up Jeffersons river and concealed themselves in the woods, the Minnetares pursued, attacked them, killed 4 men 4 women a number of boys, and mad prisoners of all the females and four boys, *Sah-cah-gar-we-ah* or Indian woman was one of the female prisoners taken at that time; tho' I cannot discover that she shews any immotion of sorrow in recollecting this event, or of joy in being again restored to her native country; if she has enough to eat and a few trinkets to wear I beleive she would be perfectly content anywhere.—

Point of observation No. 39.

At our encampment on Camp Island, near the junction of the three forks of the Missouri.

Observed Equal Altitudes of ☉ with Sextant.

	h	m	s		h	m	s		
A. M.	8	42	10	P. M.	4	21	46	accurate ⎫	Altd. at the
"		43	42	"		23	21	doubtfull ⎬	time of Observtn.
"		45	15	lost by Clouds				⎭	72° 8' 15"

Observed Meridian Altitude of ☉'s L. L. with Octant by the back observation—58° 35'—"

Latitude deduced from this observation 45° 24' 54"

[Clark]   *July 28th Sunday 1805*

I was verry unwell all night, Something better this morning, a very worm day untill 4 oClock when the wind rose & blew hard from the S W. and was Cloudy, The Thermometr. Stood at 90° above o in the evening a heavy thunder Shower from the S W. which continud at intervales untill after dark, Several deer killed to day   men all employed dressing Skins for Clothes & Mockersons, two men went up the East fork & reports that it is nearly the Size of the N. fork, verry rapid & has maney Islands. Our present Camp is the prosise Spot the Snake Indians were Camped at the time the Minetarries came in Sight, attacked & killed 4 men 4 women & a number of boys, & made prisoners of all the females & 4 boys.

1. See July 26, 1805, and Chuinard (OOMD), 302–4.

2. It may have been Biddle who also marked through the preceding passage, "that illustrious personage," both in pencil.

3. The rivers still retain the names applied by Lewis and Clark. See July 27, 1805, concerning names of the three forks.

4. These rivers all have steep gradients and they and their tributaries head in the mountains where there is an abundant source of rock. The gravel beds of these streams are a consequence of these gradients and the nearness of the source of rock.

5. Pierre Ménard and Andrew Henry of the Missouri Fur Company built a post at the Three Forks in 1810, either at Lewis's recommended site between the Madison and the Gallatin or, more likely, near the Corps of Discovery's campsite on the east bank of the Jefferson. Almost certainly it was not of brick or stone. The post proved impossible to maintain because of Blackfeet hostility. John Potts was killed nearby in 1808 while trapping with John Colter, and George Drouillard also died in the vicinity at the hands of the Blackfeet in 1810, while working for the Missouri Fur Company. In the same area John Colter had a series of narrow escapes from the Blackfeet, including his famous naked run from the Jefferson to the Madison on the occasion of Potts's death. Appleman (LC), 328–32; Oglesby, 93–96; James, 29–48; Harris; *Atlas* map 65.

6. The Three Forks valley is underlain by Tertiary continental deposits. Some of these deposits contain excellent clay for making pottery or brick.

7. The sandrush, scouring rush, *Equisetum hyemale* L. Sandrush refers to the habit of this plant of growing vigorously on river floodplains when periodic floods deposit sand on top of the plants, and due to their rhizomatous habit, grow and reproduce abundantly as described. Hitchcock et al., 1:41. The grass is probably a mixture of native grasses, sedges, and rushes commonly found growing in the wet meadows adjacent to the river floodplain. Perhaps it was Biddle who drew a red vertical line through the first part of this passage.

8. The mosquitoes are *Aedes vexans* and the gnats are probably the buffalo gnat, *Simulium* sp.

[Lewis]   *Monday July 29th 1805.*

This morning some of the hunters turned out and returned in a few hours with four fat bucks, the venison is now very fine   we have killed no mule deer since we lay here, they are all of the longtailed red deer which appear qu[i]te as large as those of the United States.[1]   the hunters brought in a living young sandhill crain;[2] it has nearly obtained it's growth but cannot fly; they had pursued it and caught it in the meadows.   it's colour is precisely that of the red deer.   we see a number of the old or full grown crains of this species feeding in these meadows.   this young animal is very ferce and strikes a severe blow with his beak; after amusing myself with it I had it set at liberty and it moved off apparently much pleased with being releived from his captivity.   the men have been busily engaged all day in dising [dressing?] skins and making them into various garments all are leather dressers and taylors.   we see a great abundance of fish in the stream some of which we take to be trout[3] but they will not bite at any bate we can offer them.   the King fisher[4] is common on the river since we have left the falls of the Missouri.   we have not seen the summer duck[5] since we left that place, nor do I beleive that it is an inhabitant of the Rocky mountains.   the Duckanmallard[6] were first seen with their young on the 20th inst. and I forgot to note it; they are now abundant with their young but do not breed in the missouri below the mountains.   the grasshopers and crickets[7] are abundant in the plains as are also the small birds frequently mentioned.   there is also in these plains a large ant[8] with a redish brown body and legs, and a black head and abdomen; they construct little perimids of small gravel in a conic shape, about 10 or 12 inches high without a mixture of sticks and with but little earth. Capt. Clark is much better today, is perfectly clear of fever but still very languid and complains of a general soarness in all his limbs. I prevailed on him to take the barks[9] which he has done and eate tolerably freely of our good venison.

Today I continued my observations. ⊙'s magnetic Azimt.

	Time by Chronometer			Azimuth by Circumferentor	Altitude of ⊙ L. L. with Sextant		
	h	m	s				
A. M.	8	48	9	N. 85° E	73°	—′	—″
	8	53	57	N. 86° E	74	58	15

Observed Equal Altitudes of the Sun with Sextant.

	h	m	s		h	m	s	
A. M.	8	57	5.5	P. M.	4	5	50	Altitude by Sextant
	″	58	41		″	7	24	at the time of Observts.
	9	—	14		″	8	29	77° 4′ 45″

Observed Meridian Altitude of the ⊙'s L. L. with Octant by the back observation 59° 7′—

Latitude deduced from this observation N. 45° 23′ 23.1″
Mean Latitude from 2 Merds. Altds. of ⊙'s L. L. N. 45° 24′ 8.5″
Observed time and Distance of ⊙'s and ☽'s nearest Limbs with Sextant. ⊙ West.

	Time			*Distance*		
	h	m	s			
P. M.	4	14	42	49°	43′	30″
	″	17	24	″	44	—
	″	19	34	″	44	45
	″	21	12	″	45	—
	″	22	9	″	45	54
	″	23	12	″	46	30
	″	24	14	″	46	45
	″	25	18	″	47	—
	″	26	26	″	47	15
	″	27	24	″	47	30

	Time			*Distance*		
	h	m	s			
P. M.	4	45	25	49°	54′	—″
	″	46	37	″	54	45
	″	47	40	″	55	15
	″	48	52	″	55	45
	″	49	47	″	56	15
	″	50	44	″	56	45
	″	51	36	″	57	15
	″	52	36	″	57	45
	″	53	37	″	58	—
	″	54	36	″	58	15

Observed Magnetic Azimuth of the Sun.

	Time by Chronometer			Azimuth by Circumfert	Altitude of ⊙'s L. L. by Sextant		
	h	m	s				
P. M.	5	7	47	S. 72° W.	55°	44′	30″
	5	13	4	S. 73 W.	53	52	45

Observed time and Distance of ☽'s Western limb from α Antares, with Sextant. ★ East.

	Time			Distance		
	h	m	s			
P. M.	8	42	16	68°	56'	—"
"		50	55	"	52	30
"		54	44	"	49	45
"		55	56	"	49	—
"		58	53	"	47	15

	Time			Distance		
	h	m	s			
P. M.	9	1	12	68°	46'	—"
"		3	1	"	45	30
"		4	47	"	45	—
"		6	27	"	44	—
"		8	31	"	13	45

Observed the Azimuth of the Pole Star.

Time by Chronometer		Azimuth by Circumferenter
h	m	
P. M. 9	27 —	N. 13° W.

[Clark]   *July 29 Monday 1805*[10]

A fair morning wind from the North   I feel my Self something better to day, made some Celestial observations took two Merdn. altitudes which gave for Latd. 45° 22′ 34″ N men all dressing Skins &c.

1. The "longtailed red deer" are western white-tailed deer, *Odocoileus virginianus dacotensis,* which are compared to the common, or eastern white-tailed, deer, *O. virginianus.* The mule deer is *O. hemionus.* Burroughs, 124–33; Jones et al., 320–27.

2. Sandhill crane, *Grus canadensis* [AOU, 206]. Perhaps it was Biddle who drew a red vertical line through part of this passage, from "we see" to "his beak."

3. If a trout, it is probably *Salmo clarkii,* cutthroat trout, but the fish may be some kind of mountain sucker, *Catostomus* sp. Lee et al., 105.

4. Belted kingfisher, *Ceryle alcyon* [AOU, 390]. There is a red vertical line though the remainder of this entry, perhaps drawn by Biddle.

5. Wood duck, *Aix sponsa* [AOU, 144]. Lewis was probably mistaken about the bird's range. Burroughs, 191–92.

6. Mallard, *Anas platyrhynchos* [AOU, 132]. Lewis was incorrect about the breeding range of the bird. Ibid., 188–89, 324 n. 3.

7. The grasshoppers and crickets represent too many varieties to be identified with any certainty.

8. Probably the western harvester ant, *Pogonomyrmex occidentalis*. Borror, Delong, & Triplehorn, 674–75.

9. Peruvian bark, or *cinchona*, was a general remedy for fevers. Chuinard (OOMD), 65, 156–57 n. 18.

10. A small symbol after the date appears to represent the sun.

[Lewis]   *Tuesday July 30th 1805.*

Capt. Clark being much better this morning and having completed my observations we reloaded our canoes and set out, ascending Jeffersons river.   Sharbono, his woman two invalleds and myself walked through the bottom on the Lard. side of the river about 4½ miles when we again struck it at the place the woman informed us that she was taken prisoner.[1] here we halted untill Capt. Clark arrived which was not untill after one P. M. the water being strong and the river extreemly crooked.   we dined and again proceeded on; as the river now passed through the woods the invalleds got on board together with Sharbono and the Indian woman; I passed the river and continued my walk on the Stard. side.   saw a vast number of beaver in many large dams which they had maid in various bayoes of the river which are distributed to the distance of three or four miles on this side of the river over an extensive bottom of timbered and meadow lands intermixed.   in order to avoid these bayoes and beaver dams which I found difficult to pass I directed my course to the high plain to the right which I gained after some time with much difficulty and waiding many beaver dams to my waist in mud and water.   I would willingly have joined the canoes but the brush were so thick, the river crooked and bottoms intercepted in such manner by the beaver dams, that I found it uceless to attempt to find them, and therefore proceeded on up the river in order to intersept it where it came near the plain and woult be more collected into one channel.   at length about sunset I arrived at the river only about six miles from my calculation on a direct line from the place I had left the canoes but I thought they were still below me. I found the river was divided where I reached it by an Island and was therefore fearfull that they might pass without my seeing them, and went

down to the lower point of the large island; here I discovered a small Island, close under the shore on which I was; I passed the narrow channel
to the small island and examined the gravly bar along the edge of the
river for the tracks of the men, knowing from the appearance of the river
at this place that if they had passed they would have used the cord on the
side where I was. I saw no tracks and was then fully convinced that they
were below me. I fired my gun and hallooed but counld hear nothing of
them.   by this time it was getting nearly dark and a duck lit on the shore
in about 40 steps of me and I killed it; having now secured my supper I
looked our for a suitable place to amuse myself in combating the musquetoes for the ballance of the evening. I found a parsel of drift wood at
the head of the little Island on which I was and immediately set it on fire
and collected some willow brush to lye on. I cooked my duck which I
found very good and after eating it layed down and should have had a
comfortable nights lodge but for the musquetoes which infested me all
night.   late at night I was awakened by the nois of some animal runing
over the stoney bar on which I lay but did not see it; from the weight with
which it ran I supposed it to be either an Elk or a brown bear.[2]   the latter
are very abundant in this neighbourhood.   the night was cool but I felt
very little inconvenience from it as I had a large fire all night. Capt. Clark
had proceeded on after I seperated from him and encamped on a islad.
only about 2 miles below me[3] but did not hear the report of my gun nor
of my hooping.—I saw some deer and antelopes.[4]

The Courses and distances of July 30th 1805.

N. 70° W.	¼	to a Stard. bend, passing timber on both sides
S. 20° W.	½	to a Stard. bend passing an Island.
S. 80° E.	¼	to a Lard. bend.
S. 50° W.	½	to the lower point of an Island.
South—	½	to a Lard. bend
S. 45° W.	⅛	to a tree in the Lard. bend
N. 45° W.	¼	to the upper point of an island
West—	½	to a Lard. bend opposite an Island
N. 60° W.	⅛	to a channel passing through the Island

South—	¼	to a Lard. bend opposite to an Island, passing severall small Bayous on the Lard. side.
West—	½	to the upper point of an Island passing a Bayou on the Lard. side.
S. 70° W.	¼	to the entrance of a Bayou on Lard. side
West—	1	to the upper point of an Island, passing the upper point of another Island ¼, one at ¾ and two bayous on Lard. side.
S. 60° W.	1	to a high bank in a Stard. bend.
S. 35° W.	¾	to the upper point of a bluff in a Stard. bend opposite to an Island.
S. 45° E.	¾	to a Lard. bend, passing the upr pt. of an Isld. and a bayou Lard.
S. 35° W.	¼	to a Lard. bend opposite an Island.
West—	¼	to a Stard. bend opposite an Isd. having passed another
S. 30° W.	¾	to an Island in a Stard. bend opposite a high plain Stard.
S. 20° W.	1 ¼	to a clift of rocks under a mountain Stard. side having passed an Island.
South—	½	to a point on the Stard. side.
S. 30° W.	½	to a high clift of craiggey rocks on the Stard. opt. 1 Isld.
S. 45° W.	⅛	to a Stard. bend under a Clift.
S. 45° E.	¼	to a Bayou in a Lard. bend passing an Island
S. 60° W.	⅛	to a Bayou in a Stard. bend above an Island
S. 50° E.	¼	to a. Bayou in a Lard. bend, opposite several small Islds.
S. 45° W.	¼	to the mouth of a Bayou in a Lard. bend.
S. 20° W.	¼	to a Bayou in a Lard. bend, passing the upper point of an Isld. on Lard.—
S. 70° W.	¼	to a Stard. bend where the party encamped for the night—

[Clark]   *July 30th Monday 1805*[5]

We Set out 8 oClock and proceeded on 13½ miles up the N. fork   the river verry rapid & Sholey   the Channel entirely Corse gravel[6] ⟨passed the⟩ many Islands and a number of Chanels in different directions thro' the bottom &c.   passed the place the Squar interpretress was taken, one man with his Sholder Strained,[7] 2 with Tumers, we Camped on the Std. Side the evening Cool. Capt Lewis who walkd on Shore did not join me this evening

1. Probably in the vicinity of the town of Three Forks, Gallatin County, Montana. *Atlas* map 65.

2. Black bear, *Ursus americanus.*

3. Clark camped in Jefferson County, Montana, just below a mouth of Philosophy River (present Willow Creek), and about two miles north of the town of Willow Creek. *Atlas* map 65.

4. Pronghorn, *Antilocapra americana.*

5. For Clark's courses, see a note at his entry of July 31, 1805.

6. Although the Jefferson River meanders extensively here through a wide floodplain, its bed is dominantly coarse gravel and cobbles. These are carried downstream from mountain sources during the flood flows of the main river and its tributaries.

7. Perhaps Sergeant Pryor, who suffered repeated injuries of this kind. See above, November 29, 1804.

[Lewis]   *Wednesday July 31st 1805.*

This morning I waited at my camp very impatiently for the arrival of Capt. Clark and party; I observed by my watch that it was 7 A. M. and they had not come in sight. I now became very uneasy and determined to wait until 8 and if they did not arrive by that time to proceed on up the river taking it as a fact that they had passed my camp some miles last evening.   just as I set out to pursue my plan I discovered Charbono walking up shore some distance below me and waited untill arrived   I now learnt that the canoes were behind, they arrived shortly after.   their detention had been caused by the rapidity of the water and the circuitous rout of the river.   they halted and breakfasted after which we all set out again and I continued my walk on the Stard. shore   the river now becomes more collected   the islands tho' numerous ar generally small.   the river continues rapid and is from 90 to 120 yd. wide has a considerable quantity of timber in it's bottoms.   towards evening the bottoms became much narrower and the timber much more scant.   high hills set in close on the Lard. and the plain high waivy or reather broken on the Stard. and approach the river closely for a shot distance vally above 1½ M wd.   About one mile above Capt. Clark's encampment of the last evening the principall entrance of a considerable river discharges itself into Jefferson's river. this stream is a little upwards of 30 yd. wide discharges a large quantity of very clear water it's bed like that of Jefferson's river is pebble and gravel. it takes it's rise in the snowclad mountains between Jefferson's and Madison's Rivers to the S. W. and discharges itself into the former by seven mouths it has some timber in it's bottoms and vas numbers of beaver and Otter.[1] this stream we call River Philosophy.[2] the rock of the clifts this evening is a hard black grannite like that of the clifts of most parts of the river below the limestone clifts at the 3 forks of the Missouri.[3] this evening just before we encamped Drewyer discovered a brown bear enter a small cops of bushes on the Lard. side; we surrounded the place an surched the brush but he had escaped in some manner unperceived but how we could not discover. nothing killed today and our fresh meat is out. when we have a plenty of fresh meat I find it impossible to make the men take any care of it, or use it with the least frugallity. tho' I expect that necessity will shortly teach them this art. the mountiains on both sides of the river at no great distance are very lofty. we have a lame crew just now, two with tumers or bad boils on various parts of them, one with a bad stone bruise, one with his arm accedently dislocated but fortunately well replaced, and a fifth has streigned his back by sliping and falling backwards on the gunwall of the canoe. the latter is Sergt. Gass. it gives him great pain to work in the canoe in his present situation, but he thinks he can walk with convenience, I therefore scelected him as one of the party to accompany me tomorrow, being determined to go in quest of the Snake Indians. I also directed Drewyer and Charbono to hold themselves in readiness. Charbono thinks that his ankle is sufficiently recovered to stand the march but I entertain my doubts of the fact; he is very anxious to accompany me and I therefore indulge him. There is some pine[4] on the hills on both sides of the river opposite to our encampment which is on the Lard. side upon a small island just above a run. the bull rush & Cat-tail flag[5] grow in great abundance in the moist parts of the bottoms the dryer situations are covered with fine grass, tanzy, thistles, onions and flax.[6] the bottom land fertile and of a black rich loam. the uplands poor sterile and of a light yellow clay with a mixture of small smooth pebble and gravel,[7] poducing prickley pears, sedge and the bearded grass in great abundance;[8] this grass is now so dry that it would birn like tinder.— we saw one bighorn[9] today a few antelopes and deer.—

Courses and distances of July 31st 1805.

West—	⅛	to a bayou in a Stard. bend.
South—	1	to a bayou on the Lard. side at the principal entrence of River Philosophy which is 30 yds. wide and discharges itself from hence downwards on Lard. side by five other mouths, and one above.
West—	¾	to the entrance of a bayou in a Stard. bend passing 2 small Islands one on each side.
South—	½	to a Lard. bend opposite 2 Islands.
S. 45° W.	½	to a point on Lard. side passing a bayou Lard. Sd.
West—	½	to a tree in a Stard. bend
South—	⅛	in the Stard. bend.
S. 60° E.	¼	to a prarie above some willows on the Lard. side
S. 25° W.	¼	to the lower point of an Island.
East—	⅛	to the upper entrance of Philosophy River, Lad.
South 20 W	1 ¼	to a Stard. bend passing 2 small Islands.
S. 25° E.	¼	to a Lard. bend.
S. 45° W.	⅛	to a Stard. bend.
South—	¼	to a Lard. bend.
S. 20° W.	¾	in the Lard. bend to a point opposite to an Isld.
West—	½	to a small bayou in a Lard. bend
S. 60 W.	1	to the head of an Island
S. 45° W.	1 ¼	to a clift of the mountain on Lard. side; passing an Island on Stard.
S. 80° W.	½	to the clift of a high hill on Stard. here the clifts put in close on both sides leaving narrow bottoms.—
S. 45° W.	¾	to a low bluff above a Lard. clift in a Lard. bend.
N. 45° W.	1	to a point of rock on the Stard. side, here the hills receede from the river bottoms 1 ½ me. wide

S. 80° W.	¼	to a Lard. bend, an Isld. on Lard. side.
N. 80° W.	1	to a Stard. bend passing an Isld.
S. 60° W.	¾	to a small island in the Stard bend.
South—	⅛	to a tree in a Lard. bend.
S 70° W.	¾	to a Stard. bend passing an Island.
S. 20° W.	1¾	to the foot of a mountain on a Lard. bend
N. 70° W.	¾	to a Stard. bend.
S. 70° W.	½	to some bushes in a Lard. bend, passing the entrance of
Miles	17⅝	a small run on Lard. just above which we encamped on a small Isld. near the Lard. side.—

[Clark]   *July 31st Tuesday 1805*

a fair Morning   Capt Lewis out all night, we arrived at his Camp to brackfast, he was without a blanket, & he killed a Duck whiche Suped on &c.   the river as yesterday Sholey & rapid, passed the lower mouth of a Small river on the Lard.   in the morning & the upper mouth a [*blank*] Miles above, this little river is the one I camped on the 26th & heads in the Snow mountains to[10] the S W. proceeded on verry well and Camped on a Small Island a little above the place I Camped the 25th instant at the mouth of a run on the Lard Side,[11] the bottoms from the Mouth of the river extend to 2½[2] Miles & enter a Short & high hill which is about 1 mile thro' and, the river then passes thro a 2d vallie of about 1½ Miles wide, Some Islands.   below this Knobe the river is Crouded with Islands, we are out of fresh meet, & nothing killed to day   The Mountains on either Side is high & rough   we have two men with toumers and unable to work.

Capt Lewis deturmin to proceed on with three me[n] in Serch of the Snake Indians, tomorrow[12]

1. The otter is *Lutra canadensis*.
2. Willow Creek, which heads in the Tobacco Root Mountains and joins the Jefferson River in Gallatin County, Montana. *Atlas* map 65.
3. The dominant rocks along the river in this area are light gray to yellow-gray limestones of the Mississippian-age Mission Canyon and Lodgepole formations. Smaller exposures of Pennsylvanian-age formations are also present, but there is no granite near the river.

4. Probably limber pine, *Pinus flexilis* James, which is more common in the area than ponderosa pine, *P. ponderosa* Laws. Little (CIH), 56-W, 64-W; Hahn, *P. flexilis* map.

5. The "bull rush" is possibly western bulrush, *Scirpus acutus* Muhl. ex Bigel., or tule, softstem bulrush, *S. validus* Vahl. The common cat-tail is *Typha latifolia* L. Hitchcock et al., 1:370–71, 383, 731; Hahn, *Scirpus* and *Typha* maps. Perhaps it was Biddle who drew a red vertical line through this passage.

6. The grass is again a generic description of vigorously growing meadow grasses along the bottoms. Tansy is *Tanacetum*, but it is rare in this region. Lewis refers to an unknown species with an aromatic and deeply divided leaf similar to tansy, with which he was familiar in the East. See above, June 6, 1805. Hitchcock et al., 5:318–20; Booth & Wright, 286–87. His thistles are either the wavyleaf thistle, *Cirsium undulatum* (Nutt.) Spreng, or the elk thistle, *C. foliosum* (Hook.) DC. The former is generally found in drier upland areas, while the latter is located in moister meadows. Booth & Wright, 261–62. The onion is possibly *Allium acuminatum* Hook., or *A. textile* A. Nels. & Macbr. However these two species are found on dry uplands and not in moister floodplain meadows. Hahn, *Allium* maps; Hitchcock et al., 1:742, 757. Lewis's flax is blue flax, *Linum perenne* L. var. *lewisii* (Pursh) Eat. & Wright. This species was collected by Lewis and orginally named for him by Frederick Pursh (*L. lewisii* Pursh). Hitchcock et al., 3:389; Cutright (LCPN), 173.

7. Along the river bottoms there is sufficient moisture for soil to develop and for a black or dark brown layer of humus or organic-rich material to form near the soil surface. The Tertiary deposits on the uplands and even the terrace deposits slightly elevated above the river, however, are dry and can form only an immature soil. These soils are not sterile, but produce only sparse vegetation because of lack of moisture.

8. Plains prickly pear, *Opuntia polyacantha* Haw. var. *polyacantha,* and thread-leaved sedge, *Carex filifolia* Nutt., or needle leaf sedge, *C. stenophylla* Wahl. The bearded grass refers to needle and thread grass, *Stipa comata* Trin. & Rupr. See July 26, 1805. By describing these species together, Lewis is naming characteristic species of the northern grasslands which extend upward along the Missouri River and into the valleys of the Rocky Mountains. Benson (CUSC), 382–88; Hahn, *Carex* and *Stipa* maps; Küchler, map; Mueggler & Stewart, 10.

9. Bighorn sheep, *Ovis canadensis.*

10. Clark interrupts his narrative at this point to enter course and distance material for July 20–27, 1805, that he has labeled: "Course of the Missouri from the gate to the three forks." Since these are courses for the main party from which he was separated and appear to be substantially the same as Lewis's daily course log (with deletions), and because it covers material in the preceding volume, it is not printed here.

11. The run is probably later Antelope Creek; the camp either in Gallatin or Madison County, Montana, a little downstream from the entrance to Lewis and Clark Caverns State Park, which the captains did not actually visit, and some two miles above where U.S. Highway 287 crosses the Jefferson. *Atlas* map 65.

12. Following this entry is Clark's course and distance table for the period July 27, 30–31, and part of August 1, 1805, that he has labeled: "Course and Distance up the

main North fork of the Missouri." These courses appear to be essentially the same as Lewis's daily log and may have been copied by Clark during a time when he was very ill. We do not repeat the material for July, but place the August 1 courses with the remainder, which Clark carried over to p. 46 of this journal (Codex G), interrupting his entry of August 5, the date at which they appear here. Throughout this part of the journal the narrative and course material is very cut up. We bring some sections together for ease of reading while maintaining the integrity of the document as far as possible.

[Lewis and Clark]   [*Weather, July 1805*][1]

Day of the Month [July]	State of the thermometer at ☉rise	Weather at ☉rise	Wind at ☉rise	State of the Thermometer at 4 P.M.	Weather at 4 P.M.	Wind at 4 P.M.	State of the river raised or fallen	Feet	Inches & Parts
1st	59 a	f	S. W.	74 a	f.	S. W.	r		½
2cd	60 a	f a r	S. W.	78 a	f.	S W			
3rd	58 a[2]	f	S. W	74 a	c a f & r	S W			
4th	52 a	f	S. W.	76 a	f a r	S. W.	f		¼
5th	49 a	f a h & r[3]	S W	72 a	f	S W.	f		½
6th	47 a	c a h r T & L.	S. W.	74 a	f a c	S. W	f		¼
7th	54 a	c. a. f.	S W	77 a	r. a. c.	S W	f		¼
8th	60 a	f	S W.	78 a	f. a. r	S. W.	f		¼
9th	56 a	f	S W	76 a	c. a. r	N. W.	f		¼
10th	52 a	f a. r	S. W.	66 a	f	S. W.			
11th	46 a	f	S W	70 a	f	S. W.			
12th	50 a	f	S. W.	74 a	f	S W	f		¼
13th	42 a	f	S W	76 a	f	S. W.	f		¼
14th	45 a	f	S W	78 a	c. a. r	S. W.			
15th	60 a	f. a. r	S W	76 a	f	S W	f		1½
16th	53 a	f	S W	80 a	f	S W	f		¾
17th	58 a	f	S. W.	81 a	f	S. W	f		1½
18th [4]	60 a	f	S W	84 a	f	S W			
19th	62 a	f	S W	68 a	c a h & r	S. W	f		½
20th	59 a	f a r	S W.	60 a	f	N. W			
21st	60 a	f	N W	67 a	f	N W	f		½
22nd	52 a	f	N W	80 a	f	N. E.			
23rd	54 a	f	S W.	80 a	c.	S W	f		½
24th	60 a	f	S W	90 a	f	S. W.	f		¾
25th	60 a	f	S. W.	86 a	f	S W.	f		½

26th	60 a	f	S W.	82 a	C. a. r.	S W	f	¾
27th	52 a	C	S W	80 a	C. a. r	S. W.	f	¾
28th	49 a	f. a. r	S W	90 a	f	S. W.	f	½
29th	54 a	f. a. r	N.	82 a	f	N. E.	r	½
30th	50 a	f	S. E.	80 a	f	S. E.		
31st	48 a	f	S W.	92 a	f	S. W.		

[*Remarks*][5]

[July]   1st   wind hard during greater part of the day.—

2nd   some rain just before sun rise

3rd   slight rain in the evening.

4th   heavy dew this morning.   slight sprinkle of rain at 2 P. M.[6]

5th   heavy shower of rain and hail last evening at 9 P. M.   some thunder & L[ightning]

6th   wind high all day.[7] A heavy wind from the S. W. attended with rain about the middle of the last night.   about day had a violent thunderstorm attended with Hail and rain.   the Hail Covered the ground and was about the Size of Musquet balls. I have Seen only one black bird[8] killed with the hail, and am astonished that more have not Suffered in a similar manner as they are abundant, and I Should Suppose the hail Sufficiently heavy to kill them.

7th   a Shower at 4 P. M.

8th   I finish taking the hight of the falls of the Missouri[9]

10th   wind hard all day.[10]

11th   wind hard all day

12th   wind violent all day.

13th   Wind violent in the latter part of the day

15th   Set out from our upper camp above the falls[11]

18th   I set out in Search of the Indians[12]

19th   Thunder Storm ½ after 3 P. M.

22nd   overtake Capt Clark[13]

23rd   he sets out again this morning

25th   Snow appears on the mountains ahead.

27th   a considerable fall of rain unattended with Lightning. Capt
       Clark rejoins me [14]
30th   Set out from 3 forks [15]

1. Lewis has weather notes for this month in Codex Fe and Codex P; Clark's are in Codex I. This table follows Codex Fe, with discrepancies noted.

2. Lewis in Codex P and Clark in Codex I have "56."

3. Clark has only "H & r"; Lewis has only "f H & R" in Codex P.

4. For this day Clark notes that the river fell one-half inch.

5. The remarks follow Lewis's marginal remarks in Codices Fe and P. Some of the remarks appear to be in Clark's handwriting. Clark has some marginal remarks in Codex I, other than those he copied from Lewis, which are noted below.

6. Clark in Codex I has, "everything across the portage."

7. The remainder of this entry is from a separate remark in Codices Fe and P.

8. Perhaps the common grackle, *Quiscalus quiscula* [AOU, 511], although other black birds are possible.

9. Clark's remark from Codex I.

10. Clark in Codex I has, "I took 8 men in Search of timber to build 2 canoes."

11. Clark adds, "where we built 2 canoes."

12. Clark's remark from Codex I.

13. Clark in Codex I has, "over taken by the party after being out [*blank*] Days in Search of the Indians."

14. Clark adds, "I join the party at the 3 forks verry Sick."

15. Clark's remark from Codex I.

[Lewis]   *August 1st 1805* [1]

At half after 8 A. M. we halted for breakfast and as had been previously agreed on between Capt. Clark and myself I set out with 3 men in quest of the Snake Indians.   the men I took were the two Interpreters Drewyer and Sharbono and Sergt. Gass who by an accedental fall had so disabled himself that it was with much pain he could work in the canoes tho' he could march with convenience.   the rout we took lay over a rough high range of mountains on the North side of the river. [2]   the rive entered these mountains a few miles above where we left it. [3] Capt Clark recommended this rout to me from a belief that the river as soon as it past the mountains boar to the N. of W. he having a few days before ascended these mountains to a position from which he discovered a large valley passing betwen the mountains and which boar to the N. West.   this how-

24

ever poved to be the inlet of a large creek which discharged itself into the river just above this range of mountans,[4] the river bearing to the S. W. we were therefore thrown several miles out of our rout. as soon as we discovered our mistake we directed our course to the river which we at length gained about 2 P. M. much exhausted by the heat of the day the roughnes of the road and the want of water. the mountains are extreemly bare of timber and our rout lay through the steep valleys exposed to the heat of the sun without shade and scarcely a breath of air; and to add to my fatiegue in this walk of about 11 miles I had taken a doze of glauber salts in the morning in consequence of a slight desentary with which I had been afflicted for several days; being weakened by the disorder and the opperation of the medecine I found myself almost exhausted before we reached the river. I felt my sperits much revived on our near approach to the river at the sight of a herd of Elk of which Drewyer and myself killed two. we then hurried to the river and allayed our thirst. I ordered two of the men to skin the Elk and bring the meat to the river while myself and the other prepared a fire and cooked some of the meat for our dinner. we made a comfortable meal of the Elk and left the ballance of the meat on the bank of the river the party with Capt. Clark. this supply was no doubt very acceptable to them as they had had no fresh meat for near two days except one beaver Game being very scarce and shy. we had seen a few deer and some goats but had not been fortunate enough to kill any of them. after dinner we resumed our march and encamped about 6 m. above on the Stard side of the river.[5]

[Lewis]   *Thursday August 1st 1805.*

This morning we set out early and proceeded on tolerably well untill 8 OC'k. by which time we had arrived within a few miles of a mountain through which the river passes. we halted on the Stard. side and took breakfast. after which or at ½ after 8 A. M. as had been previously concerted betwen Capt. Clark and myself I set out with three men in surch of the Snake Indians or Sosonees. our rout lay over a high range of mountains on the North side of the river. Capt. C. recommended this rout to me no doubt from a beleif that the river as soon as it passed this chain of mountains boar to the N. of W. he having on the 26th ult. ascended these mountains to a position from whence he discoved a large valley passing between the mountains which boar to the N. W. and presumed that the river passed in that direction; this however proved to be the passage of a large creek which discharged itself into the river just above this range of mountains, the river bearing to the S. W. we were therefore thrown several miles out of our rout. as soon as we discovered our error we directed our course to the river which we at length gained about 2 P. M. much exhausted by the heat of the day, the roughness of the road and the want of water. the mountains are extremly bare of timber, and our rout lay through the steep and narrow hollows of the mountains exposed to the intese heat of the midday sun without shade or scarcely a breath of air: to add to my fatiegue in this walk of about 11 miles, I had taken a doze of glauber salts in the morning in consequence of a slight disentary with which I had been afflicted for several days. being weakened by the disorder and the operation of the medicine I found myself almost exhausted before we reached the river. I felt my sperits much revived on our near approach to the river at the sight of a herd of Elk, of which Drewyer and myself soon killed a couple. we then hurryed to the river and allayed our thirst. I ordered two of the men to skin the Elk and bring the meat to the river, while myself and the other prepared a fire and cooked some of the meat for our dinner. we made a comfortable meal on the Elk, and left the ballance of the meat and skins on the bank of the river for Capt. Clark and party. this supply will no doubt be acceptable to them, as they had had no fresh meat when I left them for almost 2 days except one beaver; game being very scarce and shy above the forks. we had seen a few deer and antelopes but had not been fortunate enough to kill any of them. as I passed these mountains I saw a flock of the black or dark brown phesants;[6] the young phesant is almost grown we killed one of them. this bird is fully a third larger than the common phesant of the Atlantic states. it's form is much the same. it is booted nearly to the toes and the male has not the tufts of long black feathers on the sides of the neck which are so conspicuous in those of the Atlantic. their colour is a uniform dark brown with a small mixture of yellow or yelloish brown specks on some of the feathers particularly those of the tail, tho' the extremities of these are perfectly black for about one inch. the eye is nearly black, the iris has a small dash of yellowish brown. the feathers of the tail are reather longer than that of our phesant or pattridge as they are Called in the Eastern States; are the same in number or eighteen and all nearly of the same length, those in the intermediate part being somewhat longest. the flesh of this bird is white and agreeably flavored. I also saw near the top of the mountain among some scattering pine a blue bird[7] about the size of the common robbin. it's action and form is somewhat that of the jay bird and never rests long in any one position but constantly flying or hoping from sprey to sprey. I shot at one of them but missed it. their note is loud and frequently repeated both flying and when at rest and is char âh′, char′âh, char âh′, as nearly as letters can express it. after dinner we resumed our march and my pack felt much lighter than it had done about 2 hours before. we traveled about six miles further and encamped on the stard. bank of the river, making a distance of 17 miles for this day. the Musquetoes were troublesome but I had taken the precaution of bringing my bier.

Shortly after I left Capt. Clark this morning he proceed on and passed through the mountains; they formed tremendious clifts of ragged and nearly perpendicular rocks; the lower part of this rock is of the black grannite before mentioned and the upper part a light coloured freestone.[8] these clifts continue for 9 miles and approach the river very closely on either side. he found the current verry strong. Capt. C. killed a big horn on these clifts which himself and party dined on. after passing this range of mountains he entered this beautifull valley in which we also were it is from 6 to 8 miles wide. the river is crooked and crouded with islands, it's bottoms wide fertile and covered with fine grass from 9 inches to 2 feet high and possesses but a scant proportion of timber, which consists almost entirely of a few narrow leafed cottonwood trees[9] distributed along the verge of the river. in the evening Capt. C. found the Elk I had left him and ascended a short distance above to the entrance of a large creek which falls in on Stard. and encamped opposite to it on the Lard. side.[10] he sent out the two Fieldses to hunt this evening and they killed 5 deer, which with the Elk again gave them a plentifull store of fresh provisions. this large creek we called Field's Creek after

Reubin Fields one our party. on the river about the mountains wich Capt. C. passed today he saw some large cedar trees and some juniper also[11] just at the upper side of the mountain there is a bad rappid here the toe line of our canoe broke in the shoot of the rapids and swung on the rocks and had very nearly overset. a small distance above this rapid a large bold Creek falls in on Lard. side which we called Frazier's Creek after Robt. Frazier.[12] They saw a large brown bear feeding on currants but could not get a shoot at him.

Courses and distances as navigated with the Canoes
on the 1st of August 1805.[13]

N. 30° W.	1	to a point of rocks on the Lard. side, at this place the river passes through perpendicular Clifts.
N. 60° W.	¾	to the upper part of the rocks in a Stard. bend
S. 70° W.	½	to a clift on the Lard. side
S 45° W.	½	to a Stard. bend.
S. 26° W.	1¾	to a bluff on the Stard. side.
South—	½	to a Lard. bend, at this place the river enters a high mountain of steep and ruggid clifts on both sides.
N. 30° W.	1¼	to a Stard. bend under a high clift
N. 80° W.	¼	to a clift of high rocks in a Stard. bend a small bottom on Lard. side.
S. 60° W.	½	to a Lard. bend under a piney hill.
N. 25° W.	¼	to a small Island on the Lard. side
N. 30° E.	¼	to a Stard. bend high clifts on both sides
N. 80° W.	¾	to the entrance of a large creek on Lard. side passing an island and rapid of 6 feet fall; these we called Frazier's falls and Creek after Robert Frazier one of our party. here the river again enters a valley.—
North—	½	to a Stard. bend under a hill.
N. 45° W.	½	to a Lard. bend
N. 70° W.	1½	to the point of an Island passing several smal Islds.
North—	¼	to a Stard. bend.
West—	¾	to the lower point of an Island

N. 45° W.   ¼   to the entrance of a Large creek on Stard. w[h]ich we

   Miles <u>13</u>   called Field's Creek, after Reubin Fields one of our

                    party.—   opposite to which encamped on Lard. side.—

[Clark]   *August 1st Wednesday 1805*

A fine day   Capt. Lewis left me at 8 oClock just below the place I entered a verrey high mountain which jutted its tremedious Clifts on either
Side for 9 Miles, the rocks ragide Some verry dark & other part verry
light rock the light rocks is Sand Stone.[14] The water Swift & very Sholey. I
killed a *Ibix* on which the whole party Dined, after passing through the
Mountain we entered a wide extesive vallie of from 4 to 8 Miles wide
verry leavell a Creek falls in at the Commencement of this Vallie on the
Lard Side, the river widens & spreds into Small Chanels. W[e] encamped
on the Lard Side opposit a large Creek   I sent out Jo: & R fields to hunt
this evening they killed 5 Deer, I saw a large Bear eateing Currents this
evining   The river so rapid that the greatest exertion is required by all to
get the boats on wind S W Murckery at sun rise 50° Ab. o

1. Here begins Lewis's Codex Fa, containing what are apparently the first drafts of entries for August 1–4, 1805, the second drafts being in Codex F. Lewis probably wrote the
first drafts during his separation from the main party on these dates, perhaps in a blank
notebook carried along for the purpose. See the Introduction and Appendix C, vol. 2.

2. Lewis's route appears as a dotted line on *Atlas* map 65.

3. The Bull Mountain in Jefferson County, Montana; the river runs through between
the Bull and Tobacco Root mountains, Jefferson Canyon, in this area. *Atlas* map 65.

4. "R. Fields Creek," for Reubin Field of the party, on *Atlas* map 65, now Boulder
River in Jefferson County.

5. Lewis camped in Jefferson County, somewhere above the present village of Cardwell. *Atlas* map 65.

6. Evidently the first description of the blue grouse, *Dendragapus obscurus* [AOU, 297].
Cutright (LCPN), 177; Burroughs, 215–16. Lewis uses the ruffed grouse, *Bonasa umbellus*
[AOU, 300], for comparison. Perhaps it was Biddle who drew a red vertical line through
this passage from "I saw a flock" to "letters can express it."

7. The first description of the pinyon jay, *Gymnorhinus cyanocephalus* [AOU, 492]. Cutright (LCPN), 177. The American robin, *Turdus migratorius* [AOU, 761], and the blue jay,
Cyanocitta cristata [AOU, 477], are used for comparison.

8. The rocks adjacent to the Jefferson River along Jefferson Canyon are dominantly
light gray to yellow-gray limestone of the Mission Canyon and Lodgepole formations.
There are also some light-to-medium brown sandstones of Pennsylvanian through Cre-

taceous age, and some reddish shales of Pennsylvanian age. Near the upper end of the canyon, dark gray to gray-green sedimentary rocks of Precambrian age crop out on either side of the river. No granite is exposed in the Jefferson Canyon.

9. Narrowleaf cottonwood, *Populus angustifolia* James. Booth & Wright, 22; Little (MWH), 114.

10. Clark camped opposite the mouth of Boulder River, near the present village of Cardwell, Madison County, Montana. *Atlas* map 65.

11. Rocky Mountain juniper or red cedar, *Juniperus scopulorum* Sarg., and common juniper, *J. communis* L. Little (CIH), 30-W; Hahn, *Juniperus* maps.

12. "Frasures Creek," after Robert Frazer of the party, on *Atlas* map 65, now South Boulder Creek, in Madison County, near Cardwell.

13. Lewis evidently obtained these and other courses from Clark after they reunited. Clark's courses for August 1–5 are found at his entry of August 5, 1805.

14. During late Tertiary and early Quaternary time, the Jefferson River cut through this area leaving an imposing, rugged canyon. The exposed rocks are primarily light gray to yellow-gray Mississippian limestones, but sandstones and shales ranging in age from Pennsylvanian through Cretaceous are also present. Dark gray sedimentary rocks of Precambrian age are exposed along the upper portion of the canyon.

[Lewis]   *August 2nd 1805.*

We resumed our march this morning at sunrise   the weather was fair and wind from N. W.   finding that the river still boar to the south I determined to pass it if possible to shorten our rout   this we effected about five miles above our camp of last evening by wading it.[1]   found the current very rappid about 90 yards wide and waist deep   this is the first time that I ever dared to make the attempt to wade the river, tho' there are many places between this and the three forks where I presume it migh be attempted with equal success.   the valley though which our rout of this [day] lay and through which the river winds it's meandering course is a beatifull level plain with but little timber and that on the verge of the river.   the land is tolerably fertile, consisting of a black or dark yellow loam,[2] and covered with grass from 9 Inches to 2 feet high.   the plain ascends gradually on either side of the river to the bases of two ranges of mountains which ly parrallel to the river and which terminate ⟨it's⟩ the width of the vally.   the tops of these mountains were yet partially covered with snow while we in the valley.   were suffocated nearly with the intense heat of the midday sun.   the nights are so could that two blankets are not more than sufficient covering.   we found a great courants, two

30

kinds of which were red, others yellow deep purple and black, also black goosburies and service buries now ripe and in full perfection, we feasted suptuously on our wild fruit particularly the yellow courant and the deep purple servicebury which I found to be excellent the courrant grows very much like the red currant common to the gardens in the atlantic states tho' the leaf is somewhat different and the growth taller. the service burry grows on a smaller bush and differs from ours only in colour and the superior excellence of it's flavor and size, it is of a deep purple.[3] this day we saw an abundance of deer and goats or antelopes and a great number of the tracks of Elk; of the former we killed two. we continued our rout along this valley which is from six to eight Miles wide untill sun set when we encamped for the night on the river bank having traveled about 24 miles.[4] I feel myself perfectly recovered of my indisposition and ⟨have⟩ do not ⟨but little⟩ doubt ⟨but I⟩ being able to pursue my march with equal comfort in the morning.

[Lewis]   *Friday August 2cd 1805.*

We resumed our march this morning at sunrise; the [day] was fair and wind from N. W. finding that the river still boar to the South I determined to pass it if possible in order to shorten our rout; this we effected by wading the river about 5 miles above our encampment of the last evening. we found the current very rapid waist deep and about 90 yd. wide bottom smooth pebble with a small mixture of coarse gravel. this is the first time that I ever dared to wade the river, tho' there are many places between this and the forks where I presume it might be attempted with equal success. The vally allong which we passed today, and through which the river winds it's meandering course is from 6 to 8 miles wide and consists of a beatifull level plain with but little timber and that confined to the verge of the river; the land is tolerably fertile, and is either black or a dark yellow loam, covered with grass from 9 inches to 2 feet high. the plain ascends gradually on either side of the river to the bases of two ranges of high mountains, which lye parallel to the river and prescribe the limits of the plains. the tops of these mountains are yet covered partially with snow, while we in the valley are nearly suffocated with the intense heat of the midday sun; the nights are so cold that two blankets are not more than sufficient covering. soon after passing the river this morning Sergt. Gass lost my tommahawk in the thick brush and we were unable to find it, I regret the loss of this usefull implement, however accedents will happen in the best families, and I consoled myself with the recollection that it was not the only one we had with us. the bones of the buffaloe and their excrement of an old date are to be met with in every part of this valley but we have long since lost all hope of meeting with that animal in these mountains. we met with great quantities of currants to-day, two species of which were red, others yellow, deep perple and black; also black goosberries and serviceberries now ripe and in great perfection. we feasted sumptuously on our wild fruits, particularly the yellow currant and the deep perple serviceberries, which I found to be excellent. the serviceberry grows on a small bush and differs from ours only in colour size and superior excellence of it's flavour. it is somewhat larger than ours.[5] on our way we saw an abundance of deer Antelopes, of the former we killed 2. we also saw many tracks of the Elk and bear. no recent appearance of Indians. the Indians in this part of the country appear to construct their lodges with the willow boughs and brush; they are small of a conic figure and have a small aperture on one side through which they enter. we continued our rout up this valley on the Lard. side of the river untill sunset, at which time we encamped on the Lard. bank of the river having traveled 24 miles. we had brought with us a good stock of venison of which we eat a hearty supper. I feel myself perfectly recovered of my indisposition, and do not doubt being able to pursue my rout tomorrow with the same comfort I have done today.— we saw some very large beaver dams today in the bottoms of the river several of which wer five feet high and overflowed several acres of land; these dams are formed of willow brush mud and gravel and are so closely interwoven that they resist the water perfectly. the base of this work is thick and rises nearly perpendicularly on the lower side while the upper side or that within the dam is gently sloped. the brush appear to be laid in no regular order yet acquires a strength by the irregularity with which they are placed by the beaver that it would puzzle the engenuity of man to give them.

Capt. Clark continued his rout early this morning.   the rapidity of the current was such that his progress was slow, in short it required the utmost exertion of the men to get on, nor could they resist this current by any other means than that of the cord and pole.   in the course of the day they passed some villages of burrowing squirrels,[6] saw a number of beaver dams and the inhabitants of them, many young ducks both of the Duckanmallard and the redheaded fishing duck, gees, several rattle snakes, black woodpeckers, and a large gang of Elk;[7] they found the river much crouded with island both large and small and passed a small creek on Stard. side which we called *birth* Creek.[8] Capt. Clark discovers a tumor rising on the inner side of his ankle this evening which was painfull to him [*NB?: Rec: boils*].   they incamped in a level bottom on the Lard. side.—[9]

Courses and distances travelled by Capt. Clark
August 2cd 1805.

S. 80° W.	¾	to a Stard. bend
S. 30° W.	¼	to a Lard. bend
West—	¼	to a bayou in the Lard. bend
North—	½	to a Stard. bend passing a riffle and 2 small Islds.
S. 30° W.	¾	to a Lard. bend passing an Island
N. 45° W.	½	to a Stard. bend passing a Bayou Lard. side
West—	2	to an Island, passing two points on the Lard. side. 2 Islands and several bayous on Lard. the valley from 6 to 10 mls. wide
South—	1⅛	to a Lard. bend
N. 45° W.	¼	to a Stard. bend being the Lard. side of an Isld.
S. 40° W.	⅛	along the Stard. bend of the Island.
S. 60° E.	¼	to a Lard. bend passing the upper point of the Island on the Stard. side.
S. 45° W.	½	in the Lard. bend
N. 10° W.	¾	in the Stard. bend passing a bayou
N. 80° W.	¼	to a Stard. bend, being the Lard. side of an Island

S. 30° W.	¾	to a Lard. bend passing the Island.
North—	¼	to a Stard. bend.
S. 45° W.	1	to the mouths of three bayous in a Stard bend
S 30° E.	½	to a Lard. bend
S. 50 W.	⅛	in the Lard. bend.
N. 20° W.	½	to a bayou in a Stard. bend.
S. 20° W.	½	to a Lard. bend
N. 45° W.	¼	to a low bluff in a Stard. bend.
S. 45° W	⅛	along the Lard. bend passing a bayou on Stard. side
S. 20° E.	½	to a Lard. bend
S. 50° W.	¼	to the lower point of an Island
West—	¼	to a Lard. bend at a bayou, passing a bayou on the Stard. side and the Island. ⟨to a bayou⟩
S. 60° E.	½	to a Lard. bend passing an Island.
S. 45° W.	¼	to a bayou on the Stard. side in a bend.
South	¼	to a lard. bend.
S. 60° W.	½	to a Stard. bend, at the entrance of a bayou, [EC: Birth Cr.] which is rapid and 30 yds. wide
S. 45° E.	⅛	along the Stard. bend
East	⅛	to a Lard. bend
South	½	to the mouth of a bayou in a Stard. bend
S. 70° W.	¾	to a Stard. bend
South	¼	to a high bottom in a Stard. bend.
S. 70° E.	½	to a Lard. bend, where they encamped for the night in a smooth plain.
Miles	17	

[Clark]   *August 2dnd Friday 1805*

a fine day   Set out early   the river has much the Same kind of banks Chanel Current &c. as it had in the last vallie, I walked out this morning on Shore & Saw Several rattle Snakes in the plain, the wind from the S W   we proceeded on with great dificuelty from the rapidity of the current & rapids, abt. 15 miles and Encamped on the Lard Side, saw a large

Gangue of Elk at Sunset to the S W. passed a Small Creek on the Stard Side [*ML?: called birth Creek*] and maney large and Small Islands. Saw a number of young Ducks as we have also Seen everry Day, Some geese— I saw Black woodpeckers— I have either got my foot bitten by Some poisonous insect or a tumer is riseing on the inner bone of my ankle which is painfull

1. Lewis crossed the Jefferson River from Jefferson to Madison County, Montana, somewhere between the present towns of Cardwell and Whitehall. The dotted line on *Atlas* map 65 shows his route.

2. The bottomlands, being well watered, produce a soil with a fairly well-developed humus horizon here. The uplands, being drier, develop a thin soil having a yellow or buff color.

3. The two kinds of red currants are problematic since there is only one species of red-fruited, unarmed, currant which grows in the area, squaw, or western red, currant, *Ribes cereum* Dougl. var. *inebrians* (Lindl.) C. L. Hitchc. See above, July 25, 1805. The yellow, deep purple currant refers to golden currant, *R. aureum* Pursh, with its yellow and purple fruits in the same population as described earlier. The black currant is possibly *R. americanum* Mill., which is also known from the same area. The red currant of Eastern gardens is *R. rubrum*. The serviceberry is *Amelanchier alnifolia* Nutt. Booth & Wright, 107, 110; Hitchcock et al., 3:67–70; Little (MWH), 16-NW.

4. Lewis camped somewhere in the vicinity of present Waterloo, in Madison County. *Atlas* map 65.

5. Perhaps it was Biddle who drew a red vertical line from "we met with" to this point.

6. Prairie dogs, *Cynomys ludovicianus*.

7. The fishing duck is either the female red-breasted merganser, *Mergus serrator* [AOU, 130], or the female common merganser, *Mergus merganser* [AOU, 129]. Burroughs, 189; Holmgren, 29. The black woodpecker is Lewis's woodpecker, *Melanerpes lewis* [AOU, 408]. See descriptions at July 20, 1805, and May 27, 1806.

8. After Clark's thirty-fifth birthday, on August 1; it is later Whitetail Creek, in Jefferson County, which passes the town of Whitehall. *Atlas* map 65.

9. In Madison County, a little below Big Pipestone (Panther) Creek. *Atlas* map 65.

[Lewis]   *August the 3rd 1805.*

Set out this morning at sunrise and continued our rout through the valley on the Lard. side of the river. at eleven A. M. Drewyer killed a doe and we halted and took breakfast. the mountains continue high on either side of the valley, and are but skantily supplyed with timber; small pine[1] appears to be the prevalent growth. there is no timber in the valley except a small quantity of the narrow leafed cottonwood on the verge of the river. the underwood consists of the narrowleafed or small willow, honeysuckle rosebushes, courant, goosbury[2] and service bury bushes allso a small quantity of a species of dwarf burch[3] the leaf of which, oval, deep green, finely indented and very small. we encamped this evening after sunset having traveled by estimate 23 miles.[4] from the width and appearance of the valley at this place I concieved that the river forked not far above me and therefore resolved the next morning to examine the adjacent country more minutely.

[Lewis]   *Saturday August 3rd 1805.*

Set out early this morning, or before sunrise; still continued our march through the level valley on the lard. side of the river. the valley much as yesterday only reather wider; I think it 12 Miles wide, tho' the plains near the mountains rise higher and are more broken with some scattering pine near the mountain. in the leaveler parts of the plain and river bottoms which are very extensive there is no timber except a scant proportion of cottonwood near the river. the under wood consists of the narrow leafed or small willow, the small honeysuckle, rosebushes, currant, serviceberry, and goosbery bushes; also a small species of berch in but small quantities ⟨of a species⟩ the leaf which is oval finely, indented, small and of a deep green colour.[5] the stem is simple ascending and branching, and seldom rises higher than 10 or 12 feet. the Mountains continue high on either side of the valley, and are but scantily supplyed with timber; small pine apears to be the prevalent growth; it is of the pich kind, with a short leaf. at 11 A. M. Drewyer killed a doe and we halted about 2 hours and breakfasted, and then continued our rout untill night without halting, when we arrived at the river in a level bottom which appeared to spread to greater extent than usual. from the appearance of the timber I supposed that the river forked above us and resolved to examine this part of the river minutely tomorrow. this evening we passed through a high plain for about 8 miles covered with prickley pears and bearded grass, tho' we found this even better walking than the wide bottoms of the river, which we passed in the evening; these altho' apparently level, from some cause which I know not, were formed into meriads of deep holes as if rooted up by hogs   these the grass covered so thick that it was impossible to walk without the risk of falling down at every step. some parts of these bottoms also possess excellent terf or peat, I beleive of many feet deep.   the mineral salts also frequently mentioned on the Missouri we saw this evening in these uneven bottoms.[6]   we saw many deer, Antelopes ducks, gees, some beaver and great appearance of their work. also a small bird and the Curlooe as usual.[7]   we encamped on the river bank on Lard. side having traveled by estimate 23 Miles. The fish of this part of the river are trout and a species of scale fish of a while [white] colour and a remarkable small long mouth which one of our men inform us are the same with the species called in the Eastern states *bottlenose*.[8] the snowey region of the mountains and for some distance below has no timber or herbage of any kind; the timber is confined to the lower and middle regions. Capt. Clark set out this morning as usual.   he walked on shore a small distance this morning and killed a deer.   in the course of his walk he saw a track which he supposed to be that of an Indian from the circumstance of the large toes turning inward.   he pursued the track and found that the person had ascended a point of a hill from which his camp of the last evening was visible; this circumstance also confirmed the beleif of it's being an Indian who had thus discovered them and ran off. they found the river as usual much crouded with islands, the currant more rapid & much more shallow than usual.   in many places they were obliged to double man the canoes and drag them over the stone and gravel.   this morning they passed a small creek on Stard. at the entrance of which Reubin Fields killed a large Panther.   we called the creek after that animal Panther Creek.[9]   they also passed a handsome little stream on Lard. which is form of several large springs which rise in the bottoms and along the base of the mountains with some little rivulets from the melting snows.   the beaver have formed many large dams on this stream. they saw some deer Antelopes and the common birds of the country.   in the evening they passed a very bad rappid where the bed of the river is formed entrely of solid rock and encamped on an island just above.[10] the Panther which Fields killed measured seven and ½ feet from the nose to the extremity of the tail. it is precisely the same animal common to the western part of our country. the men wer compelled to be a great proportion of their time in the water today; they have had a severe days labour and are much fortiegued.—

Courses and distances as traveled by Capt. C and
party August 3rd 1805.

South—	½	in a Lard. bend.
West—	1¼	to a Stard. bend.
S. 45° W.	½	to the entrance of a small creek in a Stard. bend this stream heads in the mountains at a little distance. we called it Panther Creek.
S. 20° W.	½	in the Stard. bend.
S. 80° E.	1¼	to the lower point of an island.
South—	¼	to a point of the Island on it's stard. side
South 30° E.	¼	to a bayou in the Island
South—	1½	to the upper point of the island having passed two point and a Clift on Stard. and a point on Lard.
S. 10° W.	4	On a direct line to the entrance of a small creek on Lard. it being the dranes of a snowey mountain in view. river passing under this mountain leaving the bottoms to the Stard. and has several short bends in this course.
S. 25° W.	1	to a small run in a Lard. bend
S. 60° W.	1	to a low stolley bluff in a Stard. bend, opposite an island having passed one other.
S. 20° W.	1	to the lower point of an Island Lard. passing one other, and a narrow rocky channel under a bluf. encamped on this island for the evening.
	Miles 13	

[Clark]   *August 3rd Saturday 1805*

a fine morning wind from the N E   I walked on Shore & killed a Deer   in my walk I saw a fresh track which I took to be an Indian from the Shape of the foot as the toes turned in, I think it probable that this Indian Spied our fires and Came to a Situation to view us from the top of a Small knob on the Lard Side.   the river more rapid and Sholey than yesterday one R. F. man killed a large *Panthor* on the Shore   we are oblige to haul over the Canoes Sholey in maney places where the Islands are noumerous and bottom Sholey, in the evening the river more rapid and Sholey we encamped on an Island avove a part of the river which passed thro a rockey bed enclosed on both sides with thick willow current & red buries &c &c[11]   passed a bold Stream which heads in the mountains to our right and the drean of the minting Snow in the Montn. on that side ar in View—   at 4 oClock passed a bold Stream which falls from a mountn in three Channels to our left, the Greater portion of the Snow on this mountain is melted, but little remaining near us   Some Deer Elk & antelopes & Bear in the bottoms.   but fiew trees and they Small   the Mountains on our left Contain pine those on our right but verry partially Supplied and what pine & cedar it has is on the Lower region, no wood being near the Snow.   great numbers of Beaver Otter &c. Some fish trout & and bottle nose. Birds as usial. Geese young Ducks & Curlows

1. Lewis's small pine is limber pine.

2. The willow is sandbar, or coyote, willow, *Salix exigua* Nutt. ssp. *interior* (Rowlee) Conq.; honeysuckle is probably wolfberry, western snowberry, *Symphoricarpos occidentalis* Hook.; rosebushes are western wild rose, *Rosa woodsii* Lindl.; and the "goosbury" is probably swamp currant, *Ribes lacustre* (Pers.) Poir. Booth & Wright, 26, 234, 119, 107.

3. The scrub birch, *Betula glandulosa* Michx. Ibid., 30.

4. Lewis camped in Madison County, Montana, above the mouth of the Big Hole River as it was in 1805, at least. The rivers have meandered considerably in this region since Lewis and Clark's time. *Atlas* map 65.

5. Biddle probably drew the red vertical line through this passage about the birch.

6. Faulting and natural changes in the Jefferson River's course often cause swamps or waterlogged lands to form. The growth of vegetation in these areas is rapid, and the remains of plants are quickly covered by the remains of subsequent plants so that decay is incomplete. In such areas, peat bogs, several acres in extent, form. The mineral salts are those of sodium sulphate, sodium bicarbonate, and magnesium sulphate similar to those noticed earlier downstream of the Great Falls of the Missouri. These salts have formed here because they are derived from salt-rich Cretaceous formations through which the Ruby and Big Hole rivers pass.

7. Probably the long-billed curlew, *Numenius americanus* [AOU, 264].

8. Evidently the northern sucker, *Catostomus catostomus*. Lewis gave a fuller description on August 19, 1805. Burroughs, 264.

9. Later Big Pipestone Creek, in Madison County. The animal was a mountain lion, *Felis concolor. Atlas* map 65.

10. Clark's camp was in Jefferson or Madison County, a few miles below present Waterloo. *Atlas* map 65.

11. The "red buries" are buffaloberry, *Shepherdia argentea* (Pursh) Nutt. Booth & Wright, 160; Little (MWH), 191-NW.

[Lewis]   *August 4th 1805.*

Set out very early this morning and steered S. E. by E. about 4 Miles when we passed a bould runing creek about 12 yards wide the water could and remarkably clear, we then changed our course to S. E. passing obliquely across a valley which boar nearly E leaving the valley which we had pursued for the 2 precedeing days.   at the distance of 3 miles we passed a handsome little river which passes through this valley; it is about 30 yards wide affords a considerable quantity of water and I believe it may be navigated some miles.   I then changed my rout to S. W. passed a high plain which lyes between the vallies and returned to the S. valley, in passing which I fell in with a river about 45 yards wide which I waideg and then continued my rout down to it's junction with the river just mentioned, and from thence to the entrance of the creek which falls in about 2 miles below; still continuing my rout down this stream about three miles further and about 2 M. below our encampment of the last evening   this river forms a junction with a river 50 yards wide which comes from the N. W. and falling into the S. valley runs parrallel with the middle fork about 12 miles.   this is a bould rappid & clear stream it's bed so broken and obstructed by gravel bars and Islands that it appeared to me impossible to navigate it with safety.   the middle fork is gentle and possesses about ⅔ds as much water as this rappid stream, it's cours so far as I can observe it is about S. W. and it appears to be navigable; its water is much warmer than that of the rappid fork and somewhat turbid, from which I concluded that it had it's source at a greater distance in the mountains and passed through an opener country than the other.[1]   under this impression I wrote a note to Capt. Clark recommending his taking the middle fork provided he should arrive at this place before my return which I expect will be the day after tomorrow.   the note I left on a pole at the forks of the river and having refreshed ourselves and eat heartily of some venison we killed this morning I continued my rout up the Stard.

side of the N. W. fork, determining to pursue it untill 12 OC. the next day and then pass over to the middle fork and return to their junction or un- till I met Capt. Clark. we encamped this evening near the point where the river leaves the valley and enters the mountains, having traveled about 20 miles.—[2]

[Lewis]   *Sunday August 4th 1805.*

Set out very early this morning and Steered S. E. by E. 4 M. when we pased a bold runing Creek 12 yds. wide, the water of which was clear and very cold. it appears to be formed by four dranes from the snowey mountains to our left. after passing this creek we changed our direction to S. E. passing obliquely across a valley which boar E leaving the valley we had pursued for the two peceeding days. at the distance of 3 Ms. we passed a handsome little river which meanders through this valley; it is about 30 yds wide, affords a considerable quantity of water and appears as if it might be navigated some miles. the currant is not rapid nor the water very clear; the banks are low and the bed formed of stone and gravel.[3] I now changed my rout to S. W. passed a high plain which lies betwen the valleies and returned to the South valley, in passing which I fell in with a river about 45 yds. wide gravley bottom gentle currant waist deep and water of a whitish blue tinge. this stream we waded and con- tinued our rout down it to the entrance of the river just mentioned about ¾ of a mile. still continuing down we passed the entrance of the creek about 2 miles lower down; and at the distance of three miles further ar- rived at it's junction with a river 50 yds. wide which Comes from the S. W. and falling into the South valley runs parallel with the middle fork about 12 miles before it forms a junction. I now found that our encampment of the last evening was about 1½ miles above the entrance of this large river on Stard. this is a bold rappid and Clear Stream, it's bed so much bro- ken and obstructed by gravley bars and it's waters so much subdivided by Islands that it appears to me utterly impossible to navigate it with safety. the middle fork is gentle and possesses about ⅔rds as much water as this stream. it's course so far as I can observe it is about S. W., and from the opening of the valley I beleive it still bears more to the West above it may be safely navigated. it's water is much warmer then the rapid fork and it's water more turbid; from which I conjecture that it has it's sources at a greater distance in the mountains and passes through an opener country than the other. under this impression I wrote a note to Capt Clark, recommending his taking the middle fork povided he should arrive at this place before my return, which I expect will be the day after tomorrow. this note I left on a pole at the forks of the river, and having refreshed ourselves and eat heartily of some venison which we killed this morning we continued our rout up the rapid fork on the Stard side, resolving to pursue this stream untill noon tomorrow and then pass over to the middle fork and come down it to their junction or untill I meet Capt Clark. I have seen no recent Indian sign [*NB: Qu*] in the course of my rout as yet. Charbono complains much of his leg, and is the cause of considerable detention to us. we encamped on the river bank near the place at which it leaves the valley and enters the mountain having traveled about 23 miles. we saw some Antelopes deer Crains, gees, and ducks of the two species common to this country. the summer duck has ceased to appear, nor do I beleive it is an inhabitant of this part of the country. the timber &c is as heretofore tho' there is more in this valley on the rapid fork than we have seen in the same extent on the river since we entered this valley. the Indians appear on some parts of the river to have distroyed a great proportion of the little timber which there is by seting fire to the bottoms. This morning Capt. Clark set out at sunrise, and sent two hunters ahead to kill some meat. at 8 A. M. he arrived at my camp of the 2ed inst. where he breakfasted; here he found a note which I had left for him at that place informing him of the occurences of my rout &c. the river continued to be crouded with Islands, rapid and shoaly. these shoals or riffles succeeded each other every 3 or four hundred yards; at those places they are obliged to drag the canoes over the stone there not being water enough to float them, and betwen the riffles the current is so strong that they are compelled to have cecourse to the cord; and being unable to walk on the shore for the brush wade in the river along the shore and hawl them by the cord; this has increased the pain and labour extreemly; their feet soon get tender and soar by wading and walking over the stones. these are also so slipry that they frequently get severe falls. being constantly wet soon makes them feble also. their hunters killed 2 deer today and some gees and ducks wer killed by those who navigated the canoes. they saw deer antelopes Crains beaver Otter &c. Capt. Clark's ancle became so painfull to him that he was unable to walk.— This evening they encamped on the Stard. side in a bottom of cottonwood timber all much fatiegued.[4]

Courses and distances traveled by Capt. Clark and party.
August 4th 1805.

S. 45° W.	5	on a direct course to a Lard. bend passing 4 bends on the Lard. side and several bayous on either side.
S. 20° W.	4	With the river to a bluff on the Lard. side, passing 3 bends on the Stard. and two small Islands and 2 Bayous on Stard. side.
S. 60° W.	6	with the river to an island, passing six circular bends on the Stard. and several small bayous. encamped on stard. side in
Miles	15	a bottom covered with cottonwood.—

[Clark]   *August 4th Sunday 1805*

a fine morning cool   proceeded on verry early and Brackfast at the Camp Capt Lewis left yesterday morning, at this Camp he left a note informing that he discovered no fresh Sign of Indians &c. The river continued to be crouded with Islands Sholey rapid & clear, I could not walk on Shore to day as my ankle was Sore from a tumer on that part.   the method we are compelled to take to get on is fatigueing & laborious in the extreen, haul the Canoes over the rapids, which Suckceed each other every two or three hundred yards and between the water rapid oblige to towe & walke on Stones the whole day except when we have poleing men wet all day Sore feet &c. &c   Murcury at Sun rise 49 a. o,

1. Lewis's route is shown by the dotted line on *Atlas* map 65. He had arrived at the "Forks of the Jefferson." Ruby River (Lewis and Clark's Philanthropy River) comes in from the east to join the Beaverhead (which they called the Jefferson), forming the Jefferson River. A few miles downstream the Big Hole River (their Wisdom River) joins the Jefferson from the west. Between the two junctions is the present town of Twin Bridges, Madison County, Montana.

2. Lewis's route up the Big Hole (Wisdom) River is not marked on *Atlas* map 66. He camped near the Madison-Beaverhead county line on the Big Hole River, above the mouth of present Nez Perce Creek.

3. The Ruby River has a steep gradient and has its source in the mountains. Additionally, it is joined by numerous short tributaries that carry rocks down to it during their peak runoff stage. Consequently, like most streams in this area, the stream bed is composed principally of rounded stones of various sizes.

4. Clark's camp was in the vicinity of present Silver Star, Madison County. *Atlas* map 65.

[Lewis]   *August 5th 1805.*[1]

[Lewis]   *Monday August 5th 1805*

As Charbono complained of being unable to march far today I ordered him and Sergt. Gass to pass the rappid river near our camp and proceed at their leasure through the level bottom to a point of high timber about seven miles distant on the middle fork which was in view; I gave them my pack that of Drewyer and the meat which we had, directing them to remain at that place untill we joined them. I took Drewyer with me and continued my rout up the stard. side of the river about 4 miles and then waded it; found it so rapid and shallow that it was impossible to navigate it.   continued up it on the Lard. side about 1½ miles further when the mountains put in close on both sides and arrose to great hight, partially covered with snow.   from hence the course of the river was to the East of North. I took the advantage of a high projecting spur of the mountain which with some difficulty we ascended to it's summit in about half an hour.   from this eminance I had a pleasing view of the valley through which I had passed many miles below and the continuation of the middle fork through the valley equally wide above me to the distance of about 20 miles when that also appeared to enter the mountains and disappeared to my view; however the mountains which termineate the valley in this direction appeared much lower than those up either of the other forks.   on the rapid fork they appeared still to rise the one range towering above another as far as I could perceive them.   the middle fork as I suspected dose bear considerably to the West of South and the gap formed by it in the mountains after the valley terminates is in the same direction.   under these circumstances I did not hesitate in beleiving the middle fork the most proper for us to ascend.[2]   about South from me, the middle fork approached within about 5 miles. I resolved to pass

44

across the plains to it and return to Gass and Charbono, accordingly we set out and decended the mountain among some steep and difficult precipices of rocks. here Drewyer missed his step and had a very dangerous fall, he sprained one of his fingers and hirt his leg very much. in fifteen or 20 minutes he was able to proceed and we continued our rout to the river where we had desighned to interscept it. I quenched my thirst and rested a few minutes examined the river and found it still very navigable. an old indian road very large and plain leads up this fork, but I could see no tracks except those of horses which appeared to have passed early in the spring. as the river mad a great bend to the South East we again ascended the high plain and steered our course as streight as we could to the point where I had directed Gass and Sharbono to remain. we passed the plain regained the bottom and struck the river about 3 miles above them; by this time it was perfectly dark & we hooped but could hear no tidings of them. we had struck the river at the point of timber to which I had directed them, but [they] having mistaken a point of woods lower down, had halted short of the place. we continued our rout after dark down the bottom through thick brush of the pulppy leafed thorn[3] and prickly pears for about 2 hours when we arrived at their camp.[4] they had a small quantity of meat left which Drewyer and myself eat it being the first we had taisted today. we had traveled about 25 miles. I soon laid down and slept very soundly untill morning. I saw no deer today nor any game except a few Antelopes which were very shy. the soil of the plains is a light yellow clay very meager and intermixed with a large proportion of gravel,[5] producing nothing except the twisted or bearded grass, sedge and prickly pears. the dryer parts of the bottoms are also much more indifferent in point of soil to those below and are covered with the southernwood pulpy leafed thorn and prickley pears with but little grass. the moist parts are fertile and covered with fine grass and sand rushes.

This morning Capt. Clark set out at sunrise and dispatched Joseph & Reubin Fields to hunt. they killed two deer on one of which the party breakfasted. the river today they found streighter and more rapid even than yesterday, and the labour and difficulty of the navigation was proportionably increased, they therefore proceeded but slowly and with great pain as the men had become very languid from working in the water and many of their feet swolen and so painfull that they could scarcely walk. at 4 P. M. they arrived at the confluence of the two rivers where I had left the note. this note had unfortunately been placed on a green pole which the beaver had cut and carried off together with the note; the possibility of such an occurrence never onc occurred to me when I placed it on the green pole. this accedent deprived Capt. Clark of any information with ripect to the country and supposing that the rapid fork was most in the direction which it was proper we should pursue, or West, he took that stream and asscended it with much difficulty about a mile and encamped on an island that had been lately overflown and was yet damp;[6] they were therefore compelled to make beds of brush to keep themselves out of the mud. in ascending this stream for about a quarter of a mile it scattered in such a maner that they were obliged to cut a passage through the willow brush which leant over the little channels and united their tops. Capt. Clarks ankle is extreemly painfull to him this evening; the tumor has not yet mature, he has a slight fever.— The men were so much fortiegued today that they wished much that navigation was at an end that they might go by land.—

Courses and distances traveled by Capt. Clark and party
August 5th 1805.

S. 45° E.	½	to a Lard. bend passing a bayou on Lard. side.
S. 15° W.	½	to a Stard. bend passing an island.
South	1	to a Lard. bend passing a small Island, and a bayou on the Stard. side.
S. 45° W.	¼	to a Stard. bend passing an island.
S. 30° W.	2	to a low clift at the mouth of a bayou on Stard. side passing three bad rappids in this course
S. 60° E.	½	to a Lard. bend passing an Island Stard. side.
S. 30° W.	½	to a bluff in a Stard. bend
South—	¼	in the Stard. bend passing a bad rapid.
S. 45° E.	¼	to a Lard. bend.
South—	½	to a bluff in a Stard. bend.

South 45° E.	½	to a Lard. bend.
S. 15° W.	¼	to a Stard. bend under a bluff.
East—	½	to a Lard. bend passing a bayou on Stard. side.
S. 5° W.	¼	to a bayou in a Lard. bend.
S. 45° W.	½	to a Stard. bend passing an island.
West—	¼	to a bayou in a Stard. bend.
S. 45° E.	¼	to a Lard. bend passing an island
South—	½	to the forks. these forks are nearly of the same size tho'
Miles	9¼	the N. W. fork possesses the most water at this time and is infinitely the most rapid. ascended the last one mile on a course of S 30 W. and encamped on an Island.

[Clark]   *August 5th Monday 1805*

a Cold Clear morning the wind from the S. E.   the river Streight & much more rapid than yesterday, I Sent out Jo. & R. Fields to kill Some meat   they killed 2 Deer & we brackfast on one of them and proceeded on with great dificuelety from the rapidity of the Current, and numerable rapids we had to encounter, at 4 oClock P M Murcury 49 ab. o, passed the mouth[7] of principal fork which falls in on the Lard. Side, this fork is about the Size of the Stard. one less water reather not so rapid, its Course as far as can be Seen is S. E & appear to pass through between two mountains, the N W. fork being the one most in our course i. e. S 25 W. as far as I can See, deturmind me to take this fork as the principal and the one most proper the S E fork is of a Greenish Colour & contains but little timber. The S W fok contains more timber than is below for Some distance,[8] we assended this fork about one mile and Encamped on an Island which had been laterly overflown & was wet   we raised our bead on bushes, we passed a part of the river above the forks which was divided and Scattered thro the willows in Such a manner as to render it dificuelt to pass through for a ¼ of a mile, we wer oblige to Cut our way thro' the willows—   Men much fatigued from their excessive labours in hauling the Canoes over the rapids &c. verry weak being in the water all day.   my foot verry painfull

N. 30° W.	1	to a Pooint of rocks on the Lard Side, at this place the river passes thro a Spur of the Mountain of perpendicul Clifts
N 60° W	¾	to the upper part of a rock in Std bend
S. 70° W.	1 ½	to a Clift on the LardSide
S W	½	to the Stard. Bend
S. 26° W.	1 ¾	to a Bluff in the Stard Side
South	½	to the lard Bend, at this place the river enter a high mountn. of Steep uneaven Clifts
N. 30° W	1 ¼	to a Stard. Bend under a high Clift
N. 80° W	¼	to a Clift of high rocks in Std. bend a Small bottom on the Lard Side
S. 60° W.	½	to a Lard Bend under a pine hill
N. 25° W.	¼	to a Small Island on the Lard Side
N. 30° E	¼	to a Stard. Bend high Clifts both Sds.
N. 80° W	¾	to the mouth of a bold Creek on the Lard. Side passing an Isld. and riffle of 6 feet fall Frasures fall & creek here the river again enters a valle
North	½	to the Stard. bend under a hill
N W.	½	to a lard. bend
N. 70° W	1 ½	to the point of an Island passed Several Small Islands
North	¼	to a Stard. bend
West	¾	to the lower point of an Island
N W	¼	to the mouth of a large Creek Std. R. Fields Creek & valley 28 yd. wd. (*Encamped the 1st of Augt.*)
S. 80° W.	¾	to a Stard. Bend
S. 30° W.	¼	to a lard. Bend
West	¼	to a Bayou in the Lard. Bend
North	½	to a Stard bend passing a riffle and 2 Small Islands
S. 30° W.	¾	to a Lard. bend passed an Island
N. 45° W	½	to a Std. bend passed a Bayou Ld.
West	2	to an Island passing two points on the Lards. Side two Is-

lands and several Bayous on the Lard Side   the Vallee from 6 to 10 miles wide

South	1 ⅛	to a lard Bend
N W	¼	to a Stard bend on the Island
S 40 W	⅛	in the Stard. bend of the Isld.
S. 60 E.	¼	to a Lard. bend passing the point of the island on the Stard. Side
S W.	½	in the Lard. bend
N. 10° W.	¾	in the Stard bend passed a Bayou
N. 80° W.	¼	in the Stard. Bend of an Island
S. 30° W	¾	to a Lard. Bend passed the Island
North	¼	to a Stard. Bend
S W	1	to the mouth of 3 Bayous in a Std. bend
S. 30° E	½	in a Lard. Bend
S. 50° W.	⅛	in the lard Bend
N. 20° W	½	to a Bayou in the Stard. Bend
S 20° W	½	to a Lard Bend
N. W.	¼	to a low Bluff in a Stard. Bend
S. W.	⅛	in a Stard. Bend passd. a Bayou Std. Side.
S. 20° E	½	to a Lard Bend
S. 50° W	¼	to an lower point of an island
West	¼	to a Stard. Bend passing a Bayou on the Std. Side and the isd. to a Bayou Std.
S 60° E	½	to a Lard. Bend passed an isld.
S 45° W	¼	to a Bayou in the Stard. bend
South	¼	to a Lard Bend
S 60° W.	½	to a Stard. Bend at the mouth a Bayou rapid & 30 yds wide [*EC: White tail deer = Birth Cr.*]
S. E.	⅛	in the Stard. bend
East	⅛	to the Lard Bend
South	½	to the mo. of a Bayou in Stard. Bend

S. 70° W	¾	to a Stard. Bend
South	¼	to a high bottom in a Stard. Bend
S. 70° E	½	to a Lard. Bend
	23¾	(*Campd. 2d August*)

3d Augt

South	½	in a Lard. Bend
West	1¼	to a Stard. Bend
S. W.	½	to the Stard. Bend a Small ⟨run⟩ [*ML?: creek called panther C.*] [*EC: Pipestone*]
S. 20° W.	½	in the Stard. Bend
S. 80° E	1¼	to the Lower point of an island
South	¼	to a Std. point of the Island
S. 30° E	¼	to a Bayou in the Island
South	1½	to the upper point of the Island haveing passed 3 points and a Cliff
S. 10° W.	4	on a Direct line to the mouth of a Creek Small the Dreans of a mountain in which there is *Snow* in view, river passed under this mountain [*EC: S. Bould Mt.*] on the Lard Side & has several Short bends in this Course vallie wide & to the Stard Side
S. 25° W.	1	to a Small run in a Lard. bend
S. 60° W.	1	to a low Stoney bluff in a Stard. bend opposit an Island passed 1
S. 20° W.	1	to the lower point of a Island Ld. passed one and thro a narrow rockey Channel under the bluff (*Encamped the 3 of Augt.*)
S. 45° W.	5	on a Direct Course to a Lard. bend passed 4 bends to the Lard. Side & Several Bayous on either Side
S. 20° W.	4	with the river to a Bluff on the Lard. side, passed three bends on the Stard. and two Small Islands & 2 Bayoes Sd.
S. 60° W.	6	with the river to an island passed six round bends on the Stard. and Several Small Bayoes. (*Campd. 4h Augt*)

S. 45° E	½	to a Lard. bend a Bayou Ld. Side
S. 15° W	½	to a Stard. bend passed an Island
South	1	to a Lard. bend psd. a Small island and a Bayou on the Stard. Side
S. 45° W.	¼	to a Stard. Bend passed an island
S. 30° W.	2	to a low Clift at the mouth of a Bayou [*EC: Cherry Cr.*] on the Stard. Side passed 3 rapids in this course
S. 60° E.	½	to a Lard bend passed an Island Std. Side
S. 30° W.	½	to a Bluff in the Stard. bend
South	¼	in the Stard. bend passed a bad rapid
S. 45° E	¼	to a Lard bend
South	½	to a Bluff in a Stard. bend
S. 45° E.	½	to a Lard. bend
S. 15° W.	¼	to a Stard. Bend under a Bluff
East	½	to a Lard Bend passed a Bayou on Std Side
S. 5° W	¼	to a Bayou in the Lard. Bend
S. 45° W	½	to a Stard. bend passed an island
West	¼	to a Bayou in the Stard. Bend
S. 45° E	¼	to a Lard. Bend passed an Island
South	½	to the forks, passed an Island Those Forks is nearly of the Same Size the N W. fork the most rapid & Clear and the one most in our Course, the S. E. fork is Still of a Greenish Colour and appears to come from the S. E between two mountains
	61	
	37	
	98	up the North Fork

Assended the N W Fork 9 miles on a Course S. 30° W. to a Bluff on the Stard. Side   passed Several Bayous & Islands

1. The last entry in Codex Fa has the date only, followed by a blank half-page, and the back of the sheet blank also.

2. Lewis continued up the Big Hole (Wisdom) River about three miles beyond the Madison-Beaverhead county line where he climbed a ridge for a commanding view. Lewis still assumed that by reaching the head of the principal affluent of the Missouri he would

be near the headwaters of the Columbia or a main tributary. The middle fork was the Beaverhead, which modern geographers agree with Lewis in calling the main stream, and the mountains in that direction were probably the Tendoy Mountains. In the direction of the "rapid fork"—the Big Hole River—he would be looking at Pioneer Mountains. *Atlas* maps 65, 66.

3. Greasewood, *Sarcobatus vermiculatus* (Hook.) Torr. Booth & Wright, 48.

4. On the Beaverhead, in Madison County, Montana, a few miles above the mouth of the Ruby (Philanthropy) River. *Atlas* map 66.

5. The Tertiary uplands near the junction of these rivers are principally composed of sand, clay, and soft sandstone. Because this area receives only about ten inches of precipitation annually, a mature soil containing a significant humus horizon cannot develop except in the bottoms. The gravel found on these uplands was deposited by the adjacent rivers when they flowed at a higher elevation than at present.

6. Clark's camp was a mile or so up the Big Hole River from its mouth, in Madison County, northwest of the present town of Twin Bridges. *Atlas* map 65.

7. Here again Clark has placed the courses of several days (August 1–5) together and written the August 5 entry around it; we carry the material at the end of this entry. Someone, perhaps Coues, has underlined a few place-names in blue crayon. See also notes for Clark's entry of July 31, 1805.

8. Clark's terminology is somewhat confusing since he appears to refer to the Big Hole River as both the "N W" and "S W" fork. The southeast fork is the Ruby River. *Atlas* maps 65, 66.

[Lewis]   *Tuesday August 6th 1805.*

We set out this morning very early on our return to the forks.   having nothing to eat I set Drewyer to the woodlands to my left in order to kill a deer, sent Sergt. Gass to the right with orders to keep sufficiently near to discover Capt. C. and the party should they be on their way up that stream, and with Sharbono I directed my course to the main forks through the bottom directing the others to meet us there.   about five miles above the forks I head the hooping of the party to my left and changed my rout towards them; on my arrival found that they had taken the rapid fork and learnt from Capt. Clark that he had not found the note which I had left for him at that place and the reasons which had induced him to ascend this stream.   it was easeist & more in our direction, and apd. to contain as much water   he had hoever previously to my comeing up with him, met Drewyer who informed him of the state of the two rivers and was on his return.   one of their canoes had just overset and all the baggage wet, the medecine box among other articles and several articles lost a shot pouch and horn with all the implements for one rifle lost and never recovered. I walked down to the point where I waited their return. on their arrival found that two other canoes had filled with water and wet their cargoes completely. Whitehouse had been thrown out of one of the canoes as she swing in a rapid current and the canoe had rubed him and pressed him to the bottom as she passed over him and had the water been 2 inches shallower must inevitably have crushed him to death. our parched meal, corn, Indian preasents, and a great part of our most valuable stores were wet and much damaged on this ocasion. to examine, dry and arrange our stores was the first object; we therefore passed over to the lard. side opposite to the entrance of the rapid fork where there was a large gravly bar that answered our purposes; wood was also convenient and plenty. here we fixed our camp,[1] and unloaded all our canoes and opened and exposed to dry such articles as had been wet. a part of the load of each canoe consisted of the leaden canestirs of powder which were not in least injured, tho' some of them had remained upwards of an hour under water. about 20 lbs. of powder which we had in a tight Keg or at l[e]ast one which we thought sufficiently so got wet and intirely spoiled. this would have been the case with the other had it not have been for the expedient which I had fallen on of securing the powder by means of the lead having the latter formed into canesters which were filled with the necessary proportion of poder to discharge the lead when used, and those canesters well secured with corks and wax. in this country the air is so pure and dry that any vessel however well seasoned the timber may be will give way or shrink unless it is kept full of some liquid. we found that three deer skins which we had left at a considerable hight on a tree were taken off which we supposed had been done by a panther. we sent out some men to hunt this evening, they killed 3 deer and four Elk which gave us a plentifull supply om [of] meat once more. Shannon had been dispatched up the rapid fork this morning to hunt, by Capt Clark before he met with Drewyer or learnt his mistake in the rivers. when he returned he sent Drewyer in surch of him, but he rejoined us this evening and reported that he had been several miles up the river and could find nothing of him. we had the trumpet sounded and fired several guns but he did not join us this evening. I am fearful he is lost again. this is the same man who was seperated from us 15 days as we came up the Missouri and subsisted 9 days of that time on grapes only. Whitehouse is in much pain this evening with the injury one of his legs sustained from the canoe today at the time it upset and swing over him. Capt Clarks ankle is also very painfull to him.— we should have given the party a days rest some where near this place had not this accedent happened, as I had determined to take some observations to fix the Latitude and longitude of these forks. our merchandize medecine &c are not sufficiently dry this evening we covered them securely for the evening. Capt Clark had ascended the river about 9 miles from this place on a course of S 30° W. before he met with Drewyer.—

we beleive that the N. W. or rapid fork is the dane [*NB: drain*] of the melting snows of the mountains, and that it is not as long as the middle fork and dose not at all seasons of the year supply any thing like as much water as the other and that about this season it rises to it's greatest hight. this last appears from the apparent bed of the river which is now overflown and the water in many plases spreads through old channels which have their bottoms covered with grass that has grown this season and is such as appears on the parts of the bottom not innundated. we therefore determined that the middle fork was that which ought of right to bear the name we had given to the lower portion or *River Jefferson* and called the bold rapid an clear stream *Wisdom,* and the more mild and placid one which flows in from the S. E. *Philanthrophy,*[2] in commemoration of two of those cardinal virtues, which have so eminently marked that deservedly selibrated character through life.

[Clark]   *August 6th Tuesday 1805*

a Clear morning Cool wind from the S W we proceeded on with much dificuelty and fatigue over rapids & Stones; river about 40 or 50 yards wide much divided by Islands and narrow Bayoos to a low bluff on the Stard Side & Brackfast, dureing the time of Brackfast Drewyer Came to me from Capt. Lewis and informed me that they had explored both forks for 30 or 40 miles & that the one we were assending was impractiabl much further up & turned imediately to the north, The middle fork he reported was jintle and after a Short distanc turned to the S. W. and that all the Indian roades leades up the middle fork. this report deturmind me to take the middle fork, accordingly Droped down to the forks where I met with Capt Lewis & party, Capt Lewis had left a Letter on a pole in the forks informing me what he had discovered & the course of the rivers &c. this lettr was Cut down by the [beaver] as it was on a green pole & Carried off. Three Skins which was left on a tree was taken off by the Panthers or wolvers.[3] In decending to the Point one Can[o]e Struck & turned on a rapid & Sunk, and wet every thing which was in her, this misfortune obliged us to halt at the forks and dry those articles, one other Canoe nearly turning over, filled half full of water & wet our medison & Some Goods Corn &c. Several hunters out to day & killed a young Elk, Antilope, & 3 Deer, one man *Shannon* did not return to night— This evening Cool my anckle much wors than it has been— this evening a Violent wind from the N. W accompanied with rain which lasted half an hour wind N. W

1. On the larboard side of the Jefferson, opposite the mouth of the Big Hole (Wisdom) River, in Madison County, Montana, just north of the present town of Twin Bridges. *Atlas* map 65.
2. See above, August 4, 1805.
3. The gray wolf, *Canis lupus.*

[Lewis]   *Wednesday August 7th 1805.*

The morning being fair we spread our stores to dry at an early hour. Dispatched Reubin Fields in surch of Shannon. our stores were now so much exhausted that we found we could proceed with one canoe less. we therefore drew out one of them into a thicket of brush and secured her in such manner that the water could not take her off should the river rise to the hight where she is. The creek which falls in above us we called turf creek from the cercustance of it's bottoms being composed of excellent turf.[1] my air gun was out of order and her sights had been removed by some accedent I put her in order and regulated her. she shot again as well as she ever did. The clouds last night prevented my taking any lunar observations this day I took Equal Altitudes of the ☉ with Sextant.

	h	m	s			h	m	s	
A. M.	8	20	25.5	P. M.	4	38	3	Altitude by Sext at the
"		21	54	"		39	40	time of observation.
"		23	30	"		41	8	62° 9′ 45″

h m s

Chronometer too [*blank*] on Mean time [*blank*]

Observed Meridian Altd. of ☉'s L.L. with Octant by the back observation 63° 5′ —″

Latitude deduced from this observation N 45° 2′ 43.8″

At one oclock all our baggage was dry we therefore packed it up re-loaded the canoes and the party proceeded with Capt. Clark up Jefferson's river. I remained with Sergt. Gass to complete the observation of equal altitudes and joined them in the evening at their camp on the Lard. side just above the entrance of turf creek.[2] we had a shower of rain wich continued about 40 minutes attended with thunder and lightning. this shower wet me perfectly before I reached the camp. the clouds continued during the night in such manner that I was unable to obtain any lunar observations. This evening Drewyer brought in a deer which he had killed. we have not heard any thing from Shannon yet, we expect that he has pursued Wisdom river upwards for som distance probably killed some heavy animal and is waiting our arrival. the large biteing fly or hare fly as they sometimes called are very troublesome to us. I observe two kinds of them a large black species and a small brown species with a green head. the musquetoes are not as troublesome as they were below, but are still in considerable quantities. the eye knats have disappeared. the green or blowing flies are still in swarms.[3]

Courses and distances August 7th 1805

S. 45° E. 7 to the entrance of turf Creek 12 yds. wide which discharges
Miles 7 itself on Lard. side passing several bends both on Stard. and Lard. and several small bayous on either side. on the course of the R. about 7 M.

☞ the courses from the entrance of Wisdom river to the forks of Jefferson's river are taken directly to the objects mentioned and the distance set down is that by land on a direct line between the points; the estimated distances by water is also added in the body of the remarks on each course.—

[Clark]   *August 7th Wednesday 1805*[4]

a fine morning   put out our Stores &c. to dry & took equal altitudes with the Sextant,—   as our Store were a little exorsted and one Canoe became unnecessary deturmind to leave one.   we Hauled her up in the bushes on the lower Side of the main fork & fastened her So that the water could not flote her off. The Countrey in this quarter is as follows i, e a Vallie of 5 or 6 miles wide Inclosed between two high Mountains, the bottom rich Some Small timber on the Islands & bushes on the edges of the river Some *Bogs* & verry good *turf* in different places in the vallie, Some scattering Pine & ceder on the mountains in places, other Parts nacked except grass and Stone   The *Lattitude* of the Mouth of *Wisdom River* is 45° 2′ 21.6″ North, we proceeded up the Main Middle or S. E. fork, passed a Camped on the Lard. Side above the mouth of a bold running Stream 12 yards wide, which we call *turf* Creek from the number of bogs & quanty of turf in its waters.   this Creek runs thro a open Plain for Several miles, takeing its rise in a high mountain to the N E. The river Jefferson above Wisdom is gentle Crooked and about 40 yards wide, Containing but little timber, Some few Cotton willow Willow & Birch,[5] and the Srubs common to the countery and before mentioned   at 5 oClock a thunder Storm from the N. W. accompanied with rain which lasted about 40 minits.—   despatched R Fields to hunt Shannon, who was out huntg. on Wisdom river at the time I returned down that Stream, and has made o[n] up the river expecting us to follow him up that river one Deer killed this evening.   all those Streams Contain emence number of Beaver orter Muskrats &c.[6]

1. The portion of this creek seen by Lewis then occupied a former channel of the Ruby River, and the area adjacent to it, therefore, was very swampy or waterlogged. Vegetation grew profusely, died, and was covered by subsequent vegetation remains before it could decay completely. By this process, a peat or turf bog of several acres extent could easily develop.

2. In Madison County, Montana, just above Twin Bridges. *Atlas* map 65.

3. The flies of the two kinds are the horse fly (large black), *Tabanus* sp., and the deer fly (small brown), *Chrysops* sp. Borror, Delong, & Triplehorn, 581–82. The mosquitoes are still *Aedes vexans,* and the disappearance of the gnats confirms them as buffalo gnats. The blow fly is from either the family Calliphoridae or Sacrophagidae.

4. Clark's courses for August 7–14 are found with his entry of August 15, 1805.

5. "Cotton willow" refers to narrowleaf cottonwood; see June 3, 1805. Willow is the sandbar willow, and birch is probably the water, or river, birch, *Betula occidentalis* Hook., which is more common than the scrub birch cited on August 3. Booth & Wright, 30.

6. Muskrat, *Ondatra zibethicus.*

[Lewis]   *Thursday August 8th 1805.*

We had a heavy dew this morning.   as one canoe had been left we had now more hads to spear for the chase; game being scarce it requires more hunters to supply us.   we therefore dispatched four this morning.   we set out at sunrise and continued our rout up the river which we find much more gentle and deep than below the entrance of Wisdom river it is from 35 to 45 yards wide very crooked many short bends constituteing large and general bends; insomuch that altho' we travel briskly and a considerable distance yet it takes us only a few miles on our general course or rout.   there is but very little timber on this fork principally the under brush frequently mentioned. I observe a considerable quantity of the buffaloe clover in the bottoms.[1]   the sunflower, flax, green sword, thistle and several species of the rye grass some of which rise to the hight of 3 or 4 feet.[2]   there is a grass[3] also with a soft smooth leaf that bears it's seeds very much like the timothy but it dose not grow very luxouriant or appear as if it would answer so well as the common timothy for meadows. I preserved some of it's seeds which are now ripe, thinking perhaps it might answer better if cultivated, at all events is at least worth the experiment.   it rises about 3 feet high.   on a direct line about 2 miles above our encampment of this morning we passed the entrance of Philanthrophy River which discharges itself by 2 channels a small distance assunder. this river from it's size and S. Eastwardly course no doubt heads with Madisons river in the snowey mountains visible in that direction.[4]   at Noon Reubin Fields arrived and reported that he had been up Wisdom river some miles above where it entered the mountain and could find

58

nothing of Shannon, he had killed a deer and an Antelope. great quantity of beaver Otter and musk-rats in these rivers. two of the hunters we sent out this morning returned at noon had killed each a deer and an Antelope. we use the seting poles today almost altogether. we encamped on the Lard side[5] where there was but little timber were obliged to use willow brush for fuel; the rosebushes and bryers were very thick. the hunters brought in another deer this evening. te tumor on Capt. Clarks ankle has discharged a considerable quantity of matter but is still much swolen and inflamed and gives him considerable pain. saw a number of Gees ducks and some Crains today. the former begin to fly.—

the evening again proved cloudy much to my mortification and prevented my making any lunar observations. the Indian woman recognized the point of a high plain to our right which she informed us was not very distant from the summer retreat of her nation on a river beyond the mountains which runs to the west. this hill she says her nation calls the beaver's head from a conceived remblance of it's figure to the head of that animal.[6] she assures us that we shall either find her people on this river or on the river immediately west of it's source; which from it's present size cannot be very distant. as it is now all important with us to meet with those people as soon as possible, I determined ⟨to leave the charge of the party, and the care of the lunar observations to Capt. Clark; and⟩ to proceed tomorrow with a small party to the source of the principal stream of this river and pass the mountains to the Columbia; and down that river untill I found the Indians; in short it is my resolusion to find them or some others, who have horses if it should cause me a trip of one month. for without horses we shall be obliged to leave a great part of our stores, of which, it appears to me that we have a stock already sufficiently small for the length of the voyage before us.

Courses and Distances of August 8th 1805.

South	2	Miles to the upper or principal entrance of Philanthrophy River on Lard. being 5 Miles by water, passing seven bends on the Lard. side, two islands and several bayous. this river is 30 yds. wide is navigable and heads in the Roky Mountains with Madison's River.—

S. 20 W. 6
　　Miles 8
　　　　=
to a few high trees on the Stard. side, the river bending to the East two miles from this course. and the distance by water 14 miles passing an island at 1 M. another at 7 M. several small bayous and 35 bends on Strd. side the majority of the bends being short and circular.

[Clark]   *August 8th Thursday 1805*

We proceeded on early   wind from the S W. The Thermometer at 52 a o at Sunrise   at 5 miles by water & 4½ on a derect line from the forks we passed a River on the Lard Side 30 yards wide and navagable for Some distance takeing its rise in the Mountains Easterly & with the waters of Madisons River, passes thro an extensive vallie open & furtill &c.   this river we call *Philanthophy*—   above this river (which has but little timber) Jeffersons R is crooked with Short bends a fiew Islands and maney gravelly Sholes, no large timber, Small willow Birch & Srubs &c. Encamped on the Lard Side, R Fields joined us this eveng. & informes that he could not find Shannon   my foot yet verry Swore

1. The name buffalo clover is problematic. If this is a true clover, the most likely species is longstalk clover, *Trifolium longipes* Nutt. However, it is probably *Thermopsis montana* Nutt., mountain thermopsis, which is not a true clover but is common in the wet meadows of the area and has the long, narrow, trifoliate leaflets as described. See August 16, 1805, below. Booth & Wright, 141; Hitchcock et al., 3:364, 351–52.

2. The sunflower is the perennial species, Nuttall sunflower, *Helianthus nuttallii* T. & G., which is common in this habitat and is known from the area. The term greensward often refers to a lush, green meadow, but in this case may refer to a species of rush or sedge which dominates the wet meadow. One of the rye grasses is certainly basin wildrye, *Elymus cinereus* Scribn. & Merrill, which is a distinctive, tall, bunch-forming grass as described. Other wildrye species of the area include Canada wildrye, *E. canadensis* L., and several species of *Agropyron* with flower heads similar to wildrye. Booth & Wright, 274; Hitchcock et al., 5:230, 1:559–61; Hahn, *Elymus* and *Agropyron* maps.

3. Probably *Calamagrostis stricta* (Timm) Koeler (or *C. inexpansa* Gray), northern reedgrass, which has a flower structure similar to cultivated timothy, fits the ecological and morphological description, and is known from the immediate area. It could also possibly be a species of stream foxtail, *Alopecurus* sp., which is also similar to timothy in flower structure but not as common as *Calamagrostis*. Hahn, *Calamagrostis* and *Alopecurus* maps; Hitchcock et al., 1:527–29.

4. The Gravelly Range. However, the Madison River heads in the Yellowstone Plateau in northwestern Wyoming.

5. In Madison County, Montana, a few miles above the mouth of Ruby (Philanthropy) River. *Atlas* map 66.

6. Beaverhead (or Beaver's Head) Rock is in Madison County, near the Beaverhead County line, along Montana Highway 41, about twelve miles southwest of Twin Bridges and fourteen miles northeast of Dillon. It has been confused with the landmark Lewis named Rattlesnake Cliffs, farther upstream. See below, August 10, 1805. Appleman (LC), 299–301; *Atlas* map 66. Beaverhead Rock, and the narrows of the river there, are formed by a small, upfaulted block of limestone of the Madison Group. Because the limestone is more resistant to erosion than the adjacent Tertiary sediments, the block stands out in conspicious relief, rising more than three hundred and seventy feet above the floodplain of the river.

[Lewis]   *Friday August 9th 1805.*

The morning was fair and fine; we set out at an early hour and proceeded on very well.   some parts of the river more rapid than yesterday. I walked on shore across the land to a point which I presumed they would reach by 8 A. M. our usual time of halting.   by this means I acquired leasure to accomplish some wrightings which I conceived from the nature of my instructions necessary lest any accedent should befall me on the long and reather hazardous rout I was now about to take.[1]   the party did not arrive and I returned about a mile and met them, here they halted and we breakefasted; I had killed two fine gees on my return.   while we halted here Shannon arrived, and informed us that having missed the party the day on which he set out he had returned the next morning to the place from whence he had set out or furst left them and not finding that he had supposed that they wer above him; that he then set out and marched one day up wisdom river, by which time he was convinced that they were not above him as the river could not be navigated; he then returned to the forks and had pursued us up this river.   he brought the skins of three deer which he had killed which he said were in good order. he had lived very plentifully this trip but looked a good deel worried[2] with his march.   he informed us that Wisdom river still kept it's course obliquely down the Jefferson's river as far as he was up it.   immediately after breakfast I slung my pack and set out accompanyed by Drewyer Shields and McNeal who had been previously directed to hold themselves in readiness for this service. I directed my course across the bottom to the Stard. plain led left the beaver's head about 2 miles to my left and interscepted the river about 8 miles from the point at which I had left it; I then waded it and continued my rout to the point where I could observe that it entered the mountain, but not being able to reach that place, changed my direction to the river which I struck some miles below the mountain and encamped for the evening having traveled 16 M.[3] we passed a handsom little stream formed by some large spring which rise in this wide bottom on the Lard. side of the river. we killed two Antelopes on our way and brought with us as much meat as was necessary for our suppers and breakfast the next morning. we found this bottom fertile and covered with taller grass than usual. the river very crooked much divided by islands, shallow rocky in many plases and very rapid; insomuch that I have my doubts whether the canoes could get on or not, or if they do it must be with great labour.— Capt. Clark proceeded after I left him as usual, found the current of the river increasing in rapidity towards evening. his hunters killed 2 antelopes only. in the evening it clouded up and we experienced a slight rain attended with some thunder and lightning. the musquetoes very troublesome this evening. there are some soft bogs in these vallies covered with turf. the earth of which this mud is composed is white or bluish white and appears to be argillacious.[4]

Courses and distances travelled by Capt. Clark and
Party on the 9th of August 1805

S. 12° W.	4	to a Stard. bend, passing two islands and 16 short circular bends on the Stard. side the distance by way of the river being 11 Miles.—
S. 10° E.	1	to a high bottom on Lard. distance by water 3 M. passing an island, a bayou and 4 short bends on Stard. side.
Miles	5	

[Clark]   *August 9th Friday 1805*

a fine morning wind from the N. E we proceeded on verry well rapid places more noumerous than below, Shannon the man whome we lost on Wisdom River Joined us, haveing returned to the forks & prosued us up after prosueing Wisdom River one day

Capt Lewis and 3 men Set out after brackft. to examine the river above, find a portage if possible, also the Snake Indians. I Should have taken this trip had I have been able to march, from the rageing fury of a tumer on my anckle musle, in the evening Clouded up and a fiew drops of rain   Encamped on the Lard Side near a low bluff,[5] the river to day as yesterday.   the three hunters Could kill only two antelopes to day, game of every kind Scerce

1. The nature of these "wrightings" is unclear; he may have been bringing his journals up to date or preparing written instructions to Clark in case he did not return.

2. Biddle has it "wearied." Coues (HLC), 2:470.

3. Lewis's camp was in Beaverhead County, Montana, northeast of present Dillon, by his own estimate five miles below the mouth of Blacktail Deer (McNeal's) Creek. *Atlas* map 66. Two "x's" cross out lines at about this point. Not in red and not concerned with natural history the marks are probably not by Biddle, nor is their purpose clear.

4. Peat or turf bogs develop in swampy or waterlogged areas when vegetation growth is rapid enough to cover the previous year's dead vegetation before it can decompose completely. Tertiary clays are common throughout the Beaverhead Valley and are often exposed along the river banks. When these clays wash down onto the floodplain they can color the mud and silt of the bottoms a whitish color. Nevertheless, Lewis's comments on the color of the mud here are unclear. Their high organic content should make them appear black or dark brown.

5. In Madison County, Montana, a little downstream from the Beaverhead County line and the crossing of Montana Highway 41 over the Beaverhead River. *Atlas* map 66.

[Lewis]   *Saturday August 10th 1805.*

We set out very early this morning and continued our rout through the wide bottom on the Lard. side of the river   after passing a large creek[1] at about 5 miles we fel in with a plain Indian road which led towards the point that the river entered the mountain we therefore pursued the road I sent Drewyer to the wright to kill a deer which we saw feeding and halted on the river under an immencely high perpendicular clift of rocks[2] where it entered the mountain   here we kindled a fire and waited for Drewyer.   he arrived in about an hour and a half or at noon with three deer skins and the flesh of one of the best of them, we cooked and eat a haisty meal and departed, returning a shot distance to the Indian road which led us the best way over the mountains, which are not very high but ar ruggid and approach the river closely on both sides just below these mountains   I saw several bald Eagles and two large white headed fish-inghawks[3]   boath these birds were the same common to our country.

from the number of rattle snakes about the Clifts at which we halted we called them the rattle snake clifts. this serpent is the same before discribed with oval spots of yellowish brown.[4] the river below the mountains is rapid rocky, very crooked, much divided by islands and withal shallow. after it enters the mountains it's bends are not so circuetous and it's general course more direct, but it is equally shallow les divided more rocky and rapid. we continued our rout along the Indian road which led us sometimes over the hills and again in the narrow bottoms of the river till at the distance of fifteen Ms. from the rattle snake Clifts we arrived in a hadsome open and leavel vally where the river divided itself nearly into two equal branches;[5] here I halted and examined those streams and readily discovered from their size that it would be vain to attempt the navigation of either any further. here also the road forked one leading up the vally of each of these streams. I therefore sent Drewer on one and Shields on the other to examine these roads for a short distance and to return and compare their information with respect to the size and apparent plainness of the roads as I was now determined to pursue that which appeared to have been the most traveled this spring. in the mean time I wrote a note to Capt. Clark informing him of the occurrences which had taken place, recommending it to him to halt at this place untill my return and informing him of the rout I had taken which from the information of the men on their return seemed to be in favour of the S W or Left hand fork which is reather the smallest. accordingly I put up my note on a dry willow pole at the forks, and set out up the S. E. fork, after proceeding about 1½ miles I discovered that the road became so blind that it could not be that which we had followed to the forks of Jefferson's river, neither could I find the tracks of the horses which had passed early in the spring along the other; I therefore determined to return and examine the other myself, which I did, and found that the same horses had passed up the West fork which was reather largest, and more in the direction that I wished to pursue; I therefore did not hesitate about changing my rout but determined to take the western road. I now wrote a second note to Capt C. informing him of this change and sent Drewyer to put it with the other at the forks and waited untill he returned. there is scarcely any timber on the river above the R. Snake Clifts, nor is there anything larger than willow brush in sight of these forks. immediately in the level plain between the forks and about ½ a mile distance from them stands a high rocky mountain, the base of which is surrounded by the level plain; it has a singular appearance. the mountains do not appear very high in any direction tho' the tops of some of them are partially covered with snow. this convinces me that we have ascended to a great hight since we have entered the rocky Mountains, yet the ascent has been so gradual along the vallies that it was scarcely perceptable by land. I do not beleive that the world can furnish an example of a river runing to the extent which the Missouri and Jefferson's rivers do through such a mountainous country and at the same time so navigable as they are. if the Columbia furnishes us such another example, a communication across the continent by water will be practicable and safe. but this I can scarcely hope from a knowledge of its having in it comparitively short course to the ocean the same number of feet to decend which the Missouri and Mississippi have from this point to the Gulph of Mexico.—

The valley of the west fork through which we passed for four miles boar a little to N of West and was about 1 mile wide hemned in on either side by rough mountain and steep Clifts of rock at 4½ miles this stream enters a beatifull and extensive plain about ten miles long and from 5 to six in width. this plain is surrounded on all sides by a country of roling or high wavy plains through which several little rivulets extend their wide vallies quite to the Mountains which surround the whole in an apparent Circular manner; forming one of the handsomest coves [*EC: Shoshone*] I ever saw, of about 16 or 18 miles in diameter.[6] just after entering this cove the river bends to the N. W. and runs close under the Stard. hills. here we killed a deer and encamped on the Stard. side[7] and made our fire of dry willow brush, the only fuel which the country produces. there are not more than three or four cottonwood trees in this extensive cove and they are but small. the uplands are covered with prickly pears and twisted or bearded grass and are but poor; some parts of the bottom lands are covered with grass and tolerably fertile; but much the greater proportion is covered with prickly pears sedge twisted grass the pulpy leafed thorn southernwood wild sage &c and like the uplands is very inferior in point of soil.[8] we traveled by estimate 30 Ms. today, that is 10 to the Rattle snake Clift, 15 to the forks of Jefferson's river and 5 to our camp in the cove.   at the apparent extremity of the bottom above us two perpendicular clifts of considerable hight stand on either side of the river and appers [*NB: appears*] at this distance like a gate, it is about 10 M. due West.

Capt Clark set out at sunrise this morning and pursued his rout; found the river not rapid but shallow also very crooked.   they were obliged to drag the canoes over many riffles in the course of the day.   they passed the point which the natives call the beaver's head.   it is a steep rocky clift of 150 feet high near the Stard. side of the river, opposite to it at the distance of 300 yards is a low clift of about 50 feet which is the extremity of a spur of the mountains about 4 miles distant on Lard.   at 4 P.M. they experienced a heavy shower of rain attended with hail thunder and Lightning which continued about an hour.   the men defended themselves from the hail by means of the willow bushes but all the party got perfectly wet.   after the shower was over they pursued their march and encamped on the stard side.[9]   only one deer killed by their hunters today.   tho' they took up another by the way which had been killed three days before by Jos. Fields and hung up near the river.

Courses and distances traveled by Capt. Clark
August 10th 1805.

S. 30° W.	2	to a Clift of rocks on Stard. 150 feet high called by the natives the beaver's head. distance by water 6½ miles, passing 8 bends on the Stard. side and 2 small bayous on Lard.
S. 60° W.	2	to a low bluff on the Lard. side, distance by water 6½ miles,
Miles	4	passing four islands and 18 bends on Stard. side and a low bluff and several bayous on the same side or Stard.

[Clark]   *August 10th Satturday 1805*

Some rain this morning at Sun rise and Cloudy   we proceeded on passed a remarkable Clift point on the Stard. Side about 150 feet high, this Clift the Indians Call the *Beavers* head, opposit at 300 yards is a low clift of 50 feet which is a Spur from the Mountain on the Lard. about 4 miles, the river verry Crooked, at 4 oClock a hard rain from the S W accompanied with hail Continued half an hour, all wet, the men Sheltered themselves from the hail with bushes   We Encamped on the Stard Side near a Bluff, only one Deer killed to day, the one killed Jo Fields 3 Days past & hung up we made use of   river narrow, & Sholey but not rapid.

1. Blacktail Deer Creek, "McNeal's Creek," for Hugh McNeal of the party, on *Atlas* map 66, meeting the Beaverhead River at Dillon, Beaverhead County, Montana.

2. Rattlesnake Cliffs, found about ten miles southwest of Dillon, in Beaverhead County, near Barretts siding on Interstate Highway 15. The cliffs are composed of early Tertiary, extrusive volcanic rocks (largely rhyolite). The rock is often badly fractured which allows it to form numerous little hollows when it weathers. These little hollows make excellent dens for snakes. The cliff west of the river rises to a height of about six hundred feet above the floodplain.

3. The bald eagle, *Haliaeetus leucocephalus* [AOU, 352], and the osprey, *Pandion haliaetus* [AOU, 364].

4. Prairie rattlesnake, *Crotalus viridus viridus*. Perhaps it was Biddle who drew a red vertical line through this passage.

5. The point in Beaverhead County, where Horse Prairie Creek, from the west, and Red Rock River, from the east, unite to form the Beaverhead River. Lewis considered Horse Prairie Creek the ultimate headwaters of the Missouri, but modern geographers allot this role to Red Rock River. The immediate area is now inundated by Clark Canyon Dam and Reservoir. *Atlas* map 66.

6. "Snake Indian Cove" on *Atlas* map 67, otherwise Shoshone Cove in the journals; "cove" here means a narrow mountain valley. Today the village of Grant, Beaverhead County, lies in the middle of it.

7. Apparently about six miles east of Grant and the junction of Montana Route 324 with the road from Bannack to the north. Lewis is about one and one-half miles above Clark Canyon Reservoir on Horse Prairie Creek. The camp is not shown on *Atlas* map 67.

8. This ecological observation describes how the uplands and drier areas adjacent to the bottomlands are dominated by plains prickly pear, needle and thread grass, sedge (probably thread-leaved sedge), greasewood, and big sagebrush, *Artemisia tridentata* Nutt. (Lewis's "wild sage"). The vegetation is similar to that described by Lewis on July 31, 1805, but now with the addition of sagebrush which appears with increasing elevation. Booth & Wright, 252; Mueggler & Stewart, 50–51. It was probably Biddle who drew a red vertical line through this passage.

9. Near the Madison-Beaverhead county line and above Beaverhead Rock. The mountains to larboard (east) are the Ruby Range. *Atlas* map 67.

Chapter Nineteen

From Beaverhead
Rock to
the Great Divide

August 11–16, 1805

[Lewis] *Sunday August 11th 1805.*

We set out very early this morning; but the track which we had pursued last evening soon disappeared. I therefore resolved to proceed to the narrow pass on the creek about 10 miles West in hopes that I should again find the Indian road at the place, accordingly I passed the river which was about 12 yards wide and bared in several places entirely across by beaver dams and proceeded through the level plain directly to the pass. I now sent Drewyer to keep near the creek to my right and Shields to my left, with orders to surch for the road which if they found they were to notify me by placing a hat in the muzzle of their gun. I kept McNeal with me; after having marched in this order for about five miles I discovered an Indian on horse back about two miles distant coming down the plain toward us.   with my glass I discovered from his dress that he was of a different nation from any that we had yet seen, and was satisfyed of his being a Sosone; his arms were a bow and quiver of arrows, and was mounted on an eligant horse without a saddle, and a small string which was attatched to the underjaw of the horse which answered as a bridle. I

68

was overjoyed at the sight of this stranger and had no doubt of obtaining a friendly introduction to his nation provided I could get near enough to him to convince him of our being whitemen. I therefore proceeded towards him at my usual pace.   when I had arrived within about a mile he mad a halt which I did also and unloosing my blanket from my pack, I mad him the signal of friendship known to the Indians of the Rocky mountains and those of the Missouri, which is by holding the mantle or robe in your hands at two corners and then throwing up in the air higher than the head bringing it to the earth as if in the act of spreading it, thus repeating three times.   this signal of the robe has arisen from a custom among all those nations of spreading a robe or skin for ther gests to set on when they are visited.   this signal had not the desired effect, he still kept his position and seemed to view Drewyer an Shields who were now comiming in sight on either hand with an air of suspicion, I wold willingly have made them halt but they were too far distant to hear me and I feared to make any signal to them least it should increase the suspicion in the mind of the Indian of our having some unfriendly design upon him. I therefore haistened to take out of my sack some b[e]ads a looking glas and a few trinkets which I had brought with me for this purpose and leaving my gun and pouch with McNeal advanced unarmed towards him.   he remained in the same stedfast poisture untill I arrived in about 200 paces of him when he turn his hose about and began to move off slowly from me; I now called to him in as loud a voice as I could command repeating the word *tab-ba-bone,* which in their language signifyes *white man.*[1]   but loking over his sholder he still kept his eye on Drewyer and Sheilds who wer still advancing neither of them haveing segacity enough to recollect the impropriety of advancing when they saw me thus in parley with the Indian. I now made a signal to these men to halt, Drewyer obeyed but Shields who afterwards told me that he did not obseve the signal still kept on the Indian halted again and turned his hor[s]e about as if to wait for me, and I beleive he would have remained untill I came up whith him had it not been for Shields who still pressed forward.   whe I arrived within about 150 paces I again repepeated the word tab-ba-bone and held up the trinkits in my hands and striped up my shirt sleve to give him an opportunity of seeing the colour of my skin and advanced leasure towards him but he did not remain untill I got nearer than about 100 paces when he suddonly turned his hose about, gave him the whip leaped the creek and disapeared in the willow brush in an instant and with him vanished all my hopes of obtaining horses for the preasent. I now felt quite as much mortification and disappointment as I had pleasure and expectation at the first sight of this indian. I fet soarly chargrined at the conduct of the men particularly Sheilds to whom I principally attributed this failure in obtaining an introduction to the natives. I now called the men to me and could not forbare abraiding them a little for their want of attention and imprudence on this occasion.   they had neglected to bring my spye-glass which in haist I had droped in the plain with the blanket where I made the signal before mentioned. I sent Drewyer and Shields back to surche it, they soon found it and rejoined me.   we now set out on the track of the horse hoping by that means to be lead to an indian camp, the trail of inhabitants of which should they abscond we should probably be enabled to pursue to the body of the nation to which they would most probably fly for safety.   this rout led us across a large Island framed by nearly an equal division of the creek in this bottom; after passing to the open ground on the N. side of the creek we observed that the track made out toward the high hills about 3 m. distant in that direction. I thought it probable that their camp might probably be among those hills & that they would reconnoiter us from the tops of them, and that if we advanced haistily towards them that they would become allarmed and probably run off; I therefore halted in an elivated situation near the creek had a fire kindled of willow brush cooked and took breakfast.   during this leasure I prepared a small assortment of trinkits consisting of some mockkerson awls a few strans of several kinds of b[e]ads some paint a looking glass &c which I attatched to the end of a pole and planted it near our fire in order that should the Indians return in surch of us the[y] might from this token discover that we were friendly and white persons.   before we had finised our meal a heavy shower of rain came on with some hail wich continued abot 20 minutes and wet us to the skin, after this shower we pursued the track of the horse but as the rain had raised the grass which he had trodden down it was with difficulty that we could follow it. we pursued it however about 4 miles it turning up the valley to the left under the foot of the hills. we pas several places where the Indians appeared to have been diging roots today and saw the fresh tracks of 8 or ten horses but they had been wandering about in such a confused manner that we not only lost the track of the hose which we had been pursuing but could make nothing of them. in the head of this valley we passed a large bog covered with tall grass and moss in which were a great number of springs of cold pure water, we now turned a little to the left along the foot of the high hills and arrived at a small branch on which we encamped for the night,[2] having traveled in different directions about 20 Miles and about 10 from the camp of last evening on a direct line. after meeting with the Indian today I fixed a small flag of the U'S. to a pole which I made McNeal carry. and planted in the ground where we halted or encamped.—

This morning Capt Clark dispatched several hunters a head; the morning being rainy and wet did not set out untill after an early breakfast. he passed a large Island which he called the 3000 mile Island[3] from the circumstance of it's being that distance from the entrance of the Missouri by water. a considerable proportion of the bottom on Lard. side is a bog covered with tall grass and many parts would afford fine turf; the bottom is about 8 Ms. wide and the plains which succeed it on either side extend about the same distance to the base of the mountains. they passed a number of small Islands and bayous on both sides which cut and intersect the bottoms in various directions. found the river shallow and rapid, insomuch that the men wer compelled to be in the water a considerable proportion of the day in drageing the canoes over the shoals and riffles. they saw a number of geese ducks beaver & otter, also some deer and antelopes. the men killed a beaver with a seting pole and tommahawked several Otter. the hunters killed 3 deer and an Antelope. Capt. C. observed some bunches of privy near the river.[4] there are but few trees in this botom and those small narrow leafed Cottonwood. the principal growth is willow with the narrow leaf and Currant bushes. they encamped this evening on the upper point of a large Island near the Stard. shore.—[5]

Courses and distances traveled by Capt. Clark
August 11th 1805.

S. 20° W.	1	to the lower point of 3000 M. Island. distance by water being 3. M. passing three small Islds. 6 bends on Stard. and 6 bayous on either side.
S. 25° W.	1½	to the head of the Island, distance by water 3½ M. passing 7 bends on Lard. opposite to the Island & two bayous on the same side. the Stard. Channel passes near the Stard. bluff—
South	2½	to the upper point of a large Island, distance by water 7½. the main channel on the Lard. side passing 3 small, Islands, and several small bayous and 15 bends on the Stard. side.
Miles	5̲	

[Clark]   *August 11th Sunday 1805.*

a Shower of rain this morning at Sun rise, Cloudy all the morning wind from the S W passed a large Island which I call the 3000 mile Island as it is Situated that distance from the mouth of the Missouri by water, a number of Small Bayoes running in different directions thro the Bottom, which is about 5 miles wide, then rises to an ellivated plain on each Side which extends as far.[6] passed Several Small Islands and a number of Bayoes on each Side and Encamped on the upper point of a large Island, our hunters killed three Deer, one antilope, and Tomahawked Several *Orter* to day killed one *Beaver* with a Setting pole. I observed Some bunches of Privey on the banks

1. Sources disagree on this word; some say it meant "alien" or "stranger," others that it had no meaning in Shoshone. Rees, 6, says that Lewis intended to say *Ti-yo bo-nin*, meaning "I'm a white man! See!" deriving from *Ti-you*, meaning "one originating from the sun." According to Rees, Tab-ba-bone would mean "look at the sun," perhaps explaining why the man kept looking over his shoulder. Sven Liljeblad, University of Nevada-Reno (personal communication), believes the term was apparently *taibonii*, "those of the trail of the sun" (meaning "people coming from the east"), referring to white men. In modern Shoshone the word has become *taibo*, the plural suffix *-nii* having been lost historically. Lewis presumably obtained it from Sacagawea. It is quite possible that at this time the Shoshones had no specific term for "white man," having had no experiences with whites. Bakeless (LCPD), 235; Trenholm & Carley, 43–44; Ronda (LCAI), 140.

2. Near the northwest end of Shoshone Cove, in Beaverhead County, Montana. The camp may have been near Printer Creek; it is not shown on *Atlas* map 67.

3. Apparently this island, in Beaverhead County, has since disappeared, due to the river's change in course. *Atlas* map 66.

4. The privet is probably *Philadelphus lewisii* Pursh, Lewis's syringa or Lewis's mock orange, which has small, opposite, deciduous leaves much like the cultivated privet, and is known from the vicinity. This new species was collected by Lewis on the return trip in 1806 and named for him by Pursh. Cutright (LCPN), 299, 363, 413–14; Hitchcock et al., 3:86–87; Booth & Wright, 108.

5. In Beaverhead County, roughly halfway between Beaverhead Rock and present Dillon. *Atlas* map 66.

6. The wide bottoms in this area (about three and one-half miles maximum) exist because of the constriction of the river at Beaverhead Rock, which acts somewhat like a dam. The velocity of the river above the narrows is reduced, and the river is forced to drop part of its bedload, forming a wide valley. The elevated plain to the east of the river is part of the East Bench, a pediment surface developed primarily on soft Tertiary sediments.

[Lewis]   *Monday August 12th 1805*

This morning I sent Drewyer out as soon as it was light, to try and discover what rout the Indians had taken. he followed the track of the horse we had pursued yesterday to the mountain wher it had ascended, and returned to me in about an hour and a half. I now determined to pursue the base of the mountains which form this cove to the S. W. in the expectation of finding some Indian road which lead over the Mountains, accordingly I sent Drewyer to my right and Shields to my left with orders to look out for a road or the fresh tracks of horses either of which we should first meet with I had determined to pursue. at the distance of about 4 miles we passed 4 small rivulets[1] near each other on which we saw som resent bowers or small conic lodges formed with willow brush. near them the indians had geathered a number of roots from the manner in which they had toarn up the ground; but I could not discover the root which they seemed to be in surch of.[2] I [saw] several large hawks that were nearly black.[3] near this place we fell in with a large and plain Indian road which came into the cove from the N. E. and led along the foot of the mountains to the S. W. oliquely approaching the main stream which we had left yesterday. this road we now pursued to the S. W. at 5 miles it passed a stout stream[4] which is a principal fork of the man stream and falls into it just above the narrow pass between the two clifts before mentioned and which we now saw below us. here we halted and breakfasted on the last of our venison, having yet a small peice of pork in reseve. after eating we continued our rout through the low bottom of the main stream along the foot of the mountains on our right the valley for 5 mes. further in a S. W. direction was from 2 to 3 miles wide the main stream[5] now after discarding two stream on the left in this valley turns abruptly to the West through a narrow bottom betwen the mountains. the road was still plain, I therefore did not dispair of shortly finding a passage over the mountains and of taisting the waters of the great Columbia this evening. we saw an animal which we took to be of the fox kind as large or reather larger than the small wolf of the plains.[6] it's colours were a curious mixture of black, redis-brown and yellow. Drewyer shot at him about 130 yards and knocked him dow bet he recovered and got out of our reach. it is certainly a different animal from any that we have yet seen. we also saw several of the heath cock[7] with a long pointed tail and an uniform dark brown colour but could not kill one of them. they are much larger than the common dunghill fowls, and in their [h]abits and manner of flying resemble the growse or prarie hen. at the distance of 4 miles further the road took us to the most distant fountain of the waters of the mighty Missouri in surch of which we have spent so many toilsome days and wristless nights. thus far I had accomplished one of those great objects on which my mind has been unalterably fixed for many years, judge then of the pleasure I felt in allying my thirst with this pure and ice cold water which issues from the base of a low mountain or hill of a gentle ascent for ½ a mile. the mountains are high on either hand leave this gap at the head of this rivulet through which the road passes.[8] here I halted a few minutes and rested myself. two miles below McNeal had exultingly stood with a foot on each side of this little rivulet and thanked his god that he had lived to bestride the mighty & heretofore deemed endless Missouri. after refreshing ourselves we proceeded on to the top of the dividing ridge from which I discovered immence ranges of high mountains still to the West of us with their tops partially covered with snow. I now decended the mountain about ¾ of a mile which I found much steeper than on the opposite side, to a handsome bold running Creek of cold Clear water. here I first tasted the water of the great Columbia river.[9] after a short halt of a few minutes we continued our march along the Indian road which lead us over steep hills and deep hollows to a spring on the side of a mountain where we found a sufficient quantity of dry willow brush for fuel, here we encamped for the night having traveled about 20 Miles. as we had killed nothing during the day we now boiled and eat the remainder of our pork, having yet a little flour and parched meal. at the creek[10] on this side of the mountain I observed a species of deep perple currant[11] lower in its growth, the stem more branched and leaf doubly as large as that of the Missouri. the leaf is covered on it's under disk with a hairy pubersence. the fruit is of the ordinary size and shape of the currant and is supported in the usual manner, but is ascid & very inferior in point of flavor.—

this morning Capt. Clark set out early. found the river shoally, rapid shallow, and extreemly difficult. the men in the water almost all day. they are geting weak soar and much fortiegued; they complained of the fortiegue to which the navigation subjected them and wished to go by land Capt. C. engouraged them and passifyed them. one of the canoes was very near overseting in a rapid today. they proceeded but slowly. at noon they had a thunderstorm which continued about half an hour. their hunters killed 3 deer and a fawn. they encamped in a smoth plain near a few cottonwood trees on the Lard. side.—[12]

Courses and distances traveled by Capt. Clark.
August 12th 1805.

S. 8° W.	2	to the upper point of a large Island, distance by water 5½ M. passing many Bayous, 3 Islands and 9 bends on the Stard. side. the main channel on Stard. side.
S. 10° W.	2	to a Stard. bend distant by water 6½ passing 4 small and 2 large
Miles	4	Islands, several bayous and a number of short bends and a run of water on the Stard. side.—

[Clark]   *August 12th Monday 1805*

We Set out early (Wind N E) proceeded on passed Several large Islands and three Small ones, the river much more Sholey than below which obliges us to haul the Canoes over those Sholes which Suckceed each other at Short intervales emencely laborious men much fatigued and weakened by being continualy in the water drawing the Canoes over the Sholes   encamped on the Lard Side   men complain verry much of the emence labour they are obliged to undergo & wish much to leave the river.   I passify them.   the weather Cool, and nothing to eate but venison, the hunters killed three Deer to day

1. Among them perhaps Painter, Coyote, and Grimes creeks.

2. Perhaps camas, *Camassia quamash* (Pursh) Greene, or one of several other species of the same genus, a staple food of the mountain tribes. See entries for September 20, 1805, and June 11, 1806. Cutright (LCPN), 209; Hitchcock et al., 1:780–82.

3. Perhaps the melanistic color phase of one of various species of hawks, such as the red-tailed hawk, *Buteo jamaicensis* [AOU, 337], or Swainson's hawk, *B. swainsoni* [AOU, 342]. Coues (HLC), 2:486 n. 11. See also Holmgren, 30.

4. Probably Bloody Dick Creek. Peebles (RW), 4.

5. Lewis was now going up Trail Creek toward Lemhi Pass, the Continental Divide, and the Montana-Idaho border.

6. Possibly a wolverine, *Gulo luscus*. See above, June 14, 1805. Burroughs, 82–83. It was probably Biddle who drew a red vertical line through this passage.

7. Sage grouse, *Centrocercus urophasianus* [AOU, 309]. Ibid., 213–15. Lewis compares it to the barnyard chicken and the sharp-tailed grouse, *Tympanuchus phasianellus* [AOU, 308]. Again perhaps it was Biddle who drew the red vertical line through this material.

8. Lewis and his party were the first U.S. citizens to cross the Continental Divide; they went through Lemhi Pass from Beaverhead County, Montana, to Lemhi County, Idaho, leaving the Louisiana Purchase territory. The area still retains its wilderness character. Appleman (LC), 273–75; *Atlas* map 67.

9. Horseshoe Bend Creek flowing into the Lemhi River, in Lemhi County. By way of the Salmon and Snake rivers its waters do reach the Columbia. The Lemhi is "East Fork of Lewis R" on *Atlas* map 67; the word Lewis appears to be a substitution on the map. Peebles (RW), 5.

10. Possibly Agency Creek, Lemhi County. *Atlas* map 67.

11. Hudson gooseberry, *Ribes hudsonianum* Rich. Booth & Wright, 107; Hitchcock et al., 3:73–74. Again it was probably Biddle who drew the red vertical line through this material.

12. Although both captains place this camp on the larboard side, as does Ordway, on *Atlas* map 66 it appears on the starboard side. It was a few miles below the mouth of Blacktail Deer (McNeal's) Creek, north of Dillon, in Beaverhead County, a few miles downstream from the point where Interstate Highway 15 crosses the Beaverhead.

[Lewis]   Tuesday August 13th 1805.

We set out very early on the Indian road which still led us through an open broken country in a westerly direction.   a deep valley appeared to our left at the base of a high range of mountains which extended from

S. E. to N. W.[1] having their sides better clad with pine timber than we had been accustomed to see the mountains and their tops were also partially covered with snow.   at the distance of five miles the road after leading us down a long decending valley for 2 Ms. brought us to a large creek about 10 yds. wide;[2] this we passed and on rising the hill beyond it had a view of a handsome little valley to our left of about a mile in width through which from the appearance of the timber I conjectured that a river passed. I saw near the creek some bushes of the white maple, the ⟨small⟩ shumate of the small species with the winged rib, and a species of honeysuckle much in it's growth and leaf like the small honeysuckle of the Missouri only reather larger and bears a globular berry as large as a garden pea and as white as wax.[3] this berry is formed of a thin smooth pellicle which envellopes a soft white musilagenous substance in which there are several small brown seed irregularly scattered or intermixed without any sell or perceptable membranous covering.— we had proceeded about four miles through a wavy plain parallel to the valley or river bottom when at the distance of about a mile we saw two women, a man and some dogs on an eminence immediately before us.   they appeared to vew us with attention and two of them after a few minutes set down as if to wait our arrival we continued our usual pace towards them.   when we had arrived within half a mile of them I directed the party to halt and leaving my pack and rifle I took the flag which I unfurled and avanced singly towards them the women soon disappeared behind the hill, the man continued untill I arrived within a hundred yards of him and then likewise absconded.   tho' I frequently repeated the word *tab-ba-bone* sufficiently loud for him to have heard it. I now haistened to the top of the hill where they had stood but could see nothing of them.   the dogs were less shye than their masters they came about me pretty close   I therefore thought of tying a handkerchief about one of their necks with some beads and other trinkets and then let them loose to surch their fugitive owners thinking by this means to convince them of our pacific disposition towards them but the dogs would not suffer me to take hold of them; they also soon disappeared. I now made a signal fror the men to come on, they joined me and we pursued the back tarck of these Indians which lead us along the same road which we had been traveling.   the road was dusty and appeared to have been much traveled lately both by men and horses. these praries are very poor the soil is of a light yellow clay, intermixed with small smooth gravel,[4] and produces little else but prickly pears, and bearded grass about 3 inches high.   the prickley pear are of three species that with a broad leaf common to the missouri; that of a globular form also common to the upper pa[r]t of the Missouri and more especially after it enters the Rocky Mountains, also a 3rd peculiar to this country.[5] it consists of small circular thick leaves with a much greater number of thorns.   these thorns are stronger and appear to be barbed.   the leaves grow from the margins of each other as in the broad leafed pear of the missouri, but are so slightly attatched that when the thorn touches your mockerson it adhears and brings with it the leaf covered in every direction with many others.   this is much the most troublesome plant of the three.   we had not continued our rout more than a mile when we were so fortunate as to meet with three female savages.   the short and steep ravines which we passed concealed us from each other untill we arrived within 30 paces.   a young woman immediately took to flight, an Elderly woman and a girl of about 12 years old remained. I instantly laid by my gun and advanced towards them.   they appeared much allarmed but saw that we were to near for them to escape by flight they therefore seated themselves on the ground, holding down their heads as if reconciled to die which the expected no doubt would be their fate; I took the elderly woman by the hand and raised her up repeated the word *tab-ba-bone* and strip up my shirt sleve to sew her my skin; to prove to her the truth of the ascertion that I was a white man for my face and hads which have been constantly exposed to the sun were quite as dark as their own. they appeared instantly reconciled, and the men coming up I gave these women some beads a few mockerson awls some pewter looking-glasses and a little paint. I directed Drewyer to request the old woman to recall the young woman who had run off to some distance by this time fearing she might allarm the camp before we approached and might so exasperate the natives that they would perhaps attack us without enquiring who we were.[6]   the old woman did as she was requested and the fugitive soon returned almost out of breath. I bestoed an equvolent portion of trinket on her with the others. I now painted their tawny cheeks with some ver-

million which with this nation is emblematic of peace. after they had become composed I informed them by signs that I wished them to conduct
us to their camp that we wer anxious to become acquainted with the
chiefs and warriors of their nation. they readily obeyed and we set out,
still pursuing the road down the river. we had marched about 2 miles
when we met a party of about 60 warriors mounted on excellent horses
who came in nearly full speed,[7] when they arrived I advanced towards
them with the flag leaving my gun with the party about 50 paces behid
me. the chief and two others who were a little in advance of the main
body spoke to the women, and they informed them who we were and exultingly shewed the presents which had been given them these men
then advanced and embraced me very affectionately in their way which is
by puting their left arm over you wright sholder clasping your back, while
they apply their left cheek to yours and frequently vociforate the word
âh-hi'-e, âh-hi'-e[8] that is, I am much pleased, I am much rejoiced. bothe
parties now advanced and we wer all carresed and besmeared with their
grease and paint till I was heartily tired of the national hug. I now had the
pipe lit and gave them smoke; they seated themselves in a circle around
us and pulled of their mockersons before they would receive or smoke
the pipe. this is a custom among them as I afterwards learned indicative
of a sacred obligation of sincerity in their profession of friendship given
by the act of receiving and smoking the pipe of a stranger. or which is as
much as to say that they wish they may always go bearfoot if they are not
sincere; a pretty heavy penalty if they are to march through the plains of
their country. after smoking a few pipes with them I distributed some
trifles among them, with which they seemed much pleased particularly
with the blue beads and vermillion. I now informed the chief that the object of our visit was a friendly one, that after we should reach his camp I
would undertake to explain to him fully those objects, who we wer, from
whence we had come and wither we were going; that in the mean time I
did not care how soon we were in motion, as the sun was very warm and
no water at hand. they now put on their mockersons, and the principal
chief Ca-me-âh-wait[9] made a short speach to the warriors. I gave him the
flag which I informed him was an emblem of peace among whitemen and
now that it had been received by him it was to be respected as the bond of

union between us. I desired him to march on, which did and we followed
him; the dragoons moved on in squadron in our rear. after we had
marched about a mile in this order he halted them ang gave a second ha-
rang; after which six or eight of the young men road forward to their
encampment and no further regularity was observed in the order of
march. I afterwards understood that the Indians we had first seen this
morning had returned and allarmed the camp; these men had come out
armed cap a pe [10] for action expecting to meet with their enemies the Minnetares of Fort de Prarie whome they Call Pâh'-kees. [11]   they were armed
with b[o]ws arrow and Shield except three whom I observed with small
pieces such as the N. W. Company furnish the natives with which they
had obtained from the Rocky Mountain Indians [12] on the yellow stone
river with whom they are at peace.   on our arrival at their encampmen [13]
on the river in a handsome level and fertile bottom at the distance of
4 Ms. from where we had first met them they introduced us to a londge
made of willow brush and an old leather lodge which had been prepared
for our reception by the young men which the chief had dispatched for
that purpose. Here we were seated on green boughs and the skins of Antelopes.   one of the warriors then pulled up the grass in the center of the
lodge forming a smal circle of about 2 feet in diameter   the chief next
produced his pipe and native tobacco and began a long cerimony of the
pipe when we were requested to take of our mockersons, the Chief having previously taken off his as well as all the warriors present.   this we
complyed with; the Chief then lit his pipe at the fire kindled in this little
magic circle, and standing on the oposite side of the circle uttered a
speach of several minutes in length at the conclusion of which he pointed
the stem to the four cardinal points of the heavens first begining at the
East and ending with the North.   he now presented the pipe to me as if
desirous that I should smoke, but when I reached my hand to receive it,
he drew it back and repeated the same cremony three times, after which
he pointed the stem first to the heavens then to the center of the magic
circle smoked himself with three whifs and held the pipe untill I took as
many as I thought proper; he then held it to each of the white persons
and then gave it to be consumed by his warriors.   this pipe was made of a

dense simitransparent green stone[14] very highly polished about 2½ inches long and of an oval figure, the bowl being in the same direction with the stem. a small piece of birned clay is placed in the bottom of the bowl to seperate the tobacco from the end of the stem and is of an irregularly rounded figure not fitting the tube purfectly close in order that the smoke may pass. this is the form of the pipe.[15] their tobacco is of the same kind of that used by the Minnetares Mandans and Ricares of the Missouri.[16] the Shoshonees do not cultivate this plant, but obtain it from the Rocky mountain Indians and some of the bands of their own nation who live further south. I now explained to them the objects of our journey &c. all the women and children of the camp were shortly collected about the lodge to indulge themselves with looking at us, we being the first white persons they had ever seen. after the cerimony of the pipe was over I distributed the remainder of the small articles I had brought with me among the women and children. by this time it was late in the evening and we had not taisted any food since the evening before. the Chief informed us that they had nothing but berries to eat and gave us some cakes of serviceberries and Choke cherries which had been dryed in the sun; of these I made a hearty meal, and then walked to the river, which I found about 40 yards wide very rapid clear and about 3 feet deep. the banks low and abrupt as those of the upper part of the Missouri, and the bed formed of loose stones and gravel.[17] Cameahwait informed me that this stream discharged itself into another doubly as large at the distance of half a days march which came from the S. W.[18] but he added on further enquiry that there was but little more timber below the junction of those rivers than I saw here, and that the river was confined between inacessable mountains, was very rapid and rocky insomuch that it was impossible for us to pass either by land or water down this river to the great lake where the white men lived as he had been informed. this was unwelcome information but I still hoped that this account had been exagerated with a view to detain us among them. as to timber I could discover not any that would answer the purpose of constructing canoes or in short more than was bearly necessary for fuel consisting of the narrow leafed cottonwood and willow, also the red willow Choke Cherry[19] service

at the East and ending with the North. he now pre-
-ented the pipe to me as if desireous I should smoke
but when I reached my hand to receive it, he drew it
back and repeated the same cremony three times, after
which he pointed the stem first to the heavens then
to the center of the magic circle smoked himself
with three whifs and held the pipe untill I too
as many as I thought proper, he then held it to a
of the white persons and then gave it to be consu-
-ed by his warriors. this pipe was made of a dens
simltransparent green stone very highly polishe
about 2½ inches long and of an oval figure, the
bowl being in the same direction with the stem. a
small piece of birned clay is placed in the bottom o
the bowl to seperate the tobacco from the end of t
stem and is of an irregularly rounded figure not fill
the tube perfectly close in order that the smoke
may pass. this is the form of the pipe. their tobacco
is of the same kind

of that used by the Minnela
mandans and
Ricares of the Missouri. the Shoshones do not cultivate this
plant, but obtain it from the Rocky mountain Indian
and some of the bands of their own nation who live fur
ther south. I now explained to them the object of our journey &c.
all the women and children of the camp w
shortly collected about the lodge to endulge themselves in
looking at us, we being the first white persons they, ha
ever seen. after the cerimany of the pipe was over I di
-tributed the remainder of the small articles I had
braught with me among the women and children
by this time it was late in the evening and we had n
tasted any food since the evening before. the Chief
informed us that they, had nothing but berries to ea

1. Shoshone Smoking-pipe, August 13, 1805, Codex F, p. 99

berry and a few currant bushes such as were common on the Missouri.
these people had been attacked by the Minetares of Fort de prarie this
spring and about 20 of them killed and taken prisoners. on this occasion they lost a great part of their horses and all their lodges except that
which they had erected for our accomodation; they were now living in
lodges of a conic figure made of willow brush. I still observe a great number of horses feeding in every direction around their camp and therefore
entertain but little doubt but we shall be enable to furnish ourselves with
an adiquate number to transport our stores even if we are compelled to
travel by land over these mountains. on my return to my lodge an indian called me in to his bower and gave me a small morsel of the flesh of
an antelope boiled, and a peice of a fresh salmon roasted;[20] both which I
eat with a very good relish. this was the first salmon I had seen and perfectly convinced me that we were on the waters of the Pacific Ocean. the
course of this river is a little to the North of west as far as I can discover it;
and is bounded on each side by a range of high Mountains. tho' those on
the E. side are lowest and more distant from the river.—[21]

This evening the Indians entertained us with their dancing nearly all
night. at 12 O'Ck. I grew sleepy and retired to rest leaving the men to
amuse themselves with the Indians. I observe no essential difference between the music and manner of dancing among this nation and those of
the Missouri. I was several times awoke in the course of the night by their
yells but was too much fortiegued to be deprived of a tolerable sound
night's repose.

This morning Capt Clark set out early having previously dispatched
some hunters ahead. it was cool and cloudy all the forepart of the day.
at 8 A. M. they had a slight rain. they passed a number of shoals over
which they were obliged to drag the canoes; the men in the water ¾ths of
the day, the[y] passed a bold runing stream 7 yds. wide on the Lard. side
just below a high point of Limestone rocks. this stream we call McNeal's
Creek after Hugh McNeal one of our party.[22] this creek heads in the
Mountains to the East and forms a handsome valley for some miles between the mountains. from the top of this limestone Clift above the
creek The beaver's head boar N 24° E. 12 Ms. the course of Wisdom
river or that which the opening of it's valley makes through the moun-

tains is N. 25 W. to the gap through which Jefferson's river enters the mountains above is S 18° W 10 M. they killed one deer only today. saw a number of Otter some beaver Antelopes ducks gees and Crains. they caught a number of fine trout as they have every day since I left them. they encamped on Lrd. in a smooth level prarie near a few cottonwood trees,[23] but were obliged to make use of the dry willow brush for fuel.—

Courses and distances travelled by Capt. Clark.
August 13th 1805.

South	1	to a point of rocks about 70 feet high on Stard. distance by water 4 Mt passing the head of the Island. at 2½ Ms. opposite to which we encamped last evening. also the entrance of a bold Creek 7 Yds. wide on Lard. behind an Isld. this we called McNeal's Creek, after Hugh McNeal of our party.—
S. 30° W. Miles 5	4	to a Clift of high rocks on the Stard. side distance by water 12 M. passing several islds. and bayous on either side the river very crooked and bends short.

[Clark]   *August 13th Tuesday 1805*

a verry Cool morning   the Thermometer Stood at 52 a 0 all the fore part of the day. Cloudy at 8 oClock a mist of rain   we proceeded on passed inumerable Sholes   obliged to haul the boat ¾ of the Day over the Shole water.   passed the mouth of a bold running Stream 7 yards wide on the Lard Side below a high Point of Limestone rocks on the Stard Side   this Creek heads in the mountains to the easte and forms a Vallie between two mountains. Call this stream McNeal Creek From the top of this rock the—

Point of the Beaver head hill bears	N. 24° E 12 ms.
The Course of the Wisdom river is—	N. 25° W.
The gap at the place the river passes thro' a mountain in advance is—	S. 18° W. 10 ms.

proceeded on and Encamped on the Lard side   no wood except dry willows and them Small, one Deer killed to day. The river obliges the men to undergo great fatigue and labour in hauling the Canoes over the Sholes in the Cold water naked.

1. Lewis was looking at the Lemhi Range and the valley of the Lemhi River, "Lewis's River" on *Atlas* map 67.

2. Perhaps Pattee Creek, Lemhi County, Idaho. Peebles (RW), 5; *Atlas* map 67.

3. The white maple is Rocky Mountain maple, *Acer glabrum* Torr. The "shumate" may be either skunkbush sumac, *Rhus trilobata* (Nutt.) Gray, or poison ivy, *R. radicans* L., neither of which have been verified for the locality but which are to be expected. Lewis's honeysuckle is the first mention of common snowberry, *Symphoricarpos albus* (L.) Blake. The honeysuckle of the Missouri used for comparison is wolfberry; it is very similiar and also grows in western Montana. Seeds of the snowberry were collected, taken back, and later grown in Thomas Jefferson's garden and widely introduced into the horticultural trade from gardens in Philadelphia. Lewis's ability to distinguish between these two species based on leaf and fruit characteristics again demonstrates his remarkable botanical powers of observation. Booth & Wright, 150, 149, 234; Hitchcock et al., 3:407–9, 4:464–65; Cutright (LCPN), 210, 212, 372, 374–75. Perhaps it was Biddle who drew a red vertical line from "shumate" to "membranous covering."

4. Tertiary sediments predominate on the uplands on the north side of the Lemhi River; river deposits are in the bottomlands. The soil here is immature because of the aridity and is only slightly altered from the parent sand, silt, and clay of the underlying sediments. Most of the gravel was derived from the Lemhi River and was deposited here before the river was lowered to its present level.

5. The three species of cacti in this region are plains prickly pear; pink pincushion cactus, *Coryphantha vivipara* (Nutt.) Britton & Rose; and brittle, or little, prickly pear, *Opuntia fragilis* (Nutt.) Haw. Booth & Wright, 159–60; Hitchcock et al., 3:458–59; Benson (CUSC), 822–23, 394–99. It was again probably Biddle who drew the red vertical line through this passage about cacti.

6. In the absence of Sacagawea and Charbonneau the conversation must have been in sign language, in which Drouillard was proficient. See below, August 14, 1805.

7. Lewis had met the Lemhi Shoshones, a division of the Northern Shoshones of the Rocky Mountains, known to the Great Plains tribes as "Snakes" or "Grass Lodges." The history and etymology of the name "Shoshone," historically the name of one of the bands of that tribe, are unknown. Today, Northern Shoshone speakers pronounce it *şóş·ni*, a borrowing from English. They call themselves *nimi* (singular), "person" or *niminii* (plural), "the people." Sven Liljeblad, personal communication. Unlike the Western Shoshones of the Great Basin, the Northern Shoshones had acquired horses in the years after 1700 and had become buffalo hunters on the plains; hence, they were strongly influenced by plains culture. Having lived on the northern plains in Montana, they were driven west of the Continental Divide by the time of Lewis and Clark, by Blackfeet and other tribes. Lewis observed how they mixed traits of mountains and plains culture, living part of the year on salmon and roots in the mountain valleys, then hunting buffalo on the western edge of the plains the rest of the time. They were still subject to raids west of the divide, and their hunts on the plains were attended with great risk. Apparently their meeting with Lewis was their first direct contact with whites, although they possessed trade goods, including a

few guns, that had come to them from other Indians. Trenholm & Carley; Hyde (IHP), 175–81; Ronda (LCAI), 150–51.

8. The expression "âh-hi'-e, â-hi'-e" is still used in modern Shoshone in the form *ahuu*, "thank you," said upon receiving a gift. Sven Liljeblad, personal communication.

9. Evidently the first use in the journals of the chief's name. Rees, 7, interprets it to mean "not inclined to go" and believes the Shoshones gave it to him on this occasion because of their fear of going to meet Clark and the main body of the Corps, as Lewis urged. Rees says his real name was Too-ite-coon, "fires black gun." See below, August 24, 1805. Sven Liljeblad, personal communication, gives the names as *kee miawaiti*, "he does not walk," and *tuu'edikandi*, "black weapon owner," that is, "He Never Walks" and "Musket Owner."

10. From the Medieval French *cap-à-pie*, literally "head to foot," referring to knights in full armor.

11. Here, as earlier, the Atsinas. Rees, 4, interprets the Shoshone name as *Pahkeeks*, meaning "the place where the water falls," an allusion to the Great Falls of the Missouri, from whence they were known as "Fall Indians." See above, Estimate of Eastern Indians, vol. 3, and May 28, 1805. Sven Liljeblad, personal communication, believes the term is *pakihi'i*, "stiff, hardened blanket," referring to rawhide armor that the Shoshones called "rawhide blankets," which were carried into battle by their enemies to the north—Blackfeet, Arapahoes, Atsinas, and Assiniboines. The term was used historically to designate all of these tribes, but in modern times it has come to be applied exclusively to the Piegan Blackfeet.

12. Probably the Crows, who would have obtained the weapons at the Mandan-Hidatsa villages.

13. The village at this time was about seven miles north of present Tendoy, Lemhi County, on the east bank of the Lemhi River, probably just north of Sandy Creek. Appleman (LC), 270; *Atlas* map 67.

14. The pipe was made either from a piece of pale green talc or, more likely, from a darker green, massive serpentine. The source of either of these materials was probably the area of the Ruby Range near Dillon, Beaverhead County, Montana.

15. See fig. 1, a sketch appearing in Codex F, p. 99, at this point.

16. *Nicotiana quadrivalvis* Pursh. Goodspeed, 451; Gilmore (UPI), 61–62.

17. The steep gradient of the Lemhi and its tributaries and the proximity of a source of indurated rock combine to produce a bed containing rounded gravel and cobbles.

18. The Salmon River. On *Atlas* map 67, the Salmon below the junction is Lewis's River.

19. The red willow is red osier dogwood, *Cornus sericea* L. Choke cherry is *Prunus virginiana* L. var. *melanocarpa* (A. Nels.) Sarg. Kartesz & Kartesz, 169; Hitchock et al., 3:161–62.

20. The salmon would be *Oncorhynchus* sp.

21. The Lemhi Range lay to the west and the Beaverhead Mountains to the east. *Atlas* map 67.

22. Blacktail Deer Creek reaches the Beaverhead at present Dillon, Beaverhead County, heading in the Snowcrest Range. The cliff is formed of limestone of the Mississippian-age Madison Group. It rises about forty feet above the floodplain of the Beaverhead River. It is shown as "rock Clift" on *Atlas* map 66 and is known locally as Clark's Lookout.

23. A few miles southwest of Dillon, in Beaverhead County, and north of where Montana Highway 41 crosses the Beaverhead and joins Interstate Highway 15 today. *Atlas* map 66.

[Lewis]   *Wednesday August 14th*

In order to give Capt. Clark time to reach the forks of Jefferson's river I concluded to spend this day at the Shoshone Camp and obtain what information I could with rispect to the country.   as we had nothing but a little flour and parched meal to eat except the berries with which the Indians furnished us I directed Drewyer and Shields to hunt a few hours and try to kill something, the Indians furnished them with horses and most of their young men also turned out to hunt.   the game which they principally hunt is the Antelope which they pursue on horseback and shoot with their arrows.   this animal is so extreemly fleet and dureable that a single horse has no possible chance to overtake them or run them down.   the Indians are therefore obliged to have recorce to strategem when they discover a herd of the Antelope they seperate and scatter themselves to the distance of five or six miles in different directions arround them generally scelecting some commanding eminence for a stand; some one or two now pursue the herd at full speed over the hills vallies gullies and the sides of precipices that are tremendious to view. thus after runing them from five to six or seven miles the fresh horses that were in waiting head them and drive them back persuing them as far or perhaps further quite to the other extreem of the hunters who now in turn pursue on their fresh horses thus ⟨finally⟩ worrying the poor animal down and finally killing them with their arrows.   forty or fifty hunters will be engaged for half a day in this manner and perhaps not kill more than two or three Antelopes.   they have but few Elk or black tailed deer, and the common red deer they cannot take as they secrete themselves in the brush when pursued, and they have only the bow and arrow wich is a very slender dependence for killing any game except such as they can run down with their horses. I was very much entertained with a view of this indian chase; it was after a herd of about 10 Antelope and about 20 hunters. it lasted about 2 hours and considerable part of the chase in view from my tent. about 1 A. M. the hunters returned had not killed a single Antelope, and their horses foaming with sweat. my hunters returned soon after and had been equally unsuccessfull. I now directed McNeal to make me a little paist with the flour and added some berries to it which I found very pallateable.

The means I had of communicating with these people was by way of Drewyer who understood perfectly the common language of jesticulation or signs which seems to be universally understood by all the Nations we have yet seen.[1] it is true that this language is imperfect and liable to error but is much less so than would be expected.[2] the strong parts of the ideas are seldom mistaken.

I now prevailed on the Chief to instruct me with rispect to the geography of his country. this he undertook very cheerfully, by delienating the rivers on the ground. but I soon found that his information fell far short of my expectation or wishes. he drew the river on which we now are to which he placed two branches just above us,[3] which he shewed me from the openings of the mountains were in view; he next made it discharge itself into a large river which flowed from the S. W. about ten miles below us,[4] then continued this joint stream in the same direction of this valley or N. W. for one days march and then enclined it to the West for 2 more days march, here he placed a number of heeps of sand on each side which he informed me represented the vast mountains of rock eternally covered with snow through which the river passed.[5] that the perpendicular and even juting rocks so closely hemned in the river that there was no possibilyte of passing along the shore; that the bed of the river was obstructed by sharp pointed rocks and the rapidity of the stream such that the whole surface of the river was beat into perfect foam as far as the eye could reach. that the mountains were also inaccessible to man or horse. he said that this being the state of the country in that direction that himself nor none of his nation had ever been further down the river than these mountains. I then enquired the state of the country on either side of the river but he could not inform me. he said there was

an old man of his nation a days march below who could probably give me
some information of the country to the N. W. and refered me to an old
man then present for that to the S. W.— the Chief further informed me
that he had understood from the persed nosed Indians[6] who inhabit this
river below the rocky mountains that it ran a great way toward the seting
sun and finally lost itself in a great lake of water which was illy taisted, and
where the white men lived. I next commenced my enquiries of the old
man to whom I had been refered for information relative the country
S W. of us. this he depicted with horrors and obstructions scarcely inferior to that just mentioned. he informed me that the band of this nation to which he belonged resided at the distance of 20 days march from
hence not far from the white people[7] with whom they traded for horses
mules cloth metal beads and the shells which they woar as orniment being
those of a species of perl oister. that the course to his relations was a
little to the West of South. that in order to get to his relations the first
seven days we should be obliged to climb over steep and rocky mountains
where we could find no game to kill nor anything but roots such as a ferce
and warlike nation lived on whom he called the broken mockersons[8] or
mockersons with holes, and said inhabited those mountains and lived like
the bear of other countries among the rocks and fed on roots or the flesh
of such horses as they could take or steel from those who passed through
their country. that in passing this country the feet of our horses would
be so much wounded with the stones many of them would give out. the
next part of the rout was about 10 days through a dry and parched sandy
desert[9] in which no food at this season for either man or horse, and in
which we must suffer if not perish for the want of water. that the sun
had now dryed up the little pools of water which exist through this desert
plain in the spring season and had also scorched all the grass. that no
animal inhabited this plain on which we could hope to subsist. that
about the center of this plain a large river passed from S. E. to N. W.
which was navigable but afforded neither Salmon nor timber.[10] that beyond this plain thee or four days march his relations lived in a country
tolerable fertile and partially covered with timber on another large river
which ran in the same direction of the former.[11] that this last discharged
itself into a large river[12] on which many numerous nations lived with

whom his relations were at war but whether this last discharged itself into the great lake or not he did not know. that from his relations it was yet a great distance to the great or stinking lake as they call the Ocean. that the way which such of his nation as had been to the Stinking lake traveled was up the river on which they lived and over to that on which the white people lived which last they knew discharged itself into the Ocean, and that this was the way which he would advise me to travel if I was determined to proceed to the Ocean but would advise me to put off the journey untill the next spring when he would conduct me. I thanked him for his information and advise and gave him a knife with which he appeared to be much gratifyed. from this narative I was convinced that the streams of which he had spoken as runing through the plains and that on which his relations lived were southern branches of the Columbia, heading with the rivers Apostles and Collorado, and that the rout he had pointed out was to the Vermillion Sea or gulph of Callifornia.[13] I therefore told him that this rout was more to the South than I wished to travel, and requested to know if there was no rout on the left of this river on which we now are, by means of which, I could intercept it below the mountains through which it passes; but he could not inform me of any except that of the barren plain which he said joined the mountain on that side and through which it was impossible for us to pass at this season even if we were fortunate enough to escape from the broken mockerson Indians. I now asked Cameahwait by what rout the Pierced nosed indians, who he informed me inhabited this river below the mountains, came over to the Missouri; this he informed me was to the north, but added that the road was a very bad one as he had been informed by them and that they had suffered excessively with hunger on the rout being obliged to subsist for many days on berries alone as there was no game in that part of the mountains which were broken rockey and so thickly covered with timber that they could scarcely pass. however knowing that Indians had passed, and did pass, at this season on that side of this river to the same below the mountains, my rout was instantly settled in my own mind, povided the account of this river should prove true on an investigation of it, which I was determined should be made before we would undertake the rout by land in any direction. I felt perfectly satisfyed, that if the Indians could pass these mountains with their women and Children, that we could also pass them; and that if the nations on this river below the mountains were as numerous as they were stated to be that they must have some means of subsistence which it would be equally in our power to procure in the same country. they informed me that there was no buffaloe on the West side of these mountains; that the game consisted of a few Elk deer and Antelopes, and that the natives subsisted on fish and roots principally. in this manner I spent the day smoking with them and acquiring what information I could with respect to their country. they informed me that they could pass to the Spaniards by the way of the yellowstone river in 10 days. I can discover that these people are by no means friendly to the Spaniard their complaint is, that the Spaniards will not let them have fire arms and amunition,[14] that they put them off by telling them that if they suffer them to have guns they will kill each other, thus leaving them defenceless and an easy prey to their bloodthirsty neighbours to the East of them, who being in possession of fire arms hunt them up and murder them without rispect to sex or age and plunder them of their horses on all occasions. they told me that to avoid their enemies who were eternally harrassing them that they were obliged to remain in the interior of these mountains at least two thirds of the year where the suffered as we then saw great heardships for the want of food sometimes living for weeks without meat and only a little fish roots and berries. but this added Cameahwait, with his ferce eyes and lank jaws grown meager for the want of food, would not be the case if we had guns, we could then live in the country of buffaloe and eat as our enimies do and not be compelled to hide ourselves in these mountains and live on roots and berries as the bear do. we do not fear our enimies when placed on an equal footing with them. I told them that the Minnetares Mandans & Recares of the Missouri had promised us to desist from making war on them & that we would indevour to find the means of making the Minnetares of fort d Prarie or as they call them Pahkees desist from waging war against them also. that after our finally returning to our homes towards the rising sun whitemen would come to them with an abundance of guns and every other article necessary to their defence and comfort, and that they would be enabled to supply themselves with these articles on reasonable terms in exchange for the skins of the beaver Otter and Ermin[15] so abundant in their country. they expressed great pleasure at this information and said they had been long anxious to see the whitemen that traded guns; and that we might rest assured of their friendship and that they would do whatever we wished them.[16]

I now told Cameahwait that I wished him to speak to his people and engage them to go with me tomorrow to the forks of Jeffersons river where our baggage was by this time arrived with another Chief and a large party of whitemen who would wait my return at that place. that I wish them to take with them about 30 spare horses to transport our baggage to this place where we would then remain sometime among them and trade with them for horses, and finally concert our future plans for geting on to the ocean and of the traid which would be extended to them after our return to our homes. he complyed with my request and made a lengthey harrangue to his village. he returned in about an hour and a half and informed me that they would be ready to accompany me in the morning. I promised to reward them for their trouble. Drewyer who had had a good view of their horses estimated them at 400.[17] most of them are fine horses. indeed many of them would make a figure on the South side of James River or the land of fine horses.— I saw several with spanish brands on them, and some mules which they informed me that they had also obtained from the Spaniards. I also saw a bridle bit of spanish manufactary, and sundry other articles which I have no doubt were obtained from the same source. notwithstanding the extreem poverty of those poor people they are very merry they danced again this evening untill midnight. each warrior keep one ore more horses tyed by a cord to a stake near his lodge both day and night and are always prepared for action at a moments warning. they fight on horseback altogether. I observe that the large flies[18] are extreemly troublesome to the horses as well as ourselves.

The morning being cold and the men stif and soar from the exertions of yesterday Capt. Clark did not set out this morning untill 7 A. M. the river was so crooked and rapid that they made but little way at one mile he passed a bold runing stream on Stard. which heads in a mountain to the North, on which there is snow. this we called track Creek.[19] it is

4 yard wide and 3 feet deep   at 7 Ms. passed a stout stream which heads in some springs under the foot of the mountains on Lard.   the river near the mountain they found one continued rapid, wich was extreemly laborious and difficult to ascend.   this evening Charbono struck his indian Woman for which Capt. C. gave him a severe repremand. Joseph and Reubin Fields killed 4 deer and an Antelope, Capt. C. killed a buck.   several of the men have lamed themselves by various accedents in working the canoes through this difficult part of the river, and Capt. C. was obliged personally to assist them in this labour.   they encamped this evening on Lard. side near the rattlesnake Clift.[20]

Courses and distances traveled by Capt. Clark.
August 14th 1805.

S. 14° W.   7   to the gap of the mountain at the rattlesnake Clifts where the
Miles 7   river enters the mountains.   the same being 16 miles by the meanders of the river.   the river cold shoally and one continued rapid throughout.   passed a number of small Islands and bayous on either side.   passed bold running stream on Stard. at 1 M. called track Creek.   also another at 6 M. higher up, on Lard. side and encamped on Lard. 2 Miles by water short of the extremity of this course distance by land scarcely ½ a Mile

[Clark]   *August 14th Wednesday 1805.*

a Cold morning wind from the S. W. The Thermometer Stood at 51° a 0, at Sunrise the morning being cold and men Stiff. I deturmind to delay & take brackfast at the place we Encamped.   we Set out at 7 oClock and proceeded on river verry Crooked and rapid as below Some fiew trees on the borders near the mountain, passed a bold running Stream at 1 mile on the Stard. Side which heads in a mountain to the North on which there is Snow   passed a bold running Stream on the Lard. Side which heads in a Spring undr. a mountain, the river near the mountain is one continued rapid, which requres great labour to push & haul the Canoes ⟨over the⟩ up. We Encamped on the Lard Side near the place the river passes thro' the mountain. I checked our interpreter for Strikeing his woman at their Dinner.

The hunters Jo. & R. Fields killed 4 Deer & a antilope, I killed a fat Buck in the evening, Several men have hurt themselves pushing up the Canoes. I am oblige to a pole occasionally.

1. The sign language was common among all the plains tribes, and those mountain tribes in regular communication with the plains. There were some regional variations, but proficient sign-talkers could adjust easily. As Lewis notes, the main ideas were readily communicated. Clark. Perhaps it was Biddle who drew a red vertical line through this passage.

2. It appears to be Clark who has interlined, "This part to come in the 20th related to Capt. C thro the intepreter." He also added an asterisk here and at the end of the addition. See note below. We add a paragraph indention to set off the material. Evidently the Shoshones gave Clark the following geographical information through Sacagawea on August 20, 1805, indicating that Lewis's present entry was written some time after that date. The captains were separated from August 18 to 29. Ronda (LCAI), 150–51.

3. Perhaps the two branches were Hayden Creek and the Lemhi River itself, merging near the town of Lemhi, Lemhi County, Idaho. Information of Robert N. Bergantino, Butte, Montana. Allen would place it farther south, near Leadore. Allen (PG), 295 n. 27.

4. The Salmon River.

5. The Salmon River runs through the Salmon River Mountains, the Clearwater Mountains, and other ranges in central Idaho, some of the most rugged country in the United States. It has acquired the nickname "River of No Return."

6. Probably the first written reference to the Nez Perces by the name and trait by which they became known in history. The question of whether they actually pierced their noses remains unsettled. See below, September 20, 1805.

7. These white people were almost certainly Spanish. Wherever Lewis's informant lived, it was probably a good deal farther from Spanish settlements in California or New Mexico than Lewis supposed. Rees, 12, believes the man came from the Duck Valley region between the forks of the Owyhee River in southwest Idaho. The contact may have been indirect, since there was an extensive network of intertribal trade. Also, Spanish traders may have ventured north to meet the Indians at established intertribal trade centers, such as that in southwestern Wyoming. Terrell; Ewers (ILUM), 14–33; Hyde (IHP), 157.

8. From the location, these could be the Tukudikas, a Shoshonean group or groups living in various parts of the northern Rockies, later referred to by whites as "Sheep-eaters" because they ate the bighorn sheep. As Lewis's informant indicated, they eked out a subsistence on a scanty food supply. Rees, 12, indicates that the Shoshone name arose from their moccasins being worn out by the lava rocks in their home regions. However, the "broken moccasins" have also been identified as the Bannocks, Northern Paiutes closely associated with the Northern Shoshones, and as a mythical people. Swanson, 246–64; Clark, 334–35; Hyde (IHP), 124, 157–58; Hodge, 1:129–30; Madsen, 41.

9. Probably the arid Snake River plain of southern Idaho. Allen (PG), 296 n. 30.

10. Their first information about the Snake River.

11. Probably the Owyhee River, a tributary of the Snake that runs through eastern Oregon. Ibid., 296.

12. The Snake again.

13. The Snake does head relatively near the upper Green River, a principal tributary of the Colorado, but otherwise the captains' surmises were wrong. Traveling up the Owyhee would not take one anywhere near a stream running to either the Pacific or the Gulf of California. The Rio de los Apostolos was a mythical river of the Southwest which appears on Nicholas King's map of 1803 (*Atlas* map 2) and Clark's Fort Mandan map of 1805 (*Atlas* maps 32*a*, 32*b*, 32*c*). Ibid., 296–97.

14. The Spanish followed a fairly consistent policy of refusing to trade guns to Indians, in contrast to the French, English, and Americans. Having no direct contact with the Canadian or Missouri River trade systems, the Shoshones were thus at a great disadvantage, compared to their Blackfeet, Atsina, and Hidatsa enemies in obtaining firearms. Secoy, 51–59; Hyde (IHP), 175–76; Ronda (LCAI), 152. Perhaps it was Biddle who drew a red vertical line through this passage.

15. Long-tailed weasel, *Mustela frenata*. Burroughs, 81–82. See also August 20, 1805.

16. Here apparently is the end of the geographical information gathered by Clark on August 20. See note above. Clark has interlined, "as low as this in the 20th of the mon: Spoken to Cap C." Lewis's narrative of events on August 14 then resumes. We add a paragraph indention.

17. It may have been Biddle who drew the red vertical line beginning with this sentence to the end of the paragraph.

18. Horse fly.

19. Evidently later Rattlesnake Creek, rising on Baldy Mountain, in Beaverhead County, Montana. *Atlas* map 66.

20. In Beaverhead County, about ten miles southwest of present Dillon and just downstream of Barretts siding. *Atlas* map 66.

[Lewis]   *Thursday August 15th 1805.*

This morning I arrose very early and as hungary as a wolf. I had eat nothing yesterday except one scant meal of the flour and berries except the dryed cakes of berries which did not appear to satisfy my appetite as they appeared to do those of my Indian friends. I found on enquiry of McNeal that we had only about two pounds of flour remaining.   this I directed him to divide into two equal parts and to cook the one half this morning in a kind of pudding with the burries as he had done yesterday and reserve the ballance for the evening.   on this new fashoned pudding four of us breakfasted, giving a pretty good allowance also to the Chief who declared it the best thing he had taisted for a long time.   he took a little of the flour in his hand, taisted and examined very scrutinously and asked me if we made it of roots. I explained to him the manner in which it grew. I hurried the departure of the Indians. the Chief addressed them several times before they would move they seemed very reluctant to accompany me. I at length asked the reason and he told me that some foolish persons among them had suggested the idea that we were in league with the Pahkees and had come on in order to decoy them into an ambuscade where their enimies were waiting to receive them. but that for his part he did not believe it. I readily perceived that our situation was not entirely free from danger as the transision from suspicion to the confermation of the fact would not be very difficult in the minds of these ignorant people who have been accustomed from their infancy to view every stranger as an enemy. I told Cameahwait that I was sorry to find that they had put so little confidence in us, that I knew they were not acquainted with whitemen and therefore could forgive them. that among whitemen it was considered disgracefull to lye or entrap an enimy by falsehood. I told him if they continued to think thus meanly of us that they might rely on it that no whitemen would ever come to trade with them or bring them arms and amunition and that if the bulk of his nation still entertained this opinion I still hoped that there were some among them that were not affraid to die, that were men and would go with me and convince themselves of the truth of what I had asscerted. that there was a party of whitemen waiting my return either at the forks of Jefferson's river or a little below coming on to that place in canoes loaded with provisions and merchandize. he told me for his own part he was determined to go, that he was not affraid to die. I soon found that I had touched him on the right string; to doubt the bravery of a savage is at once to put him on his metal. he now mounted his horse and haranged his village a third time; the perport of which as he afterwards told me was to inform them that he would go with us and convince himself of the truth or falsity of what we had told him if he was sertain he should be killed, that he hoped there were some of them who heard him were not affraid to die with him and if there was to let him see them mount their horses and prepare to set out. shortly after this harange he was joined by six or eight only and with these I smoked a pipe and directed the men to put on their packs being determined to set out with them while I had them in the humour at half after 12 we set out, several of the old women were crying and imploring the great sperit to protect their warriors as if they were going to inevitable distruction. we had not proceeded far before our party was augmented by ten or twelve more, and before we reached the Creek[1] which we had passed in the morning of the 13th it appeared to me that we had all the men of the village and a number of women with us. this may serve in some measure to ilustrate the capricious disposition of those people who never act but from the impulse of the moment. they were now very cheerfull and gay, and two hours ago they looked as sirly as so many imps of satturn. when we arrived at the spring on the side of the mountain where we had encamped on the 12th the Chief insited on halting to let the horses graize with which I complyed and gave the Indians smoke. they are excessively fond of the pipe; but have it not much in their power to indulge themselves with even their native tobacco as they do not cultivate it themselves.— after remaining about an hour we again set out, and by engaging to make compensation to four of them for their trouble obtained the previlege of riding with an indian myself and a similar situation for each of my party. I soon found it more tiresome riding without tirrups than walking and of course chose the latter making the Indian carry my pack. about sunset we reached the upper part of the level valley of the Cove which now called Shoshone Cove. the grass being birned on the North side of the river we passed over to the south and encamped near some willow brush about 4 miles above the narrow pass between the hills noticed as I came up this cove.[2] the river was here about six yards wide, and frequently damed up by the beaver. I had sent Drewyer forward this evening before we halted to kill some meat but he was unsuccessfull and did not rejoin us untill after dark I now cooked and among six of us eat the remaining pound of flour stired in a little boiling water.— Capt. Clark delayed again this morning untill after breakfast, when he set out and passed between low and rugged mountains which had a few pine trees distributed over them the clifts are formed of limestone and a hard black rock intermixed.[3] no trees on the river, the bottoms narrow river crooked shallow shoally and rapid. the water is as coald as that of the best springs in our country. the men as usual suffered excessively with fatiegue and the coldness of the water to which they were exposed for hours together. at the distance of 6 miles by water they passed the entrance of a bold creek on Stard. side 10 yds. wide and 3 f. 3 I. deep which we called Willard's Creek after Alexander Willard one of our party.[4]   at 4 miles by water from their encampment of las evening passed a bold branch which tumbled down a steep precipice of rocks from the mountains on the Lard.[5] Capt Clark was very near being bitten twice today by rattlesnakes, the Indian woman also narrowly escaped.   they caught a number of fine trout. Capt. Clark killed a buck which was the only game killed today. the venison has an uncommon bitter taist which is unpleasent. I presume it proceeds from some article of their food, perhaps the willow on the leaves of which they feed very much.   they encamped this evening on the Lard. side near a few cottonwood trees about which there were the remains of several old Indian brush lodges.[6]

Courses and distances traveled by Capt. Clark
August 15th 1805.

S. 25° W.	4	to the entrance of Willard's Creek on Stard. 10 Yds. wide bold current. so called from Alexander Willard one of our party. the distance by water 6 Miles. passed a point of rocks at 2 M. on Stard. a bold run on Lard. at 4 Miles; a second point of rocks on Lard. at 5 and an Island.
S. 22° E.	1	to a small bottom on the Lard. side, passing a high clift on Stard. opposite to a steep sloping hill. the same being 3 M. by water
S. 20° W.	2	M. to a small branch on Lard. side near which is a small bot-
Miles	7	tom covered with clover and a few cottonwood trees where they encamped on Lard. side for the evening.

During my absence Capt. Clark had made the following observations.

Point of Observation No. 41.

August 11th 1805 on the upper point of an island at the encampment of this evening, observed time and distance of ☽'s Western limb from Antares ★ West with Sextant.

	Time			Distance		
	h	m	s			
P. M.	9	38	1	91°	57'	—"
	"	41	20	"	56	45
	"	44	39	"	55	15
	"	47	8	"	54	30
	"	50	38	"	54	15
	"	51	52	"	53	45

	Time			Distance		
	h	m	s			
P. M.	9	54	31	91°	49'	45"
	"	56	11	"	48	30
	"	58	14	"	48	—
	10	—	23	"	47	45
	"	1	39	"	47	45
	"	2	32	"	47	—

Longitude deduced from this observation West from Greenwich—[*blank*]

Point of Observation No. 42.
August 15th 1805.

On the Lard. side of the Missouri at the rattlesnake Clifts. Observed Meridian Altitude of ☉'s L. L. with Octant by the back observation—65° 47' —"

Latitude deduced from this observation 44° —' 48.1"

☞ this place ought to stand at about 44° 50' or thereabouts

[Clark]   *August 15th Thursday 1805*

a Cool windey morning wind from the S W we proceeded on thro a ruged low mountain water rapid as usial passed a bold running Stream which falls from the mountain on the Lard. Side at 4 miles, also a bold running Stream 10 yards wide on the Stard Side 8 feet 3 In. Deep at 6 miles, Willards Creek the bottoms narrow, the Clifs of a Dark brown Stone Some limestone intermixed— an Indian road passes on the Lard Side latterly used. Took a Meridian altitude at the Comsnt. of the Mountain with Octent 65° 47' 0". The Latd. *44° 0' 48¹/₁₀"* proceeded on with great labour & fatigue to the Mouth of a Small run on the Lard. Side passed Several Spring runs, the men Complain much of their fatigue and being repetiedly in the water which weakens them much perticularly as they are obliged to live on pore Deer meet which has a Singular bitter taste. I have no accounts of Capt Lewis Sence he Set out

In walking on Shore I Saw Several rattle Snakes and narrowly escaped at two different times, as also the Squar when walking with her husband on Shore— I killed a Buck nothing else killed to day— This mountn. I call rattle Snake mountain. not one tree on either Side to day [7]

Course Distance &c above Wisdom River

August 7th

S 45° E   7   miles by water 3 miles by land to the mouth of a Creek 12 yds. wide on the Lard. Side passed Seven bends to the Stard. Side and Several Small Bayeus on each Side.

Courses of August 8th

South   5   miles by water 2 m. by land passing seven bends on the Lard Side two Islds. & several Bayoos to the mouth of *Philanthophy* river on the Lard Side 30 yds. wide & navagable

S. 20° W.   14   miles by water & 6 by land on a Direct course to a fiew high trees on the Stard. Side the river bending round to the East 2 miles from this course, passed an Island at 1 mile, another at 7 miles, Several Small Bayos & 35 binds to the Stard. most of those bends are Short & round.

(*August 9th*)

S. 12° W.   11   miles by water 4 miles direct to a Starbdbend passd. two Small Islands, 16 Short round bends on the Stard. Side we *Dined*

S. 10° E   3   miles by water 1 m direct to a high bottom on the Lard Side passed an Island, a Bayou on the Lard Side four Short bends on the Stard Side

(*August 10th*)

S. 30° W.   6½   miles by water 2 miles Direct to a Clift of rocks 150 feet high Std. Side Called by the Snake Indians the *Beavers head,* a Clift 300 distand from the Beaver head about 50 feet high passed 8 bends on the Stard. Side two Small bayous on the Lard. Side.

S 60° W.	6½	miles by water (2 miles on the Course) to a low bluff on the Lard. Side, passed four island & 18 bends on the Stard. Side passing near a low bluff on Stard. Sd. passed Several Small Bayoes.

S. 20° W.	3	miles by water 1 m. by land to the lower point of 3000 mile Island passed three Small Islands, 6 bends on the Stard. Side, 6 Bayoes on eithr Side
S. 25° W.	3½	miles by water 1½ m. by land to the head of the Island Passed Sevin bends on the Lard Side of the Island & 2 Bayous on the Lard Side. The Stard Chanel passes near the Bluffs
South	7½	miles by water 2½ m. by land to the head of a large Island the main Chanel on the Lard. Side, passed 3 Small islands and Several Small Bayoes and 15 bends on the Stard. Side

S 8° W.	5½	miles by water 2 miles direct to the head of a large Island, main Chanel on the Stard. Side passed maney Bayoes, 3 Islands & 9 bends on the Stard. Side
S. 10° W.	6½	miles by water 2 ms. by Land to a Stard. bend passed four Small Islands and 2 large Island Several Bayoes and a number of Short bends. passed a run on the Star Side

August 13th

South	4	miles by water 1 to a point of rugid rocks about 70 feet high on the Stard. Sd. Passed the head of the Island opds to which we Encamped at 2½ ms. the mouth of a creek bold running stream 7 yards wide back of an Island on the Lard Side McNeal Creek
S. 30° W.	6	miles by water 3 m by land to he Clift of high rocks on the Stard. Side passed Several Islands and Bayoes on either Side, the river verry Crooked & bends Short

S 14° W.	<u>22</u> 111	miles by water the river makeing a genl. Bend to the East (8 miles by land) to a place the river Passes ⟨enters⟩ a mountain high Clifts on either side, river crooked cold rapid & Sholey, almost one continued rapid passed a

number of *bayoes* & Small Islands. passed a bold running Stream on the Stard Side 4 yards wide & 3 feet deep
at 7 miles, passed a bold running stream from a Spring on
the Lard Side at 15 miles. Encamped the 13th of August
at 6 miles on Ld Side   Encamped 14th of august at 20
miels on the Lar Side, a high Clift on the Course 3 miles
near the upper part of which the Creek passes

1. Pattee Creek.

2. On the south side of Horse Prairie Creek, a few miles west of present Grant,
Beaverhead County, Montana. *Atlas* map 67.

3. The rocks between the lower end of the Rattlesnake Cliffs and Grasshopper Creek
are principally extrusive volcanic rocks (basalts, rhyolites, and ash-fall tuffs) of early Tertiary age. The "limestone" is probably the light colored ash-fall tuff. Between Grasshopper
Creek and Gallagher Creek, sedimentary rocks (sandstone, shale, siltstone, and some
limestone) ranging in age from Pennsylvanian to Cretaceous are present along with out-
crops of Tertiary volcanic rocks.

4. Grasshopper Creek, Beaverhead County. *Atlas* map 66.

5. Perhaps Long Gulch Creek. *Atlas* map 66.

6. Just below the mouth of the "small branch," apparently later Gallagher's Creek,
Beaverhead County. Shown as "bold run" on *Atlas* map 66.

7. At this point in Codex G (pp. 60–62) Clark has placed courses for August 7–14.
Those for August 15–17 are found at his entry of August 17, 1805. The distances for
August 13 vary from those given by Lewis.

[Lewis]   *Friday August 16th 1805.*

I sent Drewyer and Shields before this morning in order to kill some
meat as neither the Indians nor ourselves had any thing to eat. I informed the Ceif of my view in this measure, and requested that he would
keep his young men with us lest by their hooping and noise they should
allarm the game and we should get nothing to eat, but so strongly were
there suspicions exited by this measure that two parties of discovery immediately set out one on ech side of the valley to watch the hunters as I
beleive to see whether they had not been sent to give information of their
approach to an enemy that they still preswaided themselves were lying in
wait for them. I saw that any further effort to prevent their going would
only add strength to their suspicions and therefore said no more.   after
the hunters had been gone about an hour we set out.   we had just passed

through the narrows when we saw one of the spies comeing up the level plain under whip, the chief pawsed a little and seemed somewhat concerned. I felt a good deel so myself and began to suspect that by some unfortunate accedent that perhaps some of there enimies had straggled hither at this unlucky moment; but we were all agreeably disappointed on the arrival of the young man to learn that he had come to inform us that one of the whitemen had killed a deer.   in an instant they all gave their horses the whip and I was taken nearly a mile before I could learn what were the tidings; as I was without tirrups and an Indian behind me the jostling was disagreeable   I therefore reigned up my horse and forbid the indian to whip him who had given him the lash at every jum for a mile fearing he should loose a part of the feast.   the fellow was so uneasy that he left me the horse dismounted and ran on foot at full speed, I am confident a mile.   when they arrived where the deer was which was in view of me they dismounted and ran in tumbling over each other like a parcel of famished dogs each seizing and tearing away a part of the intestens which had been previously thrown out by Drewyer who killed it; the seen was such when I arrived that had I not have had a pretty keen appetite myself I am confident I should not have taisted any part of the venison shortly.   each one had a peice of some discription and all eating most ravenously.   some were eating the kidnies the melt[1] and liver and the blood runing from the corners of their mouths, others were in a similar situation with the paunch and guts but the exuding substance in this case from their lips was of a different discription.   one of the last who attacted my attention particularly had been fortunate in his allotment or reather active in the division, he had provided himself with about nine feet of the small guts one end of which he was chewing on while with his hands he was squezzing the contents out at the other. I really did not untill now think that human nature ever presented itself in a shape so nearly allyed to the brute creation. I viewed these poor starved divils with pity and compassion   I directed McNeal to skin the deer and reserved a quarter, the ballance I gave the Chief to be divided among his people; they devoured the whole of it nearly without cooking. I now boar obliquely to the left in order to interscept the creek where there was some brush to make a fire, and arrived at this stream where Drewyer had killed a second deer; here nearly the same seene was encored.   a fire being kindled we cooked and eat and gave the ballance of the two deer to the Indians who eat the whole of them even to the soft parts of the hoofs. Drewyer joined us at breakfast with a third deer.   of this I reserved a quarter and gave the ballance to the Indians.   they all appeared now to have filled themselves and were in a good humour.   this morning early soon after the hunters set out a considerable part of our escort became allarmed and returned   28 men and three women only continued with us.   after eating and suffering the horses to graize about 2 hours we renued our march and towads evening arrived at the lower part of the cove   Shields killed an Antelope on the way a part of which we took and gave the remainder to the Indians.   being now informed of the place at which I expected to meat Capt C. and the party they insisted on making a halt, which was complyed with.   we now dismounted and the Chief with much cerimony put tippets about our necks such as they temselves woar I redily perceived that this was to disguise us and owed it's origine to the same cause already mentioned.   to give them further confidence I put my cocked hat with feather on the chief and my over shirt being of the Indian form my hair deshivled and skin well browned with the sun I wanted no further addition to make me a complete Indian in appearance   the men followed my example and we were son completely metamorphosed. I again repeated to them the possibility of the party not having arrived at the place which I expected they were, but assured them they could not be far below, lest by not finding them at the forks their suspicions might arrise to such hight as to induce them to return precipitately.   we now set out and rode briskly within sight of the forks making one of the Indians carry the flag that our own party should know who we were.   when we arrived in sight at the distance of about 2 miles I discovered to my mortification that the party had not arrived, and the Indians slackened their pace. I now scarcely new what to do and feared every moment when they would halt altogether, I now determined to restore their confidence cost what it might and therefore gave the Chief my gun and told him that if his enimies were in those bushes before him that he could defend himself with that gun, that for my own part I was not affraid to die and if I deceived him he might make what uce of the gun he thought proper or in other words that he might shoot me. the men also gave their guns to other indians which seemed to inspire them with more confidence; they sent their spies before them at some distance and when I drew near the place[2] I thought of the notes which I had left and directed Drewyer to go with an Indian man and bring them to me which he did. the indian seeing him take the notes from the stake on which they had been plased I now had recource to a stratagem in which I thought myself justifyed by the occasion, but which I must confess set a little awkward. it had it's desired effect. after reading the notes which were the same I had left I told the Chief that when I had left my brother Chief with the party below where the river entered the mountain that we both agreed not to bring the ca-noes higher up than the next forks of the river above us wherever this might happen, that there he was to wait my return, should he arrive first, and that in the event of his not being able to travel as fast as usual from the difficulty of the water, that he was to send up to the first forks above him and leave a note informing me where he was, that this note was left here today and that he informed me that he was just below the mountains and was coming on slowly up, and added that I should wait here for him, but if they did not beleive me that I should send a man at any rate to the Chief and they might also send one of their young men with him, that myself and two others would remain with them at this place. this plan was readily adopted and one of the young men offered his services; I promised him a knife and some beads as a reward for his confidence in us. most of them seemed satisfyed but there were several that com-plained of the Chief's exposing them to danger unnecessarily and said that we told different stories, in short a few were much dissatisfyed. I wrote a note to Capt. Clark by the light of some willow brush and directed Drewyer to set out early being confident that there was not a moment to spare. the chief and five or six others slept about my fire and the others hid themselves in various parts of the willow brush to avoid the enimy whom they were fearfull would attack them in the course of the night. I now entertained various conjectures myself with rispect to the cause of Capt. Clarks detention and was even fearfull that he had found the river so difficult that he had halted below the Rattlesnake bluffs. I knew that if these people left me that they would immediately disperse and secrete themselves in the mountains where it would be impossible to find them or at least in vain to pursue them and that they would spread the allarm to all other bands within our reach & of course we should be disappointed in obtaining horses, which would vastly retard and increase the labour of our voyage and I feared might so discourage the men as to defeat the expedition altogether.   my mind was in reallity quite as gloomy all this evening as the most affrighted indian but I affected cheerfullness to keep the Indians so who were about me.   we finally laid down and the Chief placed himself by the side of my musquetoe bier. I slept but little as might be well expected, my mind dwelling on the state of the expedition which I have ever held in equal estimation with my own existence, and the fait of which appeared at this moment to depend in a great measure upon the caprice of a few savages who are ever as fickle as the wind. I had mentioned to the chief several times that we had with us a woman of his nation who had been taken prisoner by the Minnetares, and that by means of her I hoped to explain myself more fully than I could do by signs. some of the party had also told the Indians that we had a man with us who was black and had short curling hair, this had excited their curiossity very much.   and they seemed quite as anxious to see this monster as they wer the merchandize which we had to barter for their horses.

at 7 A M. Capt. C. set out after breakfast.   he changed the hands in some of the canoes; they proceeded with more ease than yesterday, yet they found the river still rapid and shallow insomuch that they were obliged to drag the large canoes the greater part of the day.   the water excessively cold.   in the evening they passed several bad rapids.   considerable quantities of the buffaloe clover grows along the narrow bottoms through which they passed.   there was no timber except a few scatiring small pine on the hills.   willow service berry and currant bushes were the growth of the river bottoms.   they geatherd considerable quantities of service berries, and caught some trout.   one deer was killed by the hunters who slept out last night.   and did not join the party untill 10 A. M. Capt. Clark sent the hunters this evening up to the forks of the river which he discovered from an eminence; they mus have left this place but a little time before we arrived.   this evening they encamped on the Lard.

side only a few miles below us.[3]   and were obliged like ourselves to make use of small willow brush for fuel.   the men were much fatigued and exhausted this evening.

Courses and distances traveled by Capt. Clark
August 16th 1805.

S. 18° W.	3	to a Lard. bend under a low bluff, distance by water 7 M. the river bending to the Stard. under some high land, very crooked narrow shallow and small. passed several Islands 4 of which were opposite to each other. called this service berry Valley, from the great abundance of that fruit found here.
S. 12° W.	2	to a high Clift on the Stard side, distance by water 4 M. passed several Islds. and bayous on either Side.
S. 50° E.	1	to the entrance of a bold running stream on Lard. side, distance by water 2½ M. at this place there is a very considerable rapid and clifts near on both sides
S. 45° W.	½	mile to the lower point of an Island near the center of the Valley and river.
Miles	6½	

[Clark]   *August 16th Friday 1805*

as this morning was cold and the men fatigued Stiff and Chilled deturmined me to detain & take brackfast before I Set out. I changed the hands and Set out at 7 oClock   proceeded on Something better than yesterday for the fore part of the Day   passed Several rapids in the latter part of the day near the hills river   passed between 2 hills   I saw a great number *of Service berries* now ripe.   the Yellow Current are also Common   I observe the long leaf Clover[4] in great plenty in the vallie below this vallie—   Some fiew tres on the river   no timber on the hills or mountn. except a fiew Small Pine & Cedar.[5] The Thmtr. Stood at 48° a. o at Sunrise wind S W. The hunters joined me at 1 oClock, I dispatched 2 men to prosue an Indian roade over the hills for a fiew miles, at the narrows I assended a mountain from the top of which I could See that the river forked near me   the left hand appeared the largest & bore

S. E. the right passed from the West thro' an extensive Vallie, I could See but three Small trees in any Direction from the top of this mountain. passed an Isld. and Encamped ion the Lard. Side the only wood was Small willows

1. The spleen.

2. The junction of Horse Prairie Creek and Red Rock River to form Beaverhead River. *Atlas* map 66.

3. This camp does not appear on *Atlas* map 66. It was in Beaverhead County, Montana, four miles by Clark's estimate below the forks of the Beaverhead and the present Clark Canyon Dam.

4. Clark's "long leaf Clover" is the same as Lewis's "buffaloe clover" of this day and of August 8. The term long leaf describes the elongate, trifoliate leaflets of the mountain thermopsis. The species is common in this area, growing in wet meadows as described. Since the plant was in fruit at this time of the year and lacked the typical flower head of a clover, Lewis apparently chose the term "buffalo" to distinguish either its tall stature or grazing preference by bison, and Clark chose the descriptive "long leaf" to note the long leaflets, atypical of other clover or *Trifolium* species. Booth & Wright, 138.

5. The small pine is the limber pine and the cedar is Rocky Mountain juniper. Both species grow together on the rocky slopes above the Beaverhead River in this area and in similar habitats in the region. Pfister et al., 17.

Chapter Twenty

Crossing the Great Divide

August 17–20, 1805

[Lewis]   *Saturday August 17th 1805.*

This morning I arrose very early and dispatched Drewyer and the Indian down the river.   sent Shields to hunt. I made McNeal cook the remainder of our meat which afforded a slight breakfast for ourselves and the Cheif.   Drewyer had been gone about 2 hours when an Indian who had straggled some little distance down the river returned and reported that the whitemen were coming, that he had seen them just below.   they all appeared transported with joy, & the chef repeated his fraturnal hug. I felt quite as much gratifyed at this information as the Indians appeared to be. Shortly after Capt. Clark arrived with the Interpreter Charbono, and the Indian woman, who proved to be a sister of the Chif Cameahwait.   the meeting of those people was really affecting, particularly between Sah cah-gar-we-ah and an Indian woman,[1] who had been taken prisoner at the same time with her, and who had afterwards escaped from the Minnetares and rejoined her nation. At noon the Canoes arrived, and we had the satisfaction once more to find ourselves all together, with a flattering prospect of being able to obtain as many horses shortly as would enable us to prosicute our voyage by land should that by water be deemed unadvisable.

We now formed our camp[2] just below the junction of the forks on the Lard. side in a level smooth bottom covered with a fine terf of green-

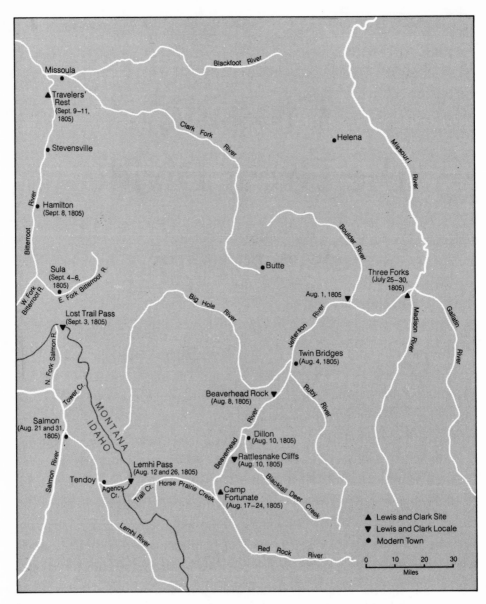

Missoula

▲ Travelers'
Rest
(Sept. 9–11,
1805)

Blackfoot River

● Stevensville

Clark Fork River

● Helena

Missouri River

Bitterroot River

Hamilton
(Sept. 8, 1805)

Sula
(Sept. 4–6,
1805)

W. Fork
Bitterroot R.

E. Fork Bitterroot R.

Butte

Big Hole River

Boulder River

Three Forks
(July 25–30,
1805) ▲

Aug. 1, 1805 ▼

Madison River

Gallatin River

Lost Trail Pass
(Sept. 3, 1805) ▼

N. Fork Salmon R.

Tower Cr.

MONTANA

IDAHO

Salmon
(Aug. 21 and 31,
1805) ●

Salmon River

Tendoy ●

Agency
Cr.

Lemhi Pass
(Aug. 12 and 26, 1805) ▼

Trail Cr.

Horse Prairie Creek

Lemhi River

Jefferson River

Twin Bridges ●
(Aug. 4, 1805)

Ruby River

Beaverhead Rock ▼
(Aug. 8, 1805)

Beaverhead River

Dillon ●
(Aug. 10, 1805)

Rattlesnake Cliffs ▼
(Aug. 10, 1805)

▲ Camp
Fortunate
(Aug. 17–24, 1805)

Blacktail Deer Creek

Red Rock River

▲ Lewis and Clark Site
▼ Lewis and Clark Locale
● Modern Town

0   10   20   30
Miles

2. From Three Forks to Travelers' Rest,
July 25–September 11, 1805

swoard. here we unloaded our canoes and arranged our baggage on shore; formed a canopy of one of our large sails and planted some willow brush in the ground to form a shade for the Indians to set under while we spoke to them, which we thought it best to do this evening. acordingly about 4 P. M. we called them together and through the medium of La-buish, Charbono and Sah-cah-gar-weah, we communicated to them fully the objects which had brought us into this distant part of the country, in which we took care to make them a conspicuous object of our own good wishes and the care of our government. we made them sensible of their dependance on the will of our government for every species of merchan-dize as well for their defence & comfort; and apprized them of the strength of our government and it's friendly dispositions towards them. we also gave them as a reason why we wished to petrate the country as far as the ocean to the west of them was to examine and find out a more di-rect way to bring merchandize to them. that as no trade could be car-ryed on with them before our return to our homes that it was mutually advantageous to them as well as to ourselves that they should render us such aids as they had it in their power to furnish in order to haisten our voyage and of course our return home. that such were their horses to transport our baggage without which we could not subsist, and that a pilot to conduct us through the mountains was also necessary if we could not decend the river by water. but that we did not ask either their horses or their services without giving a satisfactory compensation in re-turn. that at present we wished them to collect as many horses as were necessary to transport our baggage to their village on the Columbia where we would then trade with them at our leasure for such horses as they could spare us.— They appeared well pleased with what had been said. the chief thanked us for friendship towards himself and nation & declared his wish to serve us in every rispect; that he was sorry to find that it must yet be some time before they could be furnished with firearms but said they could live as they had done heretofore untill we brought them as we had promised. he said they had not horses enough with them at present to remove our baggage to their village over the mountain, but that he would return tomorrow and encourage his people to come over

with their horses and that he would bring his own and assist us.   this was
complying with all we wished at present.   we next enquired who were
chiefs among them. Cameahwait pointed out two others whom he said
were Chiefs   we gave him a medal of the small size with the likeness of
Mr. Jefferson the President of the U' States in releif on one side and clasp
hands with a pipe and tomahawk on the other, to the other Chiefs we
gave each a small medal which were struck in the Presidency of George
Washing [*NB: ton*] Esqr.   we also gave small medals of the last discription
to two young men whom the 1st Chief informed us wer good young men
and much rispected among them.   we gave the 1st Chief an uniform
coat shit [*NB: irt*] a pair of scarlet legings a carrot of tobacco and some
small articles   to each of the others we gave a shi[r]t leging handkerchief
a knife some tobacco and a few small articles   we also distributed a good
quantity paint mockerson awls knives beads lookingglasses &c among the
other Indians and gave them a plentifull meal of lyed [*NB: hull taken off by
being boiled in lye*] corn which was the first they had ever eaten in their
lives.   they were much pleased with it.   every article about us appeared
to excite astonishment in ther minds; the appearance of the men, their
arms, the canoes, our manner of working them, the back man york and
the segacity of my dog were equally objects of admiration. I also shot my
air-gun which was so perfectly incomprehensible that they immediately
denominated it the great medicine.   the idea which the indians mean to
convey by this appellation is something that eminates from or acts immediately by the influence or power of the great sperit; or that in which the
power of god is manifest by it's incomprehensible power of action.   our
hunters killed 4 deer and an Antelope this evening of which we also gave
the Indians a good proportion.   the cerimony of our council and smoking the pipe was in conformity of the custom of this nation perfomed
bearfoot.   on those occasions points of etiquet are quite as much attended to by the Indians as among scivilized nations. To keep indians in a
good humour you must not fatiegue them with too much business at one
time.   therefore after the council we gave them to eat and amused them
a while by shewing them such articles as we thought would be entertaining to them, and then renewed our enquiries with rispect to the coun-

try. the information we derived was only a repetition of that they had given me before and in which they appeared to be so candid that I could not avoid yealing confidence to what they had said. Capt. Clark and myself now concerted measures for our future operations, and it was mutually agreed that he should set out tomorrow morning with eleven men furnished with axes and other necessary tools for making canoes, their arms accoutrements and as much of their baggage as they could carry. also to take the indians Carbono and the indian woman with him; that on his arrival at the Shoshone camp he was to leave Charbono and the Indian woman to haisten the return of the Indians with their horses to this place, and to proceede himself with the eleven men down the Columbia in order to examine the river and if he found it navigable and could obtain timber to set about making canoes immediately. In the mean time I was to bring on the party and baggage to the Shoshone Camp, calculating that by the time I should reach that place that he would have sufficiently informed himself with rispect to the state of the river &c. as to determine us whether to prosicute our journey from thence by land or water. in the former case we should want all the horses which we could perchase, the latter only to hire the Indians to transport our baggage to the place at which we made the canoes. in order to inform me as early as possible of the state of the river he was to send back one of the men with the necessary information as soon as he should satisfy himself on this subject. this plan being settled we gave orders accordingly and the men prepared for an early march. the nights are very cold and the sun excessively hot in the day. we have no fuel here but a few dry willow brush. and from the appearance of country I am confident we shall not find game here to subsist us many days. these are additional reasons why I conceive it necessary to get under way as soon as possible.— this morning Capt. Clark had delayed untill 7 A. M. before he set out just about which time Drewyer arrived with the Indian; he left the canoes to come on after him, and immediately set out and joined me as has been before mentioned.— The sperits of the men were now much elated at the prospect of geting horses.

Courses and distances traveled by Capt. Clark
August 17th 1805.

S 30° W. <u>4</u>

Miles <u>4</u>

to a high Knob or hill in the forks of Jefferson's River,[3] the same being 10 M. by water. the river making a considerable bend to the Stard. the forks of this river is the most distant point to which the waters of the Missouri are navigable. of course we laid up our canoes at this place and commenced our voyage by land.—

[Clark]   *August 17th Satturday 1805*

a fair Cold morning wind S. W. the Thermometer at 42 a. 0 at Sunrise, We Set out at 7 oClock and proceeded on to the forks   I had not proceeded on one mile before I saw at a distance Several Indians on horsback Comeing towards me, The Intertrepeter & Squar who were before me at Some distance danced for the joyful Sight, and She made signs to me that they were her nation, as I aproached nearer them descovered one of Capt Lewis party With them dressed in their Dress; the met me with great Signs of joy, as the Canoes were proceeding on nearly opposit me I turned those people & Joined Capt Lewis who had Camped with 16 of those Snake Indians at the forks 2 miles in advance.   those Indians Sung all the way to their Camp where the others had provd. a cind of Shade of Willows Stuck up in a Circle   the Three Chiefs with Capt. Lewis met me with great cordialliaty embraced and took a Seat on a white robe, the Main Chief imedeately tied to my hair Six Small pieces of Shells resembling *perl* which is highly Valued by those people and is prcured from the nations resideing near the *Sea Coast*.   we then Smoked in their fassion without Shoes and without much cerimoney and form.

Capt Lewis informed me he found those people on the *Columbia* River about 40 miles from the forks at that place there was a large camp of them, he had purswaded those with him to Come and See that what he said was the truth, they had been under great apprehension all the way, for fear of their being deceived. The Great Chief of this nation proved to be the brother of the *Woman* with us and is a man of Influence Sence & easey & reserved manners, appears to possess a great deel of Cincerity. The ⟨perog⟩ Canoes arrived & unloaded—   every thing appeared to asstonish those people. the appearance of the men, their arms, the Canoes, the Clothing my black Servent & the Segassity of Capt Lewis's Dog. we Spoke a fiew words to them in the evening respecting our rout intentions our want of horses &c. & gave them a fiew presents & medals— ⟨in the eving⟩ we made a number of inquires of those people about the Columbia River the Countrey game &c. The account they gave us was verry unfavourable, that the River abounded in emence falls, one perticularly much higher than the falls of the Missouri & at the place the mountains Closed So Close that it was impracticable to pass, & that the ridge Continued on each Side of perpendicular Clifts inpenetratable, and that no Deer Elk or any game was to be found in that Countrey, aded to that they informed us that there was no timber on the river Sufficiently large to make Small Canoes, This information (if true is alarming) I deturmined to go in advance and examine the Countrey, See if those dificueltes presented themselves in the gloomey picture in which they painted them, and if the river was practiable and I could find timber to build Canoes, those Ideas & plan appeard to be agreeable to Capt Lewis's Ideas on this point, and I selected 11 men,[4] directed them to pack up their baggage Complete themselves with amunition, take each an ax and Such tools as will be Soutable to build Canoes, and be ready to Set out at 10 oClock tomorrow morning. Those people greatly pleased our hunters killed three Deer & an antilope which was eaten in a Short time the Indians being so harrassed & compelled to move about in those rugid mountains that they are half Starved liveing at this time on berries & roots which they geather in the plains. Those people are not begerley but generous, only one has asked me for anything and he for powder.

This nation Call themselves *Cho-shon-nê* the Chief is name *Too-et-te-con'l* Black Gun is his war name *Ka-me-ah-wah*— or Come & Smoke. this Chief gave me the following name and pipe *Ka-me-ah-wah*. [*NB: exchange names,*[5] *custom I was called by this name afd by the Snake Inds*]

Course and distance of the River Jefferson Continud[6]

Augt. 15th

S. 25° W.   6   miles by water (4 by land) to the Mo: of a Creek 10 yards wide bold Current I call Willard's Creek Passed a point of rocks on the Stard. Side at 2 miles, one on the Lard. at 5 miles   passed a bold running Stream at 4 miles on the Lard Side & an Isld.

S. 22° E	3	miles by water (1 mile by land) to a small bottom on the Lard Side passd. a high Clift on the Stard opposit is a high sloping hill
S. 20° W	6	miles by water (2 by land) to a Small branch on the Lard Side passed no wood except Scrub. clover bottom

16th August

S 18° W	7	miles by water (3 by land) to a Lard bend under a low bluff, the river bending to the Std. under Some high land verry Crooked Shallow rapid & Small passed Several Island 4 of them opposit each other *Service Berry Vallie*
S 12° W.	4	miles by water (2 by land) to a high Clift on the Stard Side pass several Small Isds. & Bayoes
S. 50° E.	1½	m. by water (1 by land) to the mouth of a bold running Stream on the Lard Side opposed a Considerable rapid Clifts on both Sides below high Std. ⟨Colters⟩ above rapid C. &
S. 45° W.	½	mile to the lower point of an Isld. in the middle.

17th August

S. 30° W.	10	miles by water 4 by land to a high Point in the forks of the river. river bending to the Stard. Side.— met Indians & Encamped to make a Portage
Miles	39	

1. Rees says her name was Pop-pank, "Jumping Fish," from the manner in which she jumped through the water of a stream in escaping from the Hidatsas. Rees, 4, 9.

2. "Camp Fortunate," in Beaverhead County, Montana, lies just below the forks of the Beaverhead, where a part of the party would remain until August 24. The site is now under Clark Canyon Reservoir. *Atlas* map 66.

3. Now an island surrounded by Clark Canyon Reservoir. *Atlas* map 66.

4. Including Sergeants Gass and Pryor, Privates Collins, Colter, Cruzatte, Shannon, Windsor, and four others unidentified. Sacagawea and Charbonneau accompanied Clark as far as the Shoshone village. Appleman (LC), 372 n. 111.

5. Such exchange of names, creating a ceremonial kinship between the persons concerned, was a custom of several Western tribes. However, Rees, 7, believes the name given Clark was not the chief's name but was Kim-ah-pawn, which he also interprets

as "come and smoke," which he derived from Clark's smoking with the Shoshones on August 20, 1805.

6. Here in Codex G, p. 67, Clark has inserted accumulated courses for August 15, 16, and 17, 1805.

[Lewis]   *Sunday August 18th 1805.*

This morning while Capt Clark was busily engaged in preparing for his rout, I exposed some articles to barter with the Indians for horses as I wished a few at this moment to releive the men who were going with Capt Clark from the labour of carrying their baggage and also one to keep here in order to pack the meat to camp which the hunters might kill. I soon obtained three very good horses for which I gave an uniform coat, a pair of legings, a few handkerchiefs, three knives and some other small articles the whole of which did not cost more than about 20$ in the U' States.   the Indians seemed quite as well pleased with their bargin as I was.   the men also purchased one for an old checked shirt a pair of old legings and a knife.   two of those I purchased Capt. C. took on with him. at 10 A. M. Capt. Clark departed with his detatchment and all the Indians except 2 men and 2 women who remained with us. Two of the inferior chiefs were a little displeased at not having received a present equivolent to that given the first Chief.   to releive this difficulty Capt. Clark bestoed a couple of his old coats on them and I promised that if they wer active in assisting me over the mountains with horses that I would give them an additional present; this seemed perfectly to satisfy them and they all set out in a good humour. Capt. Clark encamped this evening near the narrow pass between the hills on Jefferson's river in the Shoshone Cove.[1] his hunters killed one deer which the party with the aid of the Indians readily consumed in the course of the evening.—   after there departure this morning I had all the stores and baggage of every discription opened and aired.   and began the operation of forming the packages in proper parsels for the purpose of transporting them on horseback.   the rain in the evening compelled me to desist from my operations. I had the raw hides put in the water in order to cut them in throngs proper for lashing the packages and forming the necessary geer for pack horses, a business which I fortunately had not to learn on this occasion. Drewyer Killed one deer this evening. a beaver was also caught by one of the party. I had the net arranged and set this evening to catch some trout which we could see in great abundance at the bottom of the river. This day I completed my thirty first year, and conceived that I had in all human probability now existed about half the period which I am to remain in this Sublunary world. I reflected that I had as yet done but little, very little indeed, to further the hapiness of the human race, or to advance the information of the succeeding generation. I viewed with regret the many hours I have spent in indolence, and now soarly feel the want of that information which those hours would have given me had they been judiciously expended. but since they are past and cannot be recalled, I dash from me the gloomy thought and resolved in future, to redouble my exertions and at least indeavour to promote those two primary objects of human existence, by giving them the aid of that portion of talents which nature and fortune have bestoed on me; or in future, to live for *mankind,* as I have heretofore lived *for myself.*—

[Clark]   August 18th Sunday 1805

Purchased of the Indians three horses for which we gave a Chiefs Coat Some Handkerchiefs a Shirt Legins & a fiew arrow points &c. I gave two of my coats to two of the under Chiefs who appeared not well Satisfied that the first Chief was dressed so much finer than themselves. at 10 oClock I Set out accompanied by the Indians except 3 the interpreter and wife, the fore part of the day worm, at 12 oClock it became hasey with a mist of rain wind hard from the S. W. and Cold which increased untill night the rain Seased in about two hours. We proceeded on thro' a wide leavel vallie without wood except willows & Srubs for 15 miles and Encamped at a place the high lands approach within 200 yards in 2 points the River here only 10 yards wide Several Small Streams branching out on each Side below. all the Indians proceeded on except the 3 Chiefs & two young men. my hunters killed two Deer which we eate. The Course from the forks is West 9 miles N. 60° W. 6 miles. The Latd. of the forks agreeable to observations is 43° 30' 43" North— [EC: actually about 45°]

1. Clark's route appears as a dotted line on *Atlas* map 67. The campsite, labeled "W. C. Camp" on the map, was near Red Butte, about eight miles west of Grant, Beaverhead County, Montana. Peebles (RW), 6.

[Lewis]   *Monday August 19th 1805.*

This morning I arrose at dylight and sent out three hunters.   some of the men who were much in want of legings and mockersons I suffered to dress some skins.   the others I employed in repacking the baggage, making pack saddles &c.   we took up the net this morning but caugt no fish.   one beaver was caught in a trap.   the frost which perfectly whitened the grass this morning had a singular appearance to me at this season.   this evening I made a few of the men construct a sein of willow brush which we hawled and caught a large number of fine trout and a kind of mullet[1] about 16 Inhes long which I had not seen before.   the scales are small, the nose is long and obtusely pointed and exceedes the under jaw.   the mouth is not large but opens with foalds at the sides, the colour of it's back and sides is of a bluish brown and belley white; it has the faggot bones, from which I have supposed it to be of the mullet kind. the tongue and pallate are smooth and it has no teeth.   it is by no means as good as the trout.   the trout[2] are the same which I first met with at the falls of the Missouri, they are larger than the speckled trout of our mountains and equally as well flavored.—   The hunters returned this evening with two deer.   from what has ⟨already⟩ been said of the Shoshones it will be readily perceived that they live in a wretched stait of poverty.   yet notwithstanding their extreem poverty they are not only cheerfull but even gay, fond of gaudy dress and amusements; like most other Indians they are great egotists and frequently boast of heroic acts which they never performed.   they are also fond of games of wrisk.   they are frank, communicative, fair in dealing, generous with the little they possess, extreemly honest, and by no means beggarly.   each individual is his own sovereign master, and acts from the dictates of his own mind; the authority of the Cheif being nothing more than mere admonition supported by the influence which the propiety of his own examplery conduct may have acquired him in the minds of the individuals who compose the band. the title of cheif is not hereditary, nor can I learn that there is any cerimony of instalment, or other epoh in the life of a Cheif from which his title as such can be dated. in fact every man is a chief, but all have not an equal influence on the minds of the other members of the community, and he who happens to enjoy the greatest share of confidence is the principal Chief. The Shoshonees may be estimated at about 100 warriors, and about three times that number of woomen and children. they have more children among them than I expected to have seen among a people who procure subsistence with such difficulty. there are but few very old persons, nor did they appear to treat those with much tenderness or rispect. The man is the sole propryetor of his wives and daughters, and can barter or dispose of either as he thinks proper. a plurality of wives is common among them, but these are not generally sisters as with the Minnetares & Mandans but are purchased of different fathers. The father frequently disposes of his infant daughters in marriage to men who are grown or to men who have sons for whom they think proper to provide wives. the compensation given in such cases usually consists of horses or mules which the father receives at the time of contract and converts to his own uce. the girl remains with her parents untill she is conceived to have obtained the age of puberty which with them is considered to be about the age of 13 or 14 years. the female at this age is surrendered to her sovereign lord and husband agreeably to contract, and with her is frequently restored by the father quite as much as he received in the first instance in payment for his daughter; but this is discretionary with the father. Sah-car-gar-we-ah had been thus disposed of before she was taken by the Minnetares, or had arrived to the years of puberty. the husband was yet living and with this band. he was more than double her age and had two other wives. he claimed her as his wife but said that as she had had a child by another man, who was Charbono, that he did not want her. They seldom correct their children particularly the boys who soon become masters of their own acts. they give as a reason that it cows and breaks the Sperit of the boy to whip him, and that he never recovers his independence of mind after he is grown. They treat their women but with little rispect, and compel them to perform every species of drudgery. they collect the wild fruits and roots, attend to the horses or assist in that duty cook dreess the skins and make all their apparal, collect wood and make their fires, arrange and form their lodges, and when they travel pack the horses and take charge of all the baggage; in short the man dose little else except attend his horses hunt and fish. the man considers himself degraded if he is compelled to walk any distance, and if he is so unfortunately poor as only to possess two horses he rides the best himself and leavs the woman or women if he has more than one, to transport their baggage and children on the other, and to walk if the horse is unable to carry the additional weight of their persons— the chastity of their women is not held in high estimation, and the husband will for a trifle barter the companion of his bead for a night or longer if he conceives the reward adiquate; tho' they are not so importunate that we should caress their women as the siouxs were and some of their women appear to be held more sacred than in any nation we have seen I have requested the men to give them no cause of jealousy by having connection with their women without their knowledge, which with them strange as it may seem is considered as disgracefull to the husband as clandestine connections of a similar kind are among civilized nations. to prevent this mutual exchange of good officies altogether I know it impossible to effect, particularly on the part of our young men whom some months abstanence have made very polite to those tawney damsels. no evil has yet resulted and I hope will not from these connections.— notwithstanding the late loss of horses which this people sustained by the Minnetares the stock of the band may be very safely estimated at seven hundred of which they are perhaps about 40 coalts and half that number of mules.— these people are deminutive in stature, thick ankles, crooked legs, thick flat feet and in short but illy formed, at least much more so in general than any nation of Indians I ever saw. their complexion is much that of the Siouxs or darker than the Minnetares mandands or Shawnees. generally both men and women wear their hair in a loos lank flow over the sholders and face; tho' I observed some few men who confined their hair in two equal cues hanging over each ear and drawnn in front of the body. the cue is formed with throngs of dressed lather or Otterskin aternately crossing each other. at present most of them have cut short in the neck in consequence of the loss of their relations by the Minnetares. Cameahwait has his cut close all over his head.   this constitutes their cerimony of morning for their deceased relations.   the dress of the men consists of a robe long legings, shirt, tippet and Mockersons, that of the women is also a robe, chemise, and Mockersons; sometimes they make use of short legings.   the ornements of both men and women are very similar, and consist of several species of sea shells, blue and white beads, bras and Iron arm bands, plaited cords of the sweet grass, and collars of leather ornamented with the quills of the porcupine dyed of various colours among which I observed the red, yellow, blue, and black.   the ear is purforated in the lower part to receive various ornaments but the nose is not, nor is the ear lasserated or disvigored for this purpose as among many nations. the men never mark their skins by birning, cuting, nor puncturing and introducing a colouring matter as many nations do.   there women sometimes puncture a small circle on their forehead nose or cheeks and thus introduce a black matter usually soot and grease which leaves an indelible stane.   tho' this even is by no means common.   their arms offensive and defensive consist in the bow and arrows sheild, some lances, and a weapon called by the Cippeways who formerly used it, the pog-gar'-mag-gon'.[3] in fishing they employ wairs, gigs, and fishing hooks.   the salmon is the principal object of their pursuit.   they snair wolves and foxes. I was anxious to learn whether these people had the venerial, and made the enquiry through the intrepreter and his wife; the information was that they sometimes had it but I could not learn their remedy; they most usually die with it's effects.   this seems a strong proof that these disorders bothe gonaroehah and Louis venerae are native disorders of America.   tho' these people have suffered much by the small pox which is known to be imported and perhaps those other disorders might have been contracted from other indian tribes who by a round of communication might have obtained from the Europeans since it was introduced into that quarter of the globe.   but so much detatched on the other had from all communication with the whites that I think it most probable that those disorders are original with them.[4]   from the middle of May to the firt of September these people reside on the waters of the Columbia where they consider themselves in perfect security from their enimies as they have not as yet

ever found their way to this retreat; during this season the salmon furnish the principal part of their subsistence and as this firsh either perishes
or returns about the 1st of September they are compelled at this season in
surch of subsistence to resort to the Missouri, in the vallies of which, there
is more game even within the mountains. here they move slowly down
the river in order to collect and join other bands either of their own
nation or the Flatheads, and having become sufficiently strong as they
conceive venture on the Eastern side of the Rocky mountains into the
plains, where the buffaloe abound. but they never leave the interior of
the mountains while they can obtain a scanty subsistence, and always return as soon as they have acquired a good stock of dryed meat in the
plains; when this stock is consumed they venture again into the plains;
thus alternately obtaining their food at the risk of their lives and retiring
to the mountains, while they consume it.— These people are now on
the eve of their departure for the Missouri, and inform us that they expect to be joined at or about the three forks by several bands of their own
nation, and a band of the Flatheads. as I am now two busily engaged to
enter at once into a minute discription of the several articles which compose their dress, impliments of war hunting fishing &c I shall pursue
them at my leasure in the order they have here occurred to my mind, and
have been mentioned. This morning capt. Clark continued his rout with
his party, the Indians accompanying him as yesterday; he was obliged to
feed them. nothing remarkable happened during the day. he was met
by an Indian with two mules on this side of the dividing ridge at the foot
of the mountain, the Indian had the politeness to offer Capt. C. one of his
mules to ride as he was on foot, which he accepted and gave the fellow a
waistcoat as a reward for his politeness. in the evening he reached the
creek on this side of the Indian camp and halted for the night.[5] his
hunters killed nothing today. The Indians value their mules very highly.[6]
a good mule can not be obtained for less than three and sometimes four
horses, and the most indifferent are rated at two horses. their mules
generally are the finest I ever saw without any comparison.— today I
observed time and distance of ☉'s and ☽'s nearest limbs with sextant ☉
East. it being the

Point of Observation No. 43.

	Time			Distance		
	h	m	s			
A. M.	11	37	11	65°	53′	15″
"		39	50	"	52	—
"		44	15	"	50	45
"		46	18	"	49	—

	Time			Distance		
	h	m	s			
A. M.	11	51	37	65°	47′	15″
"		54	43	"	45	30
"		55	53	"	44	15
"		57	40	"	43	30
"		59	30	"	42	30

Observed Meridian Altitude of ☉'s L. L. with Octant by the back observation 69° 15′ ″

Latitude deduced from this observation N. 44° 37′ 57.4″

[Clark]   *August 19th Monday 1805*

A verry Cold morning Frost to be Seen   we Set out at 7 oClock and proceeded on thro a wide leavel Vallie   the Chief Shew me the place that a number of his nation was killed about 1 years past[7] this Vallie [*X: whiet vallie*] Continues 5 miles & then becoms narrow, the beaver has Damed up the River in maney places   we proceeded on up the main branch with a gradial assent to the head and passed over a low mountain and Decended a Steep Decent to a butifull Stream, passed over a Second hill of a verry Steep assent & thro' a hilley Countery for 8 miles an Encamped on a Small Stream   the Indians with us we wer oblige to feed—   one man met me with a mule & Spanish Saddle to ride, I gave him a wistoat [waistcoat]   a mule is considered a of great value among those people   we proceeded on over a verry mountanious Countery across the head of hollows & Springs ⟨and encamped⟩

1. The northern sucker; see above, August 3, 1805. It was probably Biddle who drew a red vertical line through this passage from "this evening" to "well flavored."

2. The trout which are the same as those at the Falls of the Missouri are cutthroat trout. The speckled trout used for comparison is the brook trout, *Salvelinus fontinalis,* with which Lewis was familiar. Lee et al., 114.

3. Described by Lewis below, on August 23, 1805.

4. Lewis refers to *lues venerea,* Latin for syphilis. The question of whether the disease originated in the Americas and spread to the Old World after 1492, or was native to both hemispheres, is still a subject of debate. Gonorrhea was often confused with syphilis in Lewis and Clark's time. Criswell, 54; Crosby, 122–64. Perhaps it was Biddle who drew a red vertical line through the phrase, "I was anxious . . . venerial." Another line seems to continue the first and may have been intended to strike the entire passage about venereal disease.

5. The dotted line on *Atlas* map 67 indicates Clark's route; his camp west of the divide in Lemhi County, Idaho, is marked "W. C. Camp." The stream may be Pattee Creek. Peebles (RW), 7.

6. It was probably Biddle who drew a red vertical line through this and the following lines about the mules.

7. The site is marked "Inds. Masscured 1 year [ago?]" on *Atlas* map 67.

[Lewis]   *Tuesday August 20th 1805.*

This morning I sent out the two hunters and employed the ballance of the party pretty much as yesterday. I walked down the river about ¾ of a mile and scelected a place near the river bank unperceived by the Indians for a cash, which I set three men to make, and directed the centinel to discharge his gun if he pereceived any of the Indians going down in that direction which was to be the signal for the men at work on the cash to desist and seperate, least these people should discover our deposit and rob us of the baggage we intend leaving here.   by evening the cash was completed unperceived by the Indians, and all our packages made up. the Pack-saddles and harnes is not yet complete.   in this operation we find ourselves at a loss for nails and boards; for the first we substitute throngs of raw hide which answer verry well, and for the last to cut off the blades of our oars and use the plank of some boxes which have heretofore held other articles and put those articles into sacks of raw hide which I have had made for the purpose.   by this means I have obtained as many boards as will make 20 saddles which I suppose will be sufficient for our present exegencies. The Indians with us behave themselves extreemly well; the women have been busily engaged all day making and

mending the mockersons of our party. In the evening the hunters returned unsuccessfull. Drewyer went in search of his trap which a beaver
had taken off last night; he found the beaver dead with the trap to his
foot about 2 miles below the place he had set it.   this beaver constituted
the whole of the game taken today.   the fur of this animal is as good as I
ever saw any, and beleive that they are never out of season on the upper
part of the Missouri and it's branches within the Mountains. Goodrich
caught several douzen fine trout today. I made up a small assortment of
medicines, together with the specemines of plants, minerals, seeds &c.
which, I have collected betwen this place and the falls of the Missouri
which I shall deposit here.   the robe woarn by the Shoshonees is the
same in both sexes and is loosly thrown about their sholders, and the
sides at pleasure either hanging loose or drawn together with the hands,
sometimes if the weather is cold they confine it with a girdel arround the
waist; they are generally about the size of a 2½ point blanket[1] for grown
persons and reach as low as the middle of the leg.   this robe forms a garment in the day and constitutes their only covering at night.   with these
people the robe is formed most commonly of the skins of Antelope, Bighorn, or deer, dressed with the hair on, tho' they prefer the buffaloe
when they can procure them. I have also observed some robes among
them of beaver, moonax,[2] and small wolves.   the summer robes of both
sexes are also frequently made of the Elk's skin dressed without the hair.
The shirt of the men is really a commodious and decent garment.   it
roomy and reaches nearly half way the thye, there is no collar, the apperture being sufficiently large to admit the head and is left square at top, or
most frequently, both before and behind terminate in the tails of the animals of which they are made and which foald outwards being frequently
left entire or somtimes cut into a fring on the edges and ornimented with
the quills of the Porcupine.[3]   the sides of the shirt are sewed deeply
fringed, and ornamented in a similar manner from the bottom upwards,
within six or eight inches of the sleve from whence it is left open as well as
the sleve on it's under side to the elbow nearly.   from the elbow the sleve
fits the arm tight as low as the wrist and is not ornimented with a fringe as
the sides and under parts of the sleve are above the elbow.   the sholder
straps are wide and on them is generally displayed the taste of the manu-

facterer in a variety of figures wrought with the quills of the porcupine of several colours; beads when they have them are also displayed on this part. the tail of the shirt is left in the form which the fore legs and neck give it with the addition of a slight fringe. the hair is usually left on the tail, & near the hoofs of the animal; part of the hoof is also retained to the skin and is split into a fring by way of orniment. these shirts are generally made of deer's Antelope's, Bighorn's, or Elk's skins dressed without the hair. the Elk skin is less used for this purpose than either of the others. their only thread used on this or any other occasion is the sinews taken from the back and loins of the deer Elk buffaloe &c. Their legings are most usually formed of the skins of the Antelope dressed without the hair. in the men they are very long and full each leging being formed of a skin nearly entire. the legs, tail and neck are also left on these, and the tail woarn upwards; and the neck deeply fringed and ornimented with porcupine qulls drags or trails on the ground behind the heel. the skin is sewn in such manner as to fit the leg and thye closely; the upper part being left open a sufficient distance to permit the legs of the skin to be dran underneath a girdle both before and behind, and the wide part of the skin to cover the buttock and lap before in such manner that the breechcloth is unnecessary. they are much more decent in concealing those parts than any nation on the Missouri the sides of the legings are also deeply fringed and ornimented. sometimes this part is ornimented with little fassicles of the hair of an enimy whom they have slain in battle. The tippet of the Snake Indians is the most eligant peice of Indian dress I ever saw, the neck or collar of this is formed of a strip of dressed Otter skin with the fur. it is about four or five inches wide and is cut out of the back of the skin the nose and eyes forming one extremity and the tail the other. begining a little behind the ear of the animal at one edge of this collar and proceeding towards the tail, they attatch from one to two hundred and fifty little roles of Ermin skin formed in the following manner. the skin is first dressed with the fur on it and a narrow strip is cut out of the back of the skin reaching from the nose and imbracing the tail. this is sewed arround a small cord of the silk-grass[4] twisted for the purpose and regularly tapering in such manner as to give it a just proportion to the tail which is to form the lower extremity of the stran. thus arranged they are confined at the upper point in little bundles of two—three, or more as the disign may be to make them more full; these are then attatched to the collars as before mentioned, and to conceal the connection of this part which would otherwise have a course appearance they attatch a broad fringe of the Ermin skin to the collar overlaying that part. little bundles of fine fringe of the same materials is fastened to the extremity of the tails in order to shew their black extremities to greater advantage. the center of the otterskin collar is also ornamented with the shells of the perl oister. the collar is confined arond the neck and the little roles of Ermin skin about the size of a large quill covers the solders and body nearly to the waist and has the appearance of a short cloak and is really handsome. these they esteem very highly, and give or dispose of only on important occasions. the ermin whic is known to the traiders of the N. W. by the name of the white weasel is the genuine ermine, and might no doubt be turned to great advantage by those people if they would encourage the Indians to take them. they are no doubt extreemly plenty and readily taken, from the number of these tippets which I have seen among these people and the great number of skins employed in the construction of each timppet. scarcely any of them have employed less than one hundred of these skins in their formation.—[5] This morning Capt. Clark set out at 6 in the morning and soon after arrived near their camp they having removed about 2 miles higher up the river than the camp at which they were when I first visited them. the chief requested a halt, which was complyed with, and a number of the indians came out from the village and joined them   after smoking a few pipes with them they all proceeded to the village where Capt C. was conducted to a large lodge prepared in the center of the encampment for himself and party. here they gave him one salmon and some cakes of dryed berries. he now repeated to them what had been said to them in council at this place which was repeated to the village by the Cheif. when he had concluded this address he requested a guide to accompany him down the river and an elderly man was pointed out by the Cheif who consented to undertake this task.[6] this was the old man of whom Cameahwait had spoken as a person well acquainted with the country to the North of this river. Capt. C. [*WC?: he had Conversations*][7] encouraged the Indians to come

over with their horses and assist me over with the baggage.   he distrub-
uted some presents among the Indians.   about half the men of the village turned out to hunt the antelope but were unsuccessfull.   at 3 P. M.
Capt. Clark departed, accompanyed by his guide and party except one
man[8] whom he left with orders to purchase a horse if possible and overtake him as soon as he could.   he left Charbono and the indian woman to
return to my camp with the Indians.   he passed the river about four
miles below the Indians, and encamped on a small branch, eight miles
distant.[9]   on his way he met a rispectable looking indian who returned
and continued with him all night; this indian gave them three salmon.
Capt. C. killed a cock of the plains or mountain cock.   it was of a dark
brown colour with a long and pointed tail larger than the dunghill fowl
and had a fleshey protuberant substance about the base of the upper
chap, something like that of the turkey tho' without the snout.[10]

This day I observed time and distance of ⊙'s and ☽'s nearest Limbs with Sextant. ⊙ East.

	Time			*Distance*		
	h	m	s			
A. M.	8	16	0	53°	35′	30″
	″	18	36	″	33	30
	″	21	37	″	31	45
	″	23	12	″	31	30
	″	25	—	″	30	45
	″	27	32	″	29	30
	″	29	5	″	29	—
	″	30	11	″	28	45

	Time			*Distance*		
	h	m	s			
A. M.	8	33	29	53°	27′	45″
	″	34	14	″	27	30
	″	35	31	″	27	—
	″	36	43	″	26	45
	″	37	12	″	26	—
	″	39	20	″	25	15
	″	40	32	″	25	—

Longitude deduced from this observation West of Greenwich [*blank*]

Latitude N. deduced from the Hor. ∠ of the P. M. Observation of ☉'s center 44° 33' 50.5"

Observed Equal Altitudes with Sextant of the Sun.

	h	m	s		h	m	s	
A. M.	8	45	30	P. M.	3	55	40	Altitude by Sextant
	"	47	4		"	57	16	at the time of observtn.
	"	49	40		"	58	50	68° 30' "

Observed Meridian Altitude of ☉'s L. L. with Octant by the back observation 70° ' "

Latitude deduced from this observation N. 44° 39' 43"

"So-So-ne" the Snake Indians

[Clark]   August 20th Tuesday 1805[11]

Set out at half past 6 oClock and proceeded on (met maney parties of Indians) thro' a hilley Countrey to the Camp of the Indians on a branch of the Columbia River,[12] before we entered this Camp a Serimonious hault was requested by the Chief and I Smoked with all that Came around for Several pipes, we then proceeded on to the Camp & I was introduced into the only Lodge they had which was pitched in the Center for my party all the other Lodges made of bushes, after a fiew Indian Seremonies I informed the Indians the object of our journey our good intentions towards them my consern for their distressed Situation, what we had done for them in makeing a piece with the *Minitarras Mandans Rickara* &c. for them—. and requested them all to take over their horses & assist Capt Leiwis across &c. also informing them the oject of my journey down the river and requested a ⟨pilot⟩ guide to accompany me, all of which was repeited by the Chief to the whole village.

Those pore people Could only raise a Sammon & a little dried Choke Cherris for us   half the men of the tribe with the Chief turned out to hunt the antilopes, at 3 oClock after giveing a fiew Small articles as presents I set out accompanied by an old man as a ⟨pilot⟩ Guide (I endevered to procure as much information from thos people as possible without much Suckcess they being but little acquainted or effecting to be So—[)]   I lef one man to purchase a horse and overtake me and proceeded on thro a wide rich bottom on a beaten Roade 8 miles   Crossed the river and encamped on a Small run, this evening passed a number of old lodges, and met a number of men women children & horses, met a man who appeared of Some Consideration who turned back with us, he halted a woman & gave us 3 Small Sammon, this man continued with me all night and partook of what I had which was a little Pork verry Salt. *Those* Indians are verry attentive to Strangers &c. I left our interpreter & his woman to accompany the Indians to Capt Lewis tomorrow the Day they informed me they would Set out   I killed a Pheasent at the Indian Camp larger than a dungal [dunghill] fowl with feshey protuberances about the head like a turkey. Frost last night

1. Referring to a system for measuring trade blankets by size and weight, used by the Hudson's Bay Company and other traders. The "points" were lines woven in near one corner of the blanket. A 2½ point blanket would be 5 feet 4 inches by 4 feet 3 inches, and weigh 3¹⁄₁₆ pounds. Hanson (PB).

2. Probably the yellow-bellied marmot, *Marmota flaviventris*, then new to science. Lewis's word is a variant of a Virginia Algonquian word and of the scientific name for the related woodchuck, *Marmota monax*. Jefferson used the term in his *Notes on the State of Virginia*. Cutright (LCPN), 182; Burroughs, 106; Jefferson, 50; Chamberlain, 249.

3. The yellow-haired porcupine, *Erethizon dorsatum expiranthum*.

4. Both spreading dogbane, *Apocynum androsaemifolium* L., and an unnamed dogbane, *A. medium* Greene, are known in this area and could answer for the silk grass. However, hemp dogbane, *A. cannabinum* L., is the species most often used for textile fibers, but is not recorded or abundant for this region of Montana. Hemp dogbane could have been secured from farther east in Montana. Booth & Wright, 189; Cutright (LCPN), 189 n. 10. Criswell, 78, suggests yucca as a possibility. See Gilmore (UPI), 19.

5. The artist Charles B. J. F. de Saint-Mémin painted Lewis wearing such a garment, probably the one given him by Cameahwait, after the expedition (see illustration in this volume, p. xii). Cutright (HLCJ), 92 and 92 n. 39; Cutright (LCPP), 42–43. The passages dealing with Shoshone clothing have a vertical line drawn through them, perhaps by Biddle, but not with his customary red ink.

6. This man would guide Clark on his reconnaissance of the Salmon River and conduct the entire party over the Lolo Trail to the Clearwater River country in Idaho, one of the most difficult parts of the entire journey. Although he deserves considerable credit for the success of the expedition, the captains refer to him by name only once in the journals, by the nickname "Old Toby"; see below, May 12, 1806. Rees, 11, gives the name as Tobe, an abbreviation of Tosa-tive koo-be, meaning "furnished white white-man brains," an allusion to his service as the expedition's guide (white white-man is here distinguished from black white-man or negro). According to Rees his real name was Pi-kee queen-ah, "swooping eagle."

7. Clark's interlineation refers to the geographical information he had gathered which Lewis detailed in his entry for August 14, 1805.

8. Cruzatte; see Lewis's entry for August 21, 1805, below.

9. Having crossed to the west side of the Lemhi River, Clark camped in the vicinity of Baker, Lemhi County, Idaho. On *Atlas* map 67 there is an undated campsite symbol in approximately the right area, though no "small branch" appears near it; the stream may be Withington Creek. Peebles (RW), 7.

10. Perhaps it was Biddle who drew a vertical line through this material about the sage grouse, but not in the usual red ink.

11. Clark's courses for his reconnaissance, August 20–23, are found with his entry of August 25, 1805.

12. The Shoshone camp had probably moved from its previous location to a site about four miles north of Tendoy, Lemhi County, near where Kenney Creek joins the Lemhi River. Appleman (LC), 270–72; *Atlas* map 67.

Chapter Twenty-One

Searching for Navigable Waters

August 21–26, 1805

[Lewis]   *Wednesday August 21st 1805.*

This morning was very cold.   the ice ¼ of an inch thick on the water which stood in the vessels exposed to the air.   some wet deerskins that had been spread the grass last evening are stiffly frozen.   the ink feizes in my pen.   the bottoms are perfectly covered with frost insomuch that they appear to be covered with snow. This morning early I dispatched two hunters to kill some meat if possible before the Indians arrive; Drewyer I sent with the horse into the cove for that purpose. The party pursued their several occupations as yesterday.   by evening I had all the baggage, saddles, and harness completely ready for a march.   after dark, I made the men take the baggage to the cash and deposit it. I beleve we have been unperceived by the Indians in this movement.   notwithstanding the coldness of the last night the day has proved excessively warm.   neither of the hunters returned this evening and I was obliged to issue pork and corn. The mockersons of both sexes are usually the same and are made of deer Elk or buffaloe skin dressed without the hair.   sometimes in the winter they make them of buffaloe skin dressed with the hair on and turn the hair inwards as the Mandans Minetares and most of the nations do who inhabit the buffaloe country.   the mockerson is formed with one seem on the outer edge of the foot is cut open at the instep to admit *the foot and sewed up behind. in this rispect they are the same with the Man-*

133

dans. they sometimes ornament their mockersons with various figures wrought with the quills of the Porcupine. some of the dressey young men orniment the tops of their mockersons with the skins of polecats[1] and trale the tail of that animal on the ground at their heels as they walk.— the robe of the woman is generally smaller than that of the man but is woarn in the same manner over the sholders. the Chemise is roomy and comes down below the middle of the leg the upper part of this garment is formed much like the shirt of the men except the sholder strap which is never used with the Chemise. in women who give suck, they are left open at the sides nearly as low as the waist, in others, close as high as the sleeve. the sleeve underneath as low as the elbow is open, that ⟨upper⟩ part being left very full. the sides tail and upper part of the sleeves are deeply fringed and sometimes orniminted in a similar manner with the shirts of the men with the addition of little patches of red cloth about the tail edged around with beads. the breast is usually ornament with various figures of party colours rought with the quills of the Porcupine. it is on this part of the garment that they appear to exert their greatest ingenuity. a girdle of dressed leather confines the Chemise around the waist. when either the man or woman wish to disengage their arm from the sleeve they draw it out by means of the opening underneath the arm an throw the sleeve behind the body. the legings of the women reach as high as the knee and are confined with a garter below. the mockerson covers and confins it's lower extremity. they are neither fringed nor ornamented. these legings are made of the skins of the antelope and the Chemise usually of those of the large deer Bighorn and the smallest elk.— They seldom wear the beads they possess about their necks at least I have never seen a grown person of either sex wear them on this part; some their children are seen with them in this way. the men and women were them suspen from the ear in little bunches or intermixed with triangular peices of the shells of the perl oister. the men also were them attached in a similar manner to the hare of the fore part of the crown of the head; to which they sometimes make the addition of the wings and tails of birds. the nose in neither sex is pierced nor do they wear any ornament in it. they have a variety of small sea shells of which they form collars woarn indiscriminately by both sexes. these as well as the shell of the perl oister they value very highly and inform us that they obtain them from their friends and relations who live beyond the barren plain towards the Ocean in a S. Westerly direction.[2] these friends of theirs they say inhabit a good country abounding with Elk, deer, bear, and Antelope, and possess a much greater number of horses and mules than they do themselves; or using their own figure that their horses and mules are as numerous as the grass of the plains. the warriors or such as esteem themselves brave men wear collars made of the claws of the brown bear which are also esteemed of great value and are preserved with great care. these claws are ornamented with beads about the thick end near which they are peirced through their sides and strung on a throng of dressed leather and tyed about the neck commonly with the upper edge of the tallon next the breast or neck but sometimes are reversed. it is esteemed by them an act of equal celebrity the killing one of these bear or an enimy, and with the means they have of killing this animal it must really be a serious undertaking. the sweet sented grass[3] which grows very abundant on this river is either twisted or plaited and woarn around the neck in ether sex, but most commonly by the men. they have a collar also woarn by either sex. it generally round and about the size of a man's finger; formed of leather or silk-grass twisted or firmly rolled and covered with the quills of the porcupine of different colours. the tusks of the Elk are pierced strung on a throng and woarn as an orniment for the neck, and is most generally woarn by the women and children. the men frequently wear the skin of a fox[4] or a broad strip of that of the otter around the forehead and head in form of a bando. they are also fond of the feathers of the tail of the beautifull eagle or callumet bird[5] with which they ornament their own hair and the tails and mains of their horses. [*X: also a collar of round bones which look like the joints of a fishes back*] The dress of these people is quite as desent and convenient as that of any nation of Indians I ever saw.

This morning early Capt. C. resumed his march; at the distance of five miles he arrived at some brush lodges of the Shoshones inhabited by about seven families here he halted and was very friendly received by these people, who gave himself and party as much boiled salmon as they could eat; they also gave him several dryed salmon and a considerable itself about, and were taken out by untying the small ends of the longitudinal willows, which formed the hull of the basket: the wear in the main channel was somewhat differently contrived. there were two distinct wears formed of poles and willow sticks, quite acrop the river, at no great distance from each other. each of these, were furnished with two baskets; the one to take them ascending and the other in decending. in constructing these wears, poles were first tyed together in parcels of three near the smaller extremity; these were set on end, and spread in a triangular form at the base, in such manner, that two of the three poles ranged in the direction of the intended wark, and the third down the stream. two ranges of horizontal poles, were next lashed with willow bark and wythes, to the ranging poles, and on these willow sticks were placed perpendicularly reaching from the bottom of the river to about 3 or four feet above it's surface, and placed so near each other, as not to permit the papage of the fish, and even so thick in some parts, as with the helpe of gravel and stone, to give a direction to the water which they wished. — the baskets were the same in form of the others. this is the form of the work, and disposition of the baskets.

3. Shoshone Fish Weir, August 21, 1805, Codex F, p. 147

quantity of dryed chokecherries. after smoking with them he visited their fish wear which was abut 200 yds. distant. he found the wear extended across four channels of the river which was here divided by three small islands.[6] three of these channels were narrow, and were stoped by means of trees fallen across, supported by which stakes of willow were driven down sufficiently near each other to prevent the salmon from passing. about the center of each a cilindric basket of eighteen or 20 feet in length terminating in a conic shape at it's lower extremity, formed of willows, was opposed to a small apperture in the wear with it's mouth up stream to receive the fish. the main channel of the water was conducted to this basket, which was so narrow at it's lower extremity that the fish when once in could not turn itself about, and were taken out by untying the small ends of the longitudinal willows, which frormed the hull of the basket. the wear in the main channel was somewhat differently contrived. there were two distinct wears formed of poles and willow sticks, quite across the river, at no great distance from each other. each of these, were furnished with two baskets; the one wear to take them ascending and the other in decending. in constructing these wears, poles were first tyed together in parcels of three near the smaller extremity; these were set on end, and spread in a triangular form at the base, in such manner, that two of the three poles ranged in the direction of the intended work, and the third down the stream. two ranges of horizontal poles were next lashed with willow bark and wythes to the ranging poles, and on these willow sticks were placed perpendicularly, reaching from the bottom of the river to about 3 or four feet above it's surface; and placed so near each other, as not to permit the passage of the fish, and even so thick in some parts, as with the help of gravel and stone to give a direction to the water which they wished.— the baskets were the same in form of the others. this is the form of the work, and disposition of the baskets.[7]

After examining the wears Capt. C. returned to the lodges, and shortly continued his rout and passed the river to the Lard. side[8] a little distance below the wears. he sent Collins with an Indian down the Lard. side of the river to the forks 5 me. in surch of Cruzatte who was left at the upper camp yesterday to purchase a horse and had followed on today and passed them by another road while they were at the lodges and had gone on to the forks. while Capt. Clark was at these lodges an Indian brought him a tomehawk which he said he found in the grass near the lodge where I had staid at the upper camp when I was first with his nation the tommahawk was Drewyer's he missed it in the morning before we had set out and surched for it but it was not to be found I beleive the young fellow stole it, but if he did it is the only article they have pilfered and this was now returned. Capt. C. after traveling about 20 miles through the valley with the course of the river nearly N. W. encamped on the Stard. side in a small bottom under a high Clift of rocks.[9] on his way one of the party killed a very large Salmon in a creek which they passed at the distance of 14 ms. he was joined this evening by Cruzatte and Collins who brought with them five fresh salmon which had been given them by the Indians at the forks. the forks of this river is famous as a gig fishery and is much resorted by the natives.— They killed one deer today. The Guide apeared to be a very friendly intelligent old man, Capt. C. is much pleased with him.

This day I observed Equal Altitudes of the ☉ with Sextant.

	h	m	s			h	m	s	
A. M.	8	38	36		P. M.	4	—	56	Altitude at the time
"		40	8		"		1	34	of observation.
"		42	45		"		3	5	65° 57′ 30″

Also observed Meridian Altd. of ☉'s L. L. with Octant by the back observation. 72° —′ —″

Latitude deduced from this observation North 44° 30′ 21.7″

Mean Latitude of the Forks of Jefferson's river, deduced from three observations of the Meridian Altd. of ☉'s L. L. with octant, and one calculation by means of the hor: ∠ of the ☉'s center in the P. M. observation for equal Altitudes on the 20th Instant N. 44° 35′ 28.1″

[Clark]   *August 21st Wednesday 1805*

Frost last night proceeded on with the Indians I met about 5 miles to there Camp, I entered a lodge and after Smokeing with all who Came about me I went to See the place those people take the fish, a wear across the Creek in which there is ⟨Split⟩ Stuk baskets Set in different derections

So as to take the fish either decending or assending   on my return to the Camp which was 200 yards only the different lodges (which is only bushes) brought in to the lodge   I was introduced into, Sammon boiled, and dried Choke Chers. Sufficent for all my party.—   one man brought me a *tomahawk* which we expected they had Stolen from a man of Capt Lewis's party, this man informed me he found the tomk in the grass near the place the man Slept. Crossed the River and went over a point of high land & Struck it again near a Bluff on the right Side the man I left to get a horse at the upper Camp missed me & went to the forks which is about five miles below the last Camp.

I sent one man by the forks with derections to join me to night with the one now at that place, those two men joined me at my Camp on the right Side below the 1st Clift with 5 Sammon which the Indians gave them at the forks, the place they *gig* fish at this Season. Their method of takeing fish with a *gig* or bone is with a long pole, about a foot from one End is a Strong String attached to the pole, this String is a little more than a foot long and is tied to the middle of a bone from 4 to 6 inches long, one end Sharp the other with a whole to fasten on the end of the pole with a beard[10] to the large end, the fasten this bone on one end & with the other, feel for the fish & turn and Strike them So hard that the bone passes through and Catches on the opposit Side, Slips off the End of the pole and holds the Center of the bone   Those Indians are mild in their disposition appear Sincere in their friendship, punctial, and decided.   kind with what they have, to Spare. They are excessive pore, nothing but horses   there Enemies which are noumerous on account of there horses & Defenceless Situation, have Deprived them of tents and all the Small Conveniances of life. They have only a few indifferent Knives, no ax, make use of Elk's horn Sharpened to Spit ther wood, no clothes except a Short Legins & robes of different animals, Beaver, Bear, Buffalow, wolf Panthor, Ibex, Sheep Deer, but most commonly the antilope Skins which they ware loosely about them—   Their ornements are Orter Skin dcurated with See Shells & the Skins & tales of the white weasel, Sea Shels of different size hung to their Ears hair and breast of their Shirts, beeds of Shells platted grass, and Small Strings of otter Skin dressed, they are fond of our trinkets, and give us those ornements as the most valueable of their possession. The women are held [*ML: more*] Sacred [*ML: among them than any nation we have seen*] and appear to have an equal Shere in all Conversation, which is not the Case in any othe nation I have Seen. their boeys & Girls are also admited to Speak except in Councils, the women doe all the drugery except fishing and takeing care of the horses, which the men apr. to take upon themselves.— The men ware the hair loose flowing over ther Sholders & face the women Cut Short, orniments of the back bones of fish Strung plated grass grains of Corn Strung Feathers and orniments of Birds Claws of the Bear encurcling their necks   the most Sacred of all the orniments of this nation is the Sea Shells of various Sizes and Shapes and colours, of the bassterd perl kind, which they inform us they get from the Indians to the South on the other Side of a large fork of this river in passing to which they have to pass thro Sandy & barron open plains without water to which place they can travel in 15 or 20 days— The men who passed by the forks informed me that the S W. fork was double the Size of the one I came down, and I observed that it was a handsom river at my camp   I shall in justice to Capt Lewis who was the first white man ever on this fork of the Columbia Call this Louis's river. one Deer killed this morning, and a Sammon in the last Creek 2½ feet long   The Westerley fork of the Columbia River is double the Size of the Easterley fork[11] & below those forks the river is about the Size Jeffersons River near its mouth or 100 yards wide, it is verry rapid & Sholey water Clear ⟨no⟩ but little timber. This Clift is of a redish brown Colour the rocks which fall from it is a dark brown flint tinged with that Colour. Some Gullies of white Sand Stone and Sand fine & a[s] white as Snow.[12] The mountains on each Side are high, and those on the East ruged & Contain a fiew Scattering pine, those on the West contain pine on ther tops & high up the *hollows*—[13]   The bottoms of this [day?] is wide & rich from some distance above the place I struck the East fork they are also wide on the East   Passed a large Creek which fall in on the right Side 6 miles below the forks   a road passes up this Creek & to the Missouri.

1. Probably the striped skunk, *Mephitis mephitis*.

2. There is a large "X" across this passage about the shell. It may be abalone, *Haliotis* sp. Criswell, lxxxvii.

3. Known variously as sweetgrass, holy grass, vanilla grass, or Seneca grass, *Hierochloe odorata* (L.) Beauv. Hitchcock et al., 1:599; Cutright (LCPN), 189 n. 10.

4. Probably the red fox, *Vulpes vulpes*.

5. Golden eagle, *Aquila chrysaetos* [AOU, 349].

6. The three islands and the location of the weir, marked "were for fishing," appear clearly on *Atlas* map 67, on the Lemhi a few miles southeast of present Salmon, Lemhi County, Idaho.

7. Here in Codex F, p. 147, is a drawing of the fish weir; see fig. 3.

8. If the references are based, as usual, on the direction of travel—here northwest down the Lemhi—then Clark crossed from the larboard to the starboard side of the river. Moreover, Lewis notes immediately after that Collins was sent to look for Cruzatte on the larboard side, which only makes sense if the rest of Clark's party was on the starboard side. The dotted line on *Atlas* map 67 labeled "William Clark's route" indicates the same. Clark's journal is unusually vague here, and Biddle's account does not clarify matters. Perhaps Lewis intended to write "Stard." The "forks" are the junction of the Lemhi and the Salmon. Coues (HLC), 2:527 and nn. 14, 15.

9. Clark went down the Lemhi to its junction with the Salmon ("East Fork of Lewis R" and "West Fork of Lowis's River" on *Atlas* map 67), then down the Salmon, as shown by the dotted line marked "William Clark's route" on the map. The creek where the salmon was caught may be the one labeled "Sammon run," perhaps later Carmen Creek. The camp was on the east side of the Salmon River, in Lemhi County, a few miles north of present Carmen, and below the mouth of Tower Creek. Peebles (RW), 9, and fig. 8.

10. The barb of the fish-spear. Criswell, 13. Apparently it was Biddle who drew a red vertical line through this material from "one End is" to "loosely about them." A line is also through material below, from "The men ware" to "Shapes and colours."

11. The east fork is the present Lemhi River, and the west fork and the main river below the junction are the Salmon.

12. The cliff near where Clark made his evening camp is composed of reddish-brown argillite (mudstone) of the Precambrian Belt Group. These rocks are overlain by a basal conglomerate of the Tertiary Carmen Formation. This basal conglomerate contains rocks derived from the Belt Group and from the Challis Volcanics. The white sandstones and sands are within the upper part of the Carmen Formation.

13. The Salmon River Mountains to the west, the Beaverhead Mountains to the east.

[Lewis]   *Thursday August 22ed 1805*[1]

This morning early I sent a couple of men to complete the covering of the cash which could not be done well last night in the dark, they soon accomplished their work and returned.   late last night Drewyer returned with a fawn he had killed and a considerable quantity of Indian plunder.   the anecdote with rispect to the latter is perhaps worthy of relation.   he informed me that while hunting in the Cove yesterday about

12 OCk. he came suddonly upon an Indian Camp, at which there were a young man an Old man a boy and three women, that they seemed but little supprised at seeing him and he rode up to them and dismounted turning horse out to graize.   these people had just finished their repast on some roots, he entered into conversation with them by signs, and after about 20 minutes one of the women spoke to the others of the party and they all went immediately and collected their horses brought them to camp and saddled them   at this moment he thought he would also set out and continue his hunt, and accordingly walked to catch his horse at some little distance and neglected to take up his gun which, he left at camp.   the Indians perceiving him at the distance of fifty paces imme-diately mounted their horses, the young man took the gun and the whole of them left their baggage and laid whip to their horses directing their course to the pass of the mountains.   finding himself deprived of his gun he immediately mounted his horse and pursued; after runing them about 10 miles the horses of two of the women nearly gave out and the young fellow with the gun from their frequent crys slackened his pace and being on a very fleet horse road around the women at a little dis-tance   at length Drewer overtook the women and by signs convinced them that he did not wish to hirt them   they then halted and the young fellow approached still nearer, he asked him for his gun but the only part of the answer which he could understand was pah kee which he knew to be the name by which they called their enimies.   watching his oppor-tunity when the fellow was off his guard he suddonly rode along side of him seized his gun and wrest her out of his hands.   the fellow finding Drewyer too strong for him and discovering that he must yeald the gun had pesents of mind to open the pan and cast the priming before he let the gun escape from his hands;[2] now finding himself devested of the gun he turned his horse about and laid whip leaving the women to follow him as well as they could. Drewyer now returned to the place they had left their baggage and brought it with him to my camp.   it consisted of sev-eral dressed and undressed skins; a couple of bags wove with the fingers of the bark of the silk-grass containing each about a bushel of dryed ser-vice berries some checherry cakes and about a bushel of roots of three different kinds dryed and prepared for uce which were foalded in as

many parchment hides of buffaloe. some flint and the instrument of bone for manufactureing the flint into arrow points. some of this flint was as transparent as the common black glass and much of the same colour easily broken, and flaked of[f] much like glass leaving a very sharp edge.[3] one speceis of the roots[4] were fusiform abot six inches long and about the size of a man's finger at the larger end tapering to a small point. the radicles larger than in most fusiform roots. the rind was white and thin. the body or consistence of the root was white mealy and easily reduced by pounding to a substance resembleing flour which thickens with boiling water something like flour and is agreeably flavored. this rout is frequently eaten by the Indians either green or in it's dryed state without the preparation of boiling. another speceis[5] was much mutilated but appeared to be fibrous; the parts were brittle, hard of the size of a small quill, cilindric and as white as snow throughout, except some small parts of the hard black rind which they had not seperated in the preperation. this the Indians with me informed were always boiled for use. I made the exprement, found that they became perfectly soft by boiling, but had a very bitter taste, which was naucious to my pallate, and I transfered them to the Indians who had eat them heartily. a third speceis[6] were about the size of a nutmeg, and of an irregularly rounded form, something like the smallest of the Jarusolem artichoke, which they also resemble in every other appearance. they had become very hard by being dryed these I also boiled agreeably to the instruction of the Indians and found them very agreeable. they resemble the Jerusalem Artichoke very much in their flavor and I thought them preferable, however there is some allowance to be made for the length of time I have now been without vegitable food to which I was always much attatched. these are certainly the best root I have yet seen in uce among the Indians. I asked the Indians to shew me the plant of which these roots formed a part but they informed me that neither of them grew near this place. I had set most of the men at work today to dress the deerskin belonging to those who had gone on command with Capt. Clark. at 11 A. M. Charbono the Indian Woman, Cameahwait and about 50 men with a number of women and children arrived. they encamped near us. after they had turned out their horses and arranged their camp I called the Cheifs and warriors together and addressed them a second time; gave them some further presents, particularly the second and third Cheifs who it appeared had agreeably to their promise exerted themselves in my favour. having no fresh meat and these poor devils half starved I had previously prepared a good meal for them all of boiled corn and beans which I gave them as soon as the council was over and I had distributed the presents. this was thankfully received by them. the Chief wished that his nation could live in a country where they could provide such food. I told him that it would not be many years before the whitemen would put it in the power of his nation to live in the country below the mountains where they might culti-vate corn beans and squashes.[7] he appeared much pleased with the in-formation. I gave him a few dryed squashes which we had brought from the Mandans he had them boiled and declared them to be the best thing he had ever tasted except sugar, a small lump of which it seems his sister Sah-cah-gar Wea had given him. late in the evening I made the men form a bush drag, and with it in about 2 hours they caught 528 very good fish, most of them large trout. among them I now for the first time saw ten or a douzen of a whte speceis of trout.[8] they are of a silvery colour except on the back and head, where they are of a bluish cast. the scales are much larger than the speckled trout, but in their form position of their fins teeth mouth &c they are precisely like them they are not gen-erally quite as large but equally well flavored. I distributed much the greater portion of the fish among the Indians. I purchased five good horses of them very reasonably, or at least for about the value of six dol-lars a peice in merchandize. the Indians are very orderly and do not croud about our camp nor attempt to disterb any article they see lying about. they borrow knives kettles &c from the men and always carefully return them. Capt. Clark says, "we set out early and passed a small creek at one mile,[9] also the points of four mountains which were high steep and rocky. the mountains are so steep that it is almost incredible to mention that horses had passed them. our road in many places lay over the sharp fragments of rocks which had fallen from the mountains and lay in confused heaps for miles together; yet notwithstanding our horsed trav-eled barefoot over them as fast as we could and did not detain us. passed two bold runing streams, and arrived at the entrance of a small river[10] where some Indian families resided. they had some scaffoalds of fish and burries exposed to dry. they were not acquainted with the circumstance of any whitemen being in their country and were therefore much allarmed on our approach several of the women and children fled in the woods for shelter. the guide was behind and the wood thick in which their lodges were situated we came on them before they had the least notice of us. those who remained offered us every thing they had, which was but little; they offered us collars of elks tusks which their children woar Salmon beries &c. we eat some of their fish and buries but returned them the other articles they had offered with a present of some small articles which seemed to add much to their pacification.

The guide[11] who had by this time arrived explained to them who we were and our object in visiting them; but still there were some of the women and Children inconsoleable, they continued to cry during our stay, which was about an hour. a road passes up this river which my guide informed me led over the mountains to the Missouri. from this place I continued my rout along the steep side of a mountain for about 3 miles and arrived at the river near a small Island on the lower point of which we encamped[12] in the evening we attempted to gig fish but were unsuccessfull only obtaining one small salmon. in the course of the day we had passed several women and children geathering burries who were very liberal in bestoing us a part of their collections. the river is very rapid and shoaly; many rocks lie in various derections scattered throughout it's bed. There are some few small pine scattered through the bottoms, of which I only saw one which appeared as if it would answer for a canoe and that was but small. the tops of the mountains on the Lard. side are covered with pine and some also scattered on the sides of all the mountains. I saw today a speceis of woodpecker,[13] which fed on the seeds of the pine. it's beak and tail were white, it's wings were black, and every other part of a dark brown. it was about the size of a robin—["]

[Clark]   *August 22d Thursday 1805*

We Set out early passed a Small Creek on the right at 1 mile and the points of four mountains verry Steap high & rockey, the assent of three was So Steap that it is incrediable to describe the rocks in maney places loose & Sliped from those mountains and is a ⟨Solid⟩ bed of rugid loose white and dark brown loose rock for miles.[14]   the Indian horses pass over those Clifts hills Sids & rocks as fast as a man, the three horses with me do not detain me any on account of those dificuelties, passed two bold rung. Streams on the right and a Small river [*EC: Fish Cr. also on its right*] at the mouth of Which Several families of Indians were encamped and had Several Scaffolds of fish & buries drying   we allarmed them verry much as they knew nothing of a white man being in their Countrey, and at the time we approached their lodges which was in a thick place of bushes—my guiedes were behind.—   They offered every thing they possessed (which was verry littl) to us, Some run off and hid in the bushes The first offer of theirs were Elks tuskes from around their Childrens necks, Sammon &c.   my guide ⟨Soon⟩ attempted passifyed those people and they Set before me berres, & fish to eate, I gave a fiew Small articles to those fritened people which added verry much to their pasification but not entirely as Some of the women & Childn. Cried dureing my Stay of an hour at this place, I proceeded on the Side of a verry Steep & rockey mountain for 3 miles and Encamped on the lower pt. of an Island.   we attempted to gig fish without Suckcess.   caught but one Small one.— The last Creek or Small river is on the right Side and "a road passes up it & over to the Missouri"[15]   [*NB: to Wisdom*] [*NB: From Several of these Streams roads go across to Wisdom river*]   in this day passed Several womin and Children gathering and drying buries of which they were very kind and gave us a part.   the river rapid and Sholey maney Stones Scattered through it in different directions. I Saw to day Bird of the wood pecker kind which fed on Pine burs its Bill and tale white the wings black every other part of a light brown, and about the Size of a robin. Some fiew Pine Scattered in the bottoms & Sides of the Mountains (the Top of the Motn. to the left Covered & inaxcessable) I Saw one which would make a Small Canoe.

1. This entry ends Lewis's notebook Codex F. His entries for August 23–26, 1805, are in the unbound fragment Codex Fb.

2. With a flintlock firearm, the priming powder in the "pan" on the outside of the lock caught the spark struck by the flint striking steel and in exploding set off the main charge

inside the barrel. The thief had made it impossible for Drouillard to shoot him until he had reprimed the weapon from his powder horn, giving the Indian some time to get away.

3. The stones most commonly used for making arrow points in this area were ignimbrite, chalcedony, and obsidian. Quartzite, jasper, agate, chert, and opalized wood were used to a lesser extent. The transparent flint resembling common black glass was undoubtedly obsidian, perhaps derived from sources in or near present Yellowstone National Park. The other materials were generally found locally.

4. Edible valeriana, *Valeriana edulis* Nutt. ex T. & G. The fusiform taproot of this species is just as described by Lewis and its edible uses are well known. Booth & Wright, 236; Hitchcock et al., 4:475–76. A vertical line was drawn through this passage to the bottom of the page ending with the words, "I asked the Indians to." Perhaps it was done by Biddle, but not in his usual red ink.

5. The first description of the bitterroot, *Lewisia rediviva* Pursh, named for Lewis by Pursh from specimens collected on the return trip. Hitchcock notes that the roots become bitter to the taste after early spring. Cutright (LCPN), 188 n. 8, 305; Booth & Wright, 53; Hitchcock et al., 2:235.

6. Possibly Nuttall sunflower, which has fleshy tuberous roots resembling a small Jerusalem artichoke root, *Helianthus tuberosus* L., found much farther east along the Missouri River. The similarity in root shape and taste noticed by Lewis strongly indicates this closely related, western species of sunflower. Nuttall sunflower grows in moist meadows of the Lemhi valley. Booth & Wright, 274; Hitchcock et al., 5:232.

7. The triad of foodstuffs of river Indians on the lower Missouri: corn, *Zea maise* L.; beans, *Phaseolus vulgaris* L.; and squash, *Cucurbita pepo* L. Gilmore (UPI), 15–16, 66, 84.

8. Perhaps the steelhead trout, *Salmo gairdneri,* which they refer to elsewhere as the "salmen trout." If so, this would be the first description. See below, October 26, 1805, and March 13, 1806. Burroughs, 263; Cutright (LCPN), 234. Perhaps it was Biddle who drew a vertical line through this material from "late in the evening" to "equally well flavored," but not in the usual red ink.

9. Tower Creek, Lemhi County, Idaho. Peebles (RW), 9; *Atlas* map 67.

10. North Fork Salmon River, "Fish Creek" on *Atlas* map 67; the hamlet of North Fork, Lemhi County, is now located at the junction. The two "bold runing streams" would be Fourth of July and Wagonhammer creeks. Peebles (RW), 9.

11. Here in Codex F, p. 153 (the back fly leaf), is Lewis's note "see the first page," with a pointing hand symbol. The entry is completed on the front flyleaf of the codex which Coues numbered p. 154. There the hand symbol is repeated and the words "*Continued from the last page.*"

12. Clark continued down the Salmon, as indicated by the dotted line on *Atlas* map 67; the map does not show the river's turn to the southwest immediately below the mouth of the North Fork. His campsite, a few miles southwest of North Fork, Lemhi County, does not appear on the map, and there is more than one small island indicated.

13. Clark gives the first description of a bird that now bears his name—Clark's nutcracker, *Nucifraga columbiana* [AOU, 491]. See below, May 28, 1806. Burroughs, 251–52; Holmgren, 29, 34.

14. The brown rocks near the river here are principally layered rocks belonging to the Precambrian Belt Group and basalts of the Tertiary Challis Volcanics. The white rocks are sandstones of the Carmen Formation and tuffs or rhyolites of the Challis Volcanics. Fractures or joints in the parent formations allow them to break into fragments of various sizes. These fragments then accumulate at the base of the hills in extensive talus aprons.

15. Clark apparently refers to the trail up the North Fork Salmon and over the Bitterroots, marked by a dotted line on *Atlas* map 67, which the entire party took a few days later. This trail, he had learned from the Shoshones, connected with trails leading to the Missouri. The one referred to here may have been a trail crossing the Bitterroots by Big Hole Pass, between present Gibbonsville, Lemhi County, Idaho, and Wisdom, Beaverhead County, Montana, leading to the Big Hole River. Allen (PG), 298 n. 34.

[Lewis]   *Friday August 23rd 1805.*[1]

This morning I arrose very early and despatched two hunters on horseback with orders to extend their hunt to a greater distance up the S. E. fork than they had done heretofore, in order if possible to obtain some meet for ourselves as well as the Indians who appeared to depend on us for food and our store of provision is growing too low to indulge them with much more corn or flour. I wished to have set out this morning but the cheif requested that I would wait untill another party of his nation arrived which he expected today, to this I consented from necessity, and therefore sent out the hunters as I have mentioned. I also laid up the canoes this morning in a pond near the forks; sunk them in the water and weighted them down with stone, after taking out the plugs of the gage holes in their bottoms; hoping by this means to guard against both the effects of high water, and that of the fire which is frequently kindled in these plains by the natives.   the Indians have promised to do them no intentional injury and beleive they are too lazy at any rate to give themselves the trouble to raise them from their present situation in order to cut or birn them. I reminded the chief of the low state of our stores of provision and advised him to send his young men to hunt, which he immediately recommended to them and most of them turned out. I wished to have purchased some more horses of them but they objected against disposing of any more of them untill we reach their camp beyond the mountains.   the Indians pursued a mule buck near our camp I saw this chase for about 4 miles it was really entertaining, there were about twelve of them in pursuit of it on horseback, they finally rode it down and killed it. the all came in about 1 P. M. having killed 2 mule deer and three goats. this mule buck was the largest deer of any kind I had ever seen. it was nearly as large as a doe Elk. I observed that there was but little division or distribution of the meat they had taken among themselves. some familes had a large stock and others none. this is not customary among the nations of Indians with whom I have hitherto been acquainted I asked Cameahwait the reason why the hunters did not divide the meat among themselves; he said that meat was so scarce with them that the men who killed it reserved it for themselves and their own families. my hunters arrived about 2 in the evening with two mule deer and three common deer. I distributed three of the deer among those families who appeared to have nothing to eat. at three P. M. the expected party of Indians arrived, about 50 men women and Children. I now learnt that most of them were thus far on their way down the valley towards the buffaloe country, and observed that there was a good deel of anxiety on the part of some of those who had promised to assist me over the mountains to accompany this party, I felt some uneasiness on this subject but as they still said they would return with me as they had promised I said nothing to them but resolved to set out in the morning as early as possible. I dispatched two hunters this evening into the cove to hunt and leave the meat they might kill on the rout we shall pass tomorrow.

The metal which we found in possession of these people consited of a few indifferent knives, a few brass kettles some arm bands of iron and brass, a few buttons, woarn as ornaments in their hair, a spear or two of a foot in length and some iron and brass arrow points which they informed me they obtained in exchange for horses from the Crow or Rocky Mountain Indians on the yellowstone River. the bridlebits and stirrips they obtained from the Spaniards, tho' these were but few. many of them made use of flint for knives, and with this instrument, skined the animals they killed, dressed their fish and made their arrows; in short they used it for every purpose to which the knife is applyed. this flint is of no regular form, and if they can only obtain a part of it, an inch or two in length that will cut they are satisfyed, they renew the edge by fleaking off the flint by means of the point of an Elk's or deer's horn. with the point of a deer or Elk's horn they also form their arrow points of the flint, with a quickness and neatness that is really astonishing. we found no axes nor hatchets among them; what wood they cut was done either with stone or Elk's horn. the latter they use always to rive or split their wood. their culinary eutensils exclusive of the brass kettle before mentioned consist of pots in the form of a jar made either of earth, or of a white soft stone which becomes black and very hard by birning, and is found in the hills near the three forks of the Missouri betwen Madison's and Gallitin's rivers.[2] they have also spoons made of the Buffaloe's horn and those of the Bighorn. Their bows are made of ceader or pine and have nothing remarkable about them. the back of the bow is covered with sinues and glue and is about 2½ feet long. much the shape of those used by the Siouxs Mandans Minnetares &c. their arrows are more slender generally than those used by the nations just mentioned but much the same in construction. Their Sheild is formed of buffaloe hide, perfectly arrow proof, and is a circle of 2 feet 4 I. or 2 F. 6 I. in diameter. this is frequently painted with varios figures and ornamented around the edges with feather and a fringe of dressed leather. they sometimes make bows of the Elk's horn and those also of the bighorn. those of the Elk's horn are made of a single peice and covered on the back with glue and sinues like those made of wood, and are frequently ornamented with a stran wrought porcupine quills and sinues raped around them for some distance at both extremities. the bows of the bighorn are formed of small peices laid flat and cemented with gleue, and rolled with sinews, after which, they are also covered on the back with sinews and glew, and highly ornamented as they are much prized. forming the sheild is a cerimony of great importance among them, this implement would in their minds be devested of much of its protecting power were it not inspired with those virtues by their old men and jugglers. their method of preparing it is thus, an entire skin of a bull buffaloe two years old is first provided; a feast is next prepared and all the warriors old men and jugglers invited to partake. a hole is sunk in the ground about the same in diameter with the intended sheild and about 18 inches deep. a parcel of stones are now made red hot and thrown into the hole water is next thrown in and the hot stones cause it to emit a very strong hot steem, over this they spread the green skin which must not have been suffered to dry after taken off the beast. the flesh side is laid next to the groround and as many of the workmen as can reach it take hold on it's edges and extend it in every direction. as the skin becomes heated, the hair seperates and is taken of with the fingers, and the skin continues to contract untill the whoe is drawn within the compas designed for the shield, it is then taken off and laid on a parchment hide where they pound it with their heels when barefoot. this operation of pounding continues for several days or as long as the feast lasts when it is delivered to the propryeter and declared by the jugglers and old men to be a sufficient defence against the arrows of their enimies or even bullets if feast has been a satisfactory one. many of them beleive implisitly that a ball cannot penitrate their sheilds, in consequence of certain supernaural powers with which they have been inspired by their jugglers.— The Poggamoggon is an instrument with a handle of wood covered with dressed leather about the size of a whip handle and 22 inches long; a round stone of 2 pounds weight is also covered with leather and strongly united to the leather of the handle by a throng of 2 inches long; a loop of leather united to the handle passes arond the wrist. a very heavy blow may be given with this instrument.[3] They have also a kind of armor which they form with many foalds of dressed Atelope's skin, unite with glue and sand. with this they cover their own bodies and those of their horses. these are sufficient against the effects of the arrow.— the quiver which contains their arrows and implements for making fire is formed of various skins. that of the Otter seems to be prefered. they are but narrow, of a length sufficent to protect the arrow from the weather, and are woarn on the back by means of a strap which passes over the left sholder and under the wright arm.— their impliments for making fire is nothing more than a blunt arrow and a peice of well seasoned soft spongey wood such as the willow or cottonwood. the point of this arrow they apply to this dry stick so near one edge of it that the particles of wood which are seperated from it by the friction of the arrow falls down by it's side in a little pile. the arrow is held between the palms of the hand with the fingers extended, and being pressed as much as possible against the peice is briskly rolled between the palms of the hands backwards and forwards by pressing the arrow downwards the hands of course in rolling arrow also decend; they bring them back with a quick motion and repeat the operation till the dust by the friction takes fire; the peice and arrow are then removed and some dry grass or doated wood is added. it astonished me to see in what little time these people would kindle fire in this way. in less than a minute they will produce fire.

Capt. Clark set out this morning very early and poroceeded but slowly in consequence of the difficulty of his road which lay along the steep side of a mountain over large irregular and broken masses of rocks which had tumbled from the upper part of the mountain. it was with much wrisk and pain that the horses could get on. at the distance of four miles he arrived at the river and the rocks were here so steep and juted into the river such manner that there was no other alternative but passing through the river, this he attempted with success tho' water was so deep for a short distance as to swim the horses and was very rapid; he continued his rout one mile along the edge of the river under this steep Clift to a little bot- tom,[4] below which the whole current of the river beat against the Stard. shore on which he was, and which was formed of a solid rock perfectly inaccessible to horses. here also the little track which he had been pur- suing, terminated. he therefore determined to leave the horses and the majority of the party here[5] and with his guide and three men to continue his rout down the river still further, in order more fully to satisfy himself as to it's practicability. accordingly he directed the men to hunt and fish at this place untill his return. they had not killed anything today but one goose, and the ballance of the little provision they had brought with them, as well as the five salmon they had procured yesterday were con- sumed last evening; there was of cours no inducement for his halting any time, at this place; after a few minutes he continued his rout clambering over immence rocks and along the sides of lofty precepices on the border of the river to the distance of 12 miles, at which place a large creek dis- charged itself on the Norh side 12 yds. wide and deep.[6] a short distance above the entrance of this creek there is a narrow bottom which is the first that he had found on the river from that in which he left the horses and party. a plain indian road led up this creek which the guide informed him led to a large river that ran to the North, and was frequented by another nation who occasionally visited this river for the purpose of taking fish. at this place he saw some late appearance of Indians having been encamped and the tracks of a number of horses. Capt. C. halted here about 2 hours, caught some small fish, on which, with the addition of some berries, they dined. the river from the place at which he left the party to his present station was one continued rapid, in which there were five shoals neither of which could be passed with loaded canoes nor even run with empty ones. at those several places therefore it would be necessary to unload and transport the baggage for a considerable distance over steep and almost inacassable rocks where there was no possibility of employing horses for the releif of the men; the canoes would next have to be let down by cords and even with this precaution Capt. C. conceived there would be much wriske of both canoes and men. at one of those shoals the lofty perpendicular rocks which from the bases of the mountains approach the river so nearly on each side, as to prevent the possibility of a portage, or passage for the canoes without expending much labour in removing rocks and cuting away the earth in some places. to surmount These difficulties, precautions must be observed which in their execution must necessarily consume much time and provision, neither of which we can command. the season is now far advanced to remain in these mountains as the Indians inform us we shall shortly have snow; the salmon have so far declined that they are themselves haistening from the country and not an animal of any discription is to be seen in this difficult part of the river larger than a pheasant or a squirrel and they not abundant; add to this that our stock of provision is now so low that it would not support us more than ten days. the bends of the river are short and the currant beats from side to side against the rocks with great violence. the river is about 100 yds. wide and so deep that it cannot be foarded but in a few places, and the rocks approach the river so near in most places that there is no possibility of passing between them and the water; a passage therefore with horses along the river is also impracticable. The sides of these mountains present generally one barren surface of confused and broken masses of stone. above these are white or brown and towards the base of a grey colour and so hard that when struck with a steel, yeald fire like flint.[7]   those he had just past were scarcely releived by the appearance of a tree; but those below the entrance of the creek were better covered with timber, and there were also some tall pine near the river. The sides of the mountains are very steep, and the torrents of water which roll down their sides at certain seasons appear to carry with them vast quantities of the loose stone into the river.   after dinner Capt. C. continued his rout down the river and at ½ a mile pased another creek[8] not so large as that just mentioned, or about 5 yards wide.   here his guide informed him that by ascending this creek some distance they would have a better road and would cut off a considerable bend which the river made to the south; accordingly he pursued a well beaten Indian track which led up this creek about six miles, then leaving the creek on the wright he passed over a ridge, and at the distance of a mile arrived at the river where it passes through a well timbered bottom of about eighty acres of land; they passed this bottom and asscended a steep and elivated point of a mountain,[9] from whence the guide shewed him the brake of the river through the mountains for about 20 miles further.   this view was terminated by one of the most lofty mountains, Capt. C. informed me, he had ever seen which was perfectly covered with snow.   the river directed it's course immediately to this stupendous mountain at the bace of which the gude informe him those difficulties of which himself and nation had spoken, commenced.   that after the river reached this mountain it continued it's rout to the North for many miles between high and perpendicular rocks, roling foaming and beating against innumerable rocks which crouded it's channel; that then it penetrated the mountain through a narrow gap leaving a perpendicular rock on either side as high as the top of the mountain which he beheld.   that the river here making a bend they could not see through the mountain, and as it was impossible to decend the river or clamber over that vast mountain covered with eternal snow, neither himself nor any of his nation had ever been lower in this direction, than in view of the place at which the river entered this mountain; that if Capt. C. wished him to do so, he would conduct him to that place, where he thought they could probably arrive by the next evening. Capt. C. being now perfictly satisfyed as to the impractability of this rout either by land or water, informed the old man, that he was convinced of the varacity of his assertions and would now return to the village from whence they had set out where he expected to meet myself and party. they now returned to the upper part of the last creek he had passed, and encamped.[10] it was an hour after dark before he reached this place. a small river falls into this fork of the Columbia just above the high mountain through which it passes on the south side.[11]

[Clark]   *August 23rd Friday 1805*[12]

We Set out early   proceed on with great dificuelty as the rocks were So Sharp large and unsettled and the hill sides Steep that the horses could with the greatest risque and dificulty get on, no provisions as the 5 Sammons given us yesterday by the Indians were eaten last night, one goose killed this morning; at 4 miles we came to a place the horses Could not pass without going into the river, we passed one mile to a verry bad riffle the water Confined in a narrow Channel & beeting against the left Shore, as we have no parth further and the Mounts. jut So close as to prevent the possibiley of horses proceeding down, I deturmined to delay the party here and with my guide and three men proceed on down to examine if the river continued bad or was practiable. I Set out with three men directing those left to hunt and fish until my return. I proceeded on Somtims in a Small wolf parth & at other times Climeing over the rocks for 12 miles to a large Creek on the right Side   above the mouth of this Creek for a Short distance is a narrow bottom & the first, below the place I left my partey, a road passes down this Creek which I understoode passed to the water of a River which run to Th North & was the ground of another nation, Some fresh Sign about this Creek of horse and Camps. I delayd 2 hours to fish, Cought Some Small fish on which we dined.

The River from the place I left my party to this Creek is almost one continued rapid, five verry Considerable rapids the passage of either with Canoes is entirely impossable, as the water is Confined betwen hugh Rocks & the Current beeting from one against another for Some distance below &c. &c.   at one of those rapids the mountains Close So Clost as to prevent a possibility of a portage with great labour in Cutting down the Side of the hill removeing large rocks &c. &c. all the others may be passed by takeing every thing over Slipery rocks, and the Smaller ones Passed by letting down the Canoes empty with Cords, as running them would certainly be productive of the loss of Some Canoes, those dificuelties and necessary precautions would delay us an emince time in which provisions would be necessary. (we have but little and nothing to be precured in this quarter except Choke Cheres & red haws not an animal of any kind to be seen and only the track of a Bear) below this Creek the lofty Pine is thick in the bottom hill Sides on the mountains & up the runs. The river has much the resemblance of that above bends Shorter and no passing, after a few miles between the river & the mountains & the Current So Strong that is dangerous crossing the river, and to proceed down it would rendr it necessarey to Cross almost at every bend This river is about 100 yards wide and can be forded but in a few places. below my guide and maney other Indians tell me that the Mountains Close and is a perpendicular Clift on each Side, and Continues for a great distance and that the water runs with great violence from one rock to the other on each Side foaming & roreing thro rocks in every direction, So as to render the passage of any thing impossible. [X: Game] those rapids which I had Seen he said was Small & trifleing in comparrison to the rocks & rapids below, at no great distance & The Hills or mountains were not like those I had Seen but like the Side of a tree Streight up— Those Mountains which I had passed were Steep Contain a white, a brown, & low down a Grey hard stone which would make fire, those Stone were of different Sises all Sharp and are continuly Slipping down, and in maney places one bed of those Stones inclined from the river bottom to the top of the mountains, The Torrents of water which come down aftr a rain carries with it emence numbers of those Stone into the river [13] about ½ a mile below the last mentioned Creek another Creek falls in, my guide informed me that our rout was up this Creek by which rout we would Save a considerable bend of the river to the South. we proceeded on a well beeten Indian parth up this Creak [NB?: Berry Creek] about 6 miles and passed over a ridge 1 mile to the river in a Small vally through which we passed and assended a Spur of the Mountain from which place my guide Shew me the river for about 20 [WC?: many] miles lower & pointed out

156

the dificulty we returned to the last Creek & camped about one hour after dark.

There my guide Shewed me a road from the N Which Came into the one I was in which he Said went to a large river which run to the north on which was a Nation he called Tushapass,[14] he made a map of it

1. Here begins Lewis's fragmentary Codex Fb, containing entries August 23–26, 1805, and consisting of twenty-six pages torn from one of the red notebooks. See Appendix C, vol. 2.

2. The soft, white stone is either a marly, freshwater, Tertiary limestone that is abundantly exposed in the cliffs of the Madison Plateau just east of the Madison River, southeast of the Three Forks of the Missouri, or else it is a volcanic tuff, also of Tertiary age.

3. A fairly widespread type of weapon; as Lewis notes above, on August 19, 1805, the word is Chippewa (*bgamaagan*, "cudgel, club"). Hodge, 1:313, 2:271–72; Rhodes, 40.

4. On *Atlas* map 67 the spot is marked "left the horses & 8 men 2 days." The location is perhaps near the the mouth of either Dump Creek or Moose (otherwise Little Moose) Creek, in Lemhi County, Idaho. Peebles (RW), 9.

5. One of the eight men left was Sergeant Gass. Gass notes this day that one of the sergeants, presumably with this group, was ill; since Ordway was with Lewis, the sick man must have been Pryor, perhaps suffering another of his repeated dislocations of the shoulder, and thus left behind.

6. Berry Creek on *Atlas* maps 67, 68; probably present Indian Creek in Lemhi County. Ibid.

7. The rock forming the walls of the canyon here is granite of the Cretaceous-age Idaho batholith. The colors result from slight variations in mineral composition, weathering or vegetation. The quartz and feldspar in the granite are harder than steel.

8. Squaw Creek, unnamed on *Atlas* maps 67, 68. Ibid., 10.

9. Clark was evidently three miles above present Shoup, Lemhi County. In looking down the Salmon he could see some of the most rugged and difficult country in the Rockies; much of this region of central Idaho is still primitive and roadless today. Ibid.; *Atlas* map 67.

10. Clark camped on Squaw Creek, in Lemhi County, probably near the mouth of Papoose Creek, which flows into the former. Peebles (RW), 10; *Atlas* map 67.

11. Evidently present Panther Creek, a few miles below present Shoup, Lemhi County. *Atlas* map 67.

12. Beside the date Clark has written "See Supplement anexed," probably a reference to Codex Fb; see n. 1, above.

13. The remainder of the entry in Codex G was apparently added later; it is in a smaller hand and runs over into the beginning of the next day's entry. The first part is by Clark. The next paragraph in red ink, appears also to be Clark's writing.

14. The Flatheads; see below, September 4, 1805.

[Lewis] *Saturday August 24th 1805.*

As the Indians who were on their way down the Missouri had a number of spare hoses with them I thought it probable that I could obtain some of them and therefore desired the Cheif to speak to them and inform me whether they would trade. they gave no positive answer but requested to see the goods which I was willing to give in exchange. I now produced some battle axes which I had made at Fort Mandan with which they were much pleased. knives also seemed in great demand among them. I soon purchased three horses and a mule. for each horse I gave an ax a knife handkercheif and a little paint; & for the mule the addition of a knife a shirt handkercheif and a pair of legings; at this price which was quite double that given for the horses, the fellow who sold him made a merit of having bestoed me one of his mules. I consider this mule a great acquisition. These Indians soon told me that they had no more horses for sale and I directed the party to prepare to set out. I had now nine horses and a mule, and two which I had hired made twelve these I had loaded and the Indian women took the ballance of the baggage. I had given the Interpreter some articles with which to purchase a horse for the woman which he had obtained. at twelve Oclock we set out and passed the river below the forks, directing our rout towards the cove along the track formerly mentioned.[1] most of the horses were heavily laden, and it appears to me that it will require at least 25 horses to convey our baggage along such roads as I expect we shall be obliged to pass in the mountains. I had now the inexpressible satisfaction to find myself once more under way with all my baggage and party. an Indian had the politeness to offer me one of his horses to ride which I accepted with cheerfullness as it enabled me to attend better to the march of the party. I had reached the lower part of the cove when an Indian rode up and informed me that one of my men was very sick and unable to come on. I directed the party to halt at a small run which falls into the creek on Lard. at the lower part of the Cove and rode back about 2 Miles where I found Wiser very ill with a fit of the cholic. I sent Sergt. Ordway who had remained with him for some water and gave him a doze of the essence of Peppermint and laudinum[2] which in the course of half an hour so far recovered him that he was enabled to ride my horse and I proceeded on foot and rejoined the party. the sun was yet an hour high but the Indians who had for some time impatiently waited my return at length unloaded and turned out their horses and my party had followed there example. as it was so late and the Indians had prepared their camp for the night I thought it best to acquiess and determined also to remain.[3] we had traveled only about six miles. after we encamped we had a slight shower of rain. Goodrich who is our principal fisherman caught several fine trout. Drewyer came to us late in the evening and had not killed anything. I gave the Indians who were absolutely engaged in transporting the baggage, a little corn as they had nothing to eat. I told Cameahwait that my stock of provision was too small to indulge all his people with provision and recommended it to him to advise such as were not assisting us with our baggage to go on to their camp to morrow and wait our arrival; which he did accordingly. *Cameahwait* literally translated is *one who never walks.* he told me that his nation had also given him another name by which he was signalized as a warrior which was Too-et'-te-con'-e or *black gun.* these people have many names in the course of their lives, particularly if they become distinguished characters. for it seems that every important event by which they happen to distinguish themselves intitles them to claim another name which is generally scelected by themselves and confirmed by the nation. those distinguishing acts are the killing and scalping an enemy, the killing a white bear, leading a party to war who happen to be successfull either in destroying their enemies or robing them of their horses, or individually stealing the horses of an enemy. these are considered acts of equal heroism among them, and that of killing an enemy without scalping him is considered of no importance; in fact the whole honour seems to be founded in the act of scalping, for if a man happens to slay a dozen of his enemies in action and others get the scalps or first lay their hand on the dead person the honor is lost to him who killed them and devolves on those who scalp or first touch them.[4] Among the Shoshones, as well as all the Indians of America, bravery is esteemed the primary virtue; nor can any one become eminent among them who has not at some period of his life given proofs of his possessing this virtue. with them there can be no preferment without some warelike achievement, and so completely interwoven is this principle with the earliest Elements of thought that it will in my opinion prove a serious obstruction to the restoration of a general peace among the nations of the Missouri. while at Fort Mandan I was one day addressing some cheifs of the Minetares wo visited us and pointing out to them the advantages of a state of peace with their neighbours over that of war in which they were engaged. the Chiefs who had already geathered their havest of larals, and having forceably felt in many instances some of those inconveniences attending a state of war which I pointed out, readily agreed with me in opinon. a young fellow under the full impression of the Idea I have just suggested asked me if they were in a state of peace with all their neighbours what the nation would do for Cheifs?, and added that the cheifs were now oald and must shortly die and that the nation could not exist without cheifs. taking as granted that there could be no other mode devised for making Cheifs but that which custom had established through the medium of warlike acievements.

The few guns which the Shoshones have are reserved for war almost exclusively and the bow and arrows are used in hunting. I have seen a few skins among these people which have almost every appearance of the common sheep. they inform me that they finde this animal[5] on the high mountains to the West and S. W. of them. it is about the size of the common sheep, the wool is reather shorter and more intermixed with long hairs particularly on the upper part of the neck. these skins have been so much woarn that I could not form a just Idea of the animal or it's colour. the Indians however inform me that it is white and that it's horns are lunated comprest twisted and bent backward as those of the common sheep. the texture of the skin appears to be that of the sheep. I am now perfectly convinced that the sheep as well as the Bighorn exist in these mountains. [*WC?: Capt. C Saw one at a distance to day*—]

The usual caparison of the Shoshone horse is a halter and saddle. the 1st consists either of a round plated or twisted cord of six or seven strands of buffaloe's hair, or a throng of raw hide made pliant by pounding and rubing. these cords of bufaloe's hair are about the size of a man's finger and remarkably strong. this is the kind of halter which is prefered by them. the halter of whatever it may be composed is always of great length and is never taken from the neck of the horse which they commonly use at any time. it is first attatched at one end about the neck of the horse with a knot that will not slip, it is then brought down to his under jaw and being passed through the mouth imbaces the under jaw and tonge in a simple noose formed by crossing the rope inderneath the jaw of the horse. this when mounted he draws up on the near side of the horse's neck and holds in the left hand, suffering it to trail at a great distance behind him sometimes the halter is attatched so far from the end that while the shorter end serves him to govern his horse, the other trails on the grond as before mentioned. they put their horses to their full speed with those cords trailing on the ground. when they turn out the horse to graze the noose is mearly loosed from his mouth. the saddle is made of wood and covered with raw hide which holds the parts very firmly together. it is made like the pack saddles in uce among the French and Spaniards. it consists of two flat thin boards which fit the sides of the horses back, and are held frirm by two peices which are united to them behind and before on the outer side and which rise to a considerable hight terminating sometimes in flat horizontal points extending outwards, and alwas in an accute angle or short bend underneath the upper part of these peices. a peice of buffaloe's skin with the hair on, is usually put underneath the saddle; and very seldom any covering on the saddle [*NB: but when they ride they throw on a piece of Skin*]. stirrups when used are made of wood and covered with leather. these are generally used by the elderly men and women; the young men scarcely ever use anything more than a small pad of dressed leather stuffed with hair, which is confined with a leather thong passing arond the body of the horse in the manner of a girth. they frequently paint their favorite horses, and cut their ears in various shapes. they also decorate their mains and tails, which they never draw or trim, with the feathers of birds, and sometimes suspend at the breast of the horse the finest ornaments they possess. the Spanish bridle is prefered by them when they can obtain them, but they never dispence with the cord about the neck of the horse, which serves them to take him with more ease when he is runing at large. They are excellent horsemen and extreemly expert in casting the cord about the neck of a horse. [*NB: Make a noose & catch him running &c*] the horses that have been habituated to be taken with the cord in this way, however wild they may appear at first, surrender the moment they feel the cord about their necks.— There are no horses in this quarter which can with propriety be termed wild. there are some few which have been left by the indians at large for so great a length of time that they have become shye, but they all shew marks of having been in possession of man. such is that one which Capt. Clark saw just below the three forks of the Missouri, and one other which I saw on the Missouri below the entrance of the Mussle shell river.— Capt. Clark set out very early this morning on his return, he traveled down the creek to it's entrance by the same Indian track he had ascended it; at the river he marked his name on a pine tree, then ascended to the bottom above the second creek, and brekfasted on burries, which occupyed them about one hour. he now retraced his former track and joined the party where he had left them at 4 P. M. on his way Capt. C. fell from a rock and injured one of his legs very much. the party during his absence had killed a few pheasants and caught a few small fish on which together with haws and Serviceburies they had subsisted. they had also killed one cock of the Mountains Capt. Clark now wrote me a discription of the river and country, and stated our prospects by this rout as they have been heretofore mentioned [*WC?: related the information of his guide & recomeds to me to purchase horses &c*] and dispatched Colter on horseback with orders to loose no time reaching me. he set out late with the party continued his rout about two miles and encamped.[6] Capt Clark had seen some trees which would make small canoes but all of them some distance below the Indian Caps which he passed at the entrance of fish Creek. [*WC?: he had learned from his guid that he had been on a river to the N. where he Saw people from the other Side the mountain and there was a road, the route he shewed in the Sand which gave me hope of finding a route across the m. in that direction*]

[Clark]   *August 24th Satturday 1805*

Set out verry early this morning on my return passed down the [*EC: Berry*] Creek at the mouth marked my name on a pine Tree, proceed on to the bottom above the Creek & Brackfast on buries & delayed 1 hour, then proceed on up the river by the Same rout we decended to the place I left my party where we arrived at 4 oClock, (I Sliped & bruised my leg verry much on a rock)   the party had killed Several phesents and Cought a fiew Small fish on which they had Subsisted in my absence. also a heath hen, near the Size of a Small turkey.

I wrote a letter to Capt Lewis informing him of the prospects before us and information recved of my guide which I thought favourable &c. & Stating two plans ⟨for⟩ one of which for us to pursue &c. and despatched one man & horse and directed the party to get ready to march back, every man appeared disheartened from the prospects of the river, and nothing to eate, I Set out late and Camped 2 miles above, nothing to eate but Choke Cherries & red haws[7] which act in different ways So as to make us Sick, dew verry heavy, my beding wet in passing around a rock the horses were obliged to go deep into the water.

The plan I stated to Capt Lewis if he agrees with me we shall adopt is to procure as many horses (one for each man) if possible and to hire my present guide who I sent on to him to interegate thro' the Intprtr. and proceed on by land to Some navagable part of the *Columbia* River, or to the *Ocean,* depending on what provisions we can procure by the gun aded to the Small Stock we have on hand depending on our horses as the last resort.

a second plan to divide the party one part to attempt this deficuet river with what provisions we had, and the remaindr to pass by Land on hose back Depending on our gun &c for Provisions &c. and come together occasionally on the river.

⟨a third to [send?] one party to attempt to pass the mountain by horses, & the other to return to the Missouri Collect provisions & go up Medison rivr⟩ the 1s of which I would be most pleased with &c.[8]

I saw Several trees which would make Small Canoes and by putting 2 together would make a Siseable one, all below the last Indian Camp Several miles

1. Lewis's party crossed the Beaverhead and went up Horse Prairie Creek into Shoshone Cove. His route appears as a dotted line on *Atlas* maps 66–67 and his campsites are marked.

2. The essential oil of peppermint was used as a digestive stimulant and as a carminative, that is, to expel gas from the alimentary canal. Laudanum is a tincture of opium.

3. The campsite, marked by a faint symbol on *Atlas* map 67, is a few miles east of Grant, Beaverhead County, Montana.

4. Among the plains tribes, to be first to touch an enemy was considered the bravest of war deeds. Whites called this practice "counting coup," from the French word for "blow" or "strike." The Shoshones, being strongly influenced by plains culture, had adopted the custom. Hodge, 1:354.

5. The first notice in the journals of the mountain goat, *Oreamnos americanus*, then unknown to science. Lewis and Clark were never to see one alive and at close range. Cutright (LCPN), 192. It was probably Biddle who drew a red vertical line through this passage.

6. Not marked on *Atlas* map 67, the site would be approximately two miles up the Salmon (northeast) from the place Clark left the eight men on his route downstream, in Lemhi County, Idaho, a few miles southwest of present North Fork and the mouth of the North Fork Salmon River. On *Atlas* map 67, at the mouth of present Indian (Berry) Creek, Clark has written, "Pin[e] marked W. C.," indicating where he marked his name or initials.

7. Columbia hawthorn, *Crataegus columbiana* How., is the only species of native, red-fruited hawthorn west of the Continental Divide. Hitchcock et al., 3:101; Booth & Wright, 111.

8. Having returned from the unsatisfactory reconnaissance of the Salmon River, Clark here thought out on paper the possible methods of crossing the mountains. The first and favored proposal, for hiring Old Toby as a guide and crossing the Lolo Trail on horseback, was the one the captains adopted. The second involved sending part of the party down the Salmon by canoe while the remainder traveled by horseback and attempted to stay in touch with the river party; Clark had already gained enough knowledge of the difficulties of the country to rule this course out. The third appears to be a considerably modified version of the first, prompted by the concern over the scanty sources of food in the mountains. One party would have gone down the Bitterroot River toward the Lolo Trail while the other would have returned down the Missouri to the buffalo range near the Great Falls to "collect provisions"—probably by jerking meat—and then gone up the Sun (Medicine) River to seek a way to rejoin the others. They had not known of the Sun River route, which Lewis would follow on the return trip in 1806, until they discussed the geography of the region with the Shoshones. Having set this last plan down on paper, Clark obviously found it unacceptable, probably because of the cost in time and the wide separation of the two parties, and crossed it out. The suggestions do indicate Clark's soundness of judgment and understanding of the problems the Corps of Discovery faced.

[Lewis]   *Sunday August 25th 1805.*

This morning loaded our horses and set out a little after sunrise; a few only of the Indians unengaged in assisting us went on as I had yesterday proposed to the Cheif.   the others flanked us on each side and started some Antelope which they pursued for several hours but killed none of them. we proceeded within 2 Ms. of the narrow pass or seven miles from our camp of last evening and halted for dinner. Our hunters joined us at noon with three deer the greater part of which I gave the indians. sometime after we had halted, Charbono mentioned to me with apparent unconcern that he expected to meet all the Indians from the camp on the Columbia tomorrow on their way to the Missouri. allarmed at this information I asked why he expected to meet them. he then informed me that the 1st Cheif had dispatched some of his young men this morning to this camp requesting the Indians to meet them tomorrow and that himself and those with him would go on with them down the Missouri, and consequently leave me and my baggage on the mountain or thereabouts. I was out of patience with the folly of Charbono who had not sufficient sagacity to see the consequencies which would inevitably flow from such a movement of the indians, and altho' he had been in possession of this information since early in the morning when it had been communicated to him by his Indian woman yet he never mentioned it untill the after noon. I could not forbear speaking to him with some degree of asperity on this occasion. I saw that there was no time to be lost in having those orders countermanded, or that we should not in all probability obtain any more horses or even get my baggage to the waters of the Columbia. I therefore Called the three Cheifs together and having smoked a pipe with them, I asked them if they were men of their words, and whether I could depent on the promises they had made me; they readily answered in the affermative; I then asked them if they had not promised to assist me with my baggage to their camp on the other side of the mountains, or to the place at which Capt. Clark might build the canoes, should I wish it. they acknowledged that they had. I then asked them why they had requested their people on the other side of the mountain to meet them tomorrow on the mountain where there would be no possibility of our remaining together for the purpose of trading for their horses as they had also promised. that if they had not promised to have given me their assistance in transporting my baggage to the waters on the other side of the mountain that I should not have attempted to pass the mountains but would have returned down the river and that in that case they would never have seen anymore white men in their country. that if they wished the white men to be their friends and to assist them against their enemies by furnishing them with arms and keeping their enemies from attacking them that they must never promis us anything which they did not mean to perform. that when I had first seen them they had doubted what I told them about the arrival of the party of whitemen in canoes, that they had been convinced that what I told them on that occasion was true, why then would they doubt what I said on any other point. I told them that they had witnessed my liberality in dividing the meat which my hunters killed with them; and that I should continue to give such of them as assisted me a part of whatever we had ourselves to eat. and finally concluded by telling them if they intended to keep the promises they had made me to dispatch one of their young men immediately with orders to their people to remain where they were untill our arrival. the two inferior cheifs said that they wished to assist me and be as good as their word, and that they had not sent for their people, that it was the first Chief who had done so, and they did not approve of the measure. Cameahwait remained silent for some time, at length he told me that he knew he had done wrong but that he had been induced to that measure from seeing all his people hungary, but as he had promised to give me his assistance he would not in future be worse than his word. I then desired him to send immediately and countermand his orders; acordingly a young man was sent for this purpose and I gave him a handkerchief to engage him in my interest. this matter being arranged to my satisfaction I called all the women and men together who had been assisting me in the transportation of the baggage and gave them a billet for each horse which they had imployed in that service and informed them when we arrived at the plaice where we should finally halt on the river I would take the billet back and give them merchandize for it. every one appeared now satisfyed and when I ordered the horses loaded for our departure the Indians were more than usually allert. we continued our march untill late in the evening and encamped at the upper part of the cove where the creek enters the mountains;[1] here our hunters joined us with another deer which they had killed, this I gave to the women and Children, and for my own part remained supperless. I observed considerable quantities of wild onions[2] in the bottom lands of this cove. I also saw several large hares[3] and many of the cock of the plains.

Capt. Clark set out early this morning and continued his rout to the indian camp at the entrance of fish Creek; here he halted about an hour; the indians gave himself and party some boiled salmon and burries [*WC?: tho' not half Sufficient &c*].   these people appeared extreemly hospitable tho' poor and dirty in the extreem.   he still pursued the track up the river by which he had decended and in the evening arrived at the bluff on the river where he had encamped on the 21st Inst.   it was late in the evening before he reached this place.[4]   they formed their camp, and Capt. C. sent them in different directions to hunt and fish.   some little time after they halted a party of Indians passed by on their way down the river, consisting of a man a woman and several boys; from these people the guide obtained 2 salmon which together with some small fish they caught and a beaver which Shannon killed furnished them with a plentifull supper.   the pine grows pretty abundantly high up on the sides of the mountains on the opposite side of the river.   one of the hunters saw a large herd of Elk on the opposite side of the river in the edge of the timbered land.—   Winsor was taken very sick today and detained Capt C. very much on his march.   three hunters whom he had sent on before him this morning joined him in the evening having killed nothing; they saw only one deer.

The course and the distances, of Capt. Clark's rout down this branch of the Columbia below this bluff, commencing opposite to an Island, are as follow.

N. 30° W.	2	To the top of a mountain the river 1 m. on the left.
N. 45° W.	10	With the general course of the river; passing over the spurs of four mountains, almost inaccessible, and two small runs from the wright, to some Indian lodges at the entrance of fish creek which discharges itself on the N. Side. a large Indian road passes up this creek. on this course Capt. C. also passed several Islands, and some small bottoms betwen the river and the mountains.—
West	3	along the river to the ascent of a mountain, passing one spur

		of the same. also 2 Islands and a bottom in which there was an abundance of burries.
S. 45° W.	5	to a very bad rapid, opposite which, a small run discharges itself on N. side passing perpendicular clifts where the[y] were compelled to pass through the water; passed over loose fragments of rocks on the side of a steep mountain also passed one Island and a number of small rapids.
N. 45° W.	3	high clifts on either side of the river, no road
West	2	no road. passed several bad rapids which it would be scarcely possible either to ascend or decend with empty canoes.
N. 45° W.	6	to a large Creek on the N. side; passing several bad rappids and a number of riffles. the mountains high steep and very rocky. no bottom except a little above the entrance of this Creek.
South	1	to the entrance of a small run on N. side opposite to a small island and a bad rapid.
N. 45° W.	6	up the run along an indian road through a piney country; steep and lofty hills on each side.
S. 45° W. Miles	1 39	to the river at a small bottom, passing a gap in the mountain from the top of which can be seen the break of the river through the mountains for 20 miles to a very high mountain on the South, at which place the guide informed Capt. C. that the impassable part of the river commenced, and was innitely worse than any part he had yet seen.—

This morning while passing through the Shoshone cove Frazier fired his musquet at some ducks in a little pond at the distance of about 60 yards from me; the ball rebounded from the water and pased within a very few feet of me. near the upper part of this cove the Shoshonees suffered a very severe defeat by the Minnetares about six years since. this part of the cove on the N. E. side of the Creek has lately been birned by the Indians as a signal on some occasion.

[Clark]   *August 25th Sunday 1805*

Set out verry early and halted one hour at the Indian Camp, they were kind gave us all a little boiled Sammon & dried buries to eate, abt. half as much as I could eate, those people are kind with what they have but excessive pore & Durtey.— we proceeded on over the mountains we had before passed to the Bluff we Encamped at on the 21s instant where we arrived late and turned out to hunt & fish, Cought Several Small fish, a party of Squars & one man with Several boys going down to guathe berries below, my guide got two Sammon from this party [(]which made about half a Supper for the party), after Dark Shannon came in with a beaver which the Party suped on Sumptiously— one man verry Sick to day which detained us verry much   I had three hunters out all day, they saw one Deer, killed nothing.   one of the Party Saw 9 Elk on a Mountain to our right assending, amongst the Pine timber which is thick on that side

Course & Distance Down Columbia [*EC: Lemhi and Salmon*] river by
Land, as I Decended &c.[5]

N. W.	18	miles from the Indian Camp to the forks [*EC: of Salmon R*] crossed the [*EC: Lemhi*] river twice, passed Several old camps
[*EC: Aug 20*		on the East Side and a Camp of Several lodges at a were [weir]
Aug 21]		on the west Side, passed a roade on the left leading up the main West fork [*EC: i.e. Salmon above the Lemhi*] below the last Camp, Several Small branches falls in on each Side [*EC: of the Lemhi*], a high mountain on each Side, [*EC: of Salmon and Lemhi together*] ⟨passed⟩
N. 15° W.	14	miles to a Island passed high red Clift on the right Side passed a large [*EC: Tower*] Creek [*EC: on the right*] at 9 miles up which
[*EC: Aug 21*		a roade passes large bottom below. Several Spring runs falling
Aug 22]		from the mountains on the left passed a Creek on the right. [*EC: Salmon ⟨Lemhi⟩ (right)*]
N. 30° W.	2	to the top of a mountain the river one mile to the left
N W	10	miles with the general Course of the river, passed over the Spurs of four mountains almost inexcessable and two Small
[*EC: Aug 22*]		runs on the right to Some Indian Camps at the mouth of a Small river [*EC: Fish cr.*] on the right up which a road passes passed Several Islands, and Small bottoms between the mountains.
West	3	miles on the right Side to the assent of a mountain, passed over one Spur of the Same Mountain passed 2 Islands, & a bottom in which berris were plenty.
S. W.	5	miles to a verry bad rapid & Camped, a Small run on the

[EC: Aug 22]		left. passed perpendicular Clift where we were obliged to go into the water passed Several places on Stones & Sides of Mountains, one Island & Several rapids, all the way rapids at intervales
N. W.	3	miles high Clifts on each side no road [EC: *left men here*]
West [EC: Aug 23]	2	miles do do passed bad rapids Scercely possible to pass down or up
N. W.	6	miles to a large Creek on the Right Side, passed verry bad rapids & a number of riffles, Mountains high and Steep verry Stoney no bottoms except the Creek & a little above
South	1	mile to the Mouth of a Small run on the right a Small Island and rapid
N. W.	6	miles up the Run [EC: *Berry Creek Aug. 23*] thro a piney countrey large & lofty hills high
S. W. miles	1 70	m. to the river at a Small bottom passed over a gap in the Mounts. from the top of which I could See the hollers of the river for 20 miles to a verry high Mountain on the left, at which place my guide made Signs that the bad part reclonnois
[EC: *End of reconnoissance*]		of the river Comsd. and much worst than any I Saw &c. &c. returned. 6 bad rapids. many others

1. West of the fork of Horse Prairie Creek and Trail Creek, in Beaverhead County, Montana, as marked on *Atlas* map 67.

2. An unknown *Allium* sp.

3. The white-tailed jackrabbit, *Lepus townsendii*. Burroughs, 120–23.

4. See above, August 21, 1805.

5. Clark's courses for his reconnaissance of August 20–23, 1805, are heavily marked by Coues in pencil but incorrect in giving some modern locations. The correct total is seventy-one miles.

[Lewis]   *Monday August 26th 1805.*

This morning was excessively cold; there was ice on the vessels of water which stood exposed to the air nearly a quarter of an inch thick. we collected our horses and set out at sunrise. we soon arrived at the extreem source of the Missouri; here I halted a few minutes, the men drank of the water and consoled themselves with the idea of having at length arrived at this long wished for point. from hence we proceeded to a fine spring on the side of the mountain where I had lain the evening before I first arrived at the Shoshone Camp. here I halted to dine and graize our horses, there being fine green grass on that part of the hillside which was moistened by the water of the spring while the grass on the other parts was perfectly dry and parched with the sun. I directed a pint of corn to be given each Indian who was engaged in transporting our baggage and about the same quantity to each of the men which they parched pounded and made into supe. one of the women who had been assisting in the transportation of the baggage halted at a little run about a mile behind us, and sent on the two pack horses which she had been conducting by one of her female friends. I enquired of Cameahwait the cause of her detention, and was informed by him in an unconcerned manner that she had halted to bring fourth a child and would soon overtake us; in about an hour the woman arrived with her newborn babe and passed us on her way to the camp apparently as well as she ever was. It appears to me that the facility and ease with which the women of the aborigines of North America bring fourth their children is reather a gift of nature than depending as some have supposed on the habitude of carrying heavy burthens on their backs while in a state of pregnancy. if a pure and dry air, an elivated and cold country is unfavourable to childbirth, we might expect every difficult incident to that operation of nature in this part of the continent; again as the snake Indians possess an abundance of horses, their women are seldom compelled like those in other parts of the continent to carry burthens on their backs, yet they have their children with equal convenience, and it is a rare occurrence for any of them to experience difficulty in childbirth. I have been several times informed by those who were conversant with the fact, that the indian women who are pregnant by whitemen experience more difficulty in childbirth than when pregnant by an Indian. if this be true it would go far in suport of the opinion I have advanced.—

the tops of the high and irregular mountains which present themselves to our view on the opposite side of this branch of the Columbia are yet perfectly covered with snow; the air which proceeds from those mountains has an agreeable coolness and renders these parched and South hillsides much more supportable at this time of the day it being now about

noon. I observe the indian women collecting the root of a speceis of fen-
nel[1] which grows in the moist grounds and feeding their poor starved
children; it is really distressing to witness the situation of those poor
wretches.   the radix of this plant is of the knob kind, of a long ovate form
terminating in a single radicle, the whole bing about 3 or four inches in
length and the thickest part about the size of a man's little finger.   it is
white firm and crisp in it's present state, when dryed and pounded it
makes a fine white meal; the flavor of this root is not unlike that of annis-
seed but not so pungent; the stem rises to the hight of 3 or four feet is
jointed smooth and cilindric; from 1 to 4 of those knobed roots are attatched to the base of this stem.   the leaf is sheathing sessile, & pultipar-
tite [multipartite], the divisions long and narrow; the whole is of a deep
green.   it is now in blume; the flowers are numerous, small, petals white,
and are of the umbellaferous kind.   several small peduncles put forth
from the main stock one at each joint above the sheathing leaf.   it has no
root leaves.   the root of the present year declines when the seeds have
been matured and the succeeding spring other roots of a similar kind put
fourth from the little knot which unites the roots and stem and grow and
decline with the stem as before mentioned. The sunflower[2] is very abundant near the watercourses the seeds of this plant are now rip and the
natives collect them in considerable quantities and reduce them to meal
by pounding and rubing them between smooth stones.   this meal is a favorite food their manner of using it has been beforementiond.   after
dinner we continued our rout towards the village.   on our near approach we were met by a number of young men on horseback. Cameahwait requested that we would discharge our guns when we arrived in
sight of the Village, accordingly when I arrived on an eminence above the
village in the plain I drew up the party at open order in a single rank and
gave them a runing fire discharging two rounds.   they appeared much
gratifyed with this exhibition.   we then proceeded to the village or encampment of brush lodges 32 in number.   we were conducted to a large
lodge which had been prepared for me in the center of their encampment which was situated in a beautifull level smooth and extensive bottom near the river about 3 miles above the place I had first found them
encamped.[3]   here we arrived at 6 in the evening arranged our baggage

near my tent and placed those of the men on either side of the baggage facing outwards. I found Colter here who had just arrived with a letter from Capt. Clark in which Capt. C. had given me an account of his peri-grination and the description of the river and country as before detailed [*WC: advised the purchase of horses, and the pursute of a rout he had learned from his guid who had promised to pilot ous to a road to the North &c*] from this view of the subject I found it a folly to think of attemping to decend this river in canoes and therefore ⟨determined⟩ to commence the purchase of horses in the morning from the indians in order to carry into execution the design ⟨we had formed of⟩ [*WC: Capt C had recomended in*] passing the rocky Mountains. I now informed Cameahwait of my intended expedi-tion overland to the great river which lay in the plains beyond the moun-tains and told him that I wished to purchase 20 horses of himself and his people to convey our baggage. he observed that the Minnetares had stolen a great number of their horses this spring but hoped his people would spear me the number I wished. I also asked a [*X: nother*] guide, he observed that he had no doubt but the old man who was with Capt. C. would accompany us if we wished him and that he was better informed of the country than any of them. matters being thus far arranged I di-rected the fiddle to be played and the party danced very merily much to the amusement and gratification of the natives, though I must confess that the state of my own mind at this moment did not well accord with the prevailing mirth as I somewhat feared that the caprice of the indians might suddenly induce them to withhold their horses from us without which my hopes of prosicuting my voyage to advantage was lost; however I determined to keep the indians in a good humour if possible, and to loose no time in obtaining the necessary number of horses. I directed the hunters to turn out early in the morning and indeavor to obtain some meat. I had nothing but a little parched corn to eat this evening.

This morning Capt. C. and party[4]

[Clark]   *August 26th Monday 1805*

a fine morning   Despatched three men a head to hunt, our horses missing   Sent out my guide and four men to hunt them, which detained me untill 9 oClock a. m. at which time I Set out and proceeded on by the way of the forks to the Indian Camps at the first were[5]   not one mouth-full to eate untill night as our hunters could kill nothing and I could See & catch no fish except a few Small ones. The Indians gave us 2 Sammon boiled which I gave to the men, one of my men Shot a Sammon in the river about Sunset those fish gave us a Supper.   all the Camp flocked about me untill I went to Sleep— and I beleve if they had a Sufficency to eate themselves and any to Spare they would be liberal of it

I derected the men to mend their Mockessons to night and turn out in the morning early to hunt Deer fish birds &c. &c. Saw great numbers of the large Black grass hopper.[6] Some hars which were verry wild, but few Birds.   a number of ground Lizards; Some fiew Pigions[7]

1. From Lewis's careful description, this is certainly Gairdner's yampah, *Perideridia gairdneri* (H. & A.) Mathias, then unknown to science. Cutright (LCPN), 188 n. 7; Hitchcock et al., 3:576. Perhaps it was Biddle who drew a red vertical line through this passage from "I observe" to "before mentioned." A similar line may have been started slightly above, perhaps in error.

2. Again Nuttall sunflower in its usual habitat of moist meadows.

3. See above, August 20, 1805.

4. Here ends Lewis's Codex Fb, except for the following notations in Clark's hand: "This Comes into No. 7 [*written over 8*] between the 23rd and 26 August 1805" and "This has been Copied from W. C. Journal and Coms in as above in No. 7." No. 7 is Biddle's designation for the journal now called Codex G. There are no more entries by Lewis until September 9, 1805.

5. The Indian camp at the fish weir, about five miles southeast of Salmon, Lemhi County, Idaho. See above, August 21, 1805. Clark's party remained here until August 29. Peebles (RW), 11; *Atlas* map 67.

6. Perhaps the Mormon cricket, *Anabrus simplex*. Coues (HLC), 2:538; Borror, Delong, & Triplehorn, 200. It was probably Biddle who drew a red vertical line from "Saw great numbers" to the end of the entry.

7. The ground lizard is probably the eastern short-horned lizard, *Phrynosoma douglassi brevirostre*, while the pigeons may be passenger pigeons, *Ectopistes migratorius* [AOU, 315], although Holmgren suggests the possibility of the band-tailed pigeon, *Columba fasciata* [AOU, 312], this far west. Benson (HLCE), 88; Burroughs, 233–34; Holmgren, 32.

Chapter Twenty-Two

Down the Lolo Trail

August 27–October 10, 1805

[Clark]   *August 27th Tuesday 1805*

Some frost this morning every Man except one,[1] out hunting, a young man Came from the upper Village & informed me that Capt Lewis would join me abt. 12 oClock to day. one man killed a Small Sammon, and the Indians gave me another which afforded us a Sleight brackfast. Those Pore people are here depending on what fish They Can Catch, without anything else to depend on; and appere Contented, my party hourly Complaining of their retched Situation and [contemplating?] doubts of Starveing in a Countrey where no game of any kind except a fiew fish can be found, an Indian brough in to the Camp 5 Sammon, two of which I purchased which afforded us a Supper.

1. Probably the sick man, Windsor. See above, August 25, 1805.

[Clark]   *August 28th Wednesday 1805*

a frost this morning. The Inds. Cought out of their traps Several Sammon and gave us two, I purchased two others which we made last us to day. Several a Camp of about 40 Indians came from the West fork and passed up to day, nothing killed by my party with every exertion in all places where game probably might be found. I dispatched one man[1] to the upper camps to enquire if Cap. Lewis was comeing &c. he returned after night with a letter from Capt. Lewis informing me of his Situation at the upper Village, and had precured 22 horses for our rout through by land on the plan which I had preposed in which he agreed with me in;

175

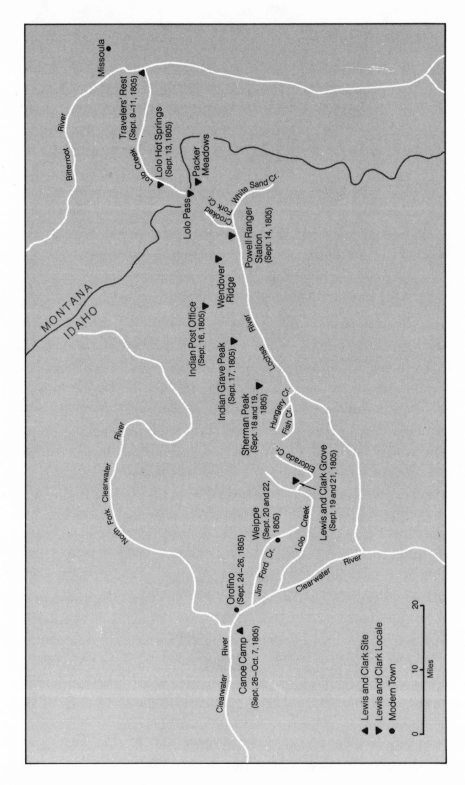

4. The Lolo Trail, September 11–22, 1805

and requsted me to ride up and get the horses the Indian informed him they had reserved for me &c. I purchased Some fish roe of those pore but kind people with whome I am Encamped for which I gave three Small fish hooks, the use of which they readily proseved, one Indian out all day & killed only one Sammon with his gig; my hunters killed nothing, I had three pack Saddles made to day for our horses which I expected Capt Lewis would purchase &c. Those Sammon which I live on at present are pleasent eateing, not with standing they weaken me verry fast and my flesh I find is declineing

Course Distance & over the portage from the Waters of the
Missouri to the Waters of the Columbia River.—[2]

N. 60° W.	5	miles to a Point of a hill on the right Passed Several points of high land bottom wide only 3 Small trees
S. 80° W	10	miles to a place the high lands approach within 200 yards, Creek 10 yds. wide
S. W.	5	miles to a narrow part of the bottom passed a Creek on each Side a place the Indians were massered, a road coms in on the right
S. 70° W.	2	miles to a Creek on the right
S. 80° W	3	miles to a rockey point opsd. a Pine thicket on the left, passed a run from the right
West	3	miles to the head Spring of the Missoui near the top of a dividing mountain at a gap
S. 80° W	6	miles to a run from the right, passed Several Small Streams & Spring runs running to my left, and down a Drean.
N. 80° W.	4	miles to the East fork of the Lewis's River 40 yds. Wide an Indian Snake Camp of 25 Lodges passed over hilley land all the way from the dividing ridge.
miles	38	

1. Sergeant Gass, according to Ordway.

2. The portage over the Continental Divide by way of Lemhi Pass. *Atlas* map 67.

[Clark]   *August 29th Thursday 1805*

a Cold morning Some frost.   the Wind from the South, I left our baggage in possession of 2 men and proceeded on up to join Capt Lewis at the upper Village of Snake Indians[1] where I arrived at 1 oClock found him much engaged in Counceling and attempting to purchase a fiew more horses. I Spoke to the Indians on various Subjects endeavoring to impress on theire minds the advantaje it would be to them for to Sell us horses and expedite the our journey the nearest and best way possibly that we might return as Soon as possible and winter with them at Some place where there was plenty of buffalow,— our ⟨object⟩ wish is to get a horse for each man to Carry our baggage and for Some of the men to ride occasionally, The horses are handsom and much acustomed to be changed as to their Parsture; we cannot Calculate on their carrying large loads & feed on the Grass which we may Calculate on finding in the Mountain Thro which we may expect to pass on our rout   made Some Selestial observations, the Lard. of this Part the Columbia River is [*blank*] North. Longtd. [*blank*] W

I purchased a horse for which I gave my Pistol 100 Balls Powder & a Knife.   our hunters Killed 2 Deer near their Camp to day.   2 yesterday & 3 The Day before, this meet was a great treat to me as I had eate none for 8 days past

1. The village site four miles north of present Tendoy, Lemhi County, Idaho. *Atlas* map 67.

[Clark]   *August 30th Friday 1805*

a fine Morning, finding that we Could purchase no more horse than we had for our goods &c. (and those not a Sufficint number for each of our Party to have one which is our wish) I Gave my Fuzee to one of the men & Sold his musket for a horse which Completed us to 29 total horses, we Purchased pack Cords Made Saddles & Set out on our rout down the [*EC: Lemhi*] river by land guided by my old guide one other who joined him, the old gude's 3 Sons followed him   before we Set out our hunters killed three Deer   proceded on 12 miles and encamped on the river South Side—   at the time we Set out from the Indian Camps the greater Part of the Band Set out over to the waters of the Missouri.   we had great attention paid to the horses, as they were nearly all Sore Backs and Several pore, & young   Those horses are indifferent, maney Sore backs and others not acustomed to pack, and as we Cannot put large loads on them are Compelled to purchase as maney as we Can to take our Small propotion of baggage of the Parties. (& Eate if necessary) Proceeded on 12 miles to day[1]

1. Their campsite, marked on *Atlas* map 67, was a few miles above the fish weir, somewhat below present Baker, Lemhi County, Idaho. Peebles (RW), 12.

[Clark]   *August 31st 1805 Satturday*[1]

A fine morning   Set out before Sun rise, as we passed the lodges at which place I had encamped for thre nights and left 2 men, Those 2 men joined us and we proceeded on in the Same rout I decended the 21st Instant, halted 3 hours on Sammon Creek to Let our horses graze   the wind hard from the S. W. I met an Indian on horse back who fled with great Speed to Some lodges below & informed them that the Enemis were Coming down, armd with guns &c.   the inhabitents of the Lodges indisceved him, we proceeded on the road on which I had decended as far as the 1st run [*EC: Tower Cr*] below & left the road & Proceeded up the Run [*NB: run*] in a tolerable road 4 miles & Encamped in Some old lodjes at the place the road leaves the Creek and assends the high Countrey[2]   Six Indians followed us four of them the Sons of our guide; our hunters killed one Deer a goose & Prarie fowl. This day warm and Sultrey, Praries or open Valies on fire in Several places—   The Countrey is Set on fire for the purpose of Collecting the different bands, and a Band of the *Flatheads* to go to the Missouri where They intend passing the winter near the Buffalow   Proceeded on 22 miles to Day, 4 miles of which up a run

1. Clark's table of courses for August 31–September 4 are found with his entry of September 2, 1805.

2. The route appears as a dotted line on *Atlas* map 67; at some points it is hard to distinguish from Clark's earlier route (marked "William Clark's route") on his Salmon River reconnaissance. Having crossed to the east side of the Lemhi, they proceeded down that river to the Salmon, traveled down that river and headed up Tower Creek. The campsite was, as Clark notes, some four miles up the creek, in Lemhi County, Idaho. Peebles (RW), 15, and fig. 13.

[Lewis and Clark]   [*Weather, August 1805*][1]

Day of the month [August]	State of the Thermometer at ☉ rise	Weather at ☉ rise	Wind at ☉ rise	State of the Thermometer at 4 P.M.	Weather at 4 P.M.	Wind at 4 P.M.	State of the River raised or fallen	Feet	Inches and parts
1st	54 a	f	S W	91 a	f	S. W.	f		½
2nd	48 a	f	N. W.	81 a	f	N. W.	f		½
3rd	50 a	f	N. E.	86 a	f	N. E.	f		½
4th	48 a	f	S	92 a	f	S	f		½
5th	49 a	f	S. E.	79 a	f	S E	f		¼
6th	52 a	f	S. W.	71 a	c	S W			
7th	54 a	c. a. r	S. W.	80 a	c	S. W.			
8th	54 a	f. a. r	S W	82 a	c a f	S W			
9th	58 a	f	N. E.	78 a	c	S. W.			
10th	60 a	C. a. r. f & L	S W	68 a	T L & r	S W			
11th	58 a	c a. r. & h	N E	70 a	f	S W.			
12th	58 a	f a r & h	W.	72 a	f. a. r a h	N W			
13th	52 a	c. a f.	N. W.	70 a	f a r	N W			
14th	51 a	f. a. r	N W.	76 a	f	N W			
15th	43 a[2]	f	S E	74 a	f	S W			
16th	48 a	f	S W.	70 a	f	S W.			
17th	42 a	f	N. E.	76 a	f	S W			
18th	45 a	C	S. W.	78 a	r	S W.			
19th	30 a	f a. r	S W	71 a	f. a. r	S W			
20th	32 a	f. a. r[3]	S W.	74 a	f	S W.			
21st	19 a	f	S E	78 a	f	E			
22nd	22 a	f	E.	70 a	f.	E.			
23rd	35 a	f	E.	72 a	f	S E			
24th	40 a	f	S. E.	76 a	f. a. r	S E			
25th	32 a	f a r	S. E	65 a	C	S E			
26th	31 a	f	S. E.	45 a	f	S. E			
27th	32 a	f	S E	56 a	f	S E			
28th	35 a	f	S W.	66 a	f	S W.			
29th	32 a	f	S W.	68 a	f	S W			
30th	34 a	C	N E	59 a	C	N E			
31st	38 a	C. a. r	N E	58 a	c a r & h	N. E.			

[August] 1st   Left the party and proceeded on a head

6th   Rejoin the party at 11 A M

7th   Thunder shower last evening from the N W.[5] The river which we are now ascending is so inconsiderable and the curant So much on a Stand that I relinquished paying further attention to it's State.

8th   a thunder Shower last evening.

9th   Encamped below the Forks Jeffersons River   Set out on a party of discovery

10th   rain Commenced at 6 P. M and continued Showery through out the night. Musqueters bad.

11th   heavy Dew last evening   killed a long tailed grouse.

12th   Saw a Snake Indian in Snake Indian Cove at 1 OC. P. M.[6]

13th   very cold last night.   passed the dividing ridge to the waters of Columbia river

14th   met with the Snake Indians, visit their camp[7]

15th   remarkably cold this morning

16th   Capt Lewis Join with the Snake Indians at the forks[8]

18th   Capt. Clark sets out with the Indians and 11 men

19th   ice on Standing water ⅛ of an inch thick.

20th   hard frost last night.[9]

21st   ice ½ an inch thick on standing water.[10] Most astonishing difference between the hight of the Murcury at ☉ rise and at 4 P. M. today   there was 59° and this in the Space of 8 hours, yet we experience this wonderfull transicion without feeling it near so Sensibly as I should have expected.

22nd   Snow yet appears on the summits of the mountains. the Indians arrive at 12 OC

23rd   white frost this morning

24th   Set out with the Indians and pack horses for the Columbia river

25th   white frost this morning[11]

26th   hard white frost and some ice on standing water this morning   arrived with baggage and party on the Columbia river at 5 P. M.

27th   hard frost white this morning.[12]

29th   Capt. Clalark joins me at the upper Indian village[13]

30th   Set out with the party by land at 2 P. M.[14]

1. Lewis has weather data for this month in Codex Fe and Codex P; Clark's is in Codex I. This table follows Codex Fe.

2. Clark has "52 a."

3. Clark has only "f."

4. Lewis (Codices Fe and P) and Clark (Codex I) both have extensive marginal remarks for this month, many of which do not refer to the weather, but to the movements of the two captains and their respective parties. Some of the remarks in Lewis's journals appear to be in Clark's handwriting. Clark's substantive differences with Lewis's remarks are noted.

5. The remainder of this entry is from a separate remark in Codices Fe and P.

6. This actually occurred on August 11, as Clark notes in his weather remarks in Codex I. Even there a line points the remark to August 12.

7. Clark in Codex I says, "Capt Lewis arrived at the Snake Indian camp on C[olumbia]." A line points the remark of August 13 to August 14.

8. Clark's remark in Codex I.

9. Clark adds, "I arrive at the Snake Indian village on the waters of Columbia River."

10. The remainder of this entry is from a separate remark in Codices Fe and P.

11. Clark writes, "I proceeded down the river 70 miles & Set out on my return."

12. Clark says simply, "on the Columbian waters."

13. Clark's version is, "I rejoin the party at the Snake Indian village & purchase horses."

14. Clark has, "Set out with the party from Snake Indian village."

[Clark]   *September 1st Sunday 1805*

a fine morning   Set out early and proceeded on over high ruged hills passing the heads of the Small runs which fall into the river on our left to a large Creek which falls into the river 6 miles to our left and encamped in the bottom,[1] Some rain to day at 12 and in the evening which obliges us to Continu all night   despatched 2 men to the mouth of the Creek to purchase fish of the Indians at that place, They returned with Some dried, we giged 4 Sammon & killed one Deer to Day. the Countrey which we passed to day is well watered & broken Pore Stoney hilly country except the bottoms of the Creek which is narrow, all the Indians leave us except our Guide, one man Shot two bear this evining unfortunately we Could git neither of them

1. They traveled across country to the North Fork Salmon River (Fish Creek on *Atlas* map 67) and camped a few miles south of Gibbonsville, Lemhi County, Idaho, in the neighborhood of the mouth of Hull Creek on the opposite side of the North Fork. Peebles (RW), 15–16, and fig. 13; Majors (LCRM), 95 n. 41.

[Clark]   *September 2nd Monday 1805*

a Cloudy Mornin, raind Some last night   we Set out early and proceeded on up the [*EC: Fish*] Creek, Crossed a large fork from the right and one from the left; and at 8 [*EC: 7½*] miles left the roade on which we were pursuing and which leads over to the Missouri; and proceeded up a West fork [*EC: of Fish Creek*] without a roade proceded on thro' thickets in which we were obliged to Cut a road, over rockey hill Sides where our horses were in pitial[1] danger of Slipping to Ther certain distruction & up & Down Steep hills, where Several horses fell, Some turned over, and others Sliped down Steep hill Sides, one horse Crippeled & 2 gave out. with the greatest dificuelty risque &c. we made five [*EC: 7½*] miles & Encamped on The left Side of the Creek in a Small Stoney bottom[2]   after night Some time before the rear Came up, one Load left, about 2 miles back, the horse on which it was Carried Crippled. Some rain at night

Course and Distance by land from the Columbia [*EC: Salmon*] River
14 miles below the forks

August 31st 1805

N. 35° E	2	miles up Tower Creek to a hill
N. 10° E	2	do do do passed remarkable rock resembling Pirimids on the Left Side
	4	

Septr. 1st Sunday

N. 80° W	1½	miles to the top of a high hill

N. 65° W.	1½	to the [top?] of a hill passing the heads of dreans passing to our left
N. 55° W.	3½	miles to the top of a high hill passd. two forks of a Crek, the first large & bold the 2d. Small
S. 80° W.	1½	mile down a raveen to a run
N. 70° W.	3½	to the top of a high hill passing a branch at ¼ & over a hill at 1 mile
N. 35° W.	2½	to the top of a high hill
N. 25° W.	1½	to ditto passed a branch at ½ mile which passes to the left
N. 80° W.	2½	decending a Steep winding hill to a large Creek which we Call Fish Creek & runs into the [EC: Salmon] river at Some lodge 6 miles below South
N. 12° W.	2	miles up the Creek to a bluff Point.
	20⟨½⟩	.

Septr. 2nd Monday

North	1½	to a large fork which falls in on the left in a pine bottom
N 45° E	2½	miles to a large fork which falls in on the right Hills Covd. with Pine
North	3½	miles to the [EC: main] forks of the Creek passed a leavel pine bottom & pine hills maney beaver Dams across the Creek
N. 60° W	2½	miles up the west fork [EC: of Fish Cr.] leaving the road on our right which passes to the Missouri [EC: Dalong Cr.] by the East fork [X: of Fish Cr.]
N. 35° W	3	miles up the west fork Crossed it Several times & passing thro' thickets brush & over rocks.
N. 50° W	2	miles over hills rocks & Steep points & hill Sides on the
miles	15	left of the [X: West fork of Fish] Creek crossing a run at 1 mile

Septr. 3rd Tuesday 1805

N. 25° W.	2½	Miles to a Small fork on the left Hilley and thick assending
N. 15° W.	2	mile to a fork on the right assending

N. 22° W.	2½	miles to a fork on the left passing one on the left Several Spring runs on the right Stoney hills & falling timber
N. 18° E.	2	miles passing over Steep points & winding ridges to a high Point passed a run on the right
N. 32° W.	2	miles to the top of a high hill passed 2 runs from the left, passing on the Side of a Steep ridge. no road
N. 40° W	3 14	miles leaveing the waters of the Creek to the right & passing over a high pine Mountn. to the head or a Drean running to the left

September 4th Wednesday 1805

N. 10° W.	6	miles on a Direct Course over a high Snow mountain & down a Drean of Flat head River [*EC: Ross Forks & Clark's rivr Divide of B. R. Mts.*] to a fork on the right. (our rout on a Dividing ridge to the right 9 *ms.* about[)] bad road
N. 18° W.	3	down the run [*EC: Camp Creek*] to a run on the left
N. 35° W	3 12	miles down the run to the river which Coms from the East, a wide Vallie. 33 tents of Flat heads

ms. 53½

1. Meant for "perpetual" or perhaps "potential."

2. Northwest of Gibbonsville, Lemhi County, Idaho, near U.S. Highway 93, somewhat above the mouth of Hammerean Creek. Peebles (RW), 16, and fig. 13; Majors (LCRM), 101 n. 54; *Atlas* map 68. However, a local historical marker places the group farther north as does a researcher who believes they may have camped beyond the mouth of Quartz Creek. Information of Robert N. Bergantino, Butte, Montana.

[Clark]   *September 3rd Tuesday 1805*

A Cloudy morning, horses verry Stiff   Sent 2 men back with the horse on which Capt Lewis rode for the load left back last night which detained us untill 8 oClock at which time we Set out. The Country is timbered with Pine Generally the bottoms have a variety of Srubs & the fur trees in Great abundance.   hills high & rockey on each Side, in the after part of the day the high mountains closed the Creek on each Side and obliged us to take on the Steep Sides of those Mountains, So Steep that the horses Could Screcly keep from Slipping down, Several Sliped & Injured themselves verry much, with great dificuelty we made [*blank*] miles [*NB: about 8 m. see Courses & Dist*] [*EC: courses and distances make 14 miles*] & Encamped on a branh of the Creek we assended after Crossing Several Steep points & one mountain,[1] but little to eate I killed 5 Pheasents & The huntes 4 with a little Corn afforded us a kind of Supper, at dusk it began to Snow ⟨& rain⟩ at 3 oClock Some rain. The ⟨last⟩ mountains [*NB: we had passed*] ⟨we had⟩ to the East Covered with Snow.   we met with a great misfortune, in haveing our last Thmometer broken by accident, This day we passed   over emence hils and Some of the worst roade that ever horses passed our horses frequently fell ⟨Country a⟩   Snow about 2 inches deep when it began to rain which termonated in a Sleet ⟨killed Seven⟩ our genl. Courses nearly North from the R

1. The party's traverse of September 3 and the camp of that night is one of the most disputed areas of the trip through the mountains. Indeed, Majors (LCRM), 106 n. 73, calls the route "the single most obscure and enigmatic of the entire Lewis and Clark expedition." The controversy surrounds the party's trip relative to references to hills and streams and to the seeming errors in Clark's course and distance table (found here with his entry of September 2). Peebles (RW), 17, and fig. 13, plots the group as following the North Fork Salmon to the entrance of Moose Creek, then move northeasterly on the west side of that stream before crossing the state line into Montana west of Lost Trail Pass, then turn northwest along the state line, and finally camp at the head of Shields Creek, in Ravalli County, Montana, southwest of Saddle Mountain. Wolf and Robert N. Bergantino, Butte, Montana (personal communication), believe that the party followed the North Fork Salmon to the entrance of Coal Gulch (Wolf) or Moose Creek (Bergantino), and then moved northeasterly along Moose Creek. Wolf has the group on the east side of Moose Creek to the Continental Divide, then follow the divide along the Montana-Idaho border, go through Chief Joseph and Lost Trail passes, continue along the state line, then cross into Montana, and camp on Shields Creek. Bergantino has a similar course for the party but on the west side of Moose Creek to a little beyond the entrance of Little Moose Creek, then northerly to hit the ridge and state line about one-quarter mile west of Lost Trail Pass, and camp farther west on a southwesterly flowing tributary of North Fork Salmon River, in Lemhi County, Idaho, and almost due south of Saddle Mountain. Fred Crandall, Nevada City, California (personal communication), has the Corps follow the North Fork Salmon to the entrance of the West Fork, pass between the streams in a northwesterly direction, then turn due north before camping in Lemhi County, somewhat west of Bergantino's proposed site. Majors (LCRM), 69, 105–16, nn. 73–81, argues for a route considerably to the west of other researchers, based on the assumption that Clark's compass readings were off. He concludes that for Clark's fourth course of the day the captain meant "N. 18° W." instead of "N. 18° E." (Wolf also thinks that Clark made an error, but in

his last course, which he says should probably read "N. 80° W" not "N. 40° W"). Majors would have the party pass between Twin and Vine creeks, follow a route to the west as they crossed over Hughes Point in Montana, and then camp at the head of Colter Creek in Montana, south of the Shields Creek camp of Wolf. Readers may want to consult the Salmon National Forest and Bitterroot National Forest maps, as well as USGS map Wisdom, Montana-Idaho, and *Atlas* map 68.

[Clark]   *September 4th Wednesday 1805*

a verry cold morning every thing wet and frosed, we detained untill 8 oClock to thaw the covering for the baggage &c. &c.   groun covered with Snow, we assended a mountain & took a Divideing ridge which we kept for Several Miles & fell on the head of a Creek which appeared to run the Course we wished to go, I was in front, & Saw Several of the Argalia or Ibex decended the mountain by verry Steep decent takeing the advantage of the points and best places to the Creek, where our hunter killed a Deer which we made use of and prosued our Course down the Creek to the forks about 5 miles[1] where we met a part of the ⟨Flat head⟩ [X: *Tushepau*] nation[2] of 33 Lodges about 80 men 400 Total and at least 500 horses, those people recved us friendly, threw white robes over our Sholders & Smoked in the pipes of peace, we Encamped[3] with them & found them friendly but nothing but berries to eate a part of which they gave us, those Indians are well dressed with Skin Shirts & robes, they Stout & light complected more So than Common for Indians, The Chiefs harangued untill late at night, Smoked our pipe and appeared Satisfied. I was the first white man who ever wer on the waters of this river.[4] [X: (*Clark's R*)]

1. From the camp of September 3 (see above), the party apparently ascended Saddle Mountain and came down into the valley between the forks of Camp Creek, in Ravalli County, Montana. Peebles (RW), 17; Majors (LCRM), 105 n. 73, 116 n. 81; *Atlas* map 68.
2. The Flatheads prefer to be called Salish. The common explanation of the English name is that they were considered flat-headed by tribes on the lower Columbia who deformed the skulls of their infants to produce a pointed head. Supposedly in the nineteenth century these mountain "Flatheads" became confused by whites with those who did practice skull deformation, and thus the term was used loosely for many Northwest tribes. Biddle does not use the term "Flathead" for these people, but the captains used the term both in their journals and in the Estimate of Eastern Indians (see Chapter 10, vol. 3), indicating that they had heard it before meeting these people, perhaps at the Mandan-

Hidatsa villages. The sign language term for the Salish suggests a flattening of the sides of the heads. Sergeant Gass used the name "Flat-head" in his published journal, perhaps helping to fasten the name on the Salish. The name "Tushepau" (or Tushepaw) apparently represents the Shoshone term *tatasiba*, "the people with shaved heads," meaning the Flatheads. Sven Liljeblad, personal communication. After acquiring the horse in the 1700s, the Flatheads became buffalo hunters on the Montana plains, but pressure from the Blackfeet and other plains tribes forced them to spend much of their time in the mountains of northwestern Montana. Their buffalo hunts were perilous excursions into enemy country. They were consistently friendly to whites from Lewis and Clark's time on. In the 1840s many were converted to Christianity by Catholic missionaries. A Flathead tradition, recorded over ninety years later, says that old Chief Three Eagles, out scouting for enemies, first spotted the explorers. Lewis and Clark were riding ahead, while the rest of the party were leading their horses. The chief was puzzled at first that the strangers did not wear blankets, as all Indians of his acquaintance did, and he wondered if York was a warrior with his face painted black as a sign of war. He finally decided that the casual manner in which they were traveling did not suggest hostile intent, so the tribe greeted the newcomers in friendly fashion. The captains gave the chiefs American tobacco mixed with kinnickinnick, which the Indians thought superior to whatever they had been smoking. Fahey; Hodge, 1:465, 2:415–16; Clark, 174–79; Wheeler, 2:65–68.

3. In the valley now called Ross, or Ross's, Hole, east of modern Sula, Ravalli County, and probably on Camp Creek near its entrance into the East Fork Bitterroot River. Majors (LCRM), 108 n. 73; *Atlas* map 68.

4. The Bitterroot River, which they at first called Flathead River but which is Clark's River on *Atlas* map 68. See *Atlas*, 10. The party will reach East Fork Bitterroot River on September 6 and the Bitterroot itself the next day above the entrance of the West Fork.

[Clark]   *September 5th Thursday 1805*

a Cloudy morning   we assembled the Chiefs & warriers and Spoke to them (with much dificuely as what we Said had to pass through Several languajes before it got in to theirs, which is a gugling kind of languaje Spoken much thro the Throught)[1]   we informed them who we were, where we Came from, where bound and for what purpose &c. &c. and requsted to purchase & exchange a fiew horses with them, in the Course of the day I purchased 11 horses & exchanged 7 for which we gave a fiew articles of merchendize.   those people possess ellegant horses.— we made 4 Chiefs whome we gave meadels & a few Small articles with Tobacco; the women brought us a few berries & roots to eate and the Principal Chief a Dressed Brarow,[2] otter & two Goat & antilope Skins

Those people wore their hair ⟨as follows⟩ the men Cewed with otter Skin on each Side falling over the Sholrs forward, the women loose promisquisly over ther Sholdrs & face long Shirts which Coms to the anckles & tied with a belt about their waste with a roabe over, the have but fiew ornaments and what they do were are Similar to the Snake Indians, They Call themselves Eoote-lash-Schute [*NB: Oat la shoot*][3] and consist of 450 Lodges in all and divided into Several bands on the heads of Columbia river & Missouri, Some low down the Columbia River

1. The language, of the Salishan family, apparently led the captains to reconsider for a time an old legend. Sergeant Ordway says, "we suppose that they are the welch Indians if their is any such from the language."

2. The badger, *Taxidea taxus*. Burroughs, 72.

3. The Indians may have referred not only to the modern Flatheads but also to linguistically related groups like the Pend d'Oreilles and Kalispells. Clark's name may represent a Flathead term, *uɫ-išú-t,* "those down below."

[Clark]   *September 6th Friday 1805*[1]

Some little rain, purchased two fine horses & took a Vocabiliary of the language litened our loads & packed up, rained contd. untill ⟨2⟩ 12 oClock   we Set out at 2 oClock at the Same time all the Indians Set out on Ther way to meet the Snake Indians at the 3 forks of the Missouri. Crossed a Small river[2] from the right we call [*blank*] [*NB: This was the main river or Clarks*] Soon after Setting out, also a Small Creek[3] from the North all three forks Comeing together below our Camp at which place the Mountains Close on each Side of the river, We proceeded on N 30 W. Crossed a Mountain and Struck the river Several miles down, at which place the Indians had Encamped two days before, we Proceeded on Down the River which is 30 yds. wide Shallow & Stoney. Crossing it Several times & Encamped in a Small bottom on the right side.[4]   rained this evening nothing to eate but berries, our flour out, and but little Corn, the hunters killed 2 pheasents only—   all our horses purchased of the ⟨flat heads⟩ oote lash Shutes we Secured well for fear of their leaveing of us, and watched them all night for fear of their leaving us or the Indians prosuing & Steeling them.

1. Clark's courses for September 6–9 are found at his entry of September 9, 1805. Again heavily marked by Coues and with some incorrect place-names.

2. East Fork Bitterroot River, unnamed on *Atlas* map 68.

3. Probably Cameron Creek.

4. A few miles northwest of Sula, Ravalli County, Montana, on the East Fork Bitterroot River, apparently above Warm Springs Creek and on the opposite side; unnamed on *Atlas* map 68. The party had apparently passed over Sula Peak on their way.

[Clark]   *September 7th Satturday 1805*

A Cloudy & rainie Day   the greater Part of the Day dark & Drisley we proceedd on down the river thro a Vallie   passed Several Small Runs on the ⟨right left⟩ [*NB: right*] & 3 creeks on the ⟨right⟩ left   The Vallie from 1 to ⟨three⟩ 2 miles wide the Snow top mountains to our left, open hilley Countrey on the right. Saw 2 horses left by the Indians   Those horses were as wild a Elk. One of our hunters Came up this morning without his horse, in the course of the night the horse broke loose & Cleared out—   we did not make Camp untill dark,[1] for the want of a good place, one of our hunters did not join us this evening.   he haveing killed an elk packed his horses & could not overtake us

1. Clark apparently mislabeled or drew in incorrectly some streams on *Atlas* map 68 above the camp of September 6. The stream labeled "West Fork of Clarks River" (today's West Fork Bitterroot River) is too far north according to his course and distance table (here found with the entry of September 9), which is more instructive for the day's route than the text. The true West Fork would be the first major stream on the east side beyond the camp of September 6, between the words "Hills" and "Pine" on the map ("Creek on the left" in the second course for the day and mislabeled "Nez Perce" by Coues). The creek in the next course would be either McCoy Creek or Tin Cup Creek, the latter according to Coues's interlineation. Coues seems to be correct in identifying the creek in the next course as Rock Creek; it is the one Clark drew in as West Fork of Clarks River. Just above that (unnamed on the map) is present Lost Horse Creek, called Little Horse Creek by Coues. The party camped southwest of Grantsdale, Ravalli County, Montana, on the east side of the Bitterroot River.

[Clark]   *September 8th Sunday 1805*

a Cloudy morning   Set out early and proceeded on through an open vallie for 23 miles   passed 4 Creeks[1] on the right Some runs on the left, The bottoms as also the hills Stoney bad land. Some pine on the Creeks and mountains, an partial on the hills to the right hand Side.   two of our hunters came up with us at 12 oClock with an Elk, & Buck— the wind from the N. W. & Cold. The foot of the Snow mountains approach the ⟨Creek⟩ River on the left Side. Some Snow on The mountain to the right also[2] proceeded on down the Vallie which is pore Stoney land and en- camped on the right Side of the river[3] a hard rain all the evening we are all Cold and wet. on this part of the river on the head of Clarks River I observe great quantities of a peculiar Sort of Prickly peare[4] grow in Clus- ters ovel & about the Size of a Pigions egge with Strong Thorns which is So birded [bearded] as to draw the Pear from the Cluster after penetrate- ing our feet. Drewyer killed a Deer. I killed a prarie fowl we found 2 mears and a Colt the mears were lame, we ventered to let our late purchase of horses loose to night

1. Including present Skalkaho Creek, Gird Creek, Willow Creek (near modern Cor- vallis, Ravalli County, Montana), Soft Rock, Birch, Spoon, and Willoughby creeks. *Atlas* map 68.

2. On the left were the Bitterroot Mountains and on the right the Sapphire Mountains. *Atlas* map 68.

3. In the neighborhood of modern Stevensville, Ravalli County. *Atlas* map 68. The "Scattered Creek" of today's last course (see with entry of September 9) could be the nu- merous streams that come into the Bitterroot River at this point, including Mill, North Spring, and Burnt Fork creeks, and the several dividing branches of the latter.

4. Brittle prickly pear, noticed by Lewis on August 13, 1805.

[Lewis]   *Monday September 9th 1805.*[1]

Set out at 7 A M. this morning and proceeded down the Flathead river leaving it on our left, the country in the valley of this river is generally a prarie and from five to 6 miles wide the growth is almost altogether pine principally of the longleafed kind, with some spruce and a kind of furr resembleing the scotch furr.[2] near the wartercourses we find a small proportion of the narrow leafed cottonwood[3] some redwood hon- eysuckle[4] and rosebushes form the scant proportion of underbrush to be seen. at 12 we halted on a small branch which falls in to the river on the E. side, where we breakfasted on a scant proportion of meat which we had reserved from the hunt of yesterday added to three geese which one of our hunters killed this morning. two of our hunters have arrived, one of them brought with him a redheaded woodpecker of the large kind common to the U States.[5]   this is the first of the kind I have seen since I left the Illinois.   just as we were seting out Drewyer arrived with two deer.   we continued our rout down the valley about 4 miles and crossed the river; it is hear a handsome stream about 100 yards wide and affords a considerable quantity of very clear water, the banks are low and it's bed entirely gravel.   the stream appears navigable, but from the circumstance of their being no sammon in it I believe that there must be a considerable fall in it below.   our guide could not inform us where this river discharged itself into the columbia river, he informed us that it continues it's course along the mountains to the N. as far as he knew it and that not very distant from where we then were it formed a junction with a stream nearly as large as itself[6] which took it's rise in the mountains near the Missouri to the East of us and passed through an extensive valley generally open prarie which forms an excellent pass to the Missouri.   the point of the Missouri where this Indian pass intersects it, is about 30 miles above the *gates of the rocky mountain,*[7] or the place where the valley of the Missouri first widens into an extensive plain after entering the rockey mountains.   the guide informed us that a man might pass to the missouri from hence by that rout in four days.   we continued our rout down the W. side of the river about 5 miles further and encamped on a large creek which falls in on the West[8]   as our guide informes that we should leave the river at this place and the weather appearing settled and fair I determined to halt the next day rest our horses and take some scelestial Observations.   we called this Creek *Travellers rest.*   it is about 20 yards wide a fine bould clear runing stream   the land through which we passed is but indifferent a could white gravley soil.[9]   we estimate our journey of this day at 19 M.

at the creek where we dined I took the Meridian Altd. of ⊙'s U. L. with Sextant fore obstn 98° 1′ 30″

Latitude deduced from this Observation 46° 41′ 38.9

Point of observation No. 46

At our encampment of this evening observed time and distance of the Moon's western limb from α Aquila ★ West with Sextant.

	Time			*Distance*		
	h	m	s			
P. M.	9	52	47	63°	33′	—″
	″	56	58	″	35	15
	″	59	41	″	36	30
	10	3	48	″	37	45
	″	6	1	″	38	30

	Time			*Distance*		
	h	m	s			
P. M.	10	6	1	63°	38′	30
	″	7	46	″	39	45
	″	9	24	″	40	30
	″	11	2	″	41	—
	″	13	27	″	41	45

☞ this set of observations cannot be much depended on as through mistake I brought the Moons Western limb in contact in stead of her Eastern limb she having passed into her third quarter and of course her Western limb somewhat imperfect.

[Clark]   *September 9th Monday 1805*

a fair morning   Set out early and proceeded on thro a plain as yesterday down the valley   Crossed a large [*NB: called*] Scattering Creek on which Cotton trees grew at 1½ miles,[10] a Small one at 10 miles, both from the right, the main river at 15 miles & Encamped on a large Creek from the left which we call Travelers rest Creek.   killed 4 deer & 4 Ducks & 3 prarie fowls.   day fair Wind N. W.   See Suplement[11]

Course Distance &c. Down *Clark's* river

Septr. 6th 1805

N. 30° W.	5	miles crossing the river [*EC: Ross' fork*] & a Creek at 1½ m. & thro a vallie to the top of a mountain Covered with pine
N. 80° W.	1½	miles down a reveen & Steep hill Sides to the river [*EC: Ross' fork*] at an old Encampment. a creek left
West	1½	miles down the Creek [*EC: River*], bottoms narrow.
N. 35° W	2 / 10	miles down the ⟨Creek⟩ River which is 25 yards wide passed a run on each side.

N. 40° W.   3   miles down the River aforesaid

N. 80° W.   3   miles down the River to a larke [*EC: large Nez Perce*] Creek on the left.   bottoms narrow.

N. 45° W.   4   down the river to a Creek [*EC: Tin Cup*] on the left.   bottoms wider, hills on the right is bald, mountains on our left is high and the tops Covered with Snow

North   4   miles to a [*EC: Rock*] Creek which runs from the Snow toped mountains, passed one on the left at 1 mile & Several Small runs on the right, and left, one Drean

N. 25° E.   8   miles down the River, passed a large [*EC: Little Horse*] Creek on the left at 2 miles.   the Vallie thro which we passed about 2 miles wide, lands pore & Stoney   The foot of the Snow toped mountains approach near the river on the left the river 50 yards wide Shallow & Stoney.   no fish to be Seen.   2 Deer 2 crains & 2 Phesents killed to day.
    22

September 8th Sunday

North   11   miles to a small run on the right Side, passed a large Creek at 1 mile one at 4 miles & a Small one at 8 miles, thro' a Call'd Horse Vally

N. 12° W   12   through the Said Vallie to a large Creek from the right divided into 4 diffierent Channels, Scattered Creek
    23

September 9th Monday

N. 15° W.   15   miles Thro a open vallie to the River, leaveing the road to our right Crossed a Small Creek from the left at 9 miles, and the river which is 100 yards wide, & passed through a pine bottom after crossing ⟨The Creek⟩ Clarks River

N. 40° W.   2   miles passing thro' a pine bottom after crossing the river to a large road on the left of the river in an open Vallie

N. 10° W.   4   miles Through an open Valle to a large Creek from the left. Caled *Travelers rest* and Encamped the 9th & 10th
    21

9th Septr. Contd.

North   12   Miles to the mouth of a lark fork [*EC: Hellgate*] which Joins from the right and heads up near the Missouri Some distance below the 3 forks,   this River has extinsive Vallies and is a good rout to the Missouri which the Indians say may be traveled in 4 days and is a good rout. The Vallie near the mouth of this fork is about 7 or 8 miles wide leavel & open, but little timber on this fork in Sight. See the Courses

[Clark]   [*undated*][12]

Moriah River	47° 29′ 10⁴⁄₁₀″ N.
Lower part of the falls is in Latd.	47° 8′ 4⁵⁄₁₀″ N.
upper part of the rapids latd. is	47° 3′ 30″ N.
Forks of Jefferson	43 30 43
Travelers rest	46 48 28

1. Here begins Lewis's fragmentary Codex Fc, consisting of four pages torn from Codex P and covering September 9 and 10, 1805. See Appendix C, vol. 2.

2. The "longleafed" pine is ponderosa pine. The spruce is Engelmann spruce, *Picea engelmannii* Parry. See September 12, 1805, where Clark refers to the latter as "spruce pine." The "furr" is probably Douglas fir, *Pseudotsuga menziesii* (Mirb.) Franco, which is typical of lower elevations in the Rocky Mountains. The "scotch furr" used for comparison may refer to either the cultivated European fir, *Abies alba* Mill., or one of the balsam fir species of the eastern United States. Little (CIH), 37-W, 80-W; Bailey, 113.

3. Probably the black cottonwood, *Populus trichocarpa* T. & G., which is the most common cottonwood species at lower elevations in Montana and Idaho. It is unclear whether Lewis was distinguishing between the two species of cottonwood which occur in the area (*P. trichocarpa* and *P. angustifolia,* the typically designated narrowleaf cottonwood), or did not observe this as a separate species. The narrowleaf cottonwood is more common at higher elevations; the black cottonwood has slightly broader leaves but is otherwise similar. Booth & Wright, 22; Little (CIH), 153-W.

4. Western trumpet, or orange, honeysuckle, *Lonicera ciliosa* (Pursh) DC., new to science and collected on the return trip. Cutright (LCPN), 210, 212, 261 n. 19, 410; Hitchcock et al. 4:458.

5. Burroughs considers this the red-headed woodpecker, *Melanerpes erythrocephalus* [AOU, 406], but Coues and Holmgren identify it as the pileated woodpecker, *Dryocopus pileatus* [AOU, 405]. Burroughs, 242; Coues (HLC), 2:590; Holmgren, 34.

6. The Bitterroot meets the Clark Fork, or Hellgate, River just west of present Missoula, Missoula County, Montana. The stream continues northwest as the Clark Fork. *Atlas* map 69.

7. In the vicinity of present Helena, Montana. The Hidatsas told them of this route, but they had not recognized its eastern approaches on the voyage up the Missouri. Appleman (LC), 171; Allen (PG), 302.

8. Lewis and Clark's Travelers' Rest Creek is now Lolo Creek. The camp was where they remained until September 11, in the vicinity of modern Lolo, Missoula County, perhaps one or two miles upstream from the Bitterroot River, on the south side of the creek. Peebles (LT), 3; Space, 4; *Atlas* map 69.

9. Although the east side of the Bitterroot Valley contains soils that are quite fertile, soils that are thin and gravelly or cobbly occur on parts of the alluvial valley bottom and on the benches east of it. Similar soils are found on alluvial fans such as the Burnt Fork fan. The white soil to which Lewis refers may be the moderately saline soils of the Burnt Fork fan, clay layers in Tertiary sediments exposed in cutbanks, or the thin wash of light-colored Tertiary clay that covers the ground in some places, especially north of Eightmile Creek.

10. See the note on Scattered Creek in the previous entry.

11. Probably a reference to Lewis's Codex Fc. See n. 1, above.

12. This note in Clark's hand, giving certain latitudes from the Marias River to Travelers' Rest, is on the front flyleaf of Codex G. It is placed here at Travelers' Rest, the last position given.

[Lewis]   *Tuesday September 10th 1805.*

The morning being fair I sent out all the hunters, and directed two of them to procede down the river as far as it's junction with the Eastern fork which heads near the missouri, and return this evening.   this fork of the river we determined to name the Valley plain river. [*NB: we called the Eastern fork of Clarkes river.*][1] I think it most probable that this river continues it's course along the rocky Mts. Northwardly as far or perhaps beyond the scources of Medecine river and then turning to the West falls into the Tacootchetessee.[2] The Minetares informed us that there mass [was] a large river west of, and at no great distance from the sources of Medecine river, which passed along the Rocky Mountains from S. to N.— this evening one of our hunters returned accompanyed by three men of the Flathead nation whom he had met in his excurtion up *travellers rest* Creek.[3]   on first meeting him the Indians were allarmed and prepared for battle with their bows and arrows, but he soon relieved their fears by laying down his gun and advancing towards them.   the Indians were mounted on very fine horses of which the Flatheads have a great abundance; that is, each man in the nation possesses from 20 to a hundred head.   our guide could not speake the language of these people but soon engaged them in conversation by signs or jesticulation, the common language of all the Aborigines of North America, it is one understood by all of them and appears to be sufficiently copious to convey with a degree of certainty the outlines of what they wish to communicate. in this manner we learnt from these people that two men which they supposed to be of the Snake nation had stolen 23 horses from them and that they were in pursuit of the theaves. they told us they were in great hast, we gave them some boiled venison, of which the eat sparingly. the sun was now set, two of them departed after receiving a few small articles which we gave them, and the third remained, having agreed to continue with us as a guide, and to introduce us to his relations whom he informed us were numerous and resided in the plain below the mountains on the columbia river, from whence he said the water was good and capable of being navigated to the sea; that some of his relation were at the sea last fall and saw an old whiteman who ⟨send given⟩ resided there by himself and who had given them some handkerchiefs such as he saw in our possession.— he said it would require five sleeps⁴ wich is six days travel, to reach his relations. the Flatheads are a very light coloured people of large stature and comely form.

[Clark]   *September 10th Tuesday 1805—*

A fair morning Concluded to Delay to day and make Some observations, as at this place the rout which we are to prosue will pass up the *Travelers rest Creek,* The day proved fair and we took equal altitudes & Some luner observations. The Latd. *46° 48′ 28″* as the guide report that no game is to be found on our rout for a long ways, ads an addition to the cause of our delay to precure Some meat, despatched all our hunters in different directions, to hunt the Deer which is the only large game to be found they killed 4 deer a Beaver & 3 Grouse which was divided, one of the hunters Colter, met with 3 ⟨flatheads⟩ Tushapaw Indians who were in pursuit of 2 Snake Indians that hade taken from ⟨the three from⟩ ther Camps on the ⟨Columbia⟩ head of Kooskooske River⁵ 21 horses, Those Indians came with Colter to our Camp & informed by Signs of their misfortune & the rout to ther villages &c. &c. one of them Concluded to return with us. ⟨I⟩ we gave them a ring fish hook & tied a pece of ribin in the hare of each which appeared to please them verry much, Cap Lewis gave them a Steel & a little Powder to make fire, after eating 2 of them proceeded on in pursute of their horses. men all much engaged preparing mockersons &c. &c. The Countrey about this place is already described in that above.

1. Biddle crossed out "we determined to name the Valley plain river" and added the interlineation in red ink. The river is the present Clark Fork above its junction with the Bitterroot. In the spring of 1806 they decided to name the Bitterroot-Clark Fork "Clark's River," having previously called it the Flathead. Thwaites (LC), 3:60, considers the interlineation Lewis's, but this is hard to accept. See the Introduction to the *Atlas*.

2. Alexander Mackenzie discovered the Tacoutche-Tesse, a large river in British Columbia west of the Continental Divide, in 1793. He believed it to be the Columbia, or a major tributary thereof, and Jefferson, Lewis, and Clark shared the assumption. It is in fact the modern Fraser River, neither the Columbia nor a tributary, but this was not discovered until 1807 by Simon Fraser. The Clark Fork, after meeting the Bitterroot, does flow northwest to Lake Pend Oreille, in northern Idaho, and from thence the Pend Oreille River flows into the Columbia. Thus the information Lewis received was essentially correct. Allen (PG), 83–86; Wallace, 445–46, 474–75.

3. The hunter was Colter. The Indians' description of their country matches the Nez Perce homeland in Idaho, and they were probably of that tribe, not Flatheads (Salish). This may be an instance of using the term "Flathead" broadly, for many tribes west of the Continental Divide. Space, 5.

4. Codex Fc, as it presently exists, ends here. The remainder of Lewis's entry of September 10 is found in Codex P, p. 80, indicating that Lewis wrote Codex Fc while the pages were still in the red notebook. The pages now in Codex Fc were probably removed in 1810, when Codex P was used to copy natural history notes. See Introduction and Appendix C, vol. 2.

5. The use of this term indicates that Clark was correcting this journal later, possibly as late as 1810 when he was conferring with Biddle. The river is the present Clearwater which the party did not reach for another ten days and which they did not name in the journals until apparently October 6.

[Clark]   September 11th Tuesday, 1805[1]

S. 45° E.   1½   miles up Travelers rest Creek to a road which passes up on the lower side & is the road to the Missouri

West   5½   miles up the Creek on the right side   hills on the right high & rugid   Snow toped mountains on the left & we passed in the vallie which is about ½ m Wide

[Clark]   *September 11th Wednesday 1805*[2]

A fair morning wind from the N W   we Set out at 3 oClock and proceeded on up the *Travelers rest Creek*, accompanied by the *flat head* or
Tushapaws Indians   about 7 miles below this Creek a large fork comes in
from the right and heads up against the waters of the Missouri below the
Three forks, this river has extensive Vallies of open leavel land, "and
passes in its Whole Course thro' a Valie" they call it ⟨Valie Plain River⟩
[Chicarluisket?] [*NB: we call it the east fork of Clark's river*][3] our Guide tels
us a fine large roade passes up this river to the Missouri— The loss of
2 of our horses detained us util'. 3 oClock. P. M.   our *Flathead* Indian
being restless thought proper to leave us and proceed on alone, Sent out
the hunters to hunt in advance as usial. (we have Selected 4 of the best
hunters to go in advance to hunt for the party. This arrangement has
been made long sinc)   we Proceeded on up the Creek [*EC: Travelers rest*]
on the right [*EC: hand*] Side [*EC: left bank*] thro a narrow valie and good
road for 7 miles and Encamped at Some old Indian Lodges,[4] nothing
killed this evening   hills on the right high & ruged, the mountains on the
left high & Covered with Snow.[5] The day Verry worm

  1. Here begins Clark's Elkskin-bound Journal, which runs to December 31, 1805. It
starts as a collection of courses and distances with numerous sketch maps; the entries
gradually expand into a regular journal, serving probably as a first draft for the notebook
journals. Because of the greater detail in the codex entries, annotation is generally to
those entries, which follow the ones in the Elkskin-bound Journal. At this point Clark's
second entries for the day are still in Codex G. See Introduction and Appendix C, vol. 2.
The sketch maps appear at the appropriate places in this present volume. The ink on the
first page is faded almost beyond reading. The edges of many pages are also badly worn.
  2. Clark's courses for September 11–25 are found after the codex entry for September 30, 1805 (see note there).
  3. Both Clark and Biddle have corrections for the material which follows the quotes.
Clark changed "we" to "they" and substituted what may be "Chicarluisket" for Vallie Plain
River, which he crossed out. Biddle crossed out the whole phrase and added his interlineation, all in red ink.
  4. They were starting west on the Lolo Trail, along Lolo Creek, the route used by the
Nez Perces to cross the Bitterroot Mountains from their homeland in Idaho to the buffalo
country in Montana. The name, thought to have derived from a French Canadian trap-
per, was not bestowed until after Lewis and Clark's time. Their camp was about one half
mile east of Woodman Creek, in Missoula County, Montana. Space, 2–3, 5; Peebles (LT),
3; *Atlas* map 69.

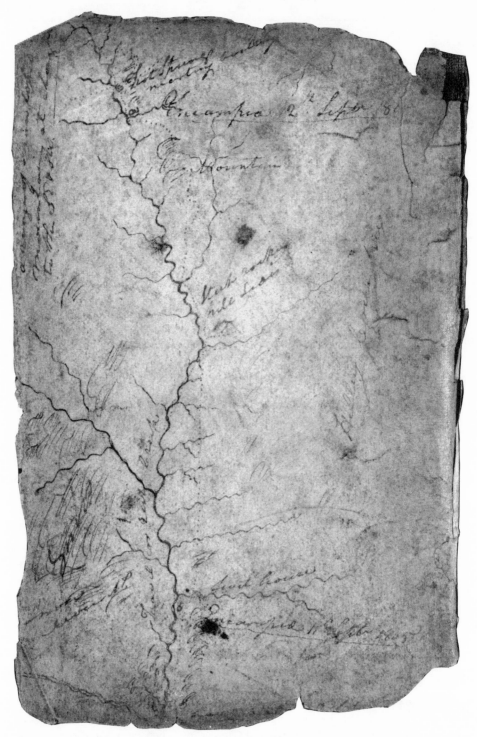

5. Route from Travelers' Rest toward Lolo Trail, Montana,
September 11–12, 1805, Elkskin-bound Journal ➔

5. On either side are portions of the Bitterroot Mountains, to the south (left) are the Lolo Mountains with Lolo Peak in the distance.

[Clark]   Septr. 12th

N. W   11   miles to the forks of the Creek   road passing through a hilley
                  countrey thickly timbered with the long leaf short leaf Spruce
                  Pine   crossed 6 branches which runs from the left the 1st the
                  largest   Killed 3 [*words illegible*] this morning   Dined at the
                  forks, passed a Hot hous covd with Earth on the 1st fork.

S. 75° W   12   miles to the Creek striking the creek at 4 mile and passing
                  over a high mountain for 8 miles   no water   the hills steep
                  & rockey & thickly timbered [*one line illegible*]

[Clark]   *September 12th Thursday 1805*

a white frost   Set out at 7 oClock & proceeded on up the Creek, passed a Fork[1] on the right on which I saw near an old Indian encampment a Swet [*NB: Sweat*] house Covered wthh earth, at 2 miles assended a high hill & proceeded through a hilley and thickly timbered Countrey for 9 miles & on the Right [*EC: hand side*] of the Creek, passing Several branches from the right of fine clear water and Struck at a fork[2] at which place the road forks, one passing up each fork. The Timber is Short & long leaf Pine Spruce Pine & fur.[3] The road through this hilley Countrey is verry bad passing over hills & thro' Steep hollows, over falling timber &c. &c.   continued on & passed Some most intolerable road on the Sides of the Steep Stoney mountains, which might be avoided by keeping up the Creek which is thickly covered with under groth & falling timber Crossed a mountain 8 miles with out water & encamped on a hill Side on the Creek after Decending a long Steep mountain,[4] Some of our Party did not git up untill 10 oClock P M. I mad camp at 8   on this roade & particularly on this Creek the Indians have pealed a number of Pine for the under bark which they eate at certain Seasons of the year, I am told in the Spring they make use of this bark[5]   our hunters Killed only one Pheasent this after noon. Party and horses much fatigued.

1. Woodman Creek, Missoula County, Montana. Space, 5; *Atlas* map 69.
2. Grave Creek, Missoula County. Space, 6; *Atlas* map 69.

3. Short-leaf pine is probably lodgepole pine, *Pinus contorta* Dougl. ex Loud. Along the Jefferson River (see August 3, 1805) and earlier, the captains used the term short-leaf pine to refer to the limber pine. Now they are out of the range of limber pine, so short-leaf must refer to a new species, lodgepole pine. Little (CIH), 50-W, 56-W; Hitchcock et al., 1 : 125–26; information of Ralph S. Space, Orofino, Idaho. Long-leaf pine remains ponderosa pine. Spruce pine is Engelmann spruce as discussed in notes for September 9. Gass used the term on September 14 and Whitehouse on September [16], when the party was in an area where Engelmann spruce is the only logical tree of reference. Fir is either subalpine fir, *Abies lasiocarpa* (Hook.) Nutt., or Douglas fir, more likely the latter. Little (CIH), 7-W.

4. Some two miles below (east of) Lolo Hot Springs, Missoula County, near U.S. Highway 12. Space, 6; Peebles (LT), 3; *Atlas* map 69.

5. Ponderosa pine has edible underbark as described here.

[Clark][1]

Course & Distance &c. Sept. 13th 1805

S. W. 2 miles up the Said Creek through an emencely bad road, rocks, Steep hill sides & fallen timber inumerable The Snow toped mountains at a long distance from S W to S E none else to be Seen in any other Directions to hot Springs on the right. Those springs come out in maney places in the rocks and nearly boiling hot

S. 30° W. 3 miles to the creek   passed a round about of 3 miles to our left of intolerable road timber &c as usial   halted to noon it & wate for Capt. Lewis who lost his horse

S. 30° W. 7 / m 12 miles over a mountain & a Dividing ridge of flat gradey land to a Creek from the left passing thro a glade of ½ a mile in width, keeping down the Creek 2 mile & Encamped. The Country as usial except the Glades which is open & boggey, water Clare and Sandey. Snow toped Mountains to the S E. at the head of this Creek which we call [*blank*] Creek. The after part of the day Cloudy. I killed 4 Pheasents & Shields killed a Black tail Deer.   a horse found in the glades left lame by Some Indians &c.

[Clark] *September 13th Wednesday [NB: Friday] 1805*

a cloudy morning   Capt Lewis and one of our guides lost their horses, Capt Lewis & 4 men detained to hunt the horses, I proceeded on with the partey up the Creek at 2 miles passed Several Springs which I observed the Deer Elk &c. had made roads to, and below one of the Indians had made a whole to bathe, I tasted this water and found it hot & not bad tasted   The last [*blank*] in further examonation I found this water nearly boiling hot at the places it Spouted from the rocks (which a hard Corse Grit, and of great size the rocks on the Side of the Mountain of the Same texture[)]   I put my finger in the water, at first could not bare it in a Second—[2]   as Several roads led from these Springs in different derections, my Guide took a wrong road and took us out of our rout 3 miles through intolerable rout, after falling into the right road I proceeded on thro tolerabl rout for abt. 4 or 5 miles and halted to let our horses graze as well as waite for Capt Lewis who has not yet Come up, The pine Countrey falling timber &c. &c. Continue. This Creek is verry much damed up with the beaver, but we can See none, dispatched two men back to hunt Capt Lewis horse, after he came up, and we proceeded over a mountain to the head of the Creek which we left to our left and at 6 miles from the place I nooned it, we fell on a Small Creek from the left which Passed through open glades Some of which ½ a mile wide,[3] we proceeded down this Creek about 2 miles to where the mountains Closed on either Side crossing the Creek Several times & Encamped.

One Deer & Some Pheasants killed this morning, I shot 4 Pheasents of the Common Kind except the taile was black.[4] The road over the last mountain was thick Steep & Stoney as usial, after passing the head of Travelers rest Creek, the road was verry fine leavel open & firm   Some mountains in view to the S E & S W. Covered with Snow.[5]

1. Opposite this entry in the Elkskin-bound Journal is a sketch map (fig. 5) showing the party's route for about September 11–12, with campsites for those days noted.

2. Lolo Hot Springs, Missoula County, Montana. Space, 6; *Atlas* map 69. The springs emerge from granitic rocks of the Cretaceous-age Idaho batholith very near the batholith's contact with rocks of the Precambrian Belt Group. The large size or texture of the crystals in the granite is indicative of the rock having cooled slowly at a great depth in the earth. The temperature of the hot springs has been measured at 111° F.

3. They crossed the present Montana-Idaho state line into Idaho County, Idaho, east of Lolo Pass, and went down Pack Creek (Glade Creek on *Atlas* map 70) to Packer Meadows. The camp was at the lower end of the meadows. Space, 6; Peebles (LT), 4; *Atlas* map 69.

4. Spruce grouse, *Dendragapus canadensis* [AOU, 298], then unknown to science. See below, September 20, 1805.

5. The Bitterroot Range, which they were now crossing. *Atlas* map 69, 70.

[Clark][1]

Course Distance &c. Septr. 14th 1805

S. 20° W.   6   miles over a high ⟨hilly⟩ mountain Countrey thickley Covered with pine to the forks ⟨passed⟩ of the Creek one of equal Size from the right Side, passed much falling timber this ⟨hi⟩ Mountain is covered with Spruce & Pitch pine fir, & what is called to the Northard Hackmatack & Tamerack, The Creeks verry stoney and has much fall

S. 60° W.[2]   9   miles over a high mountain Steep & almost inaxcessible much falling timber which ⟨cause the⟩ fatigues our men & horses exceedingly, in Slipping over So great a number of logs added to the Steep assents and decents of the Mounts. to the forks of the Creek, the one on our left which we had passed down falling into one Still larger from the left which heads in the Snowey Mountains to the S. E. & South, those two Creeks form a river of 80 yards wide, Containing much water, verry Stoney and rapid. The Creek we Came Down I call Glade Creek, the left hand fork the Killed Colt Creek from our Killing a *Colt* to eate, abov th mouth of Glade fork, the *Flatheads* has a were across to catch sammon [*one line missing, page damaged*]

S. 70° W   2   miles down the [*blank*] River to the mouth of a run on the
          m 17   right Side opposit an Island & camped   turned our horses on the Island   rained Snowed & hailed the greater part of the day all wet and Cold

[Clark]   *September 14th Thursday* [*NB: Saturday*] *1805*

  a Cloudy day in the Valies it rained and hailed, on the top of the mountains Some Snow fell   we Set out early and Crossed a high mountn on the right of the Creek for 6 miles to the forks of the Glade Creek[3] [*NB: one of the heads of the Koos koos kee*][4] the right hand fork which falls in ⟨from⟩ is about the Size of the other, we Crossed to the left Side at the foks,[5] and Crossd a verry high Steep mountain for 9 miles to a large fork from the left[6] which appears to head in the Snow toped mountains Southerley and S. E. we Crossd. Glade Creek above its mouth,[7] at a place the Tushepaws or Flat head Indians have made 2 *wears* across to Catch Sammon and have but latterly left the place I could see no ⟨Signs of⟩ fish, and the grass entirely eaten out by the horses, we proceeded on 2 miles & Encamped opposit a Small Island[8] at the mouth of a branch on the right side of the river which is at this place 80 yards wide, Swift and Stoney, here we wer compelled to kill a Colt for our men & Selves to eat for the want of meat & we named the South fork Colt killed Creek, and this river we Call *Flathead* River—[*WC: The flat head name is Koos koos ke R*][9] The Mountains which we passed to day much worst than yesterday the last excessively bad & Thickly Strowed with falling timber & Pine Spruc fur Hackmatak & Tamerack,[10] Steep & Stoney our men and horses much fatigued, The rain [*blank*]

1. Opposite this entry in the Elkskin-bound Journal is a sketch map (fig. 6) showing the party's route for about September 13–16, with campsites of those days noted.

2. The course is overwritten another illegible one, and then repeated underneath.

3. Brushy Creek, on the left, and Crooked Fork, on the right, in Idaho County, Idaho. Space, 7; *Atlas* map 69, 70.

4. Biddle's insertion refers to the captains' name for the Clearwater River; actually the stream is the Lochsa, which the captains considered a fork of the Clearwater. *Atlas* map 70.

5. Crossing Brushy Creek. Space, 7; *Atlas* map 70.

6. They called it Colt Killed or Killed Colt Creek; present White Sand Creek. Space, 7; *Atlas* map 70.

7. Crossing Lochsa River. Space, 7; *Atlas* map 70.

8. The camp was on the north bank of the Lochsa River, some two miles below the mouth of White Sand (Killed Colt) Creek, near Powell Ranger Station, in Idaho County. In going down into the valley of the Lochsa they had, probably by an error of their guide, deviated from the Lolo Trail, which follows the ridge tops. This would make the journey more difficult and probably about a day longer. Space, 7; Peebles (LT), 5; Cutright (LCPN), 200; *Atlas* map 70.

9. Again, the Lochsa River at this point and again a later insertion by Clark. "Flathead" apparently refers to the Nez Perces, not the Salish of Montana. The word "*Flathead*" appears to have been inserted in place of an erased word.

10. The major trees growing at higher elevations here are the ones noted by Clark: lodgepole pine, Engelmann spruce, and subalpine fir. In the course table Clark uses the term "Pitch pine" for the lodgepole pine, referring to the eastern species with which he

was familiar, *Pinus rigida* Mill. Earlier references to pitch-pine designated different species, but here lodgepole pine is appropriate. The last two named are apparently the same tree, known variously as western, Montana, or mountain, larch, hackmatack, and tamarack, *Larix occidentalis* Nutt. Hitchcock et al., 1:121; Little (CIH), 34-W.

[Clark]   *September 15th Friday 1805*

West   4   mile down the Creek bottoms Passing over 4 Steep high hills to a run at an old Indian Camp at a fishing place, where we wer Some time e'er, we found the proper road which assends a high mountain   road excessively bad. Take the wrong road*[1]

N. W.   4   miles assending a high Steep ruged Mountain winding in every direction, the timber has been burnt & lies in every direction, Several horses rolld down much hurt   my portable desk broken, from the top of those mountains a Snow mountain from S E to S W.   we leave the river to our left hand, found a Spring on the top of the mountain where we halted to Dine & wate for the party.   rained

N. W.   4   miles assend a Steep ruged mountain passing over high Stoney
          ___   knobs maney parts bare of timber, the[y] haveing burnt it down
           12   & as it lies on the ground in every direction we could find no water deturmd to Camp as it was late and make use of Snow for to boil our Coalt meat & make Supe.   we Camped on a high Pinical of the mountain   Two of our horses gave out to day and left.   the road as bad as it can possibly be to pass.

[Clark]   *Wednesday [NB: Sunday] Septr. 15th 1805*

   We set out early.   the morning Cloudy and proceeded on Down the right Side of [*NB: Koos koos kee*][2] River over Steep points rockey & buschey as usial for 4 miles to an old Indian fishing place, here the road leaves the river to the left and assends a *mountain* winding in every direction to get up the Steep assents[3] & to pass the emence quantity of falling timber which had falling from dift. causes i e. fire & wind and has deprived the Greater part of the Southerley Sides of this mountain of its gren timber, 4 miles up the mountain I found a Spring and halted for the rear to come up and to let our horses rest & feed, about 2 hours the rear of the party came up much fatigued & horses more So, Several horses Sliped and roled down Steep hills which hurt them verry much   The one which

Carried my desk & Small trunk Turned over & roled down a mountain for 40 yards & lodged against a tree, broke the Desk the horse escaped and appeared but little hurt   Some others verry much hurt, from this point I observed a range of high mountains Covered with Snow from S E. to S W with Their top bald or void of timber.[4]   after two hours delay we proceeded on up the mountain Steep & ruged as usial, more timber near the top, when we arrived at the top As we Conceved we could find no water and Concluded to Camp[5] and make use of the Snow we found on the top to cook the remnt. of our Colt & make our Supe, evening verry Cold and Cloudy. Two of our horses gave out, pore and too much hurt to proceed on and left in the rear—   nothing killed to day except 2 Phests.

From this mountain I could observe high ruged mountains in every direction as far as I could See.   with the greatest exertion we Could only make 12 miles up this mountain and encamped on the top of the mountain near a Bank of old Snow about 3 feet deep lying on the Northern Side of the ⟨hills⟩ mountain and in Small banks on the top & leavel parts of the mountain, we melted the Snow to drink, and Cook our horse flesh to eat.

1. The asterisk at the end of this passage is not explainable.

2. Biddle has added the name to a blank space.

3. They went down the north side of the Lochsa, paralleling modern U.S. Highway 12, to about the present location of Wendover Campground, Idaho County, Idaho, then turned north along Wendover Ridge to climb back to the Lolo Trail. Space, 9; Peebles (LT), 5; *Atlas* map 70.

4. Again, the Bitterroot Range, along the Montana-Idaho border. *Atlas* maps 69, 70.

5. They camped more or less at the point where they rejoined the Lolo Trail, in Idaho County, near present Forest Service Road #500. Space, 9; *Atlas* map 70.

[Clark]   *Septr. 16th Satturday 1805*

Course &c.

S. 75° W   13   miles over the mountain passing emince Dificuelt Knobs
            ——   Stones much falling timber and emencely Steep with great
            13   dificulty we proseeded on. The *Snow* began to fall about 3
            ==   hours before Day and Contd. all day. I found great dificulty
                  in finding the road in the evining as the Snow had fallen from
                  6 to 8 Inches deep, verry Cold and the pine which in maney

6. On the Lolo Trail, Idaho, September 13–16, 1805,
Elkskin-bound Journal ➔

places verry thick So covered with Snow, as in passing I became wet discover 8 distinct kinds of pine on those mountains   We Encamped on a Small branch running to the right.
Killed a Coalt & [eate it]¹

[Clark]   *Saturday [NB: Monday] Septr. 16th 1805*

  began to Snow about 3 hours before Day and Continud all day   the
Snow in The morning 4 Inches deep on The old Snow, and by night we
found it from 6 to 8 Inches deep   I walked in front to keep the road and
found great dificuelty in keeping it as in maney places the Snow had entirely filled up the track, and obliged me to hunt Several minits for the
track   at 12 oClock we halted on the top of the mountain² to worm & dry
our Selves a little as well as to let our horses rest and graze a little on Some
long grass which I observed, (on) The South ⟨Knobs⟩ Steep hills Side &
falling timber Continue to day, and a thickly timbered Countrey of 8 different kinds of pine,³ which are So covered with Snow, that in passing
thro them we are continually covered with Snow, I have been wet and as
cold in every part as I ever was in my life, indeed I was at one time fearfull my feet would freeze in the thin mockersons which I wore, after a
Short delay in the middle of the Day, I took one man and proceeded on
as fast as I could about 6 miles to a Small branch passing to the right,
halted and built fires for the party agains their arrival which was at Dusk
verry cold and much fatigued   we Encamped at this Branch in a thickly
timbered bottom which was Scercely large enough for us to lie leavil,⁴
men all wet cold and hungary. Killed a Second Colt which we all Suped
hartily on and thought it fine meat.

  I saw 4 Black tail Deer to day before we Set out which came up the
mountain and what is Singular Snaped 7 tims at a large buck.   it is Singular as my gun has a Steel frisen⁵ and never Snaped 7 times before   in
examining her found the flint loose   to describe the road of this day
would be a repitition of yesterday excpt the Snow which made it much
wors to proseed as we had in maney places to derect our Selves by the
appearence of the rubbings of the Packs⁶ against the trees which have
limbs quiet low and bending downwards

1. The bracketed material is from Thwaites (LC), 3:70, as it is not apparent on the damaged page of the Elkskin-bound Journal.

2. Perhaps on Spring Hill (or Spring Mountain), in northern Idaho County, Idaho, not marked on fig. 6 or *Atlas* map 70. Space, 10.

3. Clark uses the general term "pine" for all the types of evergreen conifers. The species include: lodgepole pine, Douglas fir, subalpine fir, Englemann spruce, whitebark pine, *Pinus albicaulis* Engelm., grand fir, *Abies grandis* (Dougl.) Lindl., and mountain hemlock, *Tsuga mertensiana* (Bong.) Carr. Other possibilities at lower elevations are: ponderosa pine, western white pine, *Pinus monticola* Dougl., and western redcedar, *Thuja plicata* Donn. Space, 10–11; Cutright (LCPN), 203–4; Little (CIH), 43-W, 6-W, 62-W, 93-W, 90-W; Daubenmire, 301, 314–15; Pfister et al., 17.

4. Near the rock mounds later called Indian Post Office (which none of the journals mentions), perhaps on Moon Creek, Idaho County. Space, 10; Peebles (LT), 6; Cutright (LCPN), 205 n. 14; *Atlas* map 70.

5. The frizzen is the upright piece of metal against which the flint in a flintlock firearm strikes to produce the spark that fires the powder. The repeated misfires were probably due to the wet conditions as well as the loose flint. Russell (GEF), 288–89.

6. The packs of the Indians who had passed by, going east or west. There is a blank half-page following this entry. The next entry starts at the top of a new page (p. 116) in Codex G.

[Clark] [1]

Course Dist &c. 17th Septr 1805 Sunday

S. 50° W.   12   miles over high knobs of the mountain   passed three Dreans
to right and Encamped on one to the left. Springs at all those
drians &.   road emencely bad as usial, no Snow in the hollers   all the high knobs of the mounts Covered   passed on
a Divideing ridge on which we had to Cross over emensely
high Knobs.   roads bad   Killed a few Phesants only. Killd. a
colt to eate.

[Clark]   *Sunday [NB: Tuesday] 17th Septr. 1805*

Cloudy morning   our horses much Scattered which detained us untill
one oClock P. M. at which time we Set out the falling Snow & Snow
⟨falling⟩ from the trees which kept us wet all the after noon   passed over
Several high ruged Knobs and Several dreans & Springs passing to the
right, & passing on the ridge devideing the waters of two Small rivers.[2]
road excessively bad   Snow on the Knobs, no Snow in the vallies   Killed

a fiew Pheasents which was not Sufficient for our Supper which compelled us to kill Something. a coalt being the most useless part of our
Stock he fell a Prey to our appetites. The after part of the day fare, we
made only 10 miles to day two horses fell & hurt themselves very ⟨well⟩
much. we Encamped on the top of a high Knob of the mountain at a
run passing to the left.[3] we proceed on as yesterday, & with dificulty
found the road

1. Opposite this entry in the Elkskin-bound Journal is a sketch map (fig. 7) showing the
party's route for about September 16–18, with campsites of those days noted. Some
mileage notes are also annexed.

2. Perhaps Gravey and Serpent creeks. Space, 11; *Atlas* map 70.

3. Whitehouse says they camped at a "Sinque hole full of water." The description fits a
site on the first saddle east of Indian Grave Peak, in Idaho County, Idaho. Space, 11–12;
Peebles (LT), 6; *Atlas* map 70.

[Lewis]   *Wednesday September 18th 1805.*[1]

Cap Clark set out this morning to go a head with six hunters.[2] there
being no game in these mountains we concluded it would be better for
one of us to take the hunters and hurry on to the leavel country a head
and there hunt and provide some provision ⟨for⟩ while the other remained with and brought on the party the latter of these was my part;
accordingly I directed the horses to be gotten up early being determined
to force my march as much as the abilities of our horses would permit.
the negligence of one of the party Willard who had a spare horse ⟨in⟩ not
attending to him and bringing him up last evening was the cause of our
detention this morning untill ½ after 8 A M when we set out. I sent
willard back to serch for his horse, and proceeded on with the party at
four in the evening he overtook us without the horse, we marched 18
miles this day and encamped on the side of a steep mountain;[3] we suffered for water this day passing one rivulet only; we wer fortunate in
finding water in a steep raviene about ½ maile from our camp. this
morning we finished the remainder of our last coult. we dined & suped
on a skant proportion of portable soupe,[4] a few canesters of which, a little
bears oil and about 20 lbs. of candles form our stock of provision, the

7. On the Lolo Trail, Idaho, September 16–18, 1805,
Elkskin-bound Journal ⊕

only recources being our guns & packhorses. the first is but a poor dependance in our present situation where there is nothing upon earth exept
ourselves and a few small pheasants, small grey Squirrels, and a blue bird
of the vulter kind about the size of a turtle dove or jay bird.[5] our rout lay
along the ridge of a high mountain course S. 20 W. 18 m. used the snow
for cooking.—

[Clark][6]

Course Distance 18th Septr. 1805 Monday

S 85 W   32[7]   miles nearly I proceeded on with the hunters to a Creek
running from the right which I call hungary Creek as we have
nothing to eate   passed a run & Several Springs which pass to
the right, Keep on a Dividg ridge & Crossed Several high and
Steep Knobs   a great quantity of falling timber   at 20 miles I
beheld a wide and extencive vallie in a West & S W Direction
about [*blank*] miles. a high mountain beyond   Drewyer shot
at a Deer   we did not get it.   Killed nothing in those emence
mountains of stones falling timber & brush

[Clark]   *Monday [NB: Wednesday] 18th Septr. 1805*[8]
    [*WC: The want of provisions together with the dificuely of passing those emence
mountains dampened the Spirits of the party which induced us to resort to Some
plan of reviving ther Sperits. I deturmined to take a party of the hunters and proceed on in advance to Some leavel Country, where there was game kill Some meat
& Send it back, &c.*] a fair morning cold   I proceded on in advance with
Six hunters [*WC: and let it be understood that my object was*] to try and find
deer or Something to kill [*WC: & Send back to the party*]   we passed over a
countrey Similar to the one of yesterday more falling timber passed Several runs & Springs passing to the right   from the top of a high part of
the mountain at 20 miles I had a view of an emence Plain and leavel
Countrey to the S W. & West at a great distance[9]   a high mountain in
advance beyond the Plain,[10] Saw ⟨but little⟩ [*WC: no*] Sign of deer and
nothing else, much falling timber, made 32 miles and Encamped on a
bold running Creek passing to the left which I call *Hungery Creek*[11] as at

that place we had nothing to eate. I halted only one hour to day to let our horses feed on Grass ⟨and rest⟩ [WC: hill side] and rest

1. Here begins Lewis's fragmentary Codex Fd, consisting of eight pages from one of the red books, covering September 18–22, 1805, dates on which the captains were separated while Clark was scouting ahead of the main party. See Introduction and Appendix C, vol. 2.

2. Including Reubin Field and John Shields.

3. About three miles west of Bald Mountain, in Idaho County, Idaho. Space, 13. It is marked "Party Camped 18th" on *Atlas* map 70. On *Atlas* maps 70 and 71, during this period of separation, Clark notes both the campsites of his advance party and the main body under Lewis, with dates. Clark's camps are noted with "Encamped" and the others with "Party camped" or simply "Camped." Lewis's camps were, of course, considerably behind Clark's for the same date.

4. The soup, purchased by Lewis in Philadelphia, may have been either in the form of dry powder or a thick liquid. Such preparations had apparently been in use by armies for some years. Presumably water was added. Supplies from Private Vendors [June 1803], Jackson (LLC), 1:81–82; Summary of Purchases [June 1803], ibid., 1:97; Chuinard (OOMD), 160–62.

5. The squirrel may be Richardson's red squirrel, *Tamiasciurus hudsonicus richardsoni;* see below, February 24 and 25, 1806. Burroughs, 98–99; Coues (HLC), 2:600 n. 32. The blue bird may be the pinyon jay of August 1, 1805, but some sources give it as the scrub jay, *Aphelocoma coerulescens* [AOU, 481], or Steller's jay, *Cyanocitta stelleri* [AOU, 478]. Holmgren, 31; Space, 13. Each choice creates problems when compared with Lewis's entry of September 20 (see below), but the scrub jay seems the least likely possibility. The turtle dove used for comparison is the mourning dove, *Zenaida macroura* [AOU, 316].

6. The entries in Clark's Elkskin-bound Journal expand each day from simple courses and distances; this is particularly noticeable from this date, when the two captains separated. It seems likely that Clark was using the sheets later bound in elkskin as the first draft for his notebook journals, but at what point he ceased writing in the notebook Codex G is not clear. See Introduction, vol. 2.

7. This was "36," the latter number converted to "2."

8. For the next few entries of Clark in Codex G, there is much writing by him in red ink. These words may have been added in 1810 to assist Biddle. This material is here set off with brackets and Clark's initials. Some slight rearrangement has been made for clarity.

9. Standing on Sherman Peak, Clark was viewing the open prairies in Lewis and Idaho counties, Idaho, northwest of Grangeville, including Camas and Nez Perce prairies. Space, 13; *Atlas* maps 70, 71.

10. Probably Cottonwood Butte, but perhaps also the Blue Mountains in Oregon. Space, 13.

11. Clark camped on Hungery Creek, just above the entrance of Doubt Creek, in Idaho County. Hungery Creek was for many years known as Obia Creek, but Clark's

name has been restored. Only Clark's campsites, not those of the main party during the separation period, appear on the sketch maps in the Elkskin-bound Journal; see fig. 7. Space, 13; *Atlas* map 70.

[Lewis]   *Thursday September 19th 1805.*

Set out this morning a little after sun rise and continued our rout about the same course of yesterday or S. 20 W. for 6 miles when the ridge terminated and we to our inexpressable joy discovered a large tract of Prairie country lying to the S. W. and widening as it appeared to extend to the W.[1] through that plain the Indian informed us that the Columbia river, in which we were in surch run.   this plain appeared to be about 60 Miles distant, but our guide assured us that we should reach it's borders to-morrow   the appearance of this country, our only hope for subsistance greatly revived the sperits of the party already reduced and much weakened for the want of food.   the country is thickly covered with a very heavy growth of pine of which I have ennumerated 8 distinct species. after leaving the ridge we asscended and decended several steep mountains in the distance of 6 miles further when we struck a Creek about 15 yards wide.[2]   our course being S. 35 W. we continued our rout 6 miles along the side of this creek upwards passing 2 of it's branches which flowed in from the N. 1st at the place we struck the creek and the other 3 miles further.[3]   the road was excessively dangerous along this creek being a narrow rockey path generally on the side of steep precipice, from which in many places if ether man or horse were precipitated they would inevitably be dashed in pieces. Fraziers horse fell from this road in the evening, and roled with his load near a hundred yards into the Creek. we all expected that the horse was killed but to our astonishment when the load was taken off him he arose to his feet & appeared to be but little injured, in 20 minutes he proceeded with his load.   this was the most wonderfull escape I ever witnessed, the hill down which he roled was almost perpendicular and broken by large irregular and broken rocks. the course of this Creek upwards due W.   we encamped on the Stard. side of it in a little raviene,[4] having traveled 18 miles over a very bad road. we took a small quantity of portable soup, and retired to rest much fatiegued.   several of the men are unwell of the disentary.   brakings out, or irruptions of the Skin, have also been common with us for some time.

[Clark][5]

Cours Distance & 19th Septr. Tuesday

S 60 W nearly ⟨30 22⟩ 12[6] miles on a Direct Course & at doubl the distance wind around falling timber to a branch running to the left & Camped at 6 miles found a horse on the head of the Creek in Some glades, he was not fat the me[n] beg leave to kill him which I granted, after they filled themselves, I had the ballance hung up for Capt Lewis and proceeded on, in the time the one half of the party was skining Cooking &c. the others were hunting, without seeing a track of any animal. The road up this Creek is much wors than any other part as the hills Sides are Steep and at maney places obliged for Several yds. to pass on the Sides of rocks where one false Step of a horse would be certan. destruction. Crossed over a mountain and the heads of a branch of hungary Creek over ridges and much falling timber, and a 2d high mountain of like description to a large Creek running west for 4 miles then turned South. I keped down 4 miles & turned up to the right over a mountain which was bad as usial to a branch which runs to the left and Camped. The road to day wors than usial owing to the falling timber &c. we killed 2 phsts. but few birds. the Blue jay & Small white headed Hawk Some Crows & ravins.

[Clark] *Tuesday [NB: Thursday] 19th Septr. 1805*

Set out early proceeded on up the [EC: *Hungry*] Creek passing through a Small glade at 6 miles at which place we found a horse. I derected him killed and hung up for the party after takeing a brackfast off for our Selves which we thought fine after Brackfast proceed on up the Creek two miles & left it to our right passed over a mountain, and the heads of branch of hungary Creek,[7] two high mountains, ridges and through much falling timber (which caused our road of to day to be double the derect distance on the Course[)] Struck a large Creek[8] passing to our left which I Kept down for 4 miles and left it to our left & passed ⟨over a⟩ [WC: *down the*] mountain bad falling timber to a Small Creek passing to our left and Encamped.[9] I killed 2 Pheasents, but fiew birds [WC: *are to be Seen*] Blue jay, Small white headed hawk,[10] Some Crows & ravins & large hawks. road bad. [WC: *as we decend the mountain the heat becomes more proseptable every mile*]

216

1. The same prairie country viewed by Clark's party on September 18, apparently seen from the same viewpoint, Sherman Peak, Idaho County, Idaho. The route for about September 18–20 is sketched in fig. 8. Space, 14; *Atlas* map 70.

2. Hungery creek at the mouth of Doubt Creek. Space, 14; *Atlas* map 70.

3. Doubt Creek and Bowl Creek. Space, 14; Peebles (LT), 9; *Atlas* map 70.

4. On Hungery Creek, near the mouth of a small, nameless stream. Space, 14; *Atlas* map 70.

5. Opposite this entry in the Elkskin-bound Journal is a sketch map (fig. 8) showing the party's route for about September 18–20, with campsites of those days noted.

6. It is not clear whether Clark is choosing twelve or twenty-two miles.

7. Fish Creek. Space, 14; *Atlas* map 70.

8. Present Eldorado Creek. Space, 14; Peebles (LT), 7.

9. Cedar Creek, near the present Lewis and Clark Grove. Space, 14; Peebles (LT), 7; *Atlas* map 71.

10. Perhaps the black-shouldered kite, *Elanus caeruleus* [AOU, 328]. Holmgren, 31.

[Lewis]   *Friday September 20th 1805.*

This morning my attention was called to a species of bird[1] which I had never seen before. [NB: *Copy for Dr Barton*] It was reather larger than a robbin, tho' much it's form and action. the colours were a blueish brown on the back the wings and tale black, as wass a stripe above the croop ¾ of an inch wide in front of the neck, and two others of the same colour passed from it's eyes back along the sides of the head. the top of the head, neck brest and belley and butts of the wing were of a fine yellowish brick ⟨yellow⟩ reed. it was feeding on the buries of a species of shoe-make or ash[2] which grows common in country & which I first observed on 2d of this month. I have also observed two birds of a blue colour both of which I believe to be of the haulk or vulter kind. the one[3] of a blue shining colour with a very high tuft of feathers on the head a long tale, it feeds on flesh the beak and feet black. it's note is chă-ăh, chă-ăh. it is about the size of a pigeon; and in shape and action resembles the jay bird.— another bird[4] of very similar genus, the note resembling the mewing of the cat, with a white head and a light blue colour is also common, as are a black species of woodpecker about the size of the lark woodpecker[5] Three species of Pheasants,[6] a large black species, with some white feathers irregularly scattered on the brest neck and belley a smaller kind of a dark uniform colour with a red stripe above the eye, and a brown and yellow species that a good deel resembles the phesant common to the Atlantic States. we were detained this morning untill ten oclock in consequence of not being enabled to ⟨get up⟩ collect our horses. we had proceeded about 2 miles when we found the greater part of a horse which Capt Clark had met with and killed for us.[7] he informed me by note that he should proceed as fast as possible to the leavel country which lay to the S. W. of us, which we discovered from the hights of the mountains on the 19th there he intended to hunt untill our arrival. at one oclock we halted [*X: on a small branch runing to the left*][8] and made a hearty meal on our horse beef much to the comfort of our hungry stomachs. here I larnt that one of the Packhorses with his load was missing and immediately dispatched Baptiest Lapage who had charge of him, to surch for him. he returned at 3 OC. without the horse. The load of the horse was of considerable value consisting of merchandize and all my stock of winter cloathing. I therefore dispatched two of my best woodsmen in surch of him, and proceeded with the party. Our rout lay through a thick forrest of large pine the general course being S. 25 W. and distance about 15 miles. our road was much obstructed by fallen timber particularly in the evening we encamped on a ridge[9] where ther was but little grass for our horses, and at a distance from water. however we obtained as much as served our culinary purposes and suped on our beef. the soil as you leave the hights of the mountains becomes gradually more fertile. the land through which we passed this evening is of an excellent quality tho very broken, it is a dark grey soil. a grey free stone appearing in large masses above the earth in many places.[10] saw the hucklebury, [*NB: Copy for Dr Barton*] honeysuckle, and alder common to the Atlantic states, also a kind of honeysuckle which bears a white bury and rises about 4 feet high not common but to the western side of the rockey mountains. a growth which resembles the choke cherry bears a black bury with a single stone of a sweetish taste, it rises to the hight of 8 or 10 feet and grows in thick clumps. the Arborvita is also common and grows to an immence size, being from 2 to 6 feet in diameter.[11]

[Clark] [12]

Course Dist. Friday 20th Septr 1805

Nearly S W	12	miles over a mountain to a low ridgey Countrey covered with large pine, passed into the forks of a large Creek which we kept down about 2 miles & left it to the left hand and crossed the heads of Som Dreans of the Creek & on a ruged Deviding ridge, road as bad as usial no game of Sign to day
West	3 17	miles to an Indian Camp in a leavel rich open Plain I met 3 boys who I gave a pice of ribin to each & Sent them to the ⟨Ca⟩ Villages, I Soon after met a man whome I gave a handkerchief and he escorted me to the grand Chiefs Lodge, who was with the most of the nation gorn to war those people treated us well gave us to eate roots dried roots made in bread, roots boiled, one Sammon, Berries of red haws some dried, my arrival raised great Confusion, all running to See us, after a Delay of an hour I deturmined to go lower & turn out & hunt, a principal man informed me his Camp was on my way and there was fish I concluded to go to his village, and Set out accompd. by about 100 men womin & boys 2 mile across the Plains, & halted tuned. out 4 men to hunt, he gave us a Sammon to eate, I found that his Situation was not on the river as I expected & that this Sammon was dried, & but fiew— This course is N. 70° W. 2 miles across a rich leavel Plain in which grt quantities of roots have been geathered and in heaps. those roots are like onions, Sweet when Dried, and tolerably good in bread, I eate much & am Sick in the evening. those people have an emence quantities of Roots which is their Principal food. The hunters discovered Som Signs but killed nothing

[Clark]   *Wednesday [NB: Friday] 20th September 1805*

I Set out early and proceeded on through a Countrey as ruged as usial   passed over a low mountain into the forks of a large Creek which I kept down 2 miles [13] and assended a Steep mountain leaveing the Creek to our left hand   passed the head of Several dreans on a divideing ridge,

8. On the Lolo Trail, Idaho, September 18–20, 1805,
Elkskin-bound Journal ⊕

9. On the Lolo Trail to Canoe Camp at the Junction
of the North Fork Clearwater and Clearwater Rivers, Idaho,
September 20–October 7, 1805, Elkskin-bound Journal ⊕

and at 12 miles decended the mountain to a leavel pine Countrey proceeded on through a butifull Countrey for three miles to a Small Plain in
which I found maney Indian lodges,[14] at the distance of 1 mile from the
lodges I met 3 [WC: Indian] boys, when they Saw me ran and *hid* themselves [WC: *in the grass I dismounted gave my gun & horse to one of the men,*]
searched [WC: *in the grass and*] found [WC: *2 of the boys*] gave them Small
pieces of ribin & Sent them forward to the village [WC: *Soon after*] a
man Came out to meet me with great Caution & Conducted ⟨me⟩ us to a
large Spacious Lodge which he told me (by Signs) was the Lodge of his
great Chief who had Set out 3 days previous with all the Warriers of the
nation to war on a South West derection & would return in 15 or 18 days.
the fiew men that were left in the Village aged, great numbers of women
geathered around me with much apparent Signs of fear, and apr. pleased
they ⟨those people⟩ gave us a Small piece of Buffalow meat, Some dried
Salmon beries & roots in different States, Some round and much like an
onion which they call ⟨*Pas she co*⟩ quamash the Bread or Cake is called Pas-
she-co Sweet, of this they make bread & Supe[15] they also gave us the
bread made of this root all of which we eate hartily, I gave them a fiew
Small articles as preasents, and proceeded on with a Chief to his Village
2 miles in the Same Plain, where we were treated kindly in their way and
continued with them all night[16] Those two Villages consist of about 30
double lodges, but fiew men a number of women & children; They call
themselves *Cho pun-nish* or *Pierced Noses;*[17] their dialect appears verry different from the ⟨flat heads⟩ Tushapaws altho origneally the Same people[18]
They are darker than the ⟨Flat heads⟩ Tushapaws ⟨I have seen⟩ Their
dress Similar, with more beads white & blue principally, brass & Copper
in different forms, Shells and ware their haire in the Same way. they are
large Portley men Small women & handsom fetued [NB?: *& featured*]
Emence quantity of the quawmash or *Pas-shi-co* root gathered & in piles
about the plains, those roots[19] grow much an onion in marshey places the
seed are in triangular Shell on the Stalk. they Sweat them in the following manner i. e. dig a large hole 3 feet deep Cover the bottom with Split
wood on the top of which they lay Small Stones of about 3 or 4 Inches
thick, a Second layer of Splited wood & Set the whole on fire which heats

the Stones, after the fire is extinguished they lay grass & mud mixed on the Stones, on that dry grass which Supports the Pâsh-Shi-co root a thin Coat of the Same grass is laid on the top, a Small fire is kept when necessary in the Center of the kile &c.

I find myself verry unwell all the evening from eateing the fish & roots too freely. Sent out the hunters   they killed nothing   Saw Some Signs of deer.

1. The varied thrush, *Ixoreus naevius* [AOU, 763], already known to science but not to Lewis. He gave a longer description on January 31, 1806. Burroughs, 252–54. It was probably Biddle who drew a red vertical line through this material.

2. *Sorbus stichensis* Roem., Pacific, or Sitka, mountain ash, which has red-scarlet berries attractive to birds at this time of year. It also occurs on the North Fork Salmon River in the location of the party's route of September 2, as Lewis indicates. A specimen of this new discovery was collected on September 4. Hitchcock et al., 3:189–90; Booth & Wright, 120; Little (MWH), 194-W; Cutright (LCPN), 196, 416.

3. Steller's jay and new to science. Cutright (LCPN), 210. See Lewis's full description at December 18, 1805.

4. Perhaps the gray jay, *Perisoreus canadensis* [AOU, 484]. Holmgren, 29. See also Lewis's entry of December 18, 1805.

5. The black woodpecker is Lewis's woodpecker while the lark woodpecker is the northern, or common, flicker, *Colaptes auratus* [AOU, 412]. Ibid., 34.

6. All three species were then unknown to science. The first, the blue grouse, Lewis had noted on August 1. The second is the spruce grouse, first noted on September 13, 1805. The third is the Oregon ruffed grouse, *Bonasa umbellus sabini,* now combined with *B. umbellus,* which Lewis again calls a pheasant in comparison. See also February 5 and March 3, 1806. Cutright (LCPN), 210; Burroughs, 215–19.

7. The spot on Hungery Creek, just beyond Lewis's camp of September 19, is marked on *Atlas* map 70.

8. On Fish Creek, or one of its branches in Idaho County, Idaho. Space, 17; Peebles (LT), 9; *Atlas* map 70.

9. Between Dollar and Sixbit creeks, in Idaho County. Space, 17; Peebles (LT), 9; *Atlas* map 70.

10. The short growing season and the high rate of erosion in the steeper mountains combine to produce a soil composed largely of rocky parent materials with little humus. In the forested areas the soil is acidic from decomposition of evergreen needles. This acid leaches minerals from the soil, leaving the soil light colored. The gray freestone is actually granitic rock of the Cretaceous-age Idaho batholith. The granitic rock has a tendency to spall off in slabs that are approximately parallel or conformable to the general erosion surface. This feature causes the weathered rock to appear layered in places.

11. Huckleberry is possibly mountain huckleberry, *Vaccinium membranaceum* Dougl. ex Hook., then new to science. Honeysuckle is western trumpet honeysuckle. Alder is probably Sitka, or wavyleaf, alder, *Alnus sinuata* (Regel) Rydb., if so, then new to science. The alder used for comparison is *A. serrulata* (Ait.) Willd., of the eastern United States. The honeysuckle which bears a white berry is the common snowberry. The plant which resembles the choke cherry is the choke cherry itself. Arborvita is western redcedar. Cutright (LCPN), 210, 212, 402; Hitchcock et al., 4:32, 2:74–76; Booth & Wright, 233. It was probably Biddle who drew a red vertical line through this passage.

12. Opposite Clark's entry of September 30 in the Elkskin-bound Journal is a sketch map (fig. 9) showing the party's route for about September 20–25, with some of the campsites of Clark and of the main party during this time, and with the camp of September 26–October 7 noted.

13. Clark reached the forks of Lolo and Eldorado creeks, crossed the former and went down it. Space, 15. Lolo Creek is "Collins Creek" on *Atlas* map 71, after John Collins of the party.

14. Clark went over Brown's Ridge and down Miles Creek to Weippe Prairie, in Clearwater County, Idaho. Appleman (LC), 283–85; Space, 15; *Atlas* map 71. Weippe Prairie was one of the major camas collecting grounds in the interior Pacific Northwest. Camas was an essential part of the native diet, particularly as a winter store. Not only Nez Perce, but people from as far away as the Pacific Coast came to Weippe to dig camas roots and participate in social activities. Most of the lodges Clark observed were probably late summer or early fall camps. Lodges of poles and bark mats were erected at the camas meadows and in the fall the people retired into the canyons to spend the winter. When people left in the fall, the poles were frequently cached in the area, while the mats were taken into the canyons for use there. Marshall; Ames & Marshall.

15. Camas, a member of the lily family and then new to science. See Lewis's description below, June 11, 1806. Cutright (LCPN), 209. The term *pasigoo* (Clark's "Pas-she-co") is the Shoshone designation for the camas and its edible bulb, historically a staple food. The word literally means "water sego," in reference to the sego lily, a common food in the region. Lewis and Clark wrote this word together with "quamash," that is, *qễmes,* the Nez Perce term for camas, from which the Latin and English designations derive. Sven Liljeblad, personal communication.

16. The first village Clark came to was south of present Weippe, Clearwater County. The second, where they spent the night, was about a mile southwest of Weippe; both were on a branch of Jim Ford Creek. The villages were probably seasonal camps. Appleman (LC), 283–85; *Atlas* map 71.

17. These people are now known as the Nez Perces, from the French for "pierced noses," which corresponds to their sign language designation. The Nez Perce name for themselves is *nimí·pu·,* "the people" or *cú·p'nit* or *cú·p'nitpelu·;* the etymology of the latter term is not known, but suggests pierced noses. Haro Aoki believes that Lewis and Clark's word Chopunnish may derive from *tsoopnit,* "(the act of) punching a hole with a pointed object," and by extension *tsoopnitpeloo* meaning "piercing people." The question of whether

they ever did pierce their noses is still a subject of debate. Nevertheless, Lewis and Clark saw them with ornaments in their noses and the best authorities acknowledge the practice. See Clark's entry of May 7, 1806, and Lewis's of May 13, 1806. They are noted for breeding the spotted Appaloosa horse, but again it is a disputed topic whether they developed the breed. Like many of the mountain tribes of the Northwest, after acquiring horses they made periodic trips across the Rockies to hunt buffalo and assumed many elements of plains culture. American missionaries converted a large portion of the tribe to Christianity in the 1830s and 1840s. Their long history of friendly relations with the whites, beginning with Lewis and Clark, came to an end with the war of 1877, in which a part of the tribe conducted their famous retreat over the Lolo Trail and into Montana, where they were finally captured. Nez Perce tradition says that they first considered killing the members of the Corps of Discovery but were dissuaded by a woman who first met white men while a prisoner of Indians in Canada and was kindly treated by them. See below, Clark's first entry for September 21, 1805. Aoki; Josephy (NP), 3–15, 37–38, 645–46, and passim; Josephy (NNP); Hodge 2:65–68; Space, 16; Ronda (LCAI), 158–61.

18. How Clark reached this conclusion is not apparent. The Nez Perces belong to the Shahaptian (Sahaptin) language family, the Flatheads (Salish) to the Salishan family. Hodge, 2:416–18, 519–20.

19. Someone, perhaps Biddle, has drawn a vertical line through this passage to the end of the paragraph, but not in the usual red ink.

[Lewis]   *Saturday September 21st 1805.*

We were detained this morning untill 11 OCk. in consequence of not being able to collect our horses. we then set out and proceeded along the ridge on which we had encamped, leaving which at 1½ we passed a large creek runing to the left just above it's junction with another which run parrallel with and on the left of our road before we struck the creek;[1] through the level wide and heavy timbered bottom of this creek we proceeded about 2½ miles when bearing to the right we passed a broken country heavily timbered great quantities of which had fallen and so obstructed our road that it was almost impracticable to proceed in many places. though these hills we proceeded about 5 Ms. when we passed a small creek[2] on which Capt Clark encamped on the 19th passing this creek we continued our rout 5 Ms thro' a similar country when we struck a large creek at the forks,[3] passed the Northen branch and continued down it on the West side 1 mile and encamped in a small open bottom[4] where there was tolerable food for our horses. I directed the horses to be hubbled to prevent delay in the morning being determined to make a forced march tomorrow in order to reach if possible the open country. we killed a few Pheasants, and I killd a prarie woolf[5] which together with the ballance of our horse beef and some crawfish[6] which we obtained in the creek enabled us to make one more hearty meal, not knowing where the next was to be found. the Arborvita [*NB: Copy for Dr Barton*][7] increases in quantity and size. I saw several sticks today large enough to form eligant perogues of at least 45 feet in length.— I find myself growing weak for the want of food and most of the men complain of a similar deficiency and have fallen off very much. the general course of this day S 30 W 15 M.—

[Clark]   *Septr. 21st Saturday 1805*[8]

a fine morning   Sent out all the hunters early in different directions to Kill Something and delayed with the Indians to prevent Suspicion & to acquire as much information as possible.   one of them Drew me a Chart of the river & nations below informed of one falls below which the white men lived from whome they got white beeds cloth &c. &c. The day proved warm, 2 Chifs of Bands visited me to day— the hunters all returned without any thing, I collected a horse load of roots & 3 Sammon & Sent R Fields with one Indian to meet Capt Lewis   at 4 oClock Set out with the other men to the river, passed thro a fine Pine Country   decended a Steep ruged hill verry long to a Small river which comes from our left and I suppose it to be [*blank*] River   passed down the river 2 miles on a Steep hill side   at 11 oClock P. M. arrived at a camp of 5 Squars a boy & 2 Children   those people were glad to See us & gave us drid Sammon   one had formerly been taken by the Minitarries of the north & Seen white men, our guide called the Chief who was fishing on the other Side of the river, whome I found a Cherfull man of about 65   I gave him a Medal.

[Clark]   *Thursday [NB: Saturday] 21st Septr. 1805*

A fine morning   Sent out all the hunters in different directions to hunt deer, I myself delayd with the Chief to prevent Suspission and to Collect by Signs as much information as possible about the river and

Countrey in advance. The Cheif drew me a kind of chart of the river, and informed me that a greater Cheif than himself was fishing at the river half a days march from his village called the twisted hare, and that the river forked a little below his Camp[9] and at a long distance below & below 2 large forks one from the left & the other from the right[10] the river passed thro'gh the mountains at which place was a great fall of the water passing through the rocks,[11] at those falls white people lived from whome they preceured the white Beeds & Brass &c. which the womin wore; a Chief of another band visit me to day and Smoked a pipe, I gave my handkerchief & a Silver Cord with a little Tobacco to those Chiefs, The hunters all return without any thing, I purchased as much Provisions as I could with what fiew things I chaned to have in my Pockets, Such a Salmon Bread roots & berries, & Sent one man R. Fields with an Indian to meet Capt. Lewis, and at 4 oClock P M. Set out to the river, met a man at dark on his way from the river to the village, whome I hired and gave the neck handkerchief of one of the men, to polit me to the Camp of the twisted hare,[12] we did not arrive at the Camp of the Twisted hare but oppost, untill half past 11 oClock P M.[13]   found at this Camp five Squars & 3 Children. my guide called to the Chief who was Encamped with 2 others on a Small Island in the river, he Soon joind me, I found him a Chearfull man with apparant Siencerity, I gave him a medal &c. and Smoked untill 1 oClock a. m. and went to Sleep. The Countrey from the mountains to the river hills is a leavel rich butifull Pine Countrey badly watered, thinly timbered & covered with grass—[14] The weather verry worm after decending into the low Countrey,— the river hills are verry high & Steep, Small bottoms to this little river which is Flat head[15] & is 160 yards wide and Sholey This river is the one we killed the first Coalt on near a fishing *were*

I am verry Sick to day and puke which relive me.

1. The first is Eldorado Creek, the second Dollar Creek, in Idaho County, Idaho. Space, 18; Peebles (LT), 9; *Atlas* map 71.

2. Cedar Creek. Space, 18; Peebles (LT), 9; *Atlas* map 71.

3. Present Lolo (Collins) Creek. Space, 18; Peebles (LT), 9; *Atlas* map 71.

4. On Lolo Creek, in Clearwater County, Idaho; the creek is at this point the boundary between Idaho and Clearwater counties. Space 19; *Atlas* map 71.

5. The coyote, *Canis latrans*.

6. Some variety of *Astacus,* crayfish. Pennack, 461.

7. It was apparently Biddle who drew a red vertical line through this material.

8. From this point the entries in the Elkskin-bound Journal become more like those of a regular daily journal. See the Introduction, vol. 2.

9. The junction of the North Fork Clearwater with the main stream, in Clearwater County, Idaho, west of present Orofino. *Atlas* map 71.

10. The first is probably the Snake River, the second the Columbia.

11. Celilo Falls; see below, October 22, 1805. The chief was probably misinformed about white men living there at the time. Ronda (LCAI), 159.

12. Apparently his name was Walamottinin, meaning "hair or forelock bunched and tied." Josephy (NP), 5 and n. 3. In Nez Perce it is *walamoʔtktáyniñ,* "with hair carelessly tied."

13. This camp was on the Clearwater River on the "Fishing Island" on fig. 9 and *Atlas* map 71, about a mile above present Orofino, Clearwater County. Space, 17. While there is no archaeological information on this specific locality of Fish Island, a major concentration of Nez Perces lived at the confluence of the North Fork and the Clearwater because of the salmon fishing. The area has been extensively modified by construction of Dworshak Dam on the North Fork just above the confluence, and an associated fish hatchery at the confluence itself. However, limited archaeological research in the area has exposed archaeological remains extending back several thousand years. Ames; Mattson.

14. Clark is describing parkland vegetation of the ponderosa pine where widely scattered trees appear as in an open park, with drought tolerant grasses covering the spaces between the trees. The dominant grasses of the area are Idaho fescue, *Festuca idahoensis* Elmer, and bluebunch wheatgrass, *Agropyron spicatum* (Pursh) Scribn. & Smith, the latter plant being new to science. Küchler, map; Daubenmire, 307; Cutright (LCPN), 306, 408.

15. Their first name for the combination of Whitesand (Killed Colt) Creek, Lochsa River, and the Clearwater River; they changed the name later to Kooskooskee River, as on *Atlas* map 71. The word appears to have been added to a blank space.

[Lewis]   *Sunday September 22cd 1805.*[1]

Notwithstanding my positive directions to hubble the horses last evening one of the men neglected to comply.   he plead ignorance of the order.   this neglect however detained us untill ½ after eleven OCk at which time we renewed our march, our course being about west.   we had proceeded about two and a half miles when we met Reubin Fields one of oure hunters,[2] whom Capt. Clark had dispatched to meet us with some dryed fish and roots that he had procured from a band of Indians, whose lodges were about eight miles in advance. I ordered the party to halt for the purpose of taking some refreshment. I divided the fish roots and buries, and was happy to find a sufficiency to satisfy compleatly all our appetites. Fields also killed a crow[3]   after refreshing ourselves we proceeded to the village[4] due West 7½ Miles where we arrived at 5 OCk. in the afternoon   our rout was through lands heavily timbered, the larger wood entirely pine.   the country except the last 3 miles was broken and decending   the pleasure I now felt in having tryumphed over the rocky Mountains and decending once more to a level and fertile country where there was every rational hope of finding a comfortable subsistence for myself and party can be more readily conceived than expressed, nor was the flattering prospect of the final success of the expedition less pleasing.   on our approach to the village which consisted of eighteen lodges most of the women fled to the neighbouring woods on horseback with their children, a circumstance I did not expect as Capt. Clark had previously been with them and informed them of our pacific intentions towards them and also the time at which we should most probably arrive. the men seemed but little concerned, and several of them came to meet us at a short distance from their lodges unarmed.

[Clark]   September 22nd Sunday 1805
   our first course of yesterday was nearly

N. 80° W.		winding thro a Grassy Pine Country of fine land for 12 miles
S. 70 W.	3	miles down a Steep hill & on a hill Side a Creek to the right to the river from the left at a rapid
West	2	miles down the ⟨West⟩ N Side of the River and Encamped, in
miles	17	the morning proceeded down to the Cheif Lodge on an Island, found 3 men fishing hot day

a fine morning, I proceed on down the little river to about 1½ a mile & found the Chif in a Canoe Comeing to meet me   I got into his Canoe & Crossed over to his Camp on a Small Island at a rapid   Sent out the hunters leaving one to take care of the baggage, & after eating a part of a Samn. I Set out on my return to meet Capt. Lewis with the Chief & his Son   at 2 miles met Shields with 3 Deer, I took a Small peice & Changed for his horse which was fresh & proced on   this horse threw me 3 times which hurt me Some.   at Dark met Capt Lewis   Encamped at the first

Village   men much fatigued & reduced, the Supply which I sent by R Flds. was timely, they all eate hartily of roots & fish, 2 horses lost 1 Days journey back

[Clark]   *Friday [NB: Sunday] 22nd Septr. 1805*

a verry worm day   the hunters Shild killed 3 Deer this morning. I left them on the Island and Set out with the Chief & his Son on a young horse for the Village at which place I expected to meet Capt Lewis   this young horse in fright threw himself & me 3 times on the Side of a Steep hill & hurt my hip much, Cought a Coalt which we found on the roade & I rode it for Several miles untill we saw the Chiefs horses, he cought one & we arrived at his Village at Sunset, & himself and myslf walked up to the 2d Village where I found Capt Lewis & the party Encamped, much fatigued, & hungery, much rejoiced to find something to eate of which They appeared to partake plentifully. I cautioned them of the Consequences of eateing too much &c.

The planes appeared covered with Spectators viewing the White men and the articles which we had, our party weacke and much reduced in flesh as well as Strength, The horse I left hung up they receved at a time they were in great want, and the Supply I Sent by R. Fields proved timely and gave great encouragement to the party with Captn. Lewis.   he lost 3 horses one of which belonged to our guide. Those Indians Stole out of R. F. Shot pouch his knife wipers[5] Compas & Steel, which we Could not precure from them, we attempted to have Some talk with those people but Could not for the want of an Interpreter thro' which we Could Speake, we were Compelled to converse alltogether by Signs— I got the Twisted hare to draw the river from his Camp down which he did with great cherfullness on a white Elk Skin, from the 1s fork[6] which is a few seven miles below, to the large fork[7] on which the *So So ne* or Snake Indians fish, is South 2 Sleeps; to a large river[8] which falls in on the N W. Side and into which The *Clarks*[9] *river* empties itself is 5 Sleeps   from the mouth of that river to the *falls* is 5 Sleeps   at the falls he places Establishments of white people &c. and informs that great numbers of Indians reside on all those foks as well as the main river; one other Indian gave me a like account of the Countrey, Some few drops of rain this evening. I precured maps of the Country & river with the Situation of Indians, To come from Several men of note Seperately which varied verey little.—

1. This entry is the last in Codex Fd. The following notation at the end of the journal was probably added in 1810: "(This is a part of Book No. 7 to be refured to and examined after the 9th Septr. 1805—WC[)]". "Book No. 7" refers to Codex G, Clark's notebook covering this time period. The writer of another note, "look forward 4 leaves," is not known. It is upside down to the other writing.

2. At later Crane Meadows. Space, 19; *Atlas* map 71.

3. Perhaps a subspecies of the crow, *Corvus brachyrhynchos* [AOU, 488], *C. b. hesperis*, then new to science. Burroughs, 248; Cutright (LCPN), 432.

4. The more easterly of the two Nez Perce villages on Jim Ford Creek, on Weippe Prairie about three miles southeast of present Weippe, Clearwater County, Idaho. Appleman (LC), 283–85; *Atlas* map 71.

5. Perhaps an oiled cloth or piece of soft leather used for cleaning his weapon. Criswell, 92, suggests a wiping rod, but this seems unlikely to have fit into a shot pouch. The steel mentioned below was probably used with flint to make fire.

6. The North Fork Clearwater, the "Chopunnish" River on *Atlas* map 71.

7. Probably the Snake River.

8. The Columbia, into which the Clark Fork-Pend Oreille River combination empties.

9. "Clarks" appears to have been inserted into a blank space, or possibly written in place of an erased word.

[Clark]   Septr. 23rd Sunday

Traded with the Indians, made 3 Chiefs and gave them meadels & Tobacco & Handkerchif & knives, and a flag & left a Flag & hand kerches for the great Chief when he returns from war, in the evening proceeded to the 2d Vilg 2 miles, a hard wind and rain at dark, traded for Some root Bread & Skins to make Shirts.   hot day

[Clark]   *Saturday [NB: Monday] 23rd Septr 1805.*

We assembled the principal Men as well as the Chiefs and by Signs informed them where we came from where bound our wish to inculcate peace and good understanding between all the red people &c. which appeared to Satisfy them much, we then gave 2 other Medals to other Chefs of bands, a flag to the *twisted hare,* left a flag & Handkerchief to the grand Chief gave, a Shirt to the *Twisted hare* & a knife & Handkerchif with a Small pece of Tobacco to each. Finding that those people gave no provi-

sions to day we deturmined to purchase with our Small articles of merchindize, accord we purchased all we could, Such as roots dried, in bread,
& in ther raw State, Berris of red Haws & *Fish* and in the evening Set out
and proceeded on to the 2d Village[1] 2 miles dist. where we also purchased a few articles all amounting to as much as our weak horses Could
Carry to the river   Capt. Lewis & 2 men verry Sick this evening, my hip
verry Painfull, the men trade a few old tin Canisters for dressed Elk Skin
to make themselves Shirts, at dark a hard wind from The S W accom-
paned with rain which lasted half an hour. The *twisted hare* envited Capt
Lewis & myself to his lodge which was nothin more than Pine bushes &
bark, and gave us Some broiled dried *Salmon* to eate, great numbers
about us all night at this village   the women were busily employed in
gathering and drying the *Pas-she co* root of which they had great quantites dug in piles

1. The same village at which Clark's party stayed on the night of September 20, 1805,
about a mile southwest of Weippe, Clearwater County, Idaho. Appleman (LC), 283–85;
Atlas map 71.

[Clark]   *Septr. 24th Monday 1805*

Set out early for the river and proceeded on the Same road I had prevsly
gorn to the Island at which place I had found the Chief & formed a Camp
several 8 or 9 men Sick, Capt Lewis Sick   all Complain of a *Lax* & heaviness at the Stomack, I gave rushes Pills to Several   hot day   maney Indians & thier gangues of horses follow us   hot day   Hunter had 5 Deer

[Clark]   *Sunday [NB: Tuesday] 24th Septr. 1805*

a fine morning   collected our horses despatched J. Colter back to hunt
the horses lost in the mountains & bring up Some Shot left behind, and at
10 oClock we all Set out for the river and proceeded on by the Same rout
I had previously traveled, and at Sunset We arrived at the Island on
which I found the *Twisted hare* and formed a Camp on a large Island a littl
below,[1] Capt Lewis Scercely able to ride on a jentle horse which was fur-
nishd by the Chief, Several men So unwell that they were Compelled to
lie on the Side of the road for Some time others obliged to be put on

horses.[2] I gave rushes Pills to the Sick this evening. Several Indians follow us.

1. Just below Twisted Hair's camp, which Clark first reached on September 21, 1805,
on what was China Island of the Clearwater River, about a mile above Orofino, Clearwater County, Idaho. Space, 19; Peebles (LT), 10; *Atlas* map 71.

2. Presumably the result of the change of diet, and perhaps bacteria on the dried
salmon. Cutright (LCPN), 217–19; Chuinard (OOMD), 321.

[Clark]

Septr. 25th   I with th Chief & 2 young men went down to hunt timber
for Canoes— proceeded on down to the forks   4 miles N 70° W 2 miles
S. 75° W 2 miles, halted   young men Cought 6 Sammon, the forks nearly
the Same Size, Crossed the South fork & found Timber large Pine in a
bottom   Proceeded up the South Side 3 parts of Party Sick   Capt Lewis
verry Sick   hot day

[Clark]   *Monday [NB: Wednesy] 25th of September 1805*

a verry hot day   most of the Party Complaining and 2 of our hunters
left here on the 22nd verry Sick   they had killed only two Bucks in my
absence. I Set out early with the Chief and 2 young men to hunt Some
trees Calculated to build Canoes, as we had previously deturmined to
proceed on by water, I was furnished with a horse and we proceeded on
down the river   Crossed a Creek at 1 mile from the right verry rockey
which I call rock dam Creek[1] & Passed down on the N side of the river to
a fork[2] from the North which is about the Same Size and affords about
the Same quantity of water with the other forks   we halted about an
hour, one of the young men took his guig and killed 6 fine Salmon   two
of them were roasted and we eate, two Canoes Came up loaded with the
furnitur & provisions of 2 families, those Canoes are long Stedy and without much rake   I crossed the South fork and proceeded up on the South
Side, the most of the way thro' a narrow Pine bottom in which I Saw fine
timber for Canoes[3]   one of the Indian Canoes with 2 men with Poles Set
out from the forks at the Same time I did and arrived at our Camp on the
Island within 15 minits of the Same time I did, not withstanding 3 rapids
which they had to draw the Canoe thro' in the distance, when I arrived at

Camp found Capt Lewis verry Sick, Several men also verry Sick, I gave Some Salts & Tarter emetic, we deturmined to go to where the best timbr was and there form a Camp

1. Present Orofino Creek, in Clearwater County, Idaho. Space, 19; *Atlas* map 71.
2. The junction of the North Fork Clearwater and Clearwater rivers, in Clearwater County. *Atlas* map 71.
3. Ponderosa pine, which grows to large size in the area, as Clark notes in the first entry.

[Clark]

Septr. 26th   Set out early and proceeded down the river to the bottom on the S Side opposit the forks & formed a Camp   had ax handled ground &c.   our axes all too Small, Indians caught Sammon & Sold us, 2 Chiefs & thir families came & camped near us, Several men bad, Capt Lewis Sick   I gave Pukes Salts &c. to Several, I am a little unwell. hot day

[Clark]   *Tuesday [NB: Thursday] 26th Septr. 1805* [1]

Set out early and proceeded on down the river to a bottom opposit the forks of the river on the South Side and formed a Camp.[2] Soon after our arrival a raft Came down the N. fork on which was two men, they came too, I had the axes distributed and handled and men apotned. [apportioned] ready to commence building canoes on tomorrow, our axes are Small & badly Calculated to build Canoes of the large Pine, Capt Lewis Still very unwell, Several men taken Sick on the way down, I administered *Salts* Pils Galip,[3] Tarter emetic &c. I feel unwell this evening, two Chiefs & their families follow us and encamp near us, they have great numbers of horses. This day proved verry hot, we purchase fresh Salmon of the Indians

1. The meaning of an asterisk to the side of this dateline is unknown.
2. The "Canoe Camp," at which they remained until October 7, 1805, is about five miles west of Orofino, in Clearwater County, Idaho, on the south bank of the Clearwater and opposite the mouth of the North Fork Clearwater (Lewis and Clark's Chopunnish River). It is one of the major sites in the Nez Perce National Historical Park. Appleman (LC), 281–82; Peebles (LT), 10; *Atlas* map 71.

3. Jalap, the powdered root of a Mexican plant, *Exogonium jalapa,* used as a purgative; the other medicines served a similar purpose.

[Clark]   Septr. *27th Thursday 1805*

Set all the men able to work abt. building Canoes, Colter returned and found one horse & the Canister of Shot left in the mountains   he also killed a Deer ½ of which he brought   hot day—   men Sick

[Clark]   *27th Septr. Wednesday [NB: Friday] 1805*

all the men able to work comened building 5 Canoes, Several taken Sick at work, our hunters returned Sick without meet. J. Colter returned he found only one of the lost horses, on his way killed a deer, half of which he gave the Indians the other proved nourishing to the Sick   The day verry hot, we purchase fresh Salmon of them   Several Indians Come up the river from a Camp Some distance below   Capt Lewis very Sick nearly all the men Sick.   our Shoshonee Indian Guide employed himself makeing flint points for his arrows

[Clark]   *Septr. 28th Friday*

Several men Sick   all at work which is able, nothing killed to day. Drewyer Sick   maney Indians visit us   worm day

[Clark]   *Thursday 28th Septr. 1805 [NB: Saturday]*

Our men nearly all Complaining of ther bowels, a heaviness at the Stomach & Lax, Some of those taken first getting better, a number of Indians about us gazeing &c. &c. This day proved verry worm and Sultery, nothing killed   men complaining of their diat of fish & roots.   all that is able working at the Canoes, Several Indians leave us to day, the raft continue on down the river, one old man informed us that he had been to the White peoples fort at the falls & got white beeds &c   his Story was not beleved as he Could explain nothing.—

[Clark]   *Septr. 29th Satterday*

Drewyer killed 2 deer   Collins 1 der   men Conte Sickly   at work all able to work.

[Clark]   ⟨*Friday*⟩ *Sunday 29th Septr. 1805*

a Cool morning wind from the S. W.   men Sick as usial, all The men
that are able to at work, at the Canoes   Drewyer killed 2 Deer Colter
killed 1 Deer, the after part of this day worm   Cap Lewis very Sick, and
most of the men complaning very much of ther bowels & Stomach

[Clark]   *Sunday 30th Septr. 1805* Forks[1]

a fine morning   our me[n] recruting a little   cool, all at work doing
Something except 2 which are verry Sick, Great run of Small duck passing ⟨up and⟩ down the river this morning.

Took equal altitudes with Sextent at Camp opposit the Junction of
[*blank*] River and [*blank*] River

$$
\begin{array}{lllll}
⟨\text{A M} & 8 & 41 & 45.5⟩ \\
⟨ \;'' & '' & 43 & 31⟩ \\
⟨ \;'' & '' & 4⟩ \\
\end{array}
$$

Sunday 30th Sept. 1805

	H.	M.	S.		H.	M	S
A. M	8	49	32.5	P M	4	5	23.5
"	"	51	17.5	"	4	7	9
"	"	53	8.5	"	4	8	58.5

Altitude produced from this observation is 42° 50′ 45″

Observed time and distance of Sun and Moon Nearest Limbs ☉ West. with
Sextent

		Time			distance	
	H.	M.	S			
P M	4	21	44	91°	57′	00″
	"	22	53	91	57	30
	"	23	52	91	58	0
	"	24	37	91	58	15
	"	25	35	91	58	15
	"	26	42	91	58	30
	"	27	39	91	58	45
	"	28	17	91	59	15
	"	29	43	91	59	45

"	31	10	92	50	0
"	32	15	92	0	15
"	33	8	92	0	45
"	34	23	92	1	15
"	35	30	92	1	30
"	36	20	92	1	45

Error of Enstrement 8° 45″ Sub Cronometer too fast

[Clark]   *Septr. 30th Saturday (Monday) 1805* [2]

a fine fa[i]r morning a ⟨little⟩   the men recruiting a little, all at work which are able. Great number of Small Ducks pass down the river this morning.   maney Indians passing up and down the river.

Course & Distance from *Clark's river*
to the Forks of Flat head [*EC: Kooskooskee*] river.

[*EC: Sept 11*]

S. 45° E	1½	miles up *Travelers rest* Creek to a road which joins from the right on the lower side of the Creek, which road passes from the Missouri
West	5½	miles up the creek on the right The hills high and ruged

Septr. 12

N. W.	11	miles to the forks of the Creek on a road passing over high points hilley and Covered with pine, Crosd six branches from the left, the 1st three large, psd. a hot hous of earth
S. 75° W	12	miles to the creek, passing a bend of the Creek at 4 miles & over a high mountain on which we found no water for 8 miles, the road bad much falling timber

Septr. 13

⟨S. W.	7	miles over a mountain & on a dividing ridge of flat gladey land to a Creek from the left, passing thro a glade of ½ a mile wide & keeping down the Creek for two miles.⟩
S. W.	2	miles up the Said Creek, bad road rockey Steep hill Sides falling timber to a *hot* Springs on the right of the Creek, boiling out of a corse grittey Stones &.

S. 30° W.	3	miles passing a bad falling timber to the Creek on our left passed 3 Small Streams from ou right ⟨thro' Horse Vally⟩
S. 30° W.	7	miles over a mountain and on a dividing of flat gladey land to a [EC: Glade] Creek in a glade of ½ a mile in width, & keeping down this Creek two miles

Septr. 14

S 80° W.	6	miles over a high mountanious Country thickly Covered with pine Spruce & to the forks of the Creek, one of equal Size [EC: N. fork Koosk] falling in from the right passing much falling timber
S 60° W	9	miles over a high mountain Steep and almost inexcessable, leaveing the Creek to our right hand to the forks, a [EC: Colt Killed] Creek to our right hand to the forks, a Creek of equal Size falling in from the left 2 fish dams or weares across the North fork to catch Salmon
S 70° W.	2	miles down the river Kooskooske³ to a Small branch on the right Side Killed & eate Coalt

Septr. 15th

West	4	miles down the ⟨Creek⟩ River passing over four high steep hills to a run at an old Indn. encampment.
N. W.	8	miles assending a ruged mountain winding in every direction passing over high Stoney knobs passed a Spring on our right at 4 miles to a high part of the Mountain on which was Snow.
	71	

16th Septr

S 75° W	13	miles on the mountain passing emencly high and ruged Knobs of the mounts. in Snow from 4 to 6 Inchs deep much falling timber Snow Contined to fall passed thro a Country thickly timbered with 8 destienct kinds of pine to a Small branch passing to our right

17th Septr

S. 50° W.	10	miles over high Knobs of the Mountn. emincely dificuelt, passed 3 dreans to our right to one which passes to our left on the top of a high Mountain, passing on a divide ridge

S 85° W	32	"I proced on with the hunters" 18th Septr. miles to hungary Creek passing to our left passed a branch & Several Springs which passes to our right Keeping a dividing ridge passed Several high Steep & rugid Knobs of the mountains, from the top of one view the leavel Country to the S. W. much falling timber, a branch of hungary Creek
S 80° W	22	19 Sepr miles on our course thro emencely bad falling timber the greater part of the way. Keeping up the Creek for 8 miles, at 6 passed thro a Small Plain whre we Killed a horse, the road up the Creek Stoney hill Sides much worse than any we have passed left the Creek to our right and passd. over a mountain and the heads of some branches of hungary Creek, over ridges and thro much falling timber & two other high mountains of like discription to a large Creek running West,. kept down 4 miles and left it to our left and Crossed over a mountain as bad as usial to a Branch which runs to our left
S 60° W	12 ―― 160 ══	20 Sepr miles to the Low Country at the foot of the mountain, passed over into the forks of a large Creek at 4 miles. Kept down this Creek 2 miles and left it to our left hand passing on a dividing ridge passed Some dreans to our left
West	6	miles to an Pierced nose Indian Village in a Small Plain pasd. thro a open pine Country Crossed 2 runs passing to our left
N. 70° W.	2	miles to a 2d. village passing through the open Plains Covered with horses &. & Indian womin diging roots.
N. 80° W.	12	(21s Sept) Miles thro an opin leavel rich pine Country to the top of the river hills passed no water
S. 70° W	3 ―― 188	miles down a Steep hill to the river at the mouth of a Small [X: *Village*] Creek on which the Indian village is Situated

West	3	miles down the river to the mouth of a large Creek I call *rock dam* on the right Side, passing a bad road on a Steep hill Side, and place the Indians catch fish at 2 Islands rive about 150 yds wide and is the one we killed The 1s Coalt on

25th Septr.

N. 70° W.	2	miles down the Koskoske[4] River to a rapid at a graveley Island Hills high & Steep Small bottoms covered with pine passed 2 rapids
S. 75° W.	3	miles to the forks of the river the N W. fork as large as the *Chopunnish* River. Crossed to the South side and formed a Camp to build Canoes &c. in a Small Pine bottom opposit a riffle in the Souh fok &c.

190 Miles

1. Opposite this entry in Clark's Elkskin-bound Journal is a sketch map (fig. 9). See note for September 20, 1805.

2. Clark's astronomical observations are repeated at the end of this entry (Codex G, p. 129) as apparently copied from the Elkskin-bound Journal. No differences in the figures between the two sets were found and the table is not printed here. Following that table is a course and distance table (Codex G, pp. 130–34) labeled: "Course & Distance from *Clark's river* to the Forks of Flat head river." The word "*Clark's*" appears to have been substituted for an erased word. "Flat head" also may have been added later. This covers the period September 11–25, 1805, with some days missing when the party was not on the move. We retain this table because of some differences with the Elkskin-bound Journal.

3. The word appears to have been added to a blank space.

4. Again, the word seems to have been added to a blank space, as does the word "*Chopunnish*" in the next course.

[Lewis and Clark]   [*Weather, September 1805*][1]

Day of the Month	State of the Thermometer at ☉ rise	Weather at ☉ rise	Wind at ☉ rise	State of the Thermometer at 4 P. M.	Weather at 4 P. M.	Wind at 4 P.M.
[September] 1st	38 a	c	N W	67 a	c	N W
2nd	36 a	c. a. r	N E	60 a	c a r h	N E
3rd	34 a	c. a. r	N E.	52 a	c a r	N E
4th	19 a	r. a. S.	N E	34 a	c a r	N E

5th	17 a	c. a. s	N E.	29 a	c a r & s	N E
6th		c. a. r.	N E		r	N E
7th		c. a. r	N E		c a r	N E
8th		c	N E		c a r	N E
9th		c. a. r	N E		f a r	N E
10th		f	N W		f	N W
11th		f	N W		f	N W
12th		f.	N W.		f	N E
13th		c	N E		r	N E
14th		c. a. r	S W		c a r. & S.[2]	S W
15th		c a L & s[3]	S W		s	S W
16th		c a s	S W		f	S W.
17th		f	S W		f	S W.
18th		f	S W		f	S W.
19th		f	S W		f	S W.
20th		f	S W		f	S W.
21st		f	S E		f	S W.
22nd		f	S W		f	S W
23rd		f	S W		f	S W.
24th		f a r t & L[4]	S E		f a r[5]	S E.
25th		f	E		f	S W.
26th		f	E		f	S W.
27th		f	E		f	S W.
27th		f	E		f	S W.
28th		f	E		f	S W.
29th		f	E		f	S W.
30th		f	E		f	S W.

[*Remarks*][6]

[September] 2nd   Service berries dried on the bushes abundant and very fine.   black colour.

3rd   Choke Cherries ripe and abundant.

4th   ice one inch thick.

5th   Ground Covered with Snow.

6th   *Thermometer* broke by the Box strikeing against a tree[7]

8th   Mountains Covered with Snow to the S. W.   a singular kind of Prickly Pears.

9th	arrived a[t] travelers rest Creek
10th	Met 3 flat head Indians in the pursute of 2 Snake indians who had taken their horses [8]
12th	Mounts to our left Covered with Snow
13th	a hot Spring
14th	killed and eat a colt [9]
15th	no water we are obliged to Substitute the coald Snow. [10]
16th	Snow commenced about 4 oClock A. M. and continued untill night. it is about 7 inches deep. ice one inch thick. [11]
17th	Killed & eate the 2d Coalt
18th	Capt Clark goes on a head with the hunters. hard black frost this morning
19th	rose raspberry ripe and abundant. [12]
20th	I found a horse had him killed & hung up for the party behind
21st	I arrive at the Flat head Camp of 200 lodges in a Small prarie [13]
22nd	purchased Some provisions roots &c Send Rubin Fields back with Some Provisions to meet Capt. Lewis.
23rd	I joined Capt Lewis at the flat head village last night
24th	a thunder cloud last evening. [14]
25th	I proceed to the forks worm day
26th	Form a Camp at the forks
27th	Several Indians visit us in from below. Set about building 5 canoes. day very warm
29th	¾ of the party Sick. Day very hot
30th	Great numbers of Small Ducks pass down the river. hot day

1. Lewis's weather data are in Codex Fe and Codex P; Clark's are in Codex I. This table follows Codex Fe, with discrepancies noted. There is no record of river rise or fall.

2. Lewis in Codex P and Clark in Codex I have only "c a r."

3. Lewis in Codex P and Clark in Codex I have only "c a s."

4. Lewis in Codex P has only "f."

5. Lewis in Codex P and Clark in Codex I have only "f."

6. Lewis (Codices Fe and P) and Clark (Codex I) have a number of marginal remarks for this month, many of which do not refer to the weather. Lewis is missing remarks for a number of days; Clark's are substituted for the following: September 8, 9, 10, 13, 17, 20, 21, 22, 23, 25, 27, 29, and 30.

7. Clark in Codex I adds, "in the Rock mountains." This was their last thermometer and there were, of course, no recorded temperatures for the remainder of the expedition.

8. These Flatheads were probably Nez Perces.

9. Clark adds, "Snowed rained & hailed to day."

10. Clark adds, "to boil our Colt."

11. Clark's remark reads, "the Snow fell on the old Snow 4 inches deep last night."

12. There are numerous possibilities for both the wild rose (*Rosa*) and raspberries (*Rhus*) in the area. Clark's version is, "Snow is about 4 Inches deep."

13. The Indians were actually Nez Perces.

14. Clark writes, "Capt Lewis & Several men Sick."

[Clark]   *October 1st 1805 ⟨Monday⟩ Tuesday*[1]

a cool morning wind from the N. E.   I examine & Dry all our article Cloths &. nothing to eate except Drid fish verry bad diet   Capt Lewis getting much better than for Several days past   Several Indians visit us from the different villages below and on the main fork S.   nothing killed

[Clark]   *October 1st ⟨Monday⟩ Tuesday 1805*

A cool morning wind from the East   had Examined and dried all our clothes and other articles and laid out a Small assortment of Such articles as those Indians were fond of to trade with them for Some provisions (they are remarkably fond of Beeds) nothin to eate except a little dried fish which they men complain of as working of them as as much as a dost of Salts. Capt Lewis getting much better. Several Indians visit us from the different tribes below   Some from the main South fork[2]   our hunters killed nothing to day   worm evening

1. An asterisk is at the end of this line, but for reasons unknown.

2. Probably the Snake River.

[Clark]   *Oct. 2nd ⟨Tuesday⟩ 1805* Wednesday

   dispatch 2 men & an Indian up to the villages we first Came too to purchase roots fish &c.   nothing to eate but roots.   gave a small pice of Tobacco to the Indians, 3 broachs & 2 rings with my Handkerchif divided
between 5 of them. I walked on the hills to hunt to day, Saw only one
deer, Could kill nothing   day excesively hot in the river bottom   wind
North, Burning out the hotter [hollow?] of our canoes, men Something
better   nothing except a Small Prarie wolf Killed to day, our Provisions
all out except what fiew fish we purchase of the Indians with us; we kill a
horse for the men at work to eate &c. &c.

[Clark]   *October 2nd ⟨Tuesday⟩ Wednesday 1805*

   Despatched 2 men Frasure & S. Guterich back to the village with 1 Indian & 6 horses to purchase dried fish, roots &c.   we have nothing to
eate but roots, which give the men violent pains in their bowels after eating much of them. To the Indians who visited us yesterday I gave divided
my Handkerchief between 5 of them, with a Small piece of tobacco & a
pece of riebin & to the 2 principal men each a ring & brooch. I walked out
with my gun on the hills which is verry Steep & high could kill nothing.
day hot wind N. Hunters killed nothing excep a Small Prarie wolf. Provisions all out, which Compells us to kill one of our horses to eate and make
Suep for the Sick men.

[Clark]   *October 3rd ⟨Wednesday⟩ Thursday 1805 Canoe Camp*

   a fair cool morning   wind from the East   all our men getting well and
at work at the canoes &c. ⟨The Indians Came⟩
   Took equal altitudes with Sextent

	H.	M.	S		H.	M.	S
A M.	9	8	14	P M	3	57	8
	9	10	8		3	58	58.5
	9	11	59		4	0	53

Altitude produced 44° 53′ 45″
   P M Observed time and distance of the *Moons* western Limb from α *Arietis* ★
East of the ☽

	Time			distance		
	Hs.	ms.	Sds.			
P M	8	11	49	78°	4′	00″
	″	21	6	″	2	30
	″	23	21	″	2	15
	″	25	7	″	1	45
	″	27	40	″	1	30
	″	30	10	77	59	00
	″	33	34	″	58	45
	″	35	1	″	58	15
	″	37	1	″	58	00
	″	38	28	″	57	30

[Clark] October 3rd ⟨*Wednesday*⟩ Thursday *1805* [1]

a fine morning cool wind East   all our men getting better in helth, and at work at the Canoes &c. The Indians who visited us from below Set out on their return early. Several others Came from different directions—.

1. The astronomical observation following this entry in Codex G, p. 136, is the same as that in the Elkskin-bound Journal and is not repeated here.

[Clark] October 4th ⟨*Thursday*⟩ *1805* Friday

This morning is a little cool wind from the East.   displeased an Indian by refuseing to let him have a pice of Tobacco.   thre Inds. from the S. fork visit us   Frasur and Guterich return from the village with fish roots &c. which they purchased

[Clark] October 4th ⟨*Thursday*⟩ Friday *1805*

a Cool wind from off the Eastern mountains   I displeased an Indian by refuseing him a pice of Tobacco which he tooke the liberty to take out of our Sack   Three Indians visit us from the Grat River South of us. The two men Frasure and Guterich return late from the Vllage with Fish roots &c. which they purchased   as our horse is eaten we have nothing to eate except dried fish & roots which disagree with us verry much. The after part of this day verry warm. Capt Lewis Still Sick but able to walk about a little.

[Clark]   *October 5th ⟨Friday⟩ Saturday 1805*

a Cool morning   wind from the East, Collected all our horses, & Branded them[1] 38 in No. and delivered them to the men who were to take Charge of them, each of which I gave a Knife & one a wampom Shell gorget, The Lattd. of this place the mean of 2 observations is *46° 34′ 56.3″* North.   nothing to eate but dried roots & Dried fish, Capt Lewis & my Self eate a Supper of roots boiled, which filled us So full of wind, that we were Scercely able to Breathe all night felt the effects of it. Lanced 2 Canoes to day   one proved a little leakey   the other a verry good one

[Clark]   *October 5th ⟨Friday⟩ Saty 1805*

Wind Easterley and Cool, had all our horses 38 in number Collected and branded   Cut off their fore top and delivered them to the 2 brothers and one Son of one of the Chiefs who intends to accompany us down the river   to each of those men I gave a Knife & Some Small articles &c. they promised to be attentive to our horses untill we Should return.—

Lattitude of this place from the mean of two observations is *46° 34′ 56.3″* North—

Nothing to eate except dried fish & roots. Capt Lewis & myself eate a Supper of roots boiled, which Swelled us in Such a manner that we were Scercely able to breath for Several hours—   finished and lanced [*NB: launched*] 2 of our Canoes this evening which proved to be verry good our hunters with every diligence Could kill nothing. The hills high and ruged and woods too dry to hunt the deer which is the only game in our neighbourhood. Several Squars Came with Fish and roots which we purchased of them for Beeds, which they were fond of—   Capt Lewis not So well to day as yesterday

1. Lewis's branding iron bore the legend "U.S. Capt. M. Lewis." Now in the possession of the Oregon Historical Society, it is one of the few authenticated articles associated with the expedition known to have survived. Files of the society are inexact and sources disagree on the item's provenance. It was found in 1892, 1893, or 1894, by Lineaus Winans of Hood River, Oregon, near present The Dalles, Oregon, on or below one of the Memaloose Islands before Columbia River dams inundated the area. See October 29, 1805. Wheeler, 2:118; Appleman (LC), 179–80, 373 n. 120; Oregon Historical Society files on the branding iron (courtesy of Robert E. Lange, Portland).

[Clark]   *October 6th ⟨Saturday⟩ Sunday 1805*

A cool morning   wind East for a Short time, which is always a Cool Wind, had a *cash* made for our Saddles and buried them on the Side of a Pond. [*one word, illegible*] ⟨of the Inds.⟩

Magnetic azmuth of Sun A M—

	Time		azmth.	[*ML: altitude*] ⟨distance⟩
H.	m.	S		
9	6	27	S. 75° E	42′ 58′ 00″
9	18	21	S. 73 E	45 46 45

finish all the Canoes late. I am verry Sick all night, Pane in Stomach & the bowels oweing to my diet

Equal altitudes 6th Septr. [October] with Sextent

	H.	m.	S.		H.	M	S
A M	9	16	21.5	P M.	3	45	34.5
	″	18	20.5		″	47	34.5
	″	20	17.5		″	49	26.5

Altitude produced 45° 46′ 45″—
Took time and distance of moons Western Limb and α Arquile, Star West—

		Time			*distance*	
	H.	M.	S.	d		
P M	8	25	55	58	54′	15″
	″	28	34	″	55	30
	″	32	47	″	56	45
	″	34	40	″	57	0
	″	36	53	″	57	45
	″	38	41	″	58	30
	″	40	35	″	59	15
	″	42	14	″	59	45
	″	43	37	59	1	00
	″	45	21	″	1	45

Took time and Distance of Moons ⟨Western⟩ [*ML: Western*] Limb from Alberian, Star East

	Time			Distance	
	h.	m	S.			
	9	9	52	65° 29′	15″

"	12	6	"	28	"
"	13	47	"	2	15
"	16	8	"	27	15
"	18	2	"	28	"
"	19	49	"	24	30
"	21	12	"	24	"
"	22	44	"	23	30

[Clark]   *October 6th ⟨Saturday⟩* Sunday *1805*

A Col Easterley wind which Spring up in the latter part of the night and Continues untill about 7 or 8 oClock A. M. had all our Saddles Collected a whole dug and in the night buried them, also a Canister of powder and a bag of Balls at the place the Canoe which Shields made was cut from the body of the tree— The Saddles were buried on the Side of a bend about ½ a mile below— all the Canoes finished this evening ready to be put into the water. I am taken verry unwell with a paine in the bowels & Stomach, which is certainly the effects of my diet—which last all night—.[1]

The winds blow cold from a little before day untill the Suns gets to Some hight from the Mountans East as they did from the mountans at the time we lay at the falls of Missouri from the West

The river below this forks is Called *Kos kos kee*[2] it is Clear rapid with Shoals or Swift places—

The open Countrey Commences a fiew miles below This on each side of the river, on the Lard Side below the 1st Creek.   with a few trees Scattered near the river.

1. Clark's astronomical observation here in Codex G, pp. 138–39, repeats the table found in the Elkskin-bound Journal; it is not printed here.

2. The Clearwater River. Later they adopted the spelling "Kooskooskee." There are different explanations of the name; sources differ as to whether it is the Nez Perce name for the river. A common version is that *koos keich keich* means "clear water." Josephy (NP), 5; Space, 8. Or it may represent the Nez Perce term *qu·sqú·s*, "blue gray."

[Clark]   ⟨*Sunday*⟩ *7th Oct.* [over *Septr.*] *1805* Monday

I feel my Self verry unwell, all the canoes in the water, we Load and Set out, after fixing all our Poles &c. &c. The after noon Cloudy   proced on passd maney bad rapids, one Canoe that in which I went in front Sprung a Leak in passing the 3rd rapid—

Set out at 3 oClock P M & proceeded on

N. 80° W.	1	mile, passed a bad rappid
S W.	1½	mile to the L. Side bend
West	½	mile to R. Sd. passd. a rapid
S W.	1	mile to a Left hand bend
N. 70 W.	1½	miles passed a rapid R. G.
S 60 W	1½	miles do. bad to L. S.
West	3	miles passd. a rapid ½ a Creek on the ⟨right⟩ left at 2 miles to a right hand bend
S. 10° E	1½	mile to a Left B. passed a rapid
N. 60 E	1½	m. to a R. bend passed a rapid
South	1	To a bend on the Left Side Passed a bad rapid
West	1	in the left hand bend
N W.	½	a mile to a bad rapid
S. 70° W	1½	miles to a bend on the right
S W.	2	miles to a bend on the left at the mo. of a run opposit
	20	to which we camped. from water Encamped on a pool right, narrows above for 6 miles all way

⟨N W 1 mile to a bend to right⟩

[Clark]   *October 7th ⟨Sunday⟩ Monday 1805* [1]

I continu verry unwell but obliged to attend every thing   all the Canoes put into the water and loaded, fixed our Canoes as well as possible and Set out   as we were about to Set out we missd. both of the Chiefs [2] who promised to accompany us; I also missed my Pipe Tomahawk which Could not be found.

The after part of the day Cloudy proceded on passed 10 rapids which wer danjerous   the Canoe in which I was Struck a rock and Sprung a leak in the 3rd rapid, we proceeded on 20 [*WC: 19*] miles and Encamped on a Stard point oppost a run. [3]   passed a Creek Small on the Lard. Side at 9 miles, [4] ⟨a run at⟩ a Short distanc from the river at 2 feet 4 Inches N. of a dead toped pine Treee had burid 2 Lead Canisters of Powder

Had the Canoes unloaded examined and mended a Small leake which we discovered in a thin place in her Side   passed Several ⟨old⟩ Camps of Indians to day

our Course and distance Shall be given after I get to the forks. &c.— which the Indians Say is the last of the bad water untill we get to the great falls 10 day below, where the white people live &c. The Lodges are of Sticks set in a ⟨conocal⟩ form of roof of a house & covered with mats and Straw

1. Clark's courses for October 7–10 are found in a combined table at his codex entry of October 10, 1805, where they are printed in this volume. A final course for October 10 is carried over to another table which is found following Clark's codex entry of October 16, 1805.

2. Twisted Hair and Tetoharsky. The latter's name is not recorded until May 4, 1806; nothing seems to be known of him beyond what appears in the journals.

3. Erroneously marked as the camp of October 8 on *Atlas* map 72. It was quite near present Lenore, Nez Perce County, Idaho, opposite Jacks Creek. Space, 22; Peebles (LT), 11.

4. Present Canyon Creek, meeting the Clearwater near Peck, Nez Perce County. Space, 22; *Atlas* map 72.

[Clark]   ⟨*Monday*⟩ *8th Octr.* [*over Septr.*] *1805* Tuesday

a cloudy morning   Changed Canoes and buried 2 Lead canisters of Powder 2 foot 4 In. North of a dead toped pine opposit our Camp & opposit the mouth of a run   after repareing leaks in the Canoes Sprung Coming over the rapids yesterday   Set out at 9 oClock

N. W.	1	mile to a riae in the S. bend
South	¼	thro a verry bad rappid all way
S. 70° W.	½	to a L. bend good water
N. W.	¼	thro a rapid in a Stard. bend
West	2½	miles to a Stard. bend passed a bad rapid at 1 mile pd. a rapid at 2 miles
South	1½	to a L. bend opsd. a bottom of stone
S 70° W.	2½	mile to a Stard. bend passed an Island ⟨middle of the river⟩ on the Lard. Side, a rapid at head & foot of Island end of the Course

S. W.	2	miles to a Lard bend passed a rapid & Ind camp 3 Lodges & fishing place, Lowr pt. of Isd. at which place we dined & bought fish Passed Lower pt. Isd. on Stard. Side
West	2½	miles passed an Island on which 3 Lodges of Indians were Encamped opsd. on the Lad Side a Small Creek at the Lower pt. on Std. Side 6 Lodges of Inds. we halted and took in our 2 Chiefs and bought fish & roots Psd. 2 rapids
S W	1½	ms. to a bend on Std. passed a rapid
S. 40 E	1⟨½⟩	to a bend on Lard. psd a rapid
S 60° W.	2½	miles to a bend Std Side passd. an Isd on the Lard. bad rapid
S. W.	1½	miles to a Stard bend passed an Isd. on Ld. Side a rapid at upper point and lower pt. Canoe [c]racked, a Creek falls in on the Stard. Side.[1]
West	1½	to the upper pt. of a Island Std. Side
	21⟨18⟩	

[Clark]   *October 8th* ⟨*Monday*⟩ Tuesday *1805*

A Cloudy morning   loaded our Canoes which was unloaded last night and Set out at 9 oClock   passed 15 rapids four Islands and a Creek on the Stard Side at 16 miles just below which one canoe in which Serjt. Gass was Stearing and was nearle turning over, She Sprung a leak or Split open on one Side and Bottom filled with water & Sunk on the rapid, the men, Several of which Could not Swim hung on to the Canoe, I had one of the other Canoes unloaded & with the assistance of our Small Canoe and one Indian Canoe took out every thing & ⟨got⟩ toed the empty Canoe on Shore,[2] one man Tompson a little hurt, every thing wet perticularly the greater part of our Small Stock of merchindize, had every thing opened, and two Sentinals put over them to keep off the Indians, who are enclined to theave haveing Stole Several Small articles   those people appeared disposed to give us every assistance in their power dureing our distress— We passed Several Encampments of Indians on the Islands and those near the rapids in which places they took the Salmon, at one of

Those Camps we found our two Chiefs who had promised to accompany us, we took them on board after the Serimony of Smokeing

1. "Colters Creek" on *Atlas* map 72, after John Colter of the party, now Potlatch River in Nez Perce County, Idaho. In 1899 a Jefferson peace medal, perhaps from the expedition, was discovered near the mouth of Potlatch River. It is today in the American Museum of Natural History, New York City. Wheeler, 2 : 123–24; Cutright (LCIPM), 164–65.

2. They remained at this site until October 10, as indicated on *Atlas* map 72. It was on the north side in Nez Perce County, below the confluence of the Potlatch and Clearwater rivers, a few miles from present Spalding. The party's camp was near Arrowbeach site which is located a little over half a mile below the mouth of Potlatch River. The site was excavated in the late 1960s, but it is now essentially destroyed. While the site occupation spanned at least the last three thousand years, it was probably a seasonal village during the last fifteen hundred years. Toups; Ames.

[Clark]

Octo. 9th   all day drying our roots good & articles which got wet in the Canoe last night.   our 2 Snake Indian guides left us without our knowledge, The Indians troublesom   Stole my Spoon which they returned. men merry at night & Singular acts of a Ind. woman

[Clark]   *October 9th* ⟨*Tuesday*⟩ Wednesday *1805*

The morning Cool as usial the greater part of the day proved to be Cloudy, which was unfavourable for drying our things &c. which got we[t] yesterday. In examoning our canoe found that by putting Knees & Strong *peces pined* [*NB: pieces primed*] [*EC: pinned*] to her Sides and bottom &c. She Could be made fit for Service in by the time the goods dried, Set 4 men to work at her, Serjt. Pryor & Gass, Jo Fields & Gibson, others to Collect rosin, at 1 oClock She was finished Stronger than ever   The wet articles not Sufficiently dried to pack up obliged us to delay another night dureing the time one man was tradeing for fish for our voyage, at Dark we were informed that our old guide & his Son had left us and had been Seen running up the river Several miles above, we Could not account for the Cause of his leaveing us at this time, without receiving his pay for the Services he had rendered us, or letting us know anything of his intention.

we requested the Chief to Send a horseman after our old guide to come back and recive his pay &c. which he advised us not to do as his nation would take his things from him before he passed their camps—. The Indians and our party were very mery this after noon   a woman faind madness &c. &c. Singular acts of this woman in giveing in Small potions all She had & if they were not received [*NB: or She had no more to give— pitied by Indians— She Sang*] She would Scarrify her Self in a horid manner &c.[1] Capt Lewis recovring fast.

1. What the captains regarded as madness the Indians would probably have considered the prompting of a guardian spirit. Ronda (LCAI), 162.

[Clark]   Octr. 10th ⟨Wednesday⟩ 1805 Thursday
   Set out at 7 oClock 74.26[1]

South	1	mile passed a bad rapid at the head of an Isd. on Ld. Side
S. 20° W	1½	miles to a Ld bend, passed a Isd. on Ld. Side. rapid at the Head bad. passed Lower pt. of the other [island] at the mouth of a run on Stard.
West	½	to a St. bend passed a Small Isd. Ld. Side and a rapid
S. 30° W	3	mile to a Ld. bend passed a Creek Cg [coming in] on the Ld Side at ½ a mile on which is Cotton wood bottoms Inds. Camp below the Creek
West	2	miles to the head of an Isd.[2] at bad rapid on both Sides Curt [current] on the right Side
S. 30° W.	4	mile pd. a rapd at Lower point of Isd & rapid at 1 mile, a rapd at 1½ miles rocky bottoms on each Side a rapid at 2½ miles a run[3] & (Inds. Camp) on Stard Sd at 3 miles a rapid at 3½ miles to a Lard. bend, low plain 100 ft
West	2	mile to a Stard bend, (passed an Indian bathing in hot bath) rapid an Island on the L. S. Shole waters at the head opsd. to which verry bad rapid we Call raged rapid one Canoe Struck & lodged Sprung a Leak onload Passed Several Inds camps on the Island. Took Meridian altitd. on the Island with Sextent made it 74° 26' Latd 46° 29' 21 7/10″ North
S W	1	mile to a bend on the St. Side psd 2 rapid
South	1	mile to the L. bend passed 2 rapid a large bottom on each Side

Sepulchar Island. The North
River we call Cataract River
from the number of falls which
opposed to
the Indians inform us ought Co
the Indians are afraid to
hunt or be on this Land Side
of this Columbia a great Chief ca
for fear of the Snake Inds.
who reside on a fork of
this river where falls in
about the falls a Good
Situation for Winter qu-
arters if game can be had
is just below Sepulchar
Rock on the Lard Side, high
Pine and oaker timber
the country rugged above, good
Country back, as
it appears from the river
Indian Village No. of Lodges
river ½ mile wide it Enters,

10. Confluence of the Clearwater and Snake Rivers,
Idaho-Washington border, ca. October 10, 1805,
Elkskin-bound Journal ⊕

S 80 W	3	miles to the mouth of a Large fork Caled by the Inds. *Ki-moo-e-nem* passed 2 rapids Isd. in mouth
West	1	mile to a Ld. bend ps Shore in the mouth. Wind high which
	58	obliged us to Stop. Kimooenem has two forks on the South Side, & Camps of Inds. all the way up 2d fork called *Pâr-nâsh-te* about 50 ms. camped on Std. Side to make observt

a verry worm day, Indians continue all day on the banks to view us as low as the forks. Two Indians come up in a Canoe, who means to accompany us to the Great rapids, Could get no observations, worm night— The water of the South fork is of a bluish green colour

[Clark]   *October 10th Wednesday Thursday*

a fine Morning   loaded and Set out at 7 oClock   at 2½ miles passed a run on the Stard. Side[4] haveing passed 2 Islands and two bad rapids   at 3 miles lower passed a Creek on the Lard. with wide Cotton willow bottoms haveing passed an Island and a rapid an Indian Camp of three Lodgs below the Creek[5]   at 8½ miles lower we arrived at the heade of a verry bad riffle[6] at which place we landed near 8 Lodges of Indians [*NB: Choponnesh*] [*Ed.: and one word illegible*] on the Lard Side to view the *riffle,* haveing passed two Islands & Six rapids Several of them verry bad—after view'g this riffle two Canoes were taken over verry well; the third Stuck on a rock which took us an hour to get her off which was effected without her receiving a greater injurey than a Small Split in her Side which was repared in a Short time, we purchased fish & dogs of those people, dined and proceeded on—   here we met with an Indian from the falls at which place he Sais he Saw white people, and expressd an inclination to accompany us, we passd. a fiew miles above this riffle 2 Lodges and an Indian batheing in a hot bath made by hot Stones thrown into a pon of water. at this riffle which we Call ragid rapid took meridian altitude of the Suns upper Limb with Sextt. *74° 26′ 0″* Latd. produced [*blank*] North   at five miles lower and Sixty miles below the forks arived at a large Southerly fork[7] which is the one we were on with the *Snake* or ⟨*Sho-Sho-ne*⟩ *So-So-nee* nation (haveing passed 5 rapids)   This South fork or *Lewis's River* which has two forks which fall into it on the South the 1st Small the upper large and about 2 days march up imediately parrelal to the first villages we

Came to and is called by those Indians *Pâr-nash-te*[8] on this fork a little above its mouth resides a Chief who as the Indian Say has more horses than he can Count and further Sayeth that Louises River is navagable about 60 miles up with maney rapids at which places the Indians have fishing Camps and Lodjes built of an oblong form with flat ruffs. below the 1st river on the South Side there is ten established fishing places on the 1st fork which fall in on the South Side is one fishing place, between that and the *Par nash te* River, five fishing places, above two, and one on that river all of the *Cho-pun-nish*[9] or Pierced Nose Nation many other Indians reside high up those rivers The Countrey about the forks is an open Plain on either Side I can observe at a distance on the lower Stard. Side a high ridge of Thinly timbered Countrey the water of the South fork-is a greenish blue, the north as clear as cristial

Imediately in the point is an Indian Cabin & in the South fork a Small Island, we came to on the Stard. Side below with a view to make some luner observations[10] the night proved Cloudy and we were disapointed— The Indians Came down all the Couses of this river on each Side on horses to view us as we were desending,— The man whome we saw at the *ruged rapid* and expressed an inclination to accompany us to the great rapids, came up with his Son in a Small Canoe and procisted in his intentions— worthey of remark that not one Stick of timber on the river near the forks and but a fiew trees for a great distance up the River we decended I think Lewis's[11] River is about 250 yards wide, the *Koos koos ke* River about 150 yards wide and the river below the forks about 300 yards wide. a miss understanding took place between Shabono one of our interpreters, and Jo. & R Fields which appears to have originated in just—[12] our diet extremely bad haveing nothing but roots and dried fish to eate, all the Party have greatly the advantage of me, in as much as they all relish the flesh of the dogs, Several of which we purchased of the nativs for to add to our Store of fish and roots &c. &c.—

Course Distance and remarks down the *KosKoskee* River—[13]

October 7th

N. 80° W.	1	mile to a Starboard Bend passed a rapid opsd. a Stony point on Lard.
S. W—	1½	to a Lard. bend high hills Steep

West—	½	to the Stard. Side passed a rapid
S W.—	1	to a Lard. bend. high Steep hills
N. 70° W.	1½	to a Stard. Bend passed a rapid
S. 60° W.	1½	to a Lard. Bend passed a bad rapid
West ☞	3	to a Stard. Bend passed a rapid at ½ a mile, a creek on the Lard. Side at 2 miles.
S. 10° E.	1½	to a Lard. bend passed a rapid
N. 60° E	1½	to a Stard. bend passed a rapid.
South	1	to a Lard. bend passed a bar rapid
West	1	in the Lard. bend, Cliffs high and rugid
N. W.	½	to a bad rapid in Lard bend.
S. 70° W.	1½	to a Starboard bend open Country,
S. W. ☞	2	to a Lard. bend at the mouth of a run opsd. to which 2 Lead Canisters were buried.

October 8th

N. W.	1	to a rapid in the Stard. Bend
South	¼	through a very bad rapid
S. 70° W	½	to a Lard. Bend, through good water
N. W.—	¼	through a rapid in the Stard. Bend
West	2½	to a Stard. Bend passed a bad rapid at one, and one at two miles
South	1½	to a Lard. Bend opsd. a Stoney bottom
S. 70° W.	2½	to a Stard. Bend, passed an Island on the Lard. Side, a rapid at the upper and lower point of the Island on the Lard. Side. Several Lodges on Island & on the ⟨Stard Shore⟩
S. W.	2	to a Stard. bend passed a rapid below which we ⟨pass⟩ halted at 3 Lodges, passed lower point of The Island Std. side
West ☞	2½	miles passed an Island on which three lodges of Indians were Encamped opposit a Small Creek on the Lard. Side and on the Std. Side below Six other Lodges, psd. two rapids opsd. the Island.
S. W.	1½	to a Stard. bend passed a rapid

S. 40° E	1½	to a Lard Bend passed a rapid
S. 60° W.	2	to a Stard. Bend passed an Island on the Lard. Side and a bad rapid
S. W.—	1½	to a Stard. Bend passed an Island on the Lard. Side a rapid at the upper and lower point, a large Creek Colter Creek falls in on the Std. Side above the low rapid. *Canoe Sunk* here
☞		
West	1½	to the upper point of an Island on the Stard. Side bad rapid Lard.

October 10th

South	1	mile passed a bad rapid at the head of an Island on the Lard Side
S. 20° W.	1½	to a Lard Bend passed an Island on the Lard. Side, a bad rapid at the upper point, passed the Lower point of a Second Island opsd. the mouth of a run on the Stard. Side
☞		
West	½	to a Stard. Bend passed a Small Island on the Lard. Side a rapid
S. 30° W.	3	to a Lard. Bend passed a Creek on the Lard. Side at ½ a mile Some Cotton wood in its bottom & 3 Lodges
☞		
West	2	to the head of an Island at a bad rapid on both Sides, Current on the right Side &
S. 30° W.	4 / 52	to a Lard. Bend passed a rapid at the lower point of the Island, passed rapids at one 1½, 2½ & 3½ miles, a branch and Indian Camp at three miles
West	3	miles to a Stard. bend passed a bad ragid rapid (one Canoe Stuck) above which we passed two large Indian Encampments.
S. W.	1	to a Starbd. bend passed a rapid
South	1	to a Lard Bend passed two rapids a bottom on either Side
S. 80° W.	3 / miles 60	to the mouth of *Louises River*[14] on the Lard. Side, passed two rapids—. about 250 yards wide

The *Cho-pun-nish*[15] or Pierced nose Indians are Stout likeley men, handsom women, and verry dressey in their way, the dress of the men are a white Buffalow robe or Elk Skin dressed with Beeds which are generally white, Sea Shells—i e the Mother of Pirl hung to ther hair & on a pice of otter Skin about their necks hair Cewed in two parsels hanging forward over their Sholders, feathers, and different Coloured Paints which they find in their Countrey Generally white, Green & light Blue. Some fiew were a Shirt of Dressed Skins and long legins, & Mockersons Painted, which appears to be their winters dress, with a plat of twisted grass about their necks.[16]

The women dress in a Shirt of Ibex, or ⟨Goat⟩ [X: *Argalea*] Skins which reach quite down to their anckles with ⟨out⟩ a girdle, their heads are not ornemented, their Shirts are ornemented with quilled Brass, Small peces of Brass Cut into different forms, Beeds, Shells & curios bones &c. The men expose those parts which are generally kept from few [X: *view*] by other nations but the women are more perticular than any other nation which I have passed in Screting the parts

Their amusements appear but fiew as their Situation requires the utmost exertion to prcure food they are generally employed in that pursute, all the Summer & fall fishing for the Salmon, the winter hunting the deer on Snow Shoes in the plains and takeing care of ther emence numbers of horses, & in the Spring cross the mountains to the Missouri to get Buffalow robes and meet &c. at which ⟨it⟩ time they frequent meet with their enemies & lose their horses & maney of ther people

Ther disorders are but fiew and those fiew of a Scofelous nature.[17] they make great use of Swetting. The hot and cold baethes, They are verry Selfish and Stingey of what they have to eate or ware, and they expect in return Something for everything give as presents or the Survices which they doe let it be however Small, and fail to make those returns on their part.[18]

1. Clark has scribbled a latitude reading following this line. It is in agreement with his notebook journal but in opposition to *Atlas* map 72 which gives the reading as 46° 29′ 21.7″ and which is closer to the actual location. Nearby Lewiston, Idaho, is 46° 25′.

2. Modern Hog Island shown on *Atlas* map 72 at the first extreme bend after Lapwai (Cottonwood) Creek. See later notes for this entry. Peebles (LT), 13.

3. Hatwai Creek, not shown on *Atlas* map 72. There has been no archaeological work on the south bank of the Clearwater River where mat lodges are indicated on Clark's map. Excavations at the Hatwai site at the mouth of Hatwai Creek indicate the area has been occupied for approximately eleven thousand years.

4. Nameless on *Atlas* map 72; perhaps later Catholic Creek, Nez Perce County, Idaho. Peebles (LT), 13.

5. "Cottonwood Creek" on *Atlas* map 72. Present Lapwai Creek, from the Nez Perce *Lappitwaitash*, meaning "boundary" (or *lepít wé·tes*, "two lands" or "two territories"), meeting the Clearwater at the site of Spalding, Nez Perce County. Space, 23; Peebles (LT), 13. Excavators at the Nez Perce National Historic Park at Spaulding encountered two prehistoric occupations. The earlier one dated as older than 8,000 b.p. but younger than 11,000 b.p. The second one, with two pithouses, is believed to postdate 1200 A.D. Chance & Chance.

6. "Ragid rapid" to the party, modern Reubens Rapids and shown on *Atlas* map 72 as "bad rapid Canoe Struck."

7. The Snake River, or Kimooenem of the first entry, meeting the Clearwater on the Washington-Idaho border, between present Lewiston, Nez Perce County, Idaho, and Clarkston, Asotin County, Washington. The captains, whether from guesswork or Indian information, considered it the same "Lewis's River" on which they had met the Lemhi Shoshones in August. That river, the present Lemhi River, flows into the Salmon, which flows into the Snake. Regarding the Lemhi-Salmon as the main stream, they called the Snake, from the Salmon junction on to its meeting with the Columbia, Lewis's River. Only months later did they begin to understand that the Snake above the Salmon was the major stream. An early sketch of the men's conceptions is found on fig. 10. Allen (PG), 309; *Atlas* map 72. The words *"Lewis's River"* appear to have been substituted for some erased words, which are illegible.

8. This information would have come from the Nez Perces. The first fork is probably the Grande Ronde River in northeastern Oregon and southeastern Washington. The second may be the Salmon, not recognized by the captains as their Lewis's River from the Indian description. Some of their confusion can be seen on *Atlas* map 72, particularly in the corrections. Allen (PG), 309. The word "Pâr-nash-te" is apparently *pannaiti*, the Shoshone name for the Bannock. Sven Liljeblad, personal communication, suggests that this ethnonym is used here to designate the Snake River plain.

9. This word may have been added to a blank space.

10. In Whitman County, Washington, opposite present Clarkston. *Atlas* map 72.

11. Again "Lewis's" appears to replace some erased words.

12. Probably meant for "jest."

13. See note at entry of October 7, 1805.

14. The words *"Louises River"* appear to have been substituted for some erased words.

15. The following material appears as a separate section after the table of courses. It could have been written at any time and inserted here to fill the last blank pages of Codex G. The word "Cho-pun-nish" appears to have been added to a blank space.

16. Sweetgrass, and used similarly to Lewis's description of August 21, 1805.

17. "Scrofulous," here probably alluding to skin diseases in general.

18. Here ends Clark's notebook Codex G. The remaining half-page is blank as are the last two pages. Codex H takes up on the following day. The Elkskin-bound Journal continues covering this same period.

Chapter Twenty-Three

The Rapids of the Snake and into the Columbia

October 11–20, 1805

[Clark]   *October 11h ⟨Thursday⟩ 1805* Friday[1]
  a cloudy morning wind.   Set out early   course

S. 40° W.	1½	miles to pt. of rocks on the Lbd. below a bottom & opsd. one psd. an old Lodge in the Ld. bottom
West	2	miles to a Stard. bend passed a rapd at ½ a mile 2 large Indn. houses in a bottom on the Stard Side above & below the rapid, rocky hill Sides
S. 40° W.	3	miles to the mouth of a ⟨Creek⟩ branch[2] on the Lard. bend, Several Lodges at the ⟨Creek⟩ branch and a house opposit vacant, we Purchased 7 dogs & fish roots &c to eat
S. 75° W.	1½	mile in the Lard. bend passed a rapid Point Swift water
N. 40° E	1	mile to a bend Std. at a rapid psd. a large Indn. house Std. Side
N. 60° W.	2	miles to a Lard bend at a rapid bad no timber except a fiew low Hackburry & a few willows.[3] we Purchd. Dried Cherries Pashequar root and *Pashequár marsh* or bread. Prise the shells *verry much,* also Iron wire—

N. 10° W.	2	miles to a Stard. bend at a rapid, 2 Ind. Huts on the Std Side
N. 40° W.	4	mile to a Std. bend psd. a Std. point to an Indian Camp of 3 Lodges on the Stard. Side, Dined & purchased 3 Dogs and a fiew dried fish for our voyage down one Indian accompd. us
S. 60° W.	2	miles to a Stard. bend passed a Stard point and 2 Indian House all the houses*4 are deserted the owners out in the plains killg the antelope, Saw gees & Ducks
S 30° W	1	to a Lard bend opsd. old Indn. Camp
N. 60 W	2	miles to Clift in a Stard. bend psd a rapid at ½ mile, an Indian Cabin on the Lard. Side
West	½	a mile to a Lard bend—
N. 10° W	1 ½	miles to a Std. bend passd. a cabin L. [S.?]
West	2 ½	miles to a Lard. bend passed a rapid opsd. a stoney Island from Stard opsd which S is an Indian Cabin, a rapid at the Lower point of Isd
N. W.	3 ½ ⎯⎯ 30	miles to the mouth of a run in the Stard. Bend at 2 Indian Lodges, here we *Camped*, met an Indian from below, Purchased 3 dogs and a fiew dried fish,5 this is a great fishing Island a house below, it evacuated wind a head

[Clark]   *October 11th ⟨Thursday⟩ [X: Friday] 1805*6

a cloudy morning wind from the East We Set out early and proceeded on passed a rapid at *two* miles, at 6 miles we came too at Some Indian lodges7 and took brackfast, we purchased all the fish we could and Seven dogs of those people for Stores of Provisions down the river. at this place I saw a curious Swet house under ground, with a Small whole at top to pass in or throw in the hot Stones, which those in threw on as much water as to create the temperature of heat they wished—8 at 9 mile passed a rapid at 15 miles halted at an Indian Lodge, to purchase provisions of which we precred some of the *Pash-he-quar* roots five dogs and a few fish dried, after takeing Some dinner of dog &c we proceeded on. Came to and encamped at 2 Indian Lodges at a great place of fishing9 here we met an Indian of a nation near the mouth of this river. [*NB: Qu*] we purchased three dogs and a fiew fish of those Indians, we Passed to-day nine rapids all of them great fishing places, at different places on the river saw Indian houses and Slabs & Spilt timber raised from the ground being the different parts of the houses of the natives when they reside on this river for the purpose of fishing   at this time they are out in the Plain on each side of the river hunting the antilope as we are informed by our Chiefs, ⟨at⟩ near each of those houses we observe Grave yards picketed, or pieces of wood stuck in permiscuesly over the grave or body which is Covered with earth, [*NB: wrap up dead, put them in earth & throw over earth & picket the ground about*][10]   The Country on either Side is an open plain leavel & fertile after assending a Steep assent of about 200 feet not a tree of any kind to be Seen on the river   The after part of the day the wind from the S. W. and hard. The day worm.

1. Since the Elkskin-bound Journal once again becomes chiefly courses and distances, most notes are to Codex H, which begins on this date.

2. Nameless on *Atlas* map 73; now Alpowa Creek in Asotin County, Washington.

3. Netleaf hackberry, *Celtis reticulata* Torr. (also called *C. douglasii* Planch) which is near its northernmost distributional limit along the Snake River at the Washington-Idaho border. Little (MWH), 33-NW; Hitchcock et al., 2:86–87. The willows are probably the sandbar willow.

4. Again an asterisk with no apparent reference or meaning.

5. The remainder of this entry appears to be in Lewis's hand.

6. Here begins Clark's Codex H, running to November 19, 1805. Before the text are three sketch maps of the Columbia River (figs. 22, 24, and 28). See Appendix C, vol. 2. The following notation in Biddle's hand precedes and annotates the maps: "No. 1 is the great Fall enlarged, which is marked in p. 3 of No 2 where the narrows begin—From No 2 the Narrows continue down to the word *camped* & then beginning with the word Creek in No. 3 down to Strawberry island." Coues has penciled in some dates and other words on the first two maps. Course material for October 10–16 is found after the codex entry of October 16, 1805.

7. This locality was occupied by the Alpaweyma band of the Nez Perces. Such bands were composed of several villages which took their name from the most prominent village within the territory. Archaeological research in this area has focused on three sites, one of which probably represents the lodges referred to by Clark. The area was also inhabited by the Upper Palouses, who often shared villages with the Nez Perces. The two peoples both spoke Shahaptian languages and had many similar cultural traits. Schwede; Walker (NPA), 9–18; Brauner; Trafzer & Scheuerman, 1.

8. Biddle expands at some length on the custom of the sweat bath. Coues (HLC), 2:626–27.

9. Below Almota Creek ("Brook" on *Atlas* map 73) in the vicinity of present Almota, Whitman County, Washington. Just above is Lower Granite Dam with Lower Granite Lake upstream and Lake Bryan downstream. This area was occupied by the Almotipu band of Nez Perces. Archaeological surveys have apparently failed to locate the site recorded by Clark, although several sites have been found on the south side of the river in this area. Trafzer & Scheuerman, 1, give this as the location of the Palouse village of Alamotin ("the soaring flame"). Spinden, 175; Nelson (LMLG), 11; Cleveland et al., 47.

10. Burials studied archaeologically in this general area are summarized by Sprague (ABP) and by Rodeffer. Biddle's writing is not in his customary red ink.

[Clark]   *October 12th ⟨Friday⟩ 1805* Saturday

a fair cool morning wind from E   after purchasing all the drid fish those people would Spear from their hole in which they wer buried we Set out at 7 oClock and proceeded on

S. W.	3	miles passed 4 Islands at 1½ miles ⟨three⟩ 3 nearly oppost a bad rapid on the Lard Side of those Islands, and Swift water around them to a Lard. point passed a Stard point
West	3	miles to a Lard Bend passed a Small rapid & Island on the Lard. also an Indian Cabin.
N. W.	2	miles to a Stard. Bend the bottoms are narrow from the points, the bends & high lands have Clifts of ruged rock to the river, & bottoms
S. 70° W.	2	miles to a bend on the Stard. at a rapid Isd opsd. passed a rapid on the Std. Side of a Stoney Island, opsd. to which on the Std. Side below the rapid a Small Creek[1] falls in Saw an Indian on the high land at a distance. no timber in view
South	2	miles to a pt. in Lard. bend here the Plains become low on both Sides river about 400 yards wide
S. 30° W.	2½	miles to the mouth of a Creek Ente in a Lard. bend opsd. a Small Island on the Lard Side
S. 85° W	2½	to the Stard. bend at a Swift place about half the distance of this course Cp L took Meridian altitd. on Ld. Side 72° 30′ 0″
S. 10° W.	1½	to a Lard Bend, (low open country)

S. 88° W.	3½	to a Stard. Bend wind S W. and hard. plain country rise gradually on each side passed Island and rapid an Indian house on the Stard.[2] Some Indians at it &c.
S. 60° W.	6	miles to a Stard. bend passed an Isld. at 4 miles & one at 5 miles, Swift water, and Sholey
S. 30° W.	1	mile to a Lard bend passd. a rapid at the upper pt. of a Small Stoney Isd.
West	1 / 30	mile to a Stard. bend opsd. a Small Island Close under the Lard Shore passed a run on the Std. side. here we Came too to view a falls or very bad rapid imediately below (Camped) which the Inds. informed us was very bad, we found it bad. Sent our Small Canoe over—

[Clark]   *October 12th ⟨Friday⟩ Saturday 1805*

A fair Cool morning wind from the East. after purchaseing every Speces of the provisions those Indians could Spare we Set out and proceeded on at three miles passed four Islands Swift water and a bad rapid opposit to those Islands on the Lard. Side. at 14½ miles passed the mouth of a large Creek on the Lard Side[3] opposit a Small Island here the Countrey assends with a gentle assent to the high plains, and the River is 400 yards wide about 1 mile below the Creek on the Same Side took meridian altitude which gave *72° 30′ 00″* Latitude produced [*blank*] North in the afternoon the wind Shifted to the S. W. and blew hard we passed to day [*blank*] rapids Several of them very bad and came to at the head of one (at 30 miles) on the Stard. Side to view it before we attemptd. to dsend through it. The Indians had told us was verry bad— we found long and dangerous about 2 miles in length, and maney turns necessary to Stear Clare of the rocks, which appeared to be in every direction. The Indians went through & our Small Canoe followed them, as it was late we deturmined to camp above untill the morning.[4] we passed Several Stoney Islands today Country as yesterday open plains, no timber of any kind a fiew Hack berry bushes & willows excepted, and but few drift trees to be found So that fire wood is verry Scerce—[5] The hills or assents from the water is faced with a dark ruged Stone.[6] The wind blew hard this evening.—

1. Penawawa Creek ("Brook" on *Atlas* map 73), near Penawawa, Whitman County, Washington.

2. Shown as "Cabin" on *Atlas* map 73, near present Little Goose Dam.

3. Deadman Creek ("Creek Small" on *Atlas* map 73), meeting the Snake at Central Ferry State Park, Garfield County, Washington.

4. In the vicinity of present Riparia, Whitman County, below the mouth of Alkali Flat Creek (shown as "Brook" on *Atlas* map 73).

5. They had entered the arid Great Columbian Plain, whose barren landscape offered a great contrast to the wooded mountains to the east. Allen (PG), 307–9; Meinig.

6. The dark rugged stone is Miocene-age basalt of the Columbia River Basalt Group. These rocks occupy much of the Columbia Plateau and were formed by the cooling of sheets of molten lava that extended for hundreds of miles and were each several hundred feet thick.

[Clark]   *October 13th ⟨Saturday⟩ Sunday 1805*

rained a little before day, and all the morning, a hard wind from the S West untill 9 oClock, the rained Seased & wind luled, and Capt Lewis with two Canoes Set out & ⟨Crossed⟩ passed down the rapid   The others Soon followed and we passed over this bad rapid Safe. We Should make more portages if the Season was not So far advanced and time precious with us

Course & Distance 13th

S. 20° W	2	miles to a Lard Bend passed in the greater part of the distance thro a bad rapids, rocks in every derection. Channel on the Lard Side about the center of the long rapid—
S. 70° W	3	miles to a large Creek in the Ld. bend. passed a bad rockey rapid at 2 miles many rocks
N. 50° W.	5	miles to a large Creek Std. bend [*X: at 2 Indian cabins*] passed a bad rapid for 4 miles Water Compressed in a narrow Channel not more than 25 yards for about 1½ miles Saw Several Indians, this place may be called the narrows or narrow rapid ⟨great fishery⟩
N. 75° W.	2	miles to the Stard. bend
S W.	2½	miles to a Lard. bend
N. 80° W.	3	miles to a Stard. bend
S. 60° W.	2	miles on the Std. Side passed a rapid

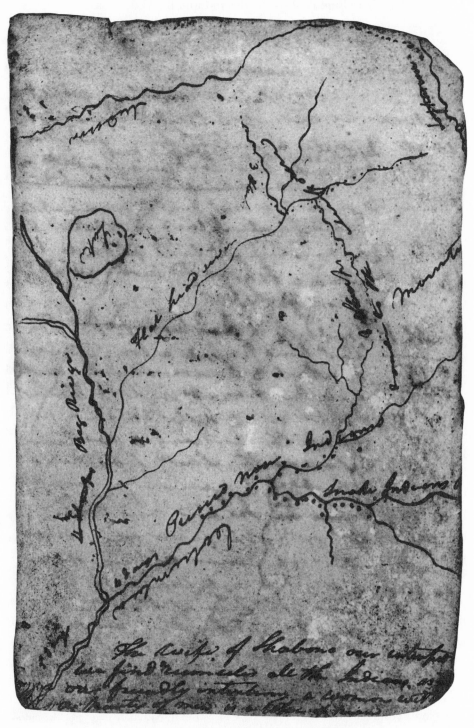

11. Columbia River and Affluents, Washington,
ca. October 13, 1805, Elkskin-bound Journal ⊕

S. 40° W.   3½   miles to a Lard. bend   high Clifts   the parts of an Indian
              23   house Scaffoled up on the Lard Sd. opposit a Picketed
                     grave yard   we Came to on the Stard. Side & Camped.
                     Two Indians whome we left at the forks over took us on
                     horsback & wishes to accompany us, no game [1]

The wife of Shabono our interpetr we find reconsiles all the Indians, as to our friendly intentions   a woman with a party of men is a token of peace

[Clark]   *October 13th ⟨Saturday⟩ Sunday 1805*

a windey dark raney morning   The rain commenced before day and Continued moderately untill near 12 oClock—   we took all our Canoes ⟨over⟩ through This rapid without any injurey.   a little below passed through another bad rapid at [*blank*] miles   passed the Mo: of a large Creek [*ML?: at 5 m in the Lard. bend we call Ki-moo-e-nimm Creek*][2]   [*ML?: 10 Ms.*] little river in a Stard. bend, imediately below a long bad rapid [*ML?: drewyers River*][3]; in which the water is Confined in a Chanel of about 20 yards between rugid rocks for the distance of a mile and a half and a rapid rockey Chanel for 2 miles above. This must be a verry bad place in high water, here is great fishing place, the timbers of Several houses piled up, and a number of wholes of fish, and the bottom appears to have been made use of as a place of deposit for their fish for ages past, here two Indians from the upper foks over took us and continued on down on horse back, two others were at this mouth of the Creek—   we passed a rapid about 9 mile lower.   at dusk came to on the Std. Side & Encamped.[4] The two Inds. on horse back Stayed with us. The Countery Thro' which we passed to day is Simlar to that of yesterday open plain no timber   passed Several houses evacuated at established fishing places,[5] wind hard from The S. W. in the evening and not very cold

1. At this point in the Elkskin-bound Journal appears a somewhat confused sketch map (fig. 11) showing the drainage of the Columbia River.

2. Now Tucannon River, Columbia County, Washington. *Atlas* map 73. "Ki-moo-e-nimm" (and similar spellings) may come from the Nez Perce term *qemúynem*. The etymology of the word is not clear but may have to do with the Wallowa valley region of the Nez Perce homeland in northeastern Oregon and apparently is unrelated to the Tucan-

non River, or at least only in a very distant geographical sense. Haruo Aoki, personal communication.

3. Present Palouse River, the boundary between Franklin and Whitman counties, Washington. This was the site of the largest Palouse village, Palus (in Nez Perce, "Palutpe"). Trafzer & Scheuerman, 2; *Atlas* map 74.

4. In Franklin County, perhaps opposite Ayer or a little lower on the opposite shore. *Atlas* map 74.

5. The burial vaults noted on *Atlas* map 74 on the east side of the Palouse (Drewyer's) River may represent an archaeological site where one burial was found, or it may represent the nearby talus burials. Nance; Sprague & Birkby, 4–6. The site mentioned on the west side of the Palouse River consisted of a large burial site involving more than two hundred individuals. The village associated with this burial ground is located nearby and to the east. Another village area, perhaps the one referred to by Clark because large circular housepit depressions are apparent on the surface, is located to the northwest of the burial ground. Sprague (PBS); Sprague (ABP), 86–101; Fryxell & Daugherty; Schalk, 141–77. A Jefferson peace medal was recovered during archaeological excavations of the area in 1964. The medal is now at Washington State University, Pullman. Chatters (LCEM); Cutright (LCIPM), 164–65. Late nineteeth-century photographs of the appearance of the piled-up house timbers may be seen in Rice (NAD), 57, 63.

[Clark]   *October 14th ⟨Sunday⟩ Monday 1805* [1]

a verry Cool morning wind from the West   Set out at 8 oClock   proceeded on

West	2½	miles to a Stard. bend Swift water opsd. a rock on Ld. pt. like a Ship
S. 10° W.	2½	miles to a Lard. bend passed a rapid ⟨and Small Island in Std. Side⟩
S. W	3	miles to a Stard. bend passed a rapid and Small Island on the Stard Side
S. 10° E.	2½	miles to a Lard. bend psd. small Isd. S.
S. 70° W.	1½	miles to a Starboard bend, wind Cold & from the S. W.—
South 18° W.	3	miles to a ⟨Stard. bend passed⟩ Lard. bend passed a long bad rapid on which 3 Canoes Struck with 2 rocky Islands in it off the Lard. Point at 3 miles, a cave in which the Indians have lived below on the Stard. Side near which is a grave yard above the ⟨passed on⟩ ⟨an⟩ Island and bad rapid ⟨opsd.⟩ on both Sides ⟨at⟩ [*blank*] ⟨miles⟩ [2]
ms.	15	

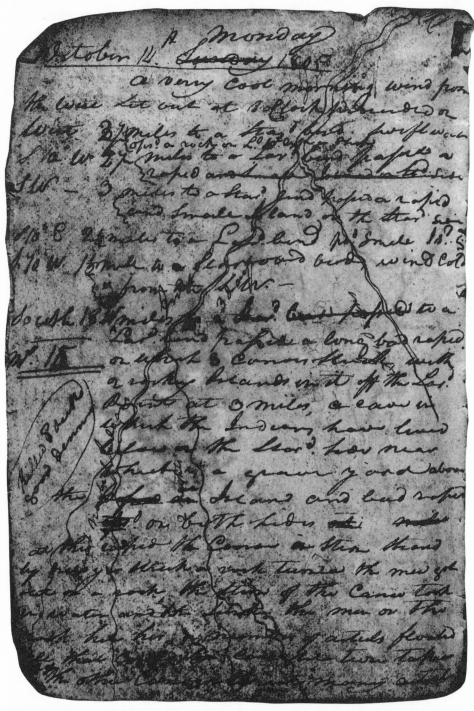

12. Indian Locales on Columbia River and Affluents,
ca. October 14, 1805, Elkskin-bound Journal ☞

at this rapid the Canoe a Stern Steared by drewyer Struck a rock turned the men got out on a rock   the Stern of the Canoe took in water and She Sunk   the men on the rock hel her, a number of articles floated   all that Could be Cought were taken by 2 of the othr Canoes, Great many articles lost among other things 2 of the mens beding Shot pouches Tomahaws &c. &c. and every article wet   of which we have great Cause to lament as all our loose Powder two Canisters, all our roots prepared in the Indian way, and one half of our goods, fortunately the lead canisters which was in the canoe was tied down, otherwise they must have been lost as the Canoe turned over   we got off the men from the rock   toed our canoe on Shore after takeing out all the Stores &c. we Could & put them out to dry on the Island on which we found Some wood which was covered with Stones, this is the Parts of an Indian house, which we used for fire wood, by the wish of our two Chiefs—   Those Chees, one of them was in the Canoe, Swam in & Saved Some property, The Inds. have buried fish on this Isld. which we are Cautious not to touch.   our Small Canoe & three Indians in another was out of Sight at the time our missfortune hapined, and did not join us.   wind hard S W.

[Clark]   *October 14th ⟨Sunday⟩ Monday 1805*

a Verry Cold morning wind from the West and Cool untill about 12 oClock When it Shifted to the S. W.   at 2½ miles passed a remarkable rock verry large and resembling the hill [hull] of a Ship[3] Situated on a Lard point at Some distance from the assending Countrey   passed rapids at 6 and 9 miles.   at 12 miles we Came too at the head of a rapid which the Indians told me was verry bad, we viewed the rapid found it bad   in decending three Stern Canoes Stuk fast for Some time on the head of the rapid and one Struk a rock in the worst part, fortunately all landed Safe below the rapid which was nearly 3 miles in length.   here we dined, and for the first time for three weeks past I had a good dinner of Blue wing Teel,[4] after dinner we Set out and had not proceded on two miles before our Stern Canoe in passing thro a Short rapid opposit the head of an Island, run on a Smoth rock and turned broad Side, the men got out on the [rock] all except one of our Indian Chiefs who Swam on Shore, The Canoe filed and Sunk   a number of articles floated out, Such as the mens bedding clothes & Skins, the Lodge &c. &c. the greater part of which were cought by 2 of the Canoes, whilst a 3rd was unloading & Steming the Swift Current to the relief of the men on the rock who could with much dificuelty hold the Canoe. however in about an hour we got the men an Canoe to Shore with the Loss of Some bedding Tomahaws Shot pouches Skins Clothes &c &c. all wet we had every articles exposed to the Sun to dry on the Island, our loss in provisions is verry Considerable all our roots was in the Canoe that Sunk, and Cannot be dried Sufficint to Save, our loose powder was also in the Canoe and is all wett This I think ⟨may⟩, we Shall saved.— In this Island[5] we found some Spilt [Split] timber the parts of a house which the Indians had verry Securely covered with Stone, we also observed a place where the Indians had buried there fish, we have made it a point at all times not to take any thing belonging to the Indians even their wood. but at this time we are Compelled to violate that rule and take a part of the Split timber we find here bured for fire wood, as no other is to be found in any direction. our Small Canoe which was a head returned at night with 2 ores which they found floating below. The wind this after noon from the S. W. as usial and hard

1. Under this entry in the Elkskin-bound Journal is a sketch map (fig. 12) showing a stylized view of the Columbia drainage system and Indian locales.

2. In the margin here, at right angles to the rest of the writing, is the phrase "killed 8 ducks, good dinner."

3. "Ship rock" on *Atlas* map 74. Now Monumental Rock, in Walla Walla County, Washington, northeast of Magallon.

4. Blue-winged teal, *Anas discors* [AOU, 140].

5. The island was at former Pine Tree Rapids, between Franklin and Walla Walla counties, Washington according to Coues (HLC), 2:631–32 n. 10. That area is just downstream from Burr Canyon and is now covered by the waters of Lake Sacajawea. The camp was also apparently in this area in Franklin County. *Atlas* map 74 shows "Indian Caves" in the cliffs of the northwest shore of the Snake River and a "Tomb." The most conspicuous caves in this general area are the Windust Caves, but they are some miles upstream from where the camp seems to have been. Clark may have misplaced the caves, found other than the Windust Caves, or the locating of the camp may be in error. In any case, archaeological excavations of these series of nine caves at Windust have proved extremely significant in studies of prehistoric cultural history and paleoenvironments of the area. Rice (CSWC); Thompson (WC).

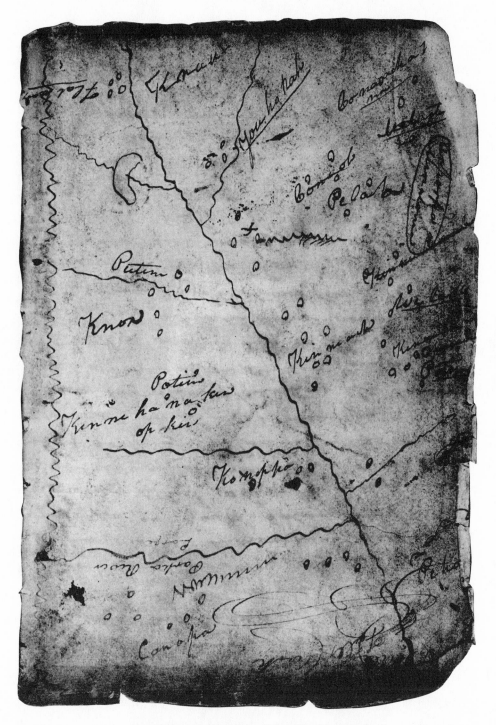

13. Indian Groups of the Columbia River Basin,
ca. October 15, 1805, Elkskin-bound Journal

273

[Clark]   *October 15th ⟨Monday⟩ Tuesday 1805* [1]

a fair morning after a Cold night. Some frost this morning and Ice. Several hunters out Saw nothing   Capt Lewis assended the hills & Saw Mountain a head bearing S. E. & N W.   a high point to the west. [2] Plain wavering. Set out at 3 oClock—

Course

South	4½	miles to the lower point of a Island close under the Std Side passed one on the Lard. & one other in the middle of the river, ⟨three⟩ 4 Small rapid at the low pt of 1st Isd. opsd. 2d & 3rd Islands—
S. E.	1½	mile to the lower point of an Isd. close under the Lard. bend opsd. the upper pt. of an Isd. on Std. point a Small rapid opposit
S. 35° W	9	miles to a Point of rocks on Lard. Sd. passed a place of Swift water at the lower point of the 1st Island a Small rapid a little below a Lard. point at 2 miles a Stard. point at 4 miles, a Lard. point at 5 miles a Stard. point 3 Small Isd. opsd. on Lard. & 2 on Stard. Side at 6 ½ a Small rapid, Several Scafles of Split timber on the Stard. Side in the bottom below the Islands a Island in the river at 8½ miles on Std. Side a fishing timber Scaffeled a willow bottom on the Lard Side above the point Country low on each side 90 to 100 [200?] feet is the hite of the plains Some Swift water at the last Isds.
South	5 / 20	miles to an Island in the head of a rapid Passed for 3 miles through good water in closed in Clifts of rocks 100 feet high. below which the river widens into a Bay nearly round. we Encamped at three Scaffles of Split timber on the Stard. Side. here we found our Pilot & one man wateing for us to Show us the ⟨rout⟩ best way thro those rapids, the evening cool, we saw no timber to day, except Small willow & Srub of Hackberry— Killed 2 Teel this evening.

[Clark]   *October 15th ⟨Monday⟩ Tuesday 1805*

a far morning   Sent out hunters to hunt in the plains, about 10 oClock they returned and informed that they could not See any Signs of game of any kind   Capt Lewis walked on the plains and informs that he could plainly See a rainge of mountains which bore S. E. & N. W. the nearest point south about 60 miles, and becoms high toward the N. W. The plaines on each Side is wavering. Labiesh killed 2 gees & 2 Ducks of the large kind. at two oClock we loaded & Set out, our Powder & Provisions of roots not Sufficently ⟨wet⟩ dry. ⟨but⟩ we Shall put them out at the forks or mouth of this river which is at no great distance, and at which place we Shall delay to make Some Selestial observations &c. passed Eleven Island and Seven rapids to day. Several of the rapids verry bad and dificuelt to pass. The Islands of different Sizes and all of round Stone and Sand, no timber of any kind in Sight of the river, a fiew Small willows excepted; in the evening the countrey becomes lower not exceding 90 or 100 feet above the water and back is a wavering Plain on each Side, passed thro: narrows for 3 miles where the Clifts of rocks juted to the river on each Side compressing the water of the river through a narrow chanel; below which it widens into a kind of bason nearly round without any proceptiable current, at the lower part of this bason is a bad dificuelt and dangerous rapid to pass, at the upper part of this rapid we over took the three Indians[3] who had Polited us thro the rapids from the forks. those people with our 2 Chiefs had proceeded on to this place where they thought proper to delay for us to warn us of the difficulties of this rapid.[4] we landed at a parcel of Split timber, the timber of a house of Indians out hunting the Antilope in the plains; and raised on Scaffolds to Save them from the Spring floods. here we were obliged for the first time to take the property of the Indians without the consent or approbation of the owner. the night was cold & we made use of a part of those boards and Split logs for fire wood. Killed two teel this evening. Examined the rapids which we found more dificuelt to pass than we expected from the Indians information. a Suckcession of Sholes, appears to reach from bank to bank for 3 miles which was also intersepted with large rocks Sticking up in every direction, and the chanel through which we must pass crooked and narrow. we only made 20 miles today, owing to the detention in passing rapids &c.

1. Opposite this entry in the Elkskin-bound Journal is a sketch map (fig. 13) of Indian groups of the Columbia River basin. Neither the tribal names nor geographic locations can be determined with any confidence.

2. Probably part of the Blue Mountains of southeast Washington and northeast Oregon.

3. These three were probably Palouse Indians. Trafzer & Scheuerman, 3.

4. Fishhook Rapids. They camped just above the rapids ("bason Rapids" on *Atlas* map 75), in Franklin County, Washington. At least two archaeological sites are known for the north shore of the Fishhook Rapids area. The downstream site appears to be the one illustrated in *Atlas* map 75; this site was a late prehistoric pit-house village that was archaeologically tested in 1959 by Daugherty.

[Clark]   *Octr. 16th ⟨Monday⟩ 1805* Wednesday

a cool morning   Set out early   passed the rapid with all the Canoes except Sgt. Pryors which run on a rock near the lower part of the rapid and Stuck fast, by the assistance of the 3 other Canoes She was unloaded and got off the rock without any further injorey than, the wetting the greater part of her loading— loaded and proceeded on   I walked around this rapid

Course

S. 12° E	3	miles to the Lard. bend passed a bad rapid all the way, here one Canoe Stuck. bad rapid
S. 60° W.	3	miles to a Stard. bend to a Scaffel of Split timber on an Island opsd. 2 other Isds. on Lard.
S 10° W.	3⟨½⟩	miles to a Point of rocks at a rapid opsd. the upper point of Small Island on th Lard. Side, passd. a rapid at the lower point of the 3 first Isds. one at the Lard. pt. 1½ mi. below Swift water
S. 50° W.	6	miles to Lard pt. opsd. a rapid and a pt. of an Island the Countrey low on both Sides Passed a rapid at 3 miles, passed a verry Bad rapid or falls, obliged to unload at 5 miles at the lower point of a Small Island Stard dined Lard. 5 Inds come to us
S. 28 W.	6½	miles to the Junction of Columbia R. in the Point Stard Passed the rapid opposit the upper Point of the Said Island and Passed a Small Isd. on Lard Side opposit, passed the lower point of the Island on Stard Side at 2½ miles a gravelley bare in the river at 3 miles, river wide Countrey on each side low, a rainge of hills on the west imedeately in front on the opposit side of Columbia [1]

We halted a Short time above the Point and Smoked with the Indians, & examined the Point and best place for our Camp, we Camped on the Columbia River a little above the point   I Saw about 200 men Comeing down from their villages & were turned back by the Chief, after we built our fires of what wood we Could Collect, & get from the Indians, the Chief brought down all his men Singing and dancing as they Came, formed a ring and danced for Some time around us   we gave them a Smoke, and they returned the village a little above, the Chief & Several delay untill I went to bead.   bought 7 dogs & they gave us Several fresh Salmon & Som horse dried

[Clark]   *October 16th Wednesday 1805*[2]

A cool morning   deturmined to run the rapids, put our Indian guide in front our Small Canoe next and the other four following each other, the canoes all passed over Safe except the rear Canoe which run fast on a rock at the lower part of the Rapids, with the early assistance of the other Canoes & the Indians, who was extreamly ellert every thing was taken out and the Canoe got off without any enjorie further than the articles which it was loaded all wet.   at 14 miles passed a bad rapid[3] at which place we unloaded and made a portage of ¾ of a mile, haveing passd. 4 Smaller rapids, three Islands and the parts of a house above, I Saw Indians & Horses on the South Side below.   five Indians[4] came up the river in great haste, we Smoked with them and gave them a piece of tobacco to Smoke with their people and Sent them back, they Set out in a run & continued to go as fast as They Could run as far as we Could See them. after getting Safely over the rapid and haveing taken Diner Set out and proceeded on Seven miles to the junction of this river and the Columbia which joins from the N. W.[5]   passd. a rapid two Islands and a graveley bare, and imediately in the mouth a rapid above an Island. In every direction from the junction of those rivers the Countrey is one Continued plain low and rises from the water gradually, except a range of high Countrey[6] which runs from S. W & N E and is on the opposit Side about 2 miles distant from the Collumbia and keeping its derection S W untill it joins a S W. range of mountains.

We halted above the point on the river Kimooenim[7] to Smoke with the Indians who had collected there in great numbers to view us,[8] here we met our 2 Chiefs who left us two days ago and proceeded on to this place to inform those bands of our approach and friendly intentions towards all nations &c.   we also met the 2 men who had passed us Several days ago on hors back, one of them we observed was a man of great influence with those Indians, harranged them; after Smokeing with the Indians who had collected to view us we formed a camp at the point[9] near which place I Saw a fiew pieces of Drift wood after we had our camp fixed and fires made, a Chief came from their Camp which was about ¼ of a mile up the Columbia river at the head of about 200 men Singing and beeting on their drums Stick and keeping time to the musik, they formed a half circle around us and Sung for Some time, we gave them all Smoke, and Spoke to their Chiefs as well as we could by Signs informing them of our friendly disposition to all nations, and our joy in Seeing those of our Children around us, Gave the principal chief[10] a large Medal Shirt and Handkf. a 2nd Chief a Meadel of Small Size, and to the Cheif who came down from the upper villages a Small *Medal* & Handkerchief.

The Chiefs then returned with the men to their camp; Soon after we purchased for our Provisions *Seven* Dogs, Some fiew of those people made us presents of fish and Several returned and delayed with us untill bedtime—   The 2 old Chiefs who accompanied us from the head of the river precured us Some fuil ⟨wood⟩ Such as ⟨woods⟩ the Stalks of weed or plant and willow bushes—   one man made me a present of a about 20 lb. of verry fat Dried horse meat.

Great quantities of a kind of prickley pares, much worst than any I have before Seen of a tapering form and attach themselves by bunches.

The Course's Distance and Remarks Decending the
Lewis's river from the mouth of *Kos kos kia*
in Latd. 46° 29′ 21.7″ N.[11]

October 10 1805

| West | 1 | mile to a bluff of high land in a bend to the Starboard Side, passed an old Encampment of Indians S. S. |

S 40° W.	1½	miles to a point of rocks in a Lard. bend opposit to a bottom an old lodge on the Larboard Side.
West	2	miles to a Starboard bend passed a rapid at ½ a mils, 2 houses on the Std. Side, ⟨passed two large Island⟩ rockey hill Sides.
S. 40° W.	3	miles to the mouth of a Brook on the Lard. Side, passed a large Camp of Alpowa Cr. Indians on the Lard Side above, a large vacant house opposit St. Side
N. 75° W.	1½	miles in the Lard Bend passed a rapid and Some Swift water
N. 40° E.	1	mile to a Stard. Bend at a *rapid* a large vacant house on the Std. Side.
N. 60° W.	2	miles to a Lard Bend at a bad *rapid* no timber except a fiew lose Hackberries.
N. 10° W.	2	miles to a Stard. Bend at a rapid Some Huts on the Stard. Side.
N 40° W.	4 / 18	miles to a Stard. Bend, passed a Std. point to *three* Lodges of Indians on the Stard. Side.
S. 60° W.	2	miles to a Stard. Bend, passed a Stard. point; two large houses vacant on the Stard. Side, Killed gees & Duck
S. 30° W.	1	miles to a lard Bend opposit an old Indian fishing encampment.
N. 60° W.	2	To a Clift in a Stard. Bend passed a rapid at ½ a mile; an Indian house on the Stard. Side.
West	½	a mile to a Lard. Bend.
N. 10° W.	1½	miles to a Stard. Bend passed a house St. S
West	2½	miles to a lard Bend passed a rapid opposit a Stoney Island from the Std. opposit to which & on the Stard Side is an Indian House, a rapid at the lower point of the Island.
N 45° W.	3½	miles to the mouth of a Brook in the Stard. Bend.

below is two Indian houses inhabited, a great fishing place. we encamped

October 12th

S. 45° W.	3	miles passed 4 Islands first at ½ a mile and the 3 others nearly opposit each other, and above a bad rapid, on the Lard Side, and Swift water, passed a Stard point.
West	3	miles to a Lard Bend passing a Small rapid and Island on the Lard. Side, a vacant House on the Lard. Side
N. 45° W.	2	miles to a Stard. Bend the bottoms are narrow in the Points, the bends now have Clifts of rugid rocks to the river, also to the bottoms.
S 70° W.	2	miles to a bend on the Stard. Side at a rapid opposit an Island and on the lard. Side, passed a rapid on the Stard. Side of a Stoney Island below which and on the Stard. Sid a Brook falls in, Saw Indians at a distance on the high lands.
South	2	miles to a point in a lard Bend, here the plains or high Countrey become much lower on both Sides, and river about 400 yeards wide.
S. 30° W.	2½	miles to the mouth of a Small Creek in a Lard Bend opposit to a Small island on the Lard Side.
S. 85° W.	2½	miles to a Stard. Bend at a Swift part of the river, at 1½ miles Took Median altitude 72° 30′ 0″
S 10° W.	1½	miles to a Lard Bend, low open countrey on each Side.
S. 88° W.	3½	miles to a Stard. Bend (wind hard from the S. W,) passed a rapid and Island. a large House of Indians opposit on the Stard. Side Countrey rise gradually on each Sides
S. 60° W.	6	miles to a Stard. Bend, passed an Island at 4 miles, one at 5 miles water Swift and Shallow.
S. 30° W.	1 / 60	mile to a Lard Bend passed a rapid at the upper point of a Small Stoney Isld.

West	1	mile to a Stard Bend opposit to a Small Island close under the Lard Side, passed a Brook on the Std. Side. Came too to View a rapid

13th October 1805

S. 20° W.	2	miles to a Lard. Bend passed in the greater part of this distance through a verry bad rapid, rocks in every direction; Chanel on the Lard. Side abt. the Center of the rapid.
S. 70° W.	3	miles to a large Creek in a Lard. Bend Ki moo o nymm C passed a bad rocky rapid at 2 miles
N. 50° W.	5	miles to a large *Creek* in a Stard. Bend Drewyers R at a great fishing establishment below the Creek at which place Several Scaffols of the parts of Indian Houses remained passing for 4 miles over a bad rapid, and through a narrow Channel, river Compressed and passes for 1½ miles thro' a Chanel not more than 25 yards wide, the other part of the river being crouded with black rough rocks, Saw Several Indians at Those narrows.
N. 75° W.	2	miles to the Starboard bend.
S. 45° W.	2½	miles to a Lardboard Bend.
N. 80° W.	3	miles to a Stard. Bend
S. 60° W	2	on the Stard. Side. passed a rapid.
S 40° W.	3½	miles to a high Clifts in a Lard bend passed the parts of a House put up on forks on the Lard. Side, a Grave yard on the Stard. Side, near which we Encamped, 2 Indians overtook us here and informed they intinded to proceed on by land to the great river. &c.—

14th October

West	2½	miles to a Stard. Bend opposit to a rock on the Lardside resembling a Ship at a Distance, passed Some Swift water
S. 10° W.	2½	miles to a Stard. Bend. passed a rapid ⟨and Small island on the Std. Side⟩

S. 45° W.	3	miles to a Stard. Bend passed a rapid & Small Isld. on the Stard. Side
S. 10° E.	2½	miles to a Lard. Bend, passed a Small Island Stard. Side.
S. 70° W.	1½	miles to a Stard. Bend (wind hard from S. W. Cool)
South 18° West	<u>3</u> ⟨99⟩ 114	miles to a Lard. Bend passed a long bad rapid on which 3 canoes Stuck fast, with 2 Small rockey Islands in the rapid, at 3 miles is a Cave in a ⟨lard point⟩ the Std. Side in which the Indians have laterly lived, a grave yard near it above the Caves is a rapid on both Sides one Canoe Struck a rock and in passing this rapid & Sunk.

15th October 1805

South	4½	miles to the lower point of an Island Close under the Stard Side passed one on the Lard Side and one in the middle of the river; four smal rapids, three of them at the lower points of the Said 3 Islands.
S. 45° E	1	mile to the lower point of an Islannd Close under the Lard Bend opsd the upper point of an Island on the Stard. Side at which place there is a Small rapid
S 35° W.	9	miles to a point of rocks on the lard. Side, passed a place of Swift water at the lower point of the 1st Island, a Small rapid a little below, a Lard point at 2 miles, a stard point at 4 miles, a Lard point at 5 miles, a Stard point and 3 Small Islands opposit ⟨near⟩ the Stard. Side and 2 Islands opds. on the lard Side at 6½ miles, a Small rapid below the Islands, Severals Scaffolds of the parts of Houses on the Stard Side, at 8½ miles passed an Island and Swift water, opposit on the Stard Side is the parts of a house raised on forks. a Small willow bottom on Lard. The Countrey becoms low on each Side Say from 90′ to 100 feet above the water
South	5	miles to an Island at the head of a rapid, passed for 3 miles thro' Still gentle water Confined between purpendicular Clifts of rocks, & then widens into a kind of basin. come to and Encamped at an old fishing place near a Saffle of the parts of a house.

S. 12° E	3	miles to a Lard. Bend passed a bad rapid in this whole. course, one Conoe Stuck & filed.
S. 60° W.	3	miles to a Stard Bend passed an Island on which the parts of a house was raised on forks &c. 2 Small Isds. on the Lard. Side.
S. 10° W	3	miles to a point of rocks at a rapid opposit to the upper point of a Small Island & on the lard. side, passed a rapid at the lower point of 3 islands; and one 1½ miles below them.
S. 60° W.	6 ‾‾‾‾ 148½	miles to a Lard. point opposit to a rapid at the upper point of an Island, passed a rapid at 3 miles, passed a (falls) or verry bad rapid at 5 miles at which place we were obliged to unlode and make a portage of ¾ of a mile. an Isd. on Std Side in the rapid.
S. 28° W.	6½ ‾‾‾ 154	miles to the junction of the *Ki moo-e nim* with the Columbia River, passed a rapid opposit to the upper point of a Sandy Isld., passed a Small Island on the Lard. Side, opposit, passed the lower point of the Island on the Std. Side at 2 miles, a graveley bare in the river at 3 miles.

1. Opposite this material is a column of figures:

$$
\begin{array}{r}
1 \\
30 \\
30 \\
23 \\
15 \\
\underline{20} \\
\underline{21} \\
140 \\
\underline{60} \\
\underline{\underline{200}}
\end{array}
$$

The figures represent mileages for October 11–16, 1805, the first number apparently being an adjustment.

2. Clark now has the days of the week correct in his codex journal; he did not get them right in the elkskin book until October 28. This may say something about the timing of his copying from one journal to the other.

3. Identified by Coues (HLC), 2:634 as Five-mile Rapids. *Atlas* map 75 shows the portage, which may be in the area of present Strawberry Island.

4. These may have been Palouse Indians. Trafzer & Scheuerman, 4.

5. The junction of the Columbia and the Snake (Lewis's) rivers.

6. The Horse Heaven Hills, or Mountains, in Yakima and Benton counties, Washington, running southwest toward the Cascade Range. *Atlas* map 75.

7. The Snake (Lewis's) River. *Atlas* map 75 has the word "Kimooenim" crossed out and "Lewis's" substituted.

8. They met Indians of two groups which the captains called Chimnapams and Sokulks, today known as the Yakimas and Wanapams respectively. The designations by Lewis and Clark are given in Shahaptian; the former is *čamnápam*, "the people of the *Chamná*," a village at the confluence of the Yakima River with the Columbia River; the term Sokulks may come from $k^w sis$ (or $k^2u'sis$), the name of a village mentioned below. The Yakimas lived in the vicinity of present Pasco, Franklin County, Washington, on both sides of the river and the Wanapams farther up the Columbia, on the west bank. They belonged to the same Shahaptian-language family as the Nez Perces, which is probably why the two Nez Perce chiefs were so useful in establishing friendly relations. A large permanent village named $k^2u'sis$, "two rivers meet," has been located approximately in the location of the village from which the chief and his men came. This village was occupied mainly by Yakima people, but many Walula and some Umatilla people lived there also. The site was an important trading center and a valuable fishing location. Trafzer & Scheuerman, 4, give Pasco as the location also of the Palouse village of Qosispah. Ray (NVCB), 144; Ronda (LCAI), 164–65.

9. In the point between the Snake and the Columbia, in Franklin County, Washington, just southeast of present Pasco and at the site of the Sacajawea State Park. *Atlas* map 75.

10. Cutssahnem, named below, October 18, 1805. Apparently all that is known of him is in the journals.

11. Here Clark gives the courses and distances from the Clearwater-Snake confluence to the Snake-Columbia confluence. There are some slight differences with the Elkskin-bound Journal. See note at October 11, 1805. The word *"Lewis's"* appears to have been substituted for an erased word.

October 17th Thursday [over Tuesday] 1805
Forks of Columbia

[Clark]

Took altitude with Sextant as follows

	h	m	s
A M.	7	40	13
"		42	58
"		43	44

altitude produced 22° 25′ 15″

Observed time and distance of Son and moon nearest Limbs the Sun East (*at the Point*)

	Time			distance		
	H.	M.	S.			
A M.	7	51	43	60°	47'	15"
"		53	33	"	46	30
"		54	35	"	45	45
"		55	55	"	45	
"		57	37	"	45	
"		58	29	"	44	
	8		26	"	43	45
"		1	22	"	43	15
"		3	8	"	43	
"		4	43	"	42	30
"		6	5	"	43	
"		7	52	"	41	30

Magnetick azmoth. Time and distance of the Sun &c.

azmth.		*Time*			*distance*	
	H.	m.	S			
S 75° ⟨W⟩ E	8	15	45	33°	4'	30"
S. 74° ⟨W⟩ E	8	19	43	34	13	

Took Equal altitudes

	H.	m	S		h	m	s
A M.	8	23		P M	3	21	53
"		24	55		"	23	50
"		26	49		"	25	42

altitude produced is 35° 9 30

This morning after the Luner observations, the old chief came down, and Several men with dogs to Sell & womin with fish &c. the Dogs we purchased the fish not good.

I took 2 men and Set out in a Small Canoe with a view to go as high up the Columbia river as the 1st forks which the Indians made Signs was but a Short distance, I set out at 2 oClock firs course was N. 83° W 6 miles to the lower point of a Island on the Lard. Side, passed an Island in the middle of the river at 5 miles, at the head of which is a rapid not bad at this rapid 3 Lodges of mats on the Lard emenc quantites of dried fish, then West 4 miles to the Lower point of an Island on the Stard. Side, 2 lodges of Indians large and built of mats— passed 3 verry large mat lodges at 2 mile on the Stard Side large Scaffols of fish drying at every lodge, and piles of Salmon lying. the Squars engaged prepareing them for the Scaffol— a Squar gave me a dried Salmon from those lodes on the Island an Indian Showed me the mouth of the river which falls in below a high hill on the Lard. N. 80° W. 8 miles from the Island.[1] The river bending ⟨Star⟩ Lard.— This river is remarkably Clear and Crouded with Salmon in maney places, I observe in assending great numbers of Salmon *dead* on the Shores, floating on the water and in the Bottoms which can be seen at the debth of 20 feet. the Cause of the emence numbers of dead Salmon I can't account for[2] So it is I must have seen 3 or 400 dead and maney living the Indians, I believe make us[e] of the [*illegible, crossed out*] fish which is not long dead as, I Struck one nearly dead and left him floating, Some Indians in a canoe behind took the fish on board his canoe

The bottoms on the ⟨West⟩ South Side as high as the Tarcouche tesse[3] is from 1 to 2 miles wide, back of the bottoms rises to hilly countrey, the Plain is low on the North & Easte for a great distance no wood to be Seen in any direction.

The Tarcouche tesse bears South of West, the Columbia N W above range of hills on the West Parrelel a range of mountains to the East which appears to run nearly North & South distance not more than 50 miles—[4] I returned to the point at Dusk followed by three canoes of Indians 20 in number— I killed a Fowl of the Pheasent kind as large as a ⟨Small⟩ turkey.[5] The length from his Beeck to the end of its tail 2 feet 6¾ Inches, from the extremity of its wings across 3 feet 6 Inches. the tail feathers 13 Inches long, feeds on grass hoppers, and the Seed of wild Isoop[6]

Those Indians are orderly, badly dressed in the Same fashions of those above except the women who wore Short Shirts and a flap over them 22 Fishing houses of Mats robes of Deer, Goat & Beaver.

[Clark]   *October 17th Thursday 1805*[7]

A fair morning made the above observations during which time the principal Chief came down with Several of his principal men and Smoked with us. Several men and woman offered Dogs and fish to Sell, we purchased all the dogs we could, the fish being out of Season and dieing in great numbers in the river, we did not think proper to use them, Send out Hunters to Shute the Prarie Cock a large fowl which I have only Seen on this river; Several of which I have killed, they are the Size of a Small turkey, of the pheasant kind, one I killed on the water edge to day measured from the Beek to the end of the toe 2 feet 6 & ¾ Inches; from the extremities of its wings 3 feet 6 inches; the tale feathers is 13 inches long: they feed on grasshoppers and the Seed of the wild plant which is also peculiar to this river and the upper parts of the Missoury somewhat resembling the whins—.[8] Capt. Lewis took a vocabelary of the Language of those people who call themselves *So kulk,* and also one of the language of a nation resideing on a Westerly fork of the Columbia which mouthes a fiew miles above this place who Call themselves *Chim nâ pum*   Some fiew of this nation reside with the *So kulks* nation, Their language differ but little from either the Sokulks or the *Chô-pun-nish* (or pierced nose) nation which inhabit the Koskoskia river and Lewis's R[9] below.

I took two men in a Small Canoe and assended the Columbia river 10 miles to an Island near the Stard. Shore on which two large Mat Lodges of Indians were drying Salmon, (as they informed me by Signs for the purpose of food and fuel, & I do not think at all improbable that those people make use of Dried fish as fuel,[)] The number of dead Salmon on the Shores & floating in the river is incrediable to Say and at this Season they have only to collect the fish Split them open and dry them on their Scaffolds on which they have great numbers, how far they have to raft their timber they make their Scaffolds of I could not lern; but there is no timber of any Sort except Small willow bushes in Sight in any direction— from this Island the natives showed me the enterance of a large Westerly fork which they Call Tâpetêtt at about 8 miles distant, the evening being late I deturmined to return to the forks, at which place I reached at Dark.   from the point up the Columbia River is N. 83° W. 6 miles to the lower point of an Island near the Lard. Side   passed a Island in the middle of the river at 5 miles at the head of which is a rapid, not dangerous   on the Lard Side opposit to this rapid is a fishing place 3 Mat Lodges, and great quants. of Salmon on Scaffolds drying. Saw great num-

bers of Dead Salmon on the Shores and floating in the water, great numbers of Indians on the banks viewing me and 18 canoes accompanied me
from the point— The Waters of this river is Clear, and a Salmon may be
Seen at the deabth of 15 or 20 feet. West 4 miles to the lower point of a
large Island near the Stard. Side at 2 Lodges, passed three large lodges[10]
on the Stard Side near which great number of Salmon was drying on
Scaffolds one of those Mat lodges I entered found it crouded with men
women and children and near the enterance of those houses I saw maney
Squars engaged Splitting and drying Salmon. I was furnished with a mat
to Sit on, and one man Set about prepareing me Something to eate, first
he brought in a piece of a Drift log of pine and with a wedge of the elks
horn, and a malet of Stone curioesly Carved he Split the log into Small
pieces and lay'd it open on the fire on which he put round Stones, a
woman handed him a basket of water and a large Salmon about half
Dried, when the Stones were hot he put them into the basket of water
with the fish which was Soon Sufficently boiled for use. it was then taken
out put on a platter of rushes neetly made, and Set before me they
boiled a Salmon for each of the men with me, dureing those prepera-
tions, I Smoked with those about me who Chose to Smoke which was but
fiew, this being a custom those people are but little accustomed to and
only Smok thro form. after eateing the boiled fish which was delicious, I
Set out & halted or came too on the Island at the two Lodges. Several fish
was given to me, in return for Which I gave Small pieces of ribbond
from those Lodges the natives Showed me the mouth of *Tap teel* River
about 8 miles above on the west Side this western fork appears to beare
nearly West, The main Columbia river N W.— a range of high land to
the S W and parralal to the river and at the distance of 2 miles on the
Lard. Side, the countrey low on the Stard. Side, and all Coverd. with a
weed or plant about 2 & three feet high and resembles the whins. I can
proceive a range of mountains to the East which appears to bare N. &
South distant about 50 or 60 miles. no wood to be Seen in any derection— On my return I was followd. by 3 canoes in which there was 20
Indians I shot a large Prairie Cock Several Grouse, Ducks and fish. on
my return found Great Numbr. of the nativs with Capt Lewis, men all
employd in dressing ther Skins mending their clothes and putting ther

arms in the best order the latter being always a matter of attention with us. The Dress of those natives differ but little from those on the Koskoskia and Lewis's[11] rivers, except the women who dress verry different in as much as those above ware long leather Shirts which highly ornimented with beeds Shells &c. &c. and those on the main Columbia river only ware a truss or pece of leather tied around them at their hips and drawn tite between ther legs and fastened before So as barly to hide those parts which are So Sacredly hid & Scured by our women. Those women are more inclined to Copulency than any we have yet Seen, with low Stature broad faces, heads flatened ⟨the eyes back⟩ and the foward compressed so as to form a Streight line from the nose to the Crown of the head,[12] their eyes are of a Duskey black, their hair of a corse black without orniments of any kind braded as above,

The orniments of each Sects are Similar, Such as large blue & white beeds, either pendant from their ears or encircling their necks, or wrists & arms. they also ware bracelets of Brass, Copper & horn, and trinkets of Shells, fish bones and curious feathers. Their ⟨Dress are as follows viz⟩ garments Consists of a short Shirt of leather and a roabe of the Skins of Deer or the Antilope but fiew of them ware Shirts all have Short robes. Those people appears to live in a State of comparitive happiness: they take a greater Share labor of the woman, than is common among Savage tribes, and as I am informd. Content with one wife (as also those on the Ki moo e nim river) Those people respect the aged with veneration, I observed an old woman in one of the Lodges which I entered She was entirely blind as I was informed by Signs, had lived more than 100 winters, She occupied the best position in the house, and when She Spoke great attention was paid to what She Said—. Those people as also those of the *flat heads* which we had passed on the Koskoske and Lewis's[13] rivers are Subject to Sore eyes, and maney are blind of one and Some of both eyes. this misfortune must be owing to the reflections of the Sun &c. on the waters in which they are continually fishing during the Spring Summer & fall, & the Snows dureing the, winter Seasons, in this open countrey where the eye has no rest.[14] I have observed amongst those, as well in all other tribes which I have passed on these waters who live on fish maney of different Sectes who have lost their teeth ⟨quit⟩ about middle age, Some have their teeth worn to the gums, perticelar those of the upper jaws, and the tribes generally have bad teeth   the cause of it I cannot account   sand attachd. to the roots &c the method they have of useing the dri'd Salmon, which is mearly worming it and eating the rine & Scales with the flesh of the fish, no doubt contributes to it[15]

The Houses or Lodges of the tribes of the main Columbia river is of large mats made of rushes, Those houses are from 15 to 60 feet in length generally of an Oblong Squar form, Suported by poles on forks in the iner Side, Six feet high, the top is covered also with mats leaveing a Seperation in the whole length of about 12 or 15 inches wide, left for the purpose of admitting light and for the Smok of the fire to pass which is made in the middle of the house.— The roughfs are nearly flat, which proves to me that rains are not common in this open Countrey

Those people appeare of a mild disposition and friendly disposed— They have in their huts independant of their nets gigs & fishing tackling each bows & large quivers of arrows on which they use flint Spikes. Theire ammusements are Similar to those of the Missouri.   they are not beggerley and receive what is given them with much joy.

I saw but fiew horses   they appeared make but little use of those animals principally useing Canoes for their uses of procureing food &c.

1. The Yakima River, "Tape-tett" on *Atlas* map 75, meeting the Columbia at modern Richland, Benton County, Washington. The name *táptat* refers to a Yakima village on the Yakima River, near Prosser, Benton County.

2. Clark was seeing the end of the annual salmon migration up the rivers from the sea; the fish were dying after having laid and fertilized their eggs. They were probably either coho (silver) salmon, *Oncorhynchus kisutch*, or sockeye (blue-backed) salmon, *O. nerka*, which are both fall breeders. Cf. Clemens & Wilby, 81–89; Cutright (LCPN), 225.

3. See above, September 10, 1805.

4. The Horse Heaven Hills to the west and the Blue Mountains to the east. See above, October 15, 1805.

5. Their first specimen of the sage grouse, a species new to science which they had seen earlier (June 5 and August 12, 1805), and which Lewis describes more fully on March 2, 1806. Burroughs, 213–15.

6. Big sagebrush.

7. Clark places the observations of both October 17 and 18 together before the first day's entry in Codex H. Being nearly identical to the ones in the Elkskin-bound Journal,

we do not print them here. On the eighteenth, however, Clark uses the term "Lewis's River" for the "*Ki-moo-e nim*" as he has it in the elkskin book. The words appear to have been substituted for some erased words.

8. Whins refers to gorse, furze, and other prickly, thorny shrubs. It is the "wild Isoop" of the other entry (big sagebrush). Since sagebrush was new to the explorers they used a variety of terms in identifying it.

9. Again, "Lewis's R" appears to have replaced some erased words.

10. Perhaps a Palouse village in Franklin County, Washington, above Pasco. Trafzer & Scheuerman, 5; *Atlas* map 75.

11. "Lewis's" apparently replaces an erased word.

12. Here was their first encounter with a custom and its results which for whites were among the most striking cultural traits of the Columbia and Northwest Coast peoples. These lower Columbia tribes placed infants in a special cradleboard with an angled board compressing the forehead; in some cases a tight headband was apparently used instead. Later, Clark sketched the headboard apparatus and examples of the results (see vol. 6). The eventual effect on the soft skull of the child was the shape noted by Clark, the head becoming decidedly pointed. Many whites applied the term "flathead" to those who practiced head deformation, although the Indians themselves apparently reserved the term for tribes in the interior who left their heads naturally "flat" on top. The deformed head shape was considered a mark of distinction, beauty, and superior status. Slaves were not allowed to deform the heads of their children. Hodge, 1:96–97; Ruby & Brown (CITC), 47–49.

13. Again, the substitution of "Lewis's" for an erased word.

14. These disorders may have been due to trachoma, gonorrhea, and perhaps also glaucoma. Chuinard (OOMD), 360–61; Cutright (LCPN), 223–24.

15. Clark was probably right in his surmise. Cutright (LCPN), 224.

[Clark]   *October 18th ⟨Wednesday⟩* Friday *1805*

a cold morning faire & wind from S E   Several Heath hens or large Pheasents lit near us & the men killed Six of them.

Took one altitude of the Suns upper Limb 28° 22′ 15″ at

    h   m   s
    8   1   24   A. M.

Several Indian Canoes Come down & joind those with us, made a Second Chief by giveing a meadel & wampom   I also gave a String of wampom to the old Chief who came down with us and informed the Indians of our views and intentions in a council

Observed time and distance of Sun & moons nearest Limbs   Sun East

Time			distance		
H	m	S			
9	37	46	47°	15′	30″
"	40	32	"	14	15
"	41	47	"	14	
"	42	55	"	13	30
"	43	44	"	12	45
"	46	2	"	12	30
"	47	18	"	12	
"	48	35	"	11	45
"	49	44	"	11	15
"	50	53	"	11	
"	52		"	9	30
"	53	46	"	9	30

Took a second altitude of the Suns upper Limb—58° 34′ 45″ at

h	m	s
10	3	59

Measured the width of the Columbia River, from the Point across to a Point of view is S 22° W   from the Point up the Columa to a Point of view is N. 84° W. 148 poles, thence across to the 1st point of view is S 28½ E

Measured the width of *Ki moo e nim* River, from the Point across to an object on the opposit side is N. 41½ E from the Point up the river is N. 8 E. 82 poles thence accross to the Point of view is N. 79° East

Distance across the *Columbia* 960¾ yds water

Distance across the *Ki-moo-e nim* 575 yds water

Names of this nation above the mouth of the *Ki-moo-e-nim* is *So-Kulk* Perced noses   The Names of the nation on the Kimoenim River is *Cho-pun-nish*   Piercd noses at the Prarie   the name of a nation at the Second forks of the *Tape tete* River, or *Nocktock* fork *Chim-nâ-pum*, Some of which reside with the *So kulks* above this—at and a few miles distance,—   4 men in a Canoe come up from below Stayed a fiew minits and returned.[1]

Took a meridian altitude 68° 57′ 30″ the Suns upper Limb. The Lattitudes produced is 46° 15′ 13⁹/₁₀″ North, Capt Lewis took a vocabillary of the So kulk or Pierced noses Language and *Chim-nâ-pum* Language whic

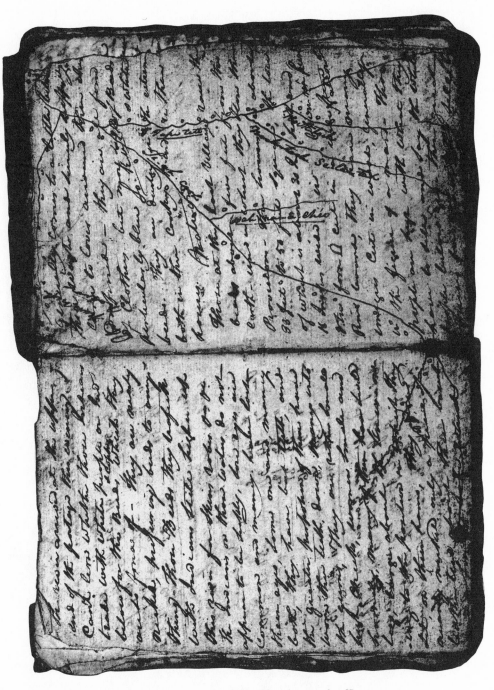

14. Indian Groups on Columbia River and Affluents,
ca. October 18, 1805, Elkskin-bound Journal ☞

is in Some words different but orriginally the Same people   The Great Chief *Cuts-Sâh nim* gave me a Sketch of the rivers & Tribes above on the great river & its waters on which he put great numbers of villages of his nation & friends, as noted on the Sketch—

The fish being very bad those which was offerd to us we had every reason to believe was taken up on the Shore dead, we thought proper not to purchase any, we purchased forty dogs for which we gave articles of little value, Such as beeds, bell, & thimbles, of which they appeard verry fond, at 4 OClock we Set out down the Great Columbia accompand by our two old Chiefs, one young man wished to accompany us, but we had no room for more, & he could be of no Service to us

The Great Chief Continued with us untill our departure.

Course

S. 55° E [2]	12	miles a Lard. bend lower part of a bad rapid and Several little Stony Islands passed an Island imediately in the mouth of the *Ki moo e-nim* one in the mid river at 8 miles this Island of Cors gravel and 3 miles long, the Columbia more than a mile wide, banks low not Subject to over flow. an Island on the Stard. Side ⟨and below⟩ from opd. the Center the last 3½ miles long. no timber in view opsd. the Center of this Island and below the last a Island [3] in the middle with 9 Lodgs and a great quantity of fish on its upper point, a Small Island imediately below opsd. the upper Pt. of which the rapid Comense Several Small on the Lard Side
S. 20° E	3½	miles to 2 Lodges of Indians on a Small Island Stard. point ⟨here the River enters Comenses a high Countrey⟩
S. E.	1½	miles to mo. of a ⟨Creek⟩ river 40 yds wide under a high Clift. in the Lard. bend here the river enters the high countrey rising abt. 200 feet above the Water large black rocks makeing out from Lard. half across the river and some distance from Stard. Side.
S. 12° W.	4 / 21	miles to a point of rocks in a Lard. Bend passed a Small Isd. passd. a 2d at 2 miles, on its upr. Point 2 Lodges of Indians fishing at a rapid opsd. the lower point psd. 9

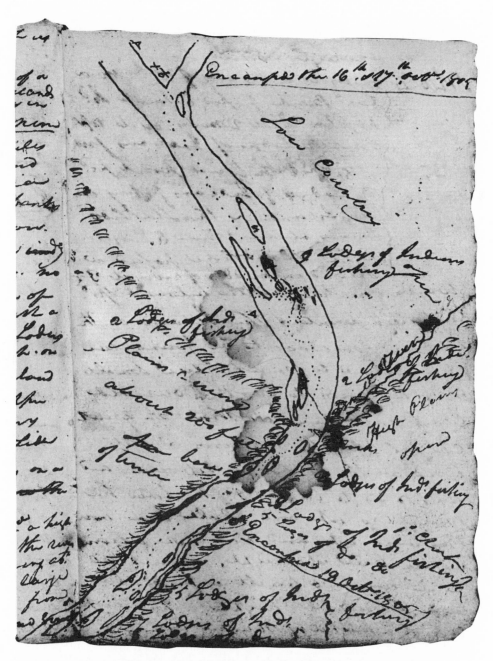

15. Columbia River near Mouth of Walla Walla River, Washington,
October 16–18, 1805, Elkskin-bound Journal ⊕

Lodges of Indians fishing on an Island on the Stard. Side below about 1 mile 5 Lodges on the Stard. Side, passed a Island in middle of river at 3 m.

we Encamped a little below & opsd. the lower point of the Island on the Lard. Side[4] no wood to be found we were obliged to make use Small drid willows to Cook— our old Chief informed us that the great Chief of all the nations about lived at the 9 Lodges above and wished us to land &c. he Said he would go up and Call him over they went up and did not return untill late at night, about 20 came down & built a fire above and Stayed all night. The chief brought a basket of mashed berries.

[Clark]   *October 18th Friday 1805*[5]

This morning Cool and fare wind from the S. E. Six of the large Prarie cock killed this morning. Several canoes of Indians Came down and joined those with us, we had a council with those in which we informed of our friendly intentions towards them and all other of our red children; of our wish to make a piece between all of our red Children in this quarter &c. &c. this was conveyed by Signs thro: our 2 Chiefs who accompanied us, and was understood, we made a 2d Chief and gave Strings of wompom to them all in remembrance of what we Said— four men in a Canoe came up from a large encampment on an Island in the River about 8 miles below, they delayed but a fiew minits and returned, without Speaking a word to us.

The Great Chief and one of the *Chim-nâ pum* nation ⟨gave⟩ drew me a Sketch of the Columbia above and the tribes of his nation, living on the bank, and its waters, and the *Tâpe têtt* river which falls in 18 miles above on the westerly side See Sketch below for the number of villages and nations &c. &c.[6]

We thought it necessary to lay in a Store of Provisions for our voyage, and the fish being out of Season, we purchased forty dogs for which we gave articles of little value, Such as bells, thimbles, knitting pins, brass wire & a few beeds all of which they appeared well Satisfied and pleased.

every thing being arranged we took in our Two Chiefs, and Set out on the great Columbia river, haveing left our guide and the two young men

16. Confluence of Snake and Columbia Rivers, Washington, ca. October 18, 1805, Codex H, p. 33 ⊕

two of them ⟨not⟩ enclined not to proceed on any further, and the 3rd
could be of no Service to us as he did not know the river below

Took our leave of the Chiefs and all those about us and proceeded on
down the great Columbia river   passed a large Island at 8 miles about 3
miles in length, a Island on the Stard. Side the upper point of which is
opposit the center of the last mentioned Island and reaches 3½ miles below the 1st. Island and opposit to this near the middle of the river nine
Lodges are Situated on the upper point at a rapid which is between the
lower point of the 1st Island and upper point of this; great numbers of
Indians appeared to be on this Island, and emence quantites of fish Scaf-
fold   we landed a few minits to view a rapid which Commenced at the
lower point, passd this rapid which was verry bad between 2 Small Islands
two Still Smaller near the Lard. Side, at this rapid on the Stard. Side is
2 Lodges of Indians Drying fish, at 2½ miles lower and 14½ below the
point passed an Island Close under the Stard. Side on which was 2 Lodges
of Indians drying fish on Scaffolds as above   at 16 miles from the point
the river passes into the range of high Countrey at which place the rocks
project into the river from the high clifts which is on ⟨both⟩ the Lard. Side
about ⅔ of the way across and those of the Stard Side about the Same
distance, the Countrey rises here about 200 feet above The water and is
bordered with black rugid rocks,[7] at the Commencement of this high
Countrey on Lard Side a Small riverlet falls in[8] which appears to passed
under the high County in its whole cose   Saw a mountain bearing S. W.
Conocal form Covered with Snow.[9]   passed 4 Islands, at the upper point
of the ⟨first⟩ 3rd is a rapid, on this Island is *two* Lodges of Indians, drying
fish, on the fourth Island Close under the Stard. Side is *nine* large Lodges
of Indians Drying fish on Scaffolds as above   at this place we were called
to land, as it was near night and no appearance of wood, we proceeded
on about 2 miles lower to Some willows, at which place we observed a
drift log   formed a Camp on the Lard Side under a high hill nearly opposit to five Lodges of Indians; Soon after we landed, our old Chiefs informed us that the large camp above "was the Camp of the 1st Chief of all
the *tribes* in this quarter, and that he had called to us to land and Stay all
night with him, that he had plenty of wood for us &"   This would have

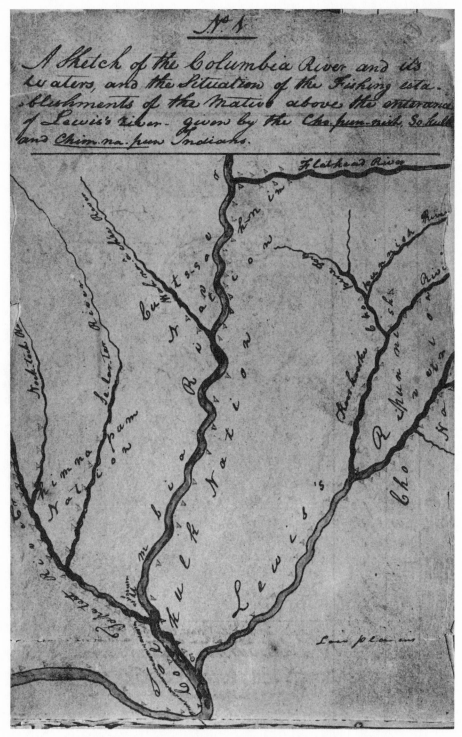

17. Confluence of Snake and Columbia Rivers, Washington,
ca. October 18, 1805, Voorhis No. 4 ⊕

been agreeable to us if it had have been understood perticelarly as we were compelled to Use drid willows for fuel for the purpose of cooking, we requested the old Chiefs to walk up on the Side we had landed and call to the Chief to come down and Stay with us all night which they did; late at night the Chief came down accompanied by 20 men, and formed a Camp a Short distance above, the chief brought with him a large basket of mashed berries which he left at our Lodge as a present. I saw on the main land opposit those Lodges a number of horses feeding, we made 21 miles to day.

1. Clark incorporated these names on a sketch map (fig. 14) of the region in his Elkskin-bound Journal (cf. fig. 16). It is under his entry of November 1.

2. Opposite this course in the Elkskin-bound Journal is a sketch map (fig. 15) of the party's route from the confluence of the Columbia and Snake rivers (unnamed on the map) to beyond the mouth of the Walla Walla River (also unnamed), for about October 16–18, 1805.

3. The island on *Atlas* map 75 noted as having "9 large Mat lodges drying fish" was probably later Rabbit Island and now apparently under the waters of Lake Wallula. The lodges probably are part of an archaeological site reported by Osborne & Crabtree and by Garth. The long island to the southwest was known as Goat Island prior to creation of Lake Wallula. On October 18 and 19, 1805, Lewis and Clark passed through what is now the reservoir (Lake Wallula) behind McNary Dam. This reservoir area has been the subject of much archaeological research. Osborne, 132; Garth; Shiner; Osborne, Bryan, & Crabtree. The tremendous number of archaeological sites in this area makes determination of the particular Indian villages which Lewis and Clark discuss difficult to assess.

4. In Walla Walla County, Washington, south of the mouth of the Walla Walla River and above the Washington-Oregon line. *Atlas* map 75.

5. Clark placed his courses for October 18 to November 16, 1805, after the entry of November 16 in Codex H, pp. 132–48, under the title "Course Distance & Remarks Descending the Columbia River from the Lewis's River in Latd. *46° 15′ 13⁹/₁₀″* N. to the Great Pacific Ocian—estimated." We divide the table across two volumes and place the material from October 18 to November 1, after the codex entry of November 1, 1805, at the end of this volume. There are some slight differences with the Elkskin-bound Journal.

6. The sketch map (fig. 16) appears in Codex H, p. 33. A more finished version appears in Voorhis No. 4 (fig. 17) with some additions and changes.

7. Just a short distance below the mouth of the Walla Walla River, a fault trending northwest-southeast cuts across the Columbia River at Wallula Gap. Southwest of the fault, resistant basalts of the middle Miocene Frenchman Springs and Rosa members of the Wanapum Basalt are at the surface. The Wanapum Basalt is part of the Yakima Basalt Subgroup of the Columbia River Basalt Group.

8. The Walla Walla River, meeting the Columbia at present Wallula, Walla Walla County. *Atlas* map 75.

9. Probably Mt. Hood, in the Cascade Range in Hood River County, Oregon, named for the British admiral Sir Samuel Hood by Lieutenant William Robert Broughton of George Vancouver's exploring expedition in 1792. Allen (PG), 312 and n. 14.

[Clark]

October 19th ⟨Thursday⟩ Saturday, The Great Chief 2d Chief and a Chief of a band below Came and Smoked with us   we gave a Meadel a String of Wampom & handkerchef to the Great Chief by name *Yel-lep-pit*[1]   The 2d Chief we gave a String of wampom, his name is [*blank*] The 3d who lives below a String of Wampom his name I did not learn. the Chief requested us to Stay untill 12 we excused our Selves and Set out at 9 oClock

Course

S W.	14	miles to a rock in a Lard. resembling a hat[2] just below a rapid at the lower Point of an Island in the Midl: of the river 7 Lodges and opposit the head of one on the Stard. Side 5 Lodges passed an Island at 8 miles 6 miles long close to Lard Side no water on Lard. a Small one opsd. and at the lower point no water Lard. passed an Isld. in middle at 8 miles on which 5 Indian Lodges, deserted at the end of this course a bad rockey ⟨rapid⟩ place plenty of water rocks in the river.— passed a Stard. point at 4 miles country a little lower
S. 80° W.	7	miles to a Point of rocks on the Stard. bend Passed the Island on Std. Side at 1 mile passed a verry bad rapid Above the end of this Course 2 miles in length with Several Small Islands in it & Banks of Mussle Shels in the rapids. here the lower Countrey Commences— Saw a high mountain covered with snow *West* this we Suppose to be Mt. ⟨Hood⟩ St Helens[3] in dist.
S. 70° W.[4]	12	Miles to a passed 20 Lodge of Indians Scattered allong the Stard. Side drying fish & Prickley pare (to Burn in winter) I went on Shore in a Small Canoe a head, landed at the first 5 Lodges, found the Indians much fritened, all got in to

18. Columbia River near Mouth of Umatilla River
(not shown), Washington and Oregon, ca. October 19, 1805,
Elkskin-bound Journal ⊕

their lodges and when I went in found Some hanging down their heads, Some Crying and others in great agitation, I took all by the hand, and distributed a few Small articles which I chanced to have in my Pockets and Smoked with them which expelled their fears, Soon after the Canoes landed & we all Smoked and were friendly. I gave a String of Wampom to the Principal man, we dined on dryed Salmon & Set out. I am confident that I could have tomahawked every Indian here. The Language is the Sam as those above, those Lodges can turn out ⟨250⟩ 350 men.[5] I shot a Crain[6] & 2 ducks and opposit to a Lodge on the Stard. Side, one mile below a rapid.   a Single Mountn. bears S. W. from the Muscle Shell rapid.

S. W. $\underline{3}$
$\underset{=}{36}$ miles to a few ⟨bushes⟩ willow Trees on the Lard. Side below the lower pt. of an Isd. Ld. opposit 24 Lodges of Indians Indians fishing.   here we came too and camped, 19 of them on the Stard. Side & 5 on an Island in the middle of the river, about 100 Inds. come over   Some brought wood and we gave Smoke to all which they were pleased at

P. Crusat played on the Violin which pleasd and astonished those reches who are badly Clad, ¾ with robes not half large enough to cover them, they are homeley high Cheeks, and but fiew orniments. I Suped on the Crane which I killed ⟨yesterday⟩ to day.

[Clark]   *October 19th Saturday 1805*

The great chief *Yel-lep-pit* two other chiefs, and a Chief of Band below presented themselves to us verry early this morning.   we Smoked with them, enformed them as we had all others above as well as we Could by Signs[7] of our friendly intentions towards our red children Perticular those who opened their ears to our Councils.   we gave a Medal, a Handkercheif & a String of Wompom to *Yelleppit* and a String of wompom to each of the others. *Yelleppit* is a bold handsom Indian, with a dignified countenance about 35 years of age, about 5 feet 8 inches high and well perpotiond.   he requested us to delay untill the Middle of the day, that his people might Come down and See us, we excused our Selves and promised to Stay with him one or 2 days on our return which appeared to

Satisfy him; great numbers of Indians Came down in Canoes to view us before we Set out which was not untill 9 oClock A M.   we proceeded on passed a Island, close under the Lard Side about Six miles in length opposit to the lower point of which two Isds. are situated on one of which five Lodges ⟨of Indians⟩ vacent & Saffolds drying fish   at the upper point of this Island Swift water.   a Short distance below passed two Islands; one near the middle of the river on which is Seven lodges of Indians drying fish,[8] at our approach they hid themselves in their Lodges and not one was to be seen untill we passed, they then Came out in greater numbers than is common in Lodges of their Size, it is probable that, the inhabitants of the 5 Lodges above had in a fright left their lodges and decended to this place to defend them Selves if attackted there being a bad rapid opposit the Island thro which we had to pass prevented our landing on this Island and passifying those people, about four miles below this fritened Island we arrived at the head of a verry bad rapid,[9] we came too on the Lard Side to view the rapid before we would venter to run it, as the Chanel appeared to be close under the oppd. Shore, and it would be necessary to liten our canoe, I deturmined to walk down on the Lard Side, with the 2 Chiefs the interpreter & his woman, and derected the Small canoe to prcede down on the Lard Side to the foot of the rapid which was about 2 miles in length   I Sent on the Indian Chiefs &c. down and I assended a high clift about 200 feet above the water from the top of which is a leavel plain extending up the river and off for a great extent, at this place the Countrey becoms low on each Side of the river, and affords a pros[pect?] of the river and countrey below for great extent both to the right and left; from this place I descovered a high mountain of emence hight covered with Snow, this must be one of the mountains laid down by Vancouver, as Seen from the mouth of the Columbia River, from the Course which it bears which is *West* I take it to be Mt. St. Helens, destant ⟨about 120⟩ 156 miles   a range of mountains in the Derection crossing, a conacal mountain S. W. toped with Snow   This rapid I observed as I passed opposit to it to be verry bad interseped with high rock and Small rockey Islands, here I observed banks of Muscle Shells banked up in the river in Several places, I Delayed at the foot of the rapid about 2 hours for the Canoes which I could See met with much dificuelty in passing down the rapid on the oposit Side maney places the men were obliged to get into the water and haul the canoes over Sholes— while Setting on a rock wateing for Capt Lewis I Shot a Crain which was flying over of the common kind. I observed a great number of Lodges on the opposit Side at Some distance below and Several Indians on the opposit bank passing up to where Capt. Lewis was with the Canoes, others I Saw on a knob nearly opposit to me at which place they delayed but a Short time before they returned to their Lodges as fast as they could run, I was fearfull that those people might not be informed of us, I deturmined to take the little Canoe which was with me and proceed with the three men in it to the Lodges, on my aproach not one person was to be Seen except three men off in the plains, and they Sheared off as I aproached near the Shore, I landed in front of five Lodges which was at no great distance from each other, Saw no person the enteranc or Dores of the Lodges wer Shut with the Same materials of which they were built a mat, I approached one with a pipe in my hand entered a lodge which was the nearest to me found 32 persons men, women and a few children Setting permiscuesly in the Lodg, ⟨Some⟩ in the greatest agutation, Some crying and ringing there hands, others hanging their heads. I gave my hand to them all and made Signs of my friendly dispotion and offered the men my pipe to Smok and distributed a fiew Small articles which I had in my pockets,—this measure passified those distressed people verry much, I then Sent one man into each lodge and entered a Second myself the inhabitants of which I found more fritened than those of the first lodge I destributed Sundrey Small articles amongst them, and Smoked with the men, I then entered the third 4h & fifth Lodge which I found Somewhat passified, the three men, Drewer Jo. & R. Fields, haveing useed everey means in their power to convince them of our friendly disposition to them, I then ⟨formd⟩ Set my Self on a rock and made Signs to the men to come and Smoke with me not one Come out untill the Canoes arrived with ⟨Some five Came out of each Lodge and Set by me and Smoked Capt Lewis at⟩ the 2 Chiefs, one of whom spoke aloud, and as was their Custom to all we had passed the Indians came out & Set by me and Smoked They said we came from the clouds &c &c ⟨which the⟩ and were not men &c. &c. this time Capt. Lewis came down with the Canoes rear in which the Indian, as Soon as they Saw the Squar wife of the interperters ⟨wife⟩ they pointed to her and informed those who continued yet in the Same position I first found them, they imediately all came out and appeared to assume new life,[10] the sight of This Indian woman, wife to one of our interprs. confirmed those people of our friendly intentions, as no woman ever accompanies a war party of Indians in this quarter— Capt Lewis joined us and we Smoked with those people in the greatest friendship, dureing which time one of our Old Chiefs informed them who we were from whence we Came and where we were going giveing them a friendly account of us, those people do not Speak prosisely the Same language of those above but understand them, I Saw Several Horses and persons on hors back in the plains maney of the men womin and children Came up from the Lodges below; all of them appeared pleased to See us, we traded some fiew articles for fish and berries, Dined, and proceeded on passed a Small rapid and 15 Lodges below the five, and Encamped below an Island Close under the Lard Side,[11] nearly opposit to 24 Lodges on an Island near the middle of the river, and the Main Stard Shor   Soon after we landed which was at a fiew willow trees about 100 [X: 5] Indians Came from the different Lodges, and a number of them brought wood which they gave us, we Smoked with all of them, and two of our Party Peter Crusat & Gibson played on the *violin* which delighted them greatly, we gave to the principal man a String of wompon treated them kindly for which they appeared greatfull, This Tribe [*NB: a branch of the nation called Pisch quit pas*] can raise about 350 men   their Dress are Similar to those at the fork except their robes are Smaller and do not reach lower than the waste and ¾ of them have Scercely any robes at all, the women have only a Small pece of a robe which Covers their Sholders neck and reaching down behind to their wastes, with a tite piece of leather about the waste, the brests are large and hang down verry low illy Shaped, high Cheeks flattened heads, & have but fiew orniments, they are all employed in fishing and drying fish of which they have great quantites on their Scaffolds, their habits customs &c. I could not lern. I killed a Duck that with the Crain afforded us a good Supper.   the Indians continued all night at our fires

This day we made 36 miles.

1. Evidently Yelleppit was chief of the Walula (or Walla Walla) tribe, although it has been suggested that he was a Cayuse leader named Ollicutt known to fur traders in the area a few years later. Ronda (LCAI), 167, 220–21; Ruby & Brown (CIIT), 22–23; Ross, 137–38; Glover, 350. The term *yelépt* means "friend, blood brother" in Nez Perce; *yalépt* means "trading partner" in Shahaptian. Sometime in the 1890s a Jefferson peace medal, perhaps from the expedition, was discovered on an island (possibly Goat Island) at the mouth of the Walla Walla River; it may be the one given to Yelleppit at this time or on the party's return trip in 1806. It is today a part of the Lewis and Clark items of the Oregon Historical Society, Portland. Cutright (LCIPM), 164; Prucha (IPM), 16–24, 90–95, Strong (SACR), 208.

2. Hat Rock retains its name from Lewis and Clark and sits prominently in Hat Rock State Park, Umatilla County, Oregon. Several miles upstream the party passed today's Washington-Oregon border.

3. Probably not Mt. St. Helens, which would not be visible from their location, but Mt. Adams, east of the main Cascade Range in Yakima County, Washington. Glover, 312 and n. 15.

4. Opposite this course in the Elkskin-bound Journal Clark sketched a map (fig. 18) showing the journey from Hat Rock to beyond the Umatilla River (not shown) and the campsite of October 19, 1805.

5. These people were Umatillas, or perhaps Cayuses, living near present Plymouth, Benton County, Washington, opposite the mouth of the Umatilla River, which the captains did not notice on the outbound journey. Ronda (LCAI), 167–68, 285 n. 14; *Atlas* map 75.

6. A crane "of the Common Kind" in Codex H; probably a sandhill crane. See above, July 21 and 29, 1805, for more description.

7. An indication, perhaps, that the sign language had penetrated this far from the Great Plains. Many Columbia Plateau tribes made buffalo-hunting trips to the plains, where they could have picked up the signs.

8. The six-mile-long island may be later Techumtas Island, while that referred to as having five lodges may be later Sheep Island. Osborne, 131, mentions the island with seven lodges. *Atlas* map 75; Osborne, Bryan, & Crabtree, 267–306; Ray (NVCB), 150–51.

9. In the area of present McNary Dam. "Muscle Shell rapid" on *Atlas* map 75.

10. At this point in Codex H (p. 41), in the right margin and at right angles to the text, Clark has written "See description." There is also a large "X" through this passage.

11. Apparently between Irrigon and Boardman, Morrow County, Oregon. *Atlas* map 75. The island could be Blalock Island, known as *amaʾama'pa* ("island") by the Umatillas. Archaeological work performed on Blalock Island in the late 1950s and 1960s has not yet been fully reported. There are several sites in this area of Plymouth, Washington, which are likely candidates for the numerous lodges noted by Clark. Ray (NVCB), 151; Alexander; Galm et al.

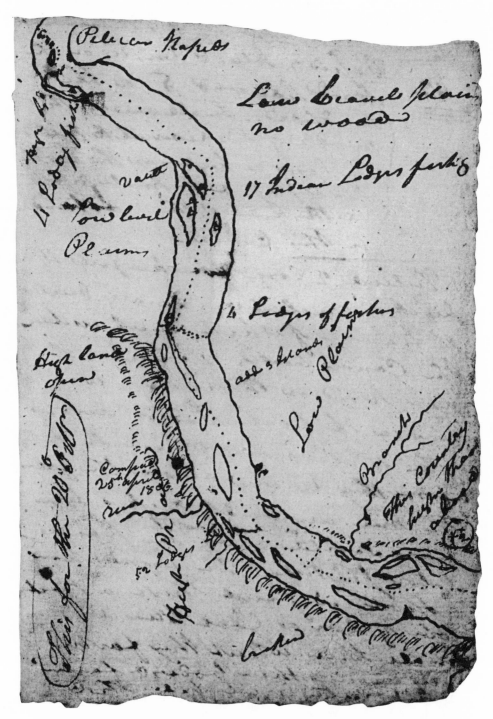

19. Columbia River, Area between Mouths of Umatilla
and John Day Rivers (not shown), Washington and Oregon,
ca. October 20, 1805, Elkskin-bound Journal ⊙

[Clark]   *October 20th ⟨Friday⟩* 1805 Sunday

a very cold morning   wind S. W.   about 100 Indians Came over this morning to See us, after a Smoke, a brackfast on Dogs flesh we Set out. about 350 men

West	6	miles to a Std. bend head of a rapd passed the Island at 1 mile 3 Indns. Lodges on Lard.
S 20° W.	10	miles passed rockey bad rapid on the Stard. a Chain of rocks from the Std. Several small Isd.— on the Lard. good water. passed an Indian fishing Camp of 4 Lodges deserted, fish hanging on Scaffels (Saw great numbers of Pelicans & Comerants, black) To a Lard. Bend opsd. a large Isd. on the Stard. Side
S. 60° W.[1]	8	miles to the Commencement of a high Countrey on the Stard. Side. passed 3 Islands nearly opposit, 2 furst on the Stard. Side Indians encd. [encamped] on each Island. we Came to at Some Camps on the lower point of the 1st & dined. purchased a fiew indifferent fish & Some berries— examined a vault &c. &c. passed 4 Lodges on a Island near the Stard. Side opsd. a bad rapid at the lower point of th Island
S. W	18 / 42̲	miles to a Point of high land in the Std. bend Passed a large Island in the middle of the R at 8 miles one on the Lard. & one on the Stard. below both Small, one other imedeately below in the middle, passed a Lard. point at 10 miles high uneavin lands on the Stard. low and leavil on the Lard. Side Passed 5 Islands Small on the Stard. Side and 5 on the Lard. Side a Small one in the middle of the river at 16 miles The land is higher on the Lard. Side passed a Small riffle at the head of the 12 Islands in this ⟨Course⟩ Day.[2]

Killed 2 large speckle guls[3] 4 Duck in Malade [duckinmallard] Small ducks the flavour of which much resembles the Canvis back[4]   no timber of any kind on the river, we Saw in the last Lodges acorns of the white oake[5] which the Inds. inform they precure above the falls   The men are badly dressed, Some have scarlet & blue cloth robes.   one has a Salors jacket,[6] The women have a Short indiferent Shirt, a Short robe of Deer or Goat Skins, & a Small Skin which they fastend. tite around their bodies &

20. Columbia River near Mouth of John Day River, Washington
and Oregon, ca. October 20, 1805, Elkskin-bound Journal ☉

fastend. between the legs to hide the[7] ⟨passed on the Stard. and on the Lard. one Small in the Middle of the river at 16 miles⟩

[Clark]   *October 20th Sunday 1805*

A cool morning wind S. W.   we concluded to delay untill after brackfast which we were obliged to make on the flesh of dog.   after brackfast we gave all the Indian men Smoke, and we Set out leaveing about 200 of the nativs at our Encampment; passd. three Indian Lodges on the Lard Side a little below our Camp which lodges ⟨we⟩ I did not discover last evening, passed a rapid at Seven miles one at a Short distance below we passed a verry bad rapid, a chane of rocks makeing from the Stard. Side and nearly Chokeing the river up entirely with hugh black rocks,[8] an Island below close under the Stard. Side on which was *four* Lodges of Indians drying fish,—   here I Saw a great number of pelicons on the wing, and black Comerants.[9]   at one oClock we landed on the lower point of ⟨Some⟩ an Island at Some Indian Lodges, a large Island on the Stard Side nearly opposit and a Small one a little below on the Lard Side   on those three Island I counted *Seventeen* Indian Lodges,[10] those people are in every respect like those above, prepareing fish for theire winter consumption   here we purchased a fiew indifferent Dried fish & a fiew berries on which we dined—(On the upper part of this Island we discovered an Indian vault[)] our curiosity induced us to examine the methot those nativs practicd in diposeing the dead, the Vaut was made by broad poads [*NB: boards*] and pieces of Canoes leaning on a ridge pole which was Suported by 2 forks Set in the ground Six feet in hight in an easterly and westerly direction and about 60 feet in length, and 12 feet wide, in it I observed great numbers of humane bones of every description perticularly in a pile near the Center of the vault, on the East End 21 Scul bomes forming a circle on Mats—; in the Westerley part of the *Vault* appeared to be appropriated for those of more resent death, as many of the bodies of the deceased *raped* up in leather robes lay [*NB: in rows*] on board covered with mats, &c   [*NB: when bones & robes rot, they are gathered in a heap & sculls placed in a circle.*]   we observed, independant of the canoes which Served as a Covering, fishing nets of various kinds, Baskets of different Sizes, wooden boles, robes Skins, trenchers, and various Kind of trinkets, in and Suspended on the ends of the pieces forming the vault; we also Saw the Skeletons of Several Horses at the vault & great number of bones about it, which Convinced me that those animals were Sacrefised as well as the above articles to the Deceased.) after diner we proceeded on to a bad rapid at the lower point of a Small Island on which four Lodges of Indians were Situated drying fish; here the high countrey Commences again on the Stard. Side leaveing a vallie of 40 miles in width, from the mustle Shel rapid. examined and passed this rapid close to the Island at 8 miles lower passed a large Island near the middle of the river a brook on the Stard. Side and 11 Islds. all in view of each other below, a riverlit [*NB: rivulet*][11] falls in on the Lard. Side behind a Small Island a Small rapid below. The Star Side is high rugid hills, the Lard. Side a low plain and not a tree to be Seen in any Direction except a fiew Small willow bushes which are Scattered partially on the Sides of the bank

The river to day is about ¼ of a mile in width; this evening the Countrey on the Lard. Side rises to the hight of that on the Starboard Side, and is wavering— we made 42 ⟨days⟩ miles to day;[12] the current much more uniform than yesterday or the day before. Killed 2 Speckle guls Severl. ducks of a delicious flavour.

1. Opposite this course in the Elkskin-bound Journal appears a sketch map (fig. 19) showing part of the route for October 20, 1805, between the mouths of the Umatilla and John Day rivers (not shown), and the camp of April 25, 1806, on the return journey.

2. Opposite this material in the Elkskin-bound Journal is a sketch map (fig. 20) showing the party's route for about October 20–21, the camp of October 20, and return campsites of April 23 and 24, 1806. It is in the area of present John Day River ("River de Page"), which they reach on October 21.

3. Coues (HLC), 2:652 n. 27, considers these immature specimens that cannot be identified.

4. Canvasback, *Aythya valisineria* [AOU, 147].

5. Oregon white, or Garry, oak, *Quercus garryana* Dougl. ex. Hook., is the only white oak species in Washington. It occurs mainly west of the Cascades but extends up the Columbia gorge to central Klickitat County, approximately twenty miles above The Dalles. It was a plant new to science. Hitchcock et al., 2:85; Little (CIH), 166-W; Cutright (LCPN), 229, 244.

6. As they neared the coast they were seeing increased signs of at least indirect white contact. Beyond the blankets and other trade goods they had seen among the mountain

tribes, sailors' clothing was a clear indication of the visits of seagoing traders on the Pacific shore.

7. Here Clark has a symbol somewhat in the form of his sun symbol and perhaps representing the women's covered parts.

8. The three Indian lodges are shown at the bottom of *Atlas* map 75 and the very bad rapid is shown as "Pelecan rapid" on *Atlas* map 76. This appears to be the area of Crow Butte State Park, Benton County, Washington. The rocks here are middle Miocene basalts belonging to the Priest Rapids Member of the Wanapum Basalt and younger members of the Saddle Mountain Basalt. Both basalts are part of the Yakima Basalt Subgroup of the Columbia River Basalt Group. Certain portions of the basalt are less fractured and hence more resistant to erosion.

9. The American white pelican, *Pelecanus erythrorhynchos* [AOU, 125], and the double-crested cormorant, *Phalacrocorax auritus* [AOU, 120]. See below, February 6, 1806, for a description of the cormorant. Burroughs, 182; Holmgren, 29. Their appearance was the reason for naming the rapids on *Atlas* map 76.

10. Shown on *Atlas* map 76.

11. Possibly later Willow Creek, in Gilliam County, Oregon. *Atlas* map 76.

12. Camp was probably in the vicinity of present Roosevelt, Klickitat County, Washington. *Atlas* map 76.

Chapter Twenty-Four

Descending the Columbia to the Cascades

October 21–November 1, 1805

[Clark]   *October 21st 1805* ⟨*Thursday*⟩ Monday

a verry Cold morning   we Set out early   wind from the S W.   we Could not Cook brakfast before we embarked as usial for the want of wood or Something to burn.—

South   3   miles to a Lard Bend

S 55° W.   17   miles to a Lard Bend below a bad rapid high ruged rock Passed a Small Island at 2 ½ miles one at 4 miles, in th middle of the river, at Smome Swift water   an Indn Camp of 8 Lodges on the Std. Side opsd. th Lower point where we Brackfast, and bought Some fine fish & Pounded rotes.   people well disposed   passed a rapid at 10 miles. Rocks out in the water passed a Stard. point & a Strd. point   at 15 [miles] passed 5 Lodges of Indians, & 2 Lodges Some distance above on Std.

N. 45° W.   4   miles to a Stard. bend   passd. the lower pt. of the Isd. at 1 mile and 2 Lodges of fishers below on the Stard Side, the rocks on th Lard. appear as if Sliped from the Clifts under which they are   passed emence rocks in differt. parts of the river which were large and too noumerous to notice. Fowl of all kinds more plentiful than above   passed a verry bad rapid at 2 miles, this rapid is Crouded with Islands of bad rocks dificuelt & crooked passage   2 Lodges of Indians below on Std. Side. I Saw Some fiew Small Pine on the tops of the high hills and bushes in the hollers

S. 60° W.	5	miles to the Stard. Bend. passed maney ruged black rocks in diffierent parts of the river, and a bad rapid at 2 miles & river narrow Several Canoes loaded with Indians (*Pierce noses*) came to See us— ⟨To⟩ at the expiration of this course a river falls in on the Lard. 40 yds. wide Islands of rocks in every direction in the river & rapids
S. 52° W.	13 $\underline{\underline{42}}$	miles to upr. point of a rocky Island 80 feet high a rapid above passed the little river rapid thro narrow channels between the rocks 4 Lodges of Indians on the Stard. Side opposit, a round toped mountain imediately in front and is the one we have been going towards & which bore S. W. from the 2d course below the Forks— passed the lower point of an Island on the Stard. at 2 miles landed at 5 Lodges of Pierced noses Indians at 4 miles where we encamped and purchased a little wood to boil our Dogs & fish, those Indians are the ⟨inhabitents⟩ relations of the falls below, fortunately for us the night was worm.

22d Octr. Course Continued[1]

fine water for 7 miles   passed a rapid of rocks nearly across above which at 6 miles   passed 6 Lodges Std., at 9 miles   passed a Bad rapid, & Lodges of Indians on Std. Side   20 piles [*one word illegible*] of fish on an Island drying, Several Indians in Canoes fishing in Canos & gigs &c.

Collins made Some excellent beer of the *Pasheco quar mash* bread of roots which was verry good   obliged to purchase wood at a high rate.[2]

[Clark]   *October 21st Monday 1805*

A verry cool morning wind from the S. W.   we Set out verry early and proceeded on, last night we could not Collect more dry willows the only fuel, than was barely Suffient to cook Supper, and not a Sufficency to cook brackfast this morning, passd. a Small Island at 5½ miles a large one

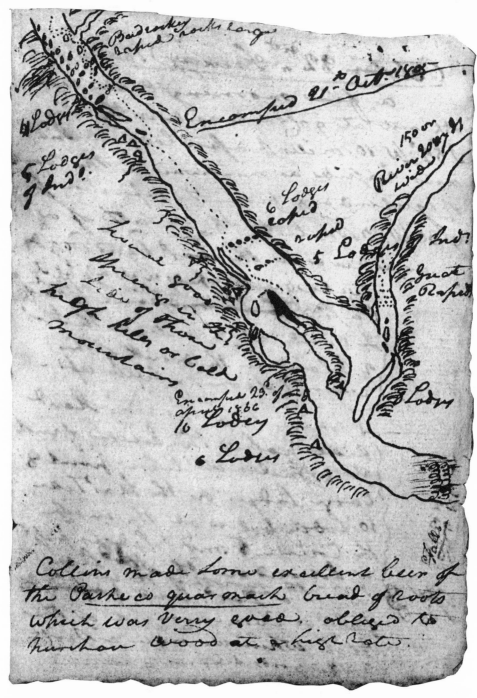

21. Columbia River near Mouth of Deschutes River, Washington
and Oregon, ca. October 21, 1805, Elkskin-bound Journal ✪

8 miles in the middle of the river, Some rapid water at the head and Eight Lodges of nativs opposit its Lower point on the Stard. Side, we came too at those lodges, bought some wood and brackfast. Those people recived us with great kindness, and examined us with much attention, their employments custom Dress and appearance Similar to those above; Speak the Same language,[3] here we Saw two Scarlet and a blue cloth blanket, also a Salors Jacket   the Dress of the men of this tribe only a Short robe of Deer or Goat Skins, and that of the womn is a Short piece of Dressed Skin which fall from the neck So as to Cover the front of the body as low as the waste, a Short robe, which is of one Deer or antilope Skin, and a flap, around their waste and Drawn tite between their legs as before described, their orniments are but fiew, and worn as those above.

we got from those people a fiew pounded rotes [*NB: roots*] fish and *Acorns* of the white oake, those Acorns they make use of as food [*NB: raw & roasted*], and inform us they precure them of the nativs who live near the falls below which place they all discribe by the term *Timm*—[4]   at 2 miles lower passed a rapid, large rocks Stringing into the river of large Size,[5] opposit to this rapid on the Stard. Shore is Situated *two* Lodges of the nativs drying fish   here we halted a fiew minits to examine the rapid before we entered it which was our constant Custom, and at all that was verry dangerous put out all who could not Swim to walk around, after passing this rapid we proceeded on passed anoothe rapid at 5 miles lower down, above this rapid on ⟨the Stard. Side⟩ *five* Lodges of Indians fishing &c.[6]   above this rapid maney large rocks on each Side at Some distance from Shore, one mile passed an Island Close to the Stard. Side, below which is *two* Lodge of nativs, a little below is a bad rapid which is bad crouded with hugh rocks Scattered in every Direction which renders the pasage verry Difficuelt   a little above this rapid on the Lard. Side emence piles of rocks appears as if Sliped from the Clifts under which they lay, passed great number of rocks in every direction Scattered in the river   5 Lodges a little below on the Stard. Side, and one lodge on an Island near the Stard. Shore opposit to which is a verry bad rapid, thro which we found much dificuelty in passing, the river is Crouded with rocks in every direction, after Passing this dificul rapid to the mouth of a Small river on the Larboard Side 40 yards wide descharges but little water at this time, and appears to take its Sourse in the Open plains to the S. E.[7]   from this place I proceved Some fiew Small pines on the tops of the high hills and bushes in the hollars.   imediately above & below this little river comences a rapid which is crouded with large rocks in every direction, the pasage both crooked and dificuelt, we halted at a Lodge to examine those noumerous Islands of rock which apd. to extend maney miles below,—. great numbs. of Indians came in Canoes to View us at this place, after passing this rapid which we accomplished without loss; ⟨we passed⟩ winding through between the hugh rocks for about 2 miles—.   (from this rapid the Conocil mountain is *S. W.* which the Indians inform me is not far to the left of the great falls; this I call the *Timm* or falls mountain it is high and the top is covered with Snow)[8]   imediately below the last rapids there is four Lodges of Indians on the Stard. Side, proceeded on about two miles lower and landed and encamped near *five* Lodges of nativs, drying fish   those are the relations of those at the *Great falls,* they are pore and have but little wood which they bring up the river from the falls as they Say, we purchased a little wood to cook our Dog meat and fish; those people did not recive us at first with the same cordiality of those above, they appear to be the Same nation Speak the Same language with a little curruption of maney words   Dress and fish in the Same way,[9] all of whome have *pierced noses* and the men when Dressed ware a long taper'd piece of Shell or beed put through the nose—[10]   this part of the river is furnished with fine Springs which either rise high up the Sides of the hills or ⟨out⟩ on the bottom near the river and run into the river.   the hills are high and rugid a fiew scattering trees to be Seen on them either Small pine or Scrubey white oke.

The probable reason of the Indians residing on the Stard. Side of this as well as the waters of Lewis's[11] River is their fear of the *Snake Indians* who reside, as they nativs Say on a great river to the South,[12] and are at war with those tribes, ⟨our to⟩ one of the Old Chiefs who accompanies us pointed out a place on the lard. Side where they had a great battle, not maney years ago, in which maney were killed on both Sides—, one of our party J. Collins presented us with Some verry good *beer* made of the *Pashi-co-quar-mash* bread, which bread is the remains of what was laid in as

[*X: a part of our*] Stores of Provisions, at the first flat heads or Cho-pun-nish Nation at the head of the *Kosskoske* river which by being frequently wet molded & Sowered &c.   we made 33 miles to day.[13]

1. Here in the Elkskin-bound Journal Clark gives the first course of the next day. There is also the number "33" by the total of "42" representing the actual miles traveled that day, that is, four instead of thirteen on the last course.

2. Above this sentence in the Elkskin-bound Journal is a sketch map (fig. 21) showing the camp of October 21, 1805, and the return camp of April 21, 1806 (misidentified as April 23). The entrances of the John Day and Deschutes rivers are also shown, but the streams are not named.

3. Referred to as "Met-cow-wes" on *Atlas* map 77 and in entries on the return journey on April 24, 1806, they may have been the Methows, although these spoke a Salishan language, not the Shahaptian of the people upstream. They lived in Klickitat County, Washington, between the present towns of Roosevelt and Blalock. Hodge, 1:850. The Shahaptian term *mítxaw* designates a Salish-speaking group closely associated with the Columbia and Okanogan rivers.

4. The Chinookan term *tṁm* is an onomatopoeic particle, derived from the Chinook jargon, meaning "(river) falls."

5. The rocks are more resistant parts of the middle Miocene Grande Ronde Basalt and the Frenchman Springs Member of the Wanapum Basalt, both part of the Columbia River Basalt Group.

6. These two groups of lodges are located near the mouth of present Rock Creek, shown entering from the north in the upper right hand corner of *Atlas* map 77. This was the location of a Umatilla village named *ḱami'łpu* ("opening through the canyon where light penetrates"). The location marked the downriver boundary of the Umatilla Indians where over one hundred persons lived. It was a popular area because wood was plentiful. Archaeological work has been extensive on the opposite (Oregon) shore in this area. Ray (NVCB), 151; Dumond & Minor.

7. The John Day River, marking the boundary between Gilliam and Sherman counties, Oregon. It is "River de Page" on fig. 20 and "River La Page" on *Atlas* map 77, after expedition member Jean Baptiste Lepage.

8. Mt. Hood; see above, October 18, 1805.

9. "Wah-how pum" on *Atlas* map 77. A small Shahaptian-language group living near the mouth of Olive Creek, in Klickitat County. Hodge, 2:890.

10. The shell belongs to a marine mollusk of the genus *Dentalium*, resembling a miniature elephant tusk, much used by tribes as far east as the Great Plains for decoration. Cutright (LCPN), 229.

11. The phrase "waters of Lewis's" appears to have been substituted for some erased words.

12. Perhaps the Deschutes River or John Day River; these "Snakes" are probably Northern Paiutes. Ray & Lurie, 361–65; Murdock.

13. Camp was in Klickitat County, in the vicinity of the present John Day Dam. *Atlas* map 77.

[Clark]   *October 22nd ⟨Friday⟩ Tuesday 1805*

a fine morning Calm.   we Set out at 9 oClock and on the Course S. 52° W. 10 miles   passed lodges & Inds. and rapids as mentioned in the Cours of yesterday, from the expiration of

S. 30° W.	3	miles to the mouth of a large river[1] in the Lard. bend 200 yds wide great rapids in it a ¼ up it long and impracticable of assent Passed [*words illegible, crossed out*] a point of rock Island at 2 miles on the Stard. 3 Islands in the mouth of this river no bottoms a little up—
West[2]	4	miles to a bend on Stard. Side passed the Island of rocks at 2 miles at Lower point 8 large Lodges, on the Stard. Side 10 Lodges, below at the end of the Course 6 more Lodges passd. a Island on the Stbd. Side.
S. W.	2 $\underline{\underline{19}}$[3]	miles to a rocky Lard. bend ⟨passed⟩ from the mouth of the river at the fall or Comencment of the Pitch where we made a portage of 457 yards & down a Slide

Took our Baggage & formed a Camp below the rapids in a cove on the Stard Side[4]   the distance 1200 yards haveing passed at the upper end of the portage 17 Lodges of Indians,[5] below the rapids & above the Camp 5 large Loges of Indians, great numbers of baskets of Pounded fish on the rocks Islands & near their Lodges   thos are neetly pounded & put in verry new baskets of about 90 or 100 pounds wight.   hire Indians to take our heavy articles across the portage   purchased a Dog for Supper Great numbers of Indians view us, we with much dificuelty purchd. as much wood as Cooked our dogs ⟨& fish⟩ this evening, our men all in helth—   The Indians have their grave yards on an Island in the rapids. The Great Chief of those Indians ⟨are⟩ is out hunting.   no Indians reside on the Lard Side for fear of the Snake Indians with whome they are at war and who reside on the large fork on the lard. a little above

[Clark]   *October 22d Tuesday 1805*

A fine morning calm and fare   we Set out at 9 oClock passed a verry
bad rapid at the head of an Island close under the Stard. Side, above this
rapid on the Stard Side is Six Lodges of nativs Drying fish,[6] at 9 mls.
passed a bad rapid at the head of a large Island of high, uneaven [rocks],
jutting over the water, a Small Island in a Stard. Bend opposit the upper
point, on which I counted 20 parcels of dryed and pounded fish; on the
main Stard Shore opposit to this Island *five* Lodges of Indians are Situated[7]   Several Indians in Canoes killing fish with gigs, ⟨and nets⟩ &c.
opposit the center of this Island of rocks which is about 4 miles long we
discovered the enterence of a large river on the Lard. Side which appeared to Come from the S. E.—   we landed at Some distance above the
mouth of this river and Capt. Lewis and my Self Set out to view this river
above its mouth, as our rout was intersepted by a deep narrow Chanel
which runs out of this river into the Columbia a little below the place we
landed, leaveing a high dry rich Island[8] of about 400 yards wide and 800
yards long   here we Seperated, I proceeded on to the river and Struck it
at the foot of a verry Considerable rapid, here I beheld an emence body
of water Compressd in a narrow Chanel of about 200 yds in width, fome-
ing over rocks maney of which presented their tops above the water,
when at this place Capt. Lewis joined me haveing delayed on the way to
examine a root of which the nativs had been digging great quantities in
the bottoms of this River.[9]   at about two miles above this River appears
to be confined between two high hils below which it divided by numbers
of large rocks, and Small Islands covered with a low groth of timber, and
has a rapid as far as the narrows   three Small Islands in the mouth of
this River, ⟨we returned⟩ this River haveing no Indian name that we
could find out, except "the River on which the Snake Indians live," we
think it best to leave the nameing of it untill our return.

we proceeded on pass the mouth of this river at which place it appears
to discharge ¼ as much water as runs down the Columbia.   at *two* miles
below this River passed Eight Lodges on the Lower point of the Rock Island aforesaid   at those Lodges we saw large logs of wood which must
have been rafted down the *To war-ne hi ooks*[10] River, below this Island on

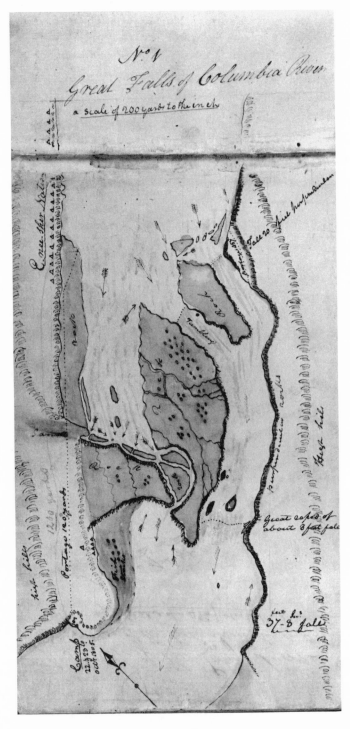

22. Great (Celilo) Falls of the Columbia River, Washington
and Oregon, October 22–23, 1805, Codex H, p. 1

the main Stard Shore is 16 Lodges of nativs; here we landed a fiew minits to Smoke, the lower point of one Island opposit which heads in the mouth of *Towarnehiooks* River which I did not observe untill after passing these lodges   about ½ a mile lower passed 6 more Lodges on the Same Side and 6 miles below the upper mouth of *Towarnehiooks* River the comencement of the pitch of the Great falls,[11] opposit on the Stard. Side is 17 Lodges of the nativs   we landed and walked down accompanied by an old man to view the falls, and the best rout for to make a portage which we Soon discovered was much nearest on the Stard. Side, and the distance 1200 yards one third of the way on a rock, about 200 yards over a loose Sand collected in a hollar blown by the winds from the bottoms below which was disagreeable to pass, as it was Steep and loose.   at the lower part of those rapids we arrived at 5 Large Lodges of nativs drying and prepareing fish for market, they gave us Philburts,[12] and berries to eate, we returned droped down to the head of the rapids and took every article except the Canoes across the portag where I had formed a camp on ellegable Situation for the protection of our Stores from Thieft, which we were more fearfull of, than their arrows.   we despatched two men to examine the river on the opposit Side, and reported that the Canoes could be taken down a narrow Chanel on the opposit Side after a Short portage at the head of the falls, at which place the Indians take over their Canoes. Indians assisted us over the portage with our heavy articles on their horses, the waters is divided into Several narrow chanels which pass through a hard black rock forming Islands of rocks at this Stage of the water,[13] on those Islands of rocks as well as at and about their Lodges I observe great numbers of Stacks of pounded Salmon ⟨butifully⟩ neetly preserved in the following manner, i e after Suffiently Dried it is pounded between two Stones fine, and put into a speces of basket neetly made of grass and rushes[14] of better than two feet long and one foot Diamiter, which basket is lined with the Skin of Salmon Stretched and dried for the purpose, in theis it is pressed down as hard as is possible, when full they Secure the open part with the fish Skins across which they fasten tho' the loops of the basket that part very Securely, and then on a Dry Situation they Set those baskets the Corded part up, their common Custom is to Set 7 as close as they can Stand and 5 on the top of them, and secure them

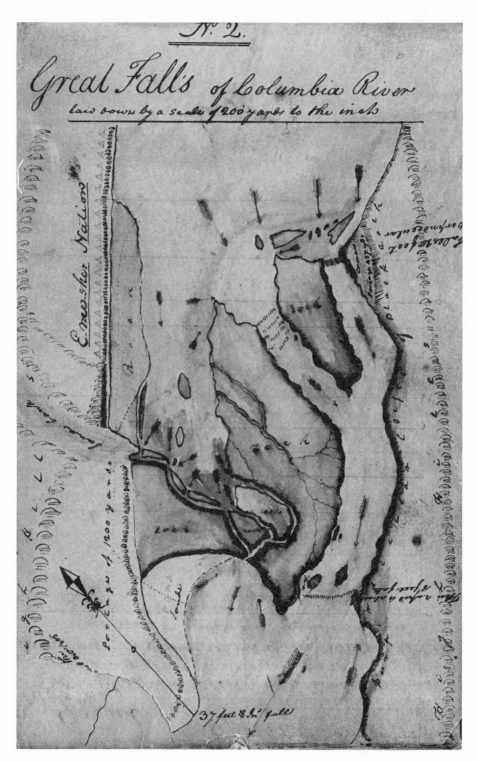

23. Great (Celilo) Falls of the Columbia River, Washington
and Oregon, October 22–23, 1805, Voorhis No. 4

with mats which is raped around them and made fast with cords and Covered also with mats, those 12 baskets of from 90 to 100 w. each ⟨basket⟩ form a Stack.   thus preserved those fish may be kept Sound and Sweet Several years, as those people inform me, Great quantities as they inform us are Sold to the whites people who visit the mouth of this river as well as to the nativs below.

on one of those Island I saw Several tooms but did not visit them— The principal Chiefs of the bands resideing about this Place is out hunting in the mountains to the S. W.—   no Indians reside on the S. W.— side of this river for fear (as we were informed) of the Snake Indians, who are at war with the tribes on this river—.   they represent the Snake Indians as being verry noumerous, and resideing in a great number of villages on Towarnehiooks River which falls in 6 miles above on the Lard. Side and is reaches a great ways and is large a little abov its mouth at which part it is not intersepted with rapids, they inform that one considerable rapid & maney Small ones in that river, and that the Snake live on Salmon, and they go to war to their first villages in 12 days, the Couse they pointed is S. E. or to the S of S. E.   we are visited by great numbers of Indians to Day to view us, we purchased a Dog for Supper, Some fish and with dificuelty precured as much wood as Cooked Supper, which we also purchased   we made 19 miles to day

1. The Deschutes River, forming the line between Wasco and Sherman counties, Oregon, where it reaches the Columbia. Nameless on fig. 21, it is "Clark's River" on *Atlas* map 77 and "Towarnahiooks" later. See also n. 10 below.

2. Opposite this course is a column of figures:

$$
\begin{array}{r}
17 \\
21 \\
36 \\
42 \\
33 \\
\underline{19} \\
168
\end{array}
$$

The figures represent mileage for October 18–22, 1805. The first number (17) may represent an adjustment.

3. The mileage figures do not add up correctly for this day. If one takes nine miles off the previous day's total (which Clark says belongs here) the total for this day is still only eighteen miles. The figures in Codex H are no help.

4. In Klickitat County, Washington, near present Wishram where the camp remained until October 24. *Atlas* map 78.

5. Lewis and Clark's Eneeshurs, perhaps the later Tapanash, a Shahaptian-language people. Ronda (LCAI), 173; Hodge, 1:422. "Eneeshurs" may represent Wishram-Wasco Chinookan *i-mi-šúxʷ*, "he (is) your relative." No known archaeological sites correspond to these locations. The portage route and the villages are now probably under the reservoir water behind The Dalles Dam. Ray (NVCB), 151, lists two villages of Wanapam people just upstream of the portage area.

6. This village is near the present location of Maryhill State Park in Washington.

7. This village seems to be located on what is now known as Bobs Point, and has been recorded as an archaeological site. Wilke et al., 27, 208–9, 238.

8. Later Miller Island, in Klickitat County. *Atlas* map 77.

9. Perhaps wapato, *Sagittaria latifolia* Willd., also called arrowhead. It could be *S. cuneata* Sheld., also named wapato and arrowhead, which is more common east of the Cascades, while *S. latifolia* grows principally west of the mountains. Hitchcock et al., 1:147–49. See Lewis's entry of November 4, 1805, in the next volume. Use of the term wapato in this edition denotes *S. latifolia*.

10. Clark probably inserted the term in this and other previously existing blanks in Codex H during or after May 1806 when the decision was apparently made to give the Deschutes River that name. *Atlas*, p. 10. The Chinookan term *[ił-]ĵtwánxa-yukš*, "enemies," refers specifically to the Paiutes; the Deschutes River leads south toward their territory.

11. Later Celilo Falls, near Wishram, Klickitat County, Washington, and Celilo, Wasco County, Oregon. The area was a great meeting place and trading site for the tribes of the Columbia, also marking a dividing line between Shahaptian and Chinookan languages. Today the falls are inundated by The Dalles Dam. Clark drew a detailed sketch map (fig. 22) of the area in Codex H, p. 1, and another version (fig. 23) in Voorhis No. 4. Ronda (LCAI), 169–71; Appleman (LC), 183–86; *Atlas* maps 77, 78.

12. Hazelnut, filbert, beaked hazel, *Corylus cornuta* Marsh. var. *californica* (DC.) Sharp, then new to science. Hitchcock et al., 2:83; Little (MWH), 54-NW: Cutright (LCPN), 229, 244.

13. The falls and channels here are cut into a more resistant basalt layer of the middle Miocene Frenchman Springs Member of the Wanapum Basalt.

14. Probably using beargrass, *Xerophyllum tenax* (Pursh) Nutt. (also called Indian basket grass), and western bulrush. Gunther, 22–23; Hitchcock et al., 1:812.

[Clark]   *October 23rd ⟨Saturday⟩ Wednesday 1805*

Took the Canoes over the Portage on the Lard. Side with much dificuelty, description on another Paper[1] one Canoe got loose & cought by the Indians which we were obliged to pay.   our old Chiefs over herd the Indians from below Say they would try to *kill* us & informed us of it, we have all the arm examined and put in order, all th Inds leave us early,

Great numbers of flees on the Lard Side— Shot a Sea Oter[2] which I did not get, Great Numbers about those rapids we purchased 8 dogs, Small & fat for our party to eate, the Indians not verry fond of Selling their good fish, compells us to make use of dogs for food Exchanged our Small canoe for a large & a very new one built for riding the waves obsd Merdn. altd. 66° 27′ 30″ Latd. prodsd. 45° 42′ 57³⁄₁₀″ North[3]

[Clark]   *October 23d Wednesday 1805*

a fine morning, I with the greater part of the men Crossed in the Canoes to opposit Side above the falls and hauled them across the portage of 457 yards which is on the Lard. Side and certainly the best side to pass the canoes I then decended through a narrow chanel of about 150 yards wide forming a kind of half circle in it course of a mile to a pitch of 8 feet in which the chanel is divided by 2 large rocks at this place we were obliged to let the Canoes down by Strong ropes of Elk Skin which we had for the purpose, one Canoe in passing this place got loose by the Cords breaking, and was cought by the Indians below. I accomplished this necessary business and landed Safe with all the Canoes at our Camp below the falls by 3 oClock P. M. nearly covered with flees which were So thick amongst the Straw and fish Skins at the upper part of the portage at which place the nativs had been Camped not long Since; that every man of the party was obliged to Strip naked dureing the time of takeing over the canoes, that they might have an oppertunity of brushing the flees of their legs and bodies—[4] Great numbers of *Sea Otters* in the river below the falls, I Shot one in the narrow chanel to day which I could not get. Great numbers of Indians visit us both from above and below—. one of the old Chiefs who had accompanied us from the head of the river, informed us that he herd the Indians Say that the nation below intended to kill us, we examined all the arms &c. complete the amunition to 100 rounds. The nativs leave us earlyer this evening than usial, which gives a Shadow of Confirmation to the information of our Old Chief, as we are at all times & places on our guard, are under no greater apprehention than is common.

we purchased 8 Small fat dogs for the party to eate the nativs not being fond of Selling their good fish, compells us to make use of Dog meat for food, the flesh of which the most of the party have become fond of from the habits of useing it for Some time past. The Altitude of this day 66° 27′ 30″ gave for Latd. *45° 42′ 57 ³/₁₀ N.*

I observed on the beach near the Indian Lodges two Canoes butifull of different Shape & Size to what we had Seen above wide in the midde and tapering to each end, on the bow curious figures were Cut in the wood &c. Capt. Lewis went up to the Lodges to See those Canoes and exchanged our Smallest Canoe for one of them by giveing a Hatchet & few trinkets to the owner who informed that he purchased it of a white man below for a horse, these Canoes are neeter made than any I have ever Seen and Calculated to ride the waves, and carry emence burthens, they are dug thin and are suported by cross pieces of about 1 inch diamuter tied with Strong bark thro' holes in the Sides.[5] our two old Chiefs appeared verry uneasy this evening.

1. Possibly a reference to the entry in Codex H for this day.

2. The sea otter, *Enhydra lutris,* never leaves salt water. They had evidently observed the harbor seal, *Phoca vitulina richardii,* a species new to science. The captains later corrected this error; see below, February 23, 1806. Cutright (LCPN), 233–34.

3. The observation may be in Lewis's hand.

4. This passage about fleas has a red vertical line through it, perhaps drawn by Biddle.

5. The Chinookan peoples of the lower Columbia and Northwest Coast were master canoe-builders, a skill which helped them immeasurably in coping with their environment. For further observations, see below, February 1, 1806. Ray (CI), 121, 126–27.

[Clark] *October 24th ⟨Sunday⟩ Thursday 1805*

a fine morning the Indians approached us with caution. our 2 old Chiefs deturmin to return home, Saying they were at war with Indians below and they would kill them we pursuaded them to Stay 2 nights longer with us, with a view to make a peace with those Indians below as well as to have them with us dureing our Delay with this tribe. Capt Lewis went to view the falls I Set out with the party at 9 oClock a m at 2½ miles passed a rock which makes from the Stard Side 4 Lodges above 1 below and Confined the river in a narrow channel of about 45 yards[1] this continued for about ¼ of a mile & widened to about 200 yards, in those narrows the water was agitated in a most Shocking manner boils

Swell & whorl pools, we passed with great risque It being impossible to make a portage of the Canoes, about 2 miles lower passed a verry Bad place between 2 rocks one large & in the middle of the river   here our Canoes took in Some water, I put all the men who Could not Swim on Shore; & Sent a fiew articles Such as guns & papers, and landed at a village of 20 houses on the Stard Side in a Deep bason where the river apprd. to be blocked up with emence rocks[2]   I walked down and examined the pass found it narrow, and one verry bad place a little ⟨below⟩ in the narrows   I pursued this Chanel which is from 50 to 100 yards wide and Swels and boils with a most Tremendeous manner; prosued this channel[3] 5 ms & returned   found Capt Lewis & a Chief from below with maney of his men on a visit to us, one of our Party Pete Crusat played on the *violin* which pleased the Savage, the men danced, Great numbers of Sea Orter Pole Cats about those fishories.   the houses of those Indians are 20 feet Square and Sunk 8 feet under ground & Covered with bark with a Small door round at top rose about 18 Inches above ground, to keep out the Snow   I saw 107 parcels of fish Stacked, and great quantites in the houses

[Clark]   *October 24th Thursday 1805*

The morning fare after a beautifull night, the nativs approached us this morning with great caution.   our two old chiefs expressed a desire to return to their band from this place, Saying "that they Could be of no further Service to us, as their nation extended no further down the river than those falls, [*NB: they could no longer understand the language of those below the falls, till then not much difference in the vocaby.*][4] and as the nation below had expressed hostile intentions against us, would Certainly kill them; perticularly as They had been at war with each other;" we requested them to Stay with us *two* nights longer, and we would See the nation below and make a peace between them, they replied they "were anxious to return and See our horses" we insisted on their Staying with us two nights longer to which they agreed; our views were to detain those Chiefs with us untill we Should pass the next falls, which we were told was verry bad, and at no great distance below, that they might inform us of any designs of the nativs, and if possible to bring about a peace between them and the tribes below.

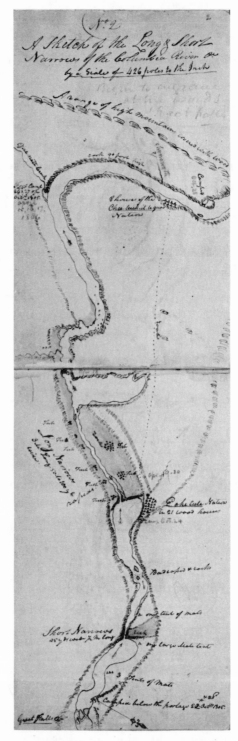

24. Long and Short Narrows (The Dalles)
of the Columbia River, Washington and Oregon,
October 22–28, 1805, Codex H, pp. 2–3

The first pitch of this falls is 20 feet perpendicular, then passing thro' a narrow Chanel for 1 mile to a rapid of about 18 feet fall below which the water has no perceptable fall but verry rapid *See Sketch* No. 1.[5] It may be proper here to remark that from Some obstruction below, the cause of which we have not yet learned, the water in high fluds (which are in the Spring) rise ⟨nearly⟩ below these falls nearly to a leavel with the water above the falls; the marks of which can be plainly trac'd around the falls. at that Stage of the water the Salmon must pass up which abounds in Such great numbers above— below those falls are Salmon trout and great numbers of the heads of a Species of trout Smaller than the Salmon. those fish they catch out of the Salmon Season, and are at this time in the act of burrying those which they had drid for winter food. the mode of buring those fish is in holes of various Sizes, lined with Straw on which they lay fish Skins in which they inclose the fish which is laid verry close, and then Covered with earth of about 12 or 15 inches thick. Capt Lewis and three men crossed the river and on the opposit Side to view the falls which he had not yet taken a full view of— At 9 oClock a. m. I Set out with the party and proceeded on down a rapid Stream of about 400 yards wide at 2½ miles the river widened into a large bason to the Stard. Side on which there is five Lodges of Indians. here a tremendious ⟨heigh⟩ black rock Presented itself high and Steep appearing to choke up the river[6] nor could I See where the water passed further than the Current was drawn with great velocity to the Lard Side of this rock at which place I heard a great roreing. I landed at the Lodges and the natives went with me to the top of this rock which makes from the Stard. Side; from the top of which I could See the dificuelties we had to pass for Several miles below; at this place the water of this great river is compressed into a Chanel between two rocks not exceeding *forty five* yards wide and continues for a ¼ of a mile when it again widens to 200 yards and continues this width for about 2 miles when it is again intersepted by rocks. This obstruction in the river accounts for the water in high floods riseing to Such a hite at the last falls. The whole of the Current of this great river must at all Stages pass thro' this narrow chanel of 45 yards wide. as the portage of our canoes over this high rock would be impossible with our Strength, and the only danger in passing thro those narrows was the whorls and

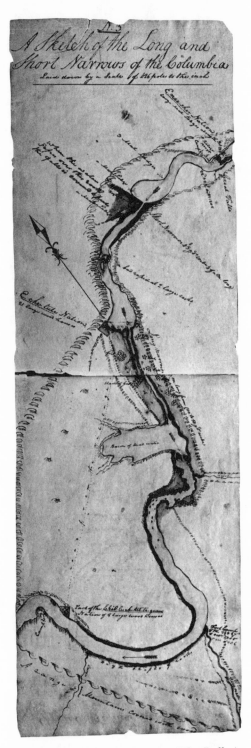

25. Long and Short Narrows (The Dalles)
of the Columbia River, Washington and Oregon,
October 22–28, 1805, Voorhis No. 4

Swills arriseing from the Compression of the water, and which I thought (as also our principal watermen Peter Crusat) by good Stearing we could pass down Safe, accordingly I deturmined to pass through this place notwithstanding the horrid appearance of this agitated gut Swelling, boiling & whorling in every direction (which from the top of the rock did not appear as bad as when I was in it;[)] however we passed Safe to the astonishment of all the Inds: of the last Lodges who viewed us from the top of the rock. passed one Lodge below this rock and halted on the Stard. Side to view a verry bad place, the Current divided by 2 Islands of rocks the lower of them large and in the middle of the river, this place being verry bad I Sent by land all the men who could not Swim and Such articles as was most valuable to us Such as papers Guns & amunition, and proceeded down with the Canoes two at a time to a village of 20 wood housies in a Deep bend to the Stard. Side below which a rugid black rock about ⟨the⟩ 20 feet hiter ⟨of⟩ than the Common high fluds of the river with Several dry Chanels which appeared to Choke the river up quite across; this I took to be the 2d falls or the place the nativs above call *timm,* The nativs of this village reived me verry kindly, one of whome envited me into his house, which I found to be large and comodious, and the first wooden houses in which Indians have lived Since we left those in the vicinty of the Illinois, they are scattered permiscuisly on a elivated Situation near a mound of about 30 feet above the Common leavel, which mound has Some remains of houses and has every appearance of being artificial— those houses are about the Same Shape Size and form 20 feet ⟨Square⟩ wide and 30 feet long with one Dore raised 18 Inches above ground, ⟨which⟩ they are 29½ inches high & 14 wide, forming in a half Circle above[7] those houses were Sunk into the earth Six feet, the roofs of them was Supported by a ridge pole resting on three Strong pieces of Split timber thro' one of which the dore was cut ⟨on which⟩ that and the walls ⟨which⟩ the top of which was just above ground Suported a certain number of Spars which are Covered with the Bark of the white Ceadar, or *Arber Vitea;* and the whole attached and Secured by the fibers of the Cedar. the eaves at or near the earth, the gable ends and Side walls are Secured with Split boards which is Seported on iner Side with Strong pieces of timber under the eves &c. to keep those pieces errect & the

18/29 Inches above ground ~~which~~, they are 9 1/2 inches ~~high~~ & 14 wide, forming in a half Circle above, thou houses were sunk into the earth Six feet, the roofs of them was Supported by ~~three~~ strong pieces of Split timber ~~on which~~, that and the walls, ~~which~~ the top of Which was just above ground Supports a certain number of Spars Which are Covered with the Bark of the White Cedar, or Arbervitea; and the whole attached and secured by the fibers of the Cedar. the eaves at or near the earth, the gable ends and side walls are Secured with Split boards which is Suported on iner Side with strong pieces of timber under the eves & to keep those pieces erect & the earth from without pressing in the boards, Suported by Strong posts at the Corners to which those pole were attached to give adetional Strength, Smale openings in the roof were left above the ground, for the purpose, as I conjectured, of discharging their arrows at a besieging enemy; light is admited thro' as opening

26. Shape of a Hut Door, October 24, 1805, Codex H, p. 63

334

earth from without pressing in the boards, Suported by Strong posts at
the Corners to which those poles were attached to give aditional Strength,
Small openings were left [*NB: in the roof*] above the ground, for the purpose, as I conjectured, of deschargeing Their arrows at a besiegeing
enimey; Light is admited Thro an opening at top which also Serves for
the Smoke to pass through.   one half of those houses is apropriated for
the Storeing away Dried & pounded fish which is the principal food
The other part next the dore is the part occupied by the nativs who have
beds raised on either Side, with a fire place in the center of this Space
each house appeared to be occupied by about three families; that part
which is apropriated for fish was crouded with that article, and a fiew baskets of burries—   I dispatched a Sufficent number of the good Swimers
back for the 2 canoes above the last rapid and with 2 men walked down
three miles to examine the river Over a bed of rocks, which the water at
verry high fluds passes over, on those rocks I Saw Several large Scaffols
on which the Indians dry fish; as this is out of Season the poles on which
they dry those fish are tied up verry Securely in large bundles and put
upon the Scaffolds, I counted 107 ⟨Scaff⟩ Stacks of dried pounded fish in
different places on those rocks which must have contained 10,000 w. of
neet fish, The evening being late I could not examine the river to my Satisfaction, the Chanel is narrow and compressed for about 2 miles, when it
widens into a deep bason to the Stard. Side, & again contracts into a narrow chanel divided by a rock   I returned through a rockey open countrey infested with pole-cats to the village where I met with Capt. Lewis the
two old Chiefs who accompanied us & the party & canoes who had all
arrived Safe; the Canoes haveing taken in Some water at the last rapids.
here we formed a Camp near the Village, The principal Chief from the
nation below with Several of his men visited us, and afforded a favourable oppertunity of bringing about a Piece and good understanding between this chief and his people and the two Chiefs who accompanied us
which we have the Satisfaction to Say we have accomplished, as we have
every reason to believe and that those two bands or nations are and will
be on the most friendly terms with each other.   gave this Great Chief a
Medal and Some other articles, of which he was much pleased, Peter

Crusat played on the *violin* and the men danced which delighted the nativs, who Shew every civility towards us. we Smoked with those people untill late at night, when every one retired to rest.

1. The Short, or Little, Narrows, with the Long Narrows, constitute The Dalles of the Columbia, located above the present town of The Dalles, Wasco County, Oregon. Once major obstacles to navigation, they are now inundated by The Dalles Dam. Clark drew a detailed sketch map (fig. 24) of the area in Codex H, pp. 2–3, and another version (fig. 25) in Voorhis No. 4. Allen (PG), 313; *Atlas* map 78. The four lodges have been reported as occurring in the vicinity of Browns Island, but the precise location has not been ascertained. This seems too far downstream, as Browns Island occurs downstream of the Lewis and Clark's Short Narrows and the lodges are shown at the upstream end on *Atlas* map 78. Wilke et al., 27–28.

2. They camped here, in Klickitat County, Washington, in the vicinity of Horsethief Lake State Park. The reason for the asterisk at the beginning of the next sentence is unknown. The Indians were Wishram-Wasco Chinookans whom Lewis and Clark called Echelutes, from the term *i-č-xlúit*, "I am a Wishram[-Wasco] Indian." Ronda (LCAI), 170; *Atlas* map 78; Sapir, 533; Curtis, 180 n. 1. The wealth of archaeological materials recorded in this general area at the head of the Long Narrows certainly could contain the village near which Lewis and Clark camped. These lodges may be near what was recorded as the Wishram village of *wa'q!Emap*. Spier & Sapir, 164. Extensive archaeological research between Horsethief Lake and The Dalles Dam has taken place since the 1920s. Duncan; Wilke et al.; Spier & Sapir; Butler (WM); Caldwell; Butler (ALCV); Cressman et al.; Strong, Schenck, & Steward.

3. The Long Narrows. *Atlas* map 78.

4. The Dalles area was a dividing point between Chinookan-language speakers downstream and Shahaptian-language speakers upstream. The two Nez Perce chiefs could no longer serve as interpreters. Ronda (LCAI), 173.

5. A reference to fig. 22 from Codex H.

6. The rocks here are composed of basalt of the middle Miocene Frenchman Springs Member of the Wanapum Basalt. A fault cuts across the eastern end of the basin raising a block of these rocks across the river.

7. Here in Codex H, p. 63, Clark inserts his drawing of the door shape (fig. 26).

[Clark]   *October 25th* ⟨*Monday*⟩ Friday 1805

A Cold morning, we deturmined to attempt the Chanel   after brackfast I took down all the party below the bad places with a load & one Canoe   passed well, a 2d passed well   I had men on the Shore with ropes to throw in in Case any acidence happened at the Whirl &c—   the Inds on the rocks veiwing us   the 3rd Canoe nearly filled with water   we got her Safe to Shore. The last Canoe Came over well which to me was truly gratifying   Set out and had not passed 2 mils before 3 Canoes run against a rock in the river with great force   no damg.   ⟨at⟩ met with a 2d Chief of the nation from hunting, we Smoked with him and his party and gave a medal of The Small Size & Set out   passed great numbers of rocks, good water and Came to at a high ⟨bluff⟩ point of rocks below the mouth of a Creek which falls in on the Lard Side and head up towards the high Snow mountain to the S W.   this Creek[1] is 20 yards wide[2] and has Some beaver Signs at its mouth   river about ½ a mile wide and Crouded with Sea otters, & drum was Seen this evening   we took possession of a high Point of rocks to defend our Selves in Case the threts of those Indians below Should be put in execution against us. Sent out Some hunters to look if any Signs of game, one man killed a Small deer & Several others Seen   I killed a goose, and Suped hartily on venison & goose. Camped on the rock[3]   guard under the hill.

Courses from the upper rapids

West	2	miles passing a Lard. point of Land and a Stard. point & 3 Lodges a deep bason to the Stard. to a pt of rocks, above a Chanel
S. 70° W.	2	miles to a rock Island in the middle of the river at a bad rapid & whols, passed thro a narrow bad Chanel 45 yds wide for ¼ of a mile.[4] a Lodge below on Stard. Side halted to look out
S. 50° W.	2	miles to a rock at the head of a narrow Chanel, a deep bason to the Stard. on which a village of 21 Lodges— passed a large rock Island in the middle of the river. The Channel nearest the Lard Side

Octr. 25

S. 34° W	3	miles thro a narrow Swift bad Chanel from 50 to 100 yards wide,[5] of Swels Whorls & bad places a verry bad place at 1 mile, a rock in the midl. at 2 miles to a rock above a Deep bason to the Stard. Side above the rock
S. 20° W.	2	miles to a high Rock Passed thro a narrow Channel on the Std. Side of a rock in the middle of the Chanel

| N. 60° W | 1 | mile to a bend, passed a bason to the Lard Side, and large ruged rocks on both Sides |
| S. 60° W. | 4 | miles to large Creek a Lard. bend under a timbered bottom & the first timber we have Seen near the river for a long distance Pine & white oake |

[Clark]   *October 25th Friday 1805*

a cool morning   Capt Lewis and my Self walked down to See the place the Indians pointed out as the worst place in passing through the gut, which we found difficuelt of passing without great danger, but as the portage was impractiable with our large Canoes, we Concluded to Make a portage of our most valuable articles and run the canoes thro   accordingly on our return divided the party Some to take over the Canoes, and others to take our Stores across a portage of a mile to a place on the Chanel below this bad whorl & Suck, with Some others I had fixed on the Chanel with roapes to throw out to any who Should unfortunately meet with difficuelty in passing through; great number of Indians viewing us from the high rocks under which we had to pass, the 3 firt Canoes passed thro very well, the 4th nearly filled with water, the last passed through by takeing in a little water, ⟨we⟩ thus Safely below what I conceved to be the worst part of this Chanel, felt my Self extreamly gratified and pleased.   we loaded the Canoes & Set out, and had not proceeded, more than two mile before the unfortunate Canoe which filled crossing the bad place above, run against a rock and was in great danger of being lost, This Chanel is through a hard rough black rock, from 50–100 yards wide.[6] Swelling and boiling in a most tremendious maner Several places on which the Indians inform me they take the Salmon as fast as they wish; we passed through a deep bason to the Stard Side of 1 mile below which the River narrows and divided by a rock   The Curent we found quit jentle, here we met with our two old Chiefs who had been to a village below to Smoke a friendly pipe, and at this place they met the Cheif & party from the village above[7] on his return from hunting all of whome were then crossing over their horses, we landed to Smoke a pipe with this Chief whome we found to be a bold pleasing looking man of about 50

years of age dressd. in a war jacket a cap Legins & mockersons. he gave
us Some meat of which he had but little and informed us he in his rout
met with a war party of Snake Indians from the great river of the S. E.
which falls in a few miles above and had a fight. we gave this Chief a
Medal, &c. a parting Smoke with our two faithful friends the Chiefs who
accompanied us from the head of the river, (who had purchased a horse
each with 2 robes and intended to return on horse back) we proceeded
on down the water fine, rocks in every derection for a fiew miles when the
river widens and becoms a butifull jentle Stream of about half a mile
wide, Great numbers of the Sea Orter [*NB: or Seals*] about those narrows
and both below and above. we Came too, under a high point of rocks on
the Lard. Side below a creek of 20 yards wide and much water, as it was
necessary to make Some Selestial observations we formed our Camp on
the top of a high point of rocks, which forms a kind of ⟨artif⟩ fortification
in the Point between the river & Creek, with a boat guard, this Situation
we Concieve well Calculated for defence, and Conveniant to hunt under
the foots of the mountain to the West & S. W.[8] where timber of different
kinds grows, and appears to be handsom Coverts for the Deer, in oke
woods, Sent out hunters to examine for game   G. D.[9] Killed a Small Deer
& other Saw much Sign, I killed a goose in the creek which was verry
fat— one of the guard saw a Drum fish[10] to day as he Conceved our
Situation well Calculated to defend ⟨us⟩ our Selves from any designs of
the natives, Should They be enclined to attack us.

This little Creek heads in the range of mountains which run S S W & N
W for a long distance on which is Scattering pine white Oake &c. The
Pinical of the round toped mountain which we Saw a Short distance below the forks of this river is S. 43° W. of us and abt 37 miles, it is at this
time toped with Snow we called this the *falls mountain* or *Timm* mountain. [*NB: This the Mount Hood of Vancouver*] The face of the Countrey,
on both Side of the river above and about the falls, is Steep ruged and
rockey open and contain but a Small preportion of erbage, no timber a
fiew bushes excepted, The nativs at the upper falls raft their timber down
Towarnehooks River & those at the narrows take theirs up the river to the
lower part of the narrows from this Creek, and Carry it over land 3 miles

to their houses &c.   at the mouth of this creek Saw Some beaver Sign, and a Small wolf in a Snare Set in the willows   The Snars of which I saw Several made for to catch wolves, are made as follows vz: a long pole which will Spring is made fast with bark to a willow, on the top of this pole a String [*NB: Described elsewhere*][11]

1. "Que-nett Creek" on *Atlas* maps 78, 86, now Mill Creek, reaching the Columbia at The Dalles, Wasco County, Oregon. The name Quenett probably comes from the Upper Chinookan *-gwánat*, "Chinook salmon."

2. Here in the Elkskin-bound Journal Clark has inserted the courses and distances for October 25, in the middle of a sentence in the main text. The two parts of the text have been brought together for ease of reading.

3. What they later called "Fort Camp" or "Fort Rock Camp," at the mouth of Mill Creek, at the present town of The Dalles. Here they camped October 25–28, 1805, and April 15–18, 1806, on the return journey. *Atlas* map 78.

4. Little Narrows of *Atlas* map 78.

5. Long Narrows of ibid.

6. The narrow channel here is cut through a downfaulted block of basalt of the middle Miocene Priest Rapids Member of the Wanapum Basalt.

7. Presumably from the "Echelute," or Wishram village above the Long Narrows, but perhaps from the "Eneeshurs" above Celilo Falls. See above, October 22 and 24, 1805. *Atlas* map 78.

8. The Cascade Range.

9. George Drouillard.

10. No species of drum fish are known in the Columbia River and it is impossible to determine what the guard was seeing. Lee et al., 756–61.

11. See below, January 15, 1806. The remaining half-page of Codex H, p. 70, is blank.

[Clark]   *October 26th 1805 ⟨Tuesday⟩ Saturday*

a fine morning   Sent out Six men to hunt ⟨to Kill⟩ deer & Collect rozin to Pitch our Canoes, had all our articles put out to dry—   Canoes drawed out and repaired, the injories recved in drawing them over the rocks, every article wet in the Canoe which nearly Sunk yesterday—

Took the Azmuth of the Sun & time this morning.

Azumuth			Time			distance		
			h	m	s			
S.	64°	E	8	41	6	41°	1′	0″
S.	63°	E	8	45	32	42	6	30
S.	62°	E	8	51	8	43	28	15

Took equal altitudes with Sextn.

	H.	m	S.		h	m	s
AM	8	54	22	PM	2	9	44
	8	56	41	"		12	5
	8	59	1				

Altitude produced from this observation 44° 14′ 15″

a number of Indians came to the opposit Side and Shew great anxiety to Come over. they delayed untill late[1]

Took time and distance of Sun and moon Sun West P M

h	m	s			
2	21	12	49°	51′	15″
"	25	45	49	51	
"	29	4	49	52	
"	31	43	49	52	30
"	33	9	49	52	45
"	36	2	49	53	30
"	37	49	49	54	30
"	39	5	49	55	
"	40	23	49	55	30
"	41	36	49	56	

Took time and distance of Moons Western limb & Fulenhalt,[2] Star East—

	Time			*distance*		
	h	m.	S			
PM	6	34	0	67°	36′	15″
	"	36	4	67	35	15
	"	39	2	67	34	30 [*letters illegible; "Cloudy" in Codex H*]

In the evening 2 Chief and 15 men came over in a Single Canoe, those Chfs proved to be the 2 great Chiefs of the tribes above, one gave me a ⟨buf⟩ dressed Elk Skin, and gave us Som deer meet, and 2 Cakes of white bread made of white roots, we gave to each Chief a Meadel of the Small Size a red Silk handkerchief & a knife to the 1st a arm ban & a pin of Paint & a Comb to his Son a Piece of riben tied to a tin gorget and 2 hams of Venison They deturmined to Stay with us all night, we had a fire made for them & one man played on the violin which pleased them much my Servent danced— our hunters killed five Deer, 4 verry large gray Squirrels,[3] a goose & Pheasent, one man giged a *Salmon trout*[4] which we had fried in a little Bears oil which a Chief gave us yesterday and I think the finest fish I ever tasted, Saw great numbers of white Crains[5] flying in Different directions verry high. The river has rose nearly 8 Inches to day and has every appearance of a tide, from what Cause I can't Say— our hunters Saw Elk & bear signs to day in the white oake woods the Country to the Lard is broken Country thinly timbered with pine and white oake, a mountain which I must call *Timm* or *falls* Mountain rises verry high and bears to S W the Course it has bore Sinc we first Saw it. our men danced to night. dried all our wet articles and repaired our Canoes

The flees[6] my Self and the men got on them in passing thro the plains the Indians had lately lived in Lodges on the Lard. Side at the falls, are very troublesom and with every exertion the men Can't get rid of them, perticilarly as they have no clothes to change those which they wore— Those Indians are at Ware with the Snake Indians on the river which falls in a few miles above this and have lately had a battle with them, their loss I cannot lern.[7]

[Clark]   *October 26th Saturday 1805*

A fine morning   Sent Six men out to hunt Deer, and Collect rozin to pitch the Canoes which has become verry leakey, by frequently hauling them over rocks &c as well Striking rocks frequently in passing down. all our articles we have exposed to the Sun to Dry; and the Canoes drawn out and turned up— maney of our Stores entirely Spoiled by being re-peetedly wet;[8]

A number of Indians came to the Oposit Side of the river in the fore part of the day and Shew that they were anxious to Cross to us, we did not think proper to cross them in our Canoes and did not Send for them. in the evening *two* Chiefs and 15 men came over in a Small Canoe, those two Chiefs proved to be the two Principal Chiefs of the tribes above at the falls, and above, who was out hunting at the time we passed their bands; one of those Chiefs made Capt Lewis and my Self each a Small present of Deer meat, and Small Cakes of white bread made of roots. we gave to each Chief a Meadel of the Small Size a red Silk handkerchief, arm band, Knife & a piece of Paint, and acknowledged them as chiefs; as we thought it necessary at this time to treat those people verry friendly & ingratiate our Selves with them, to insure us a kind & friendly reception on our return, we gave Small presents to Several, and half a Deer to them to eate. we had also a fire made for those people to Sit around in the middle of our Camp, and Peter Crusat Played on the violin, which pleased those nativs exceedingly. the two Chiefs and Several men deturmined to delay all night (yorked Danced for the Inds) with us all the others returned, leaving the horses for those who Staied on the opposit Side. our hunters returned in the evening Killed five Deer, four verry large grey Squirels and a grouse. one of the guard at the river guiged a Salmon Trout, which we had fried in a little Bears Oil which the Chief we passed below the narrows gave us: ⟨thought this⟩ this I thought one of the most delicious fish I have ever tasted

Great numbers of white Crain flying in different Directions verry high— The river rose 8 Inches to day from what cause I cannot Say certainly, as the tides cannot effect the river here as there is a falls below, I conjecture that the rise is owing to the winds which has Set up the river for 24 hours past. our hunters inform that the countrey back is broken, Stoney and thinly timbered with pine and White Oake. They Saw Elk & Bear Sign in the mountains. Dried all our wet articles and repared our Canoes to day, and the Party amused themselves at night danceing. The *Flees* which the party got on them at the upper & great falls, are very troublesom and dificuelt to get rid of, perticularly as the me[n] have not a Change of Clothes to put on, they Strip off their Clothes and kill the flees, dureing which time they remain neckid.

The nations in the vicinity of this place is at War with the Snake Indians who they Say are noumerous and live on the river we passed above the falls on the Same Side on which we have encamped, and the nearest town is about four days march they pointed nearly S. E. and informed that they had a battle with those Inds. laterly, their loss I could not assertain

1. The numbers "54 22" follow this line at the bottom of a page of the Elkskin-bound Journal. They probably represent astronomical data.
2. The star Fomalhaut.

3. Probably the western gray squirrel, *Sciurus griseus*, then new to science. For Lewis's detailed description, see below, February 25, 1806. Burroughs, 97.

4. Evidently the steelhead trout. See above, August 22, 1805.

5. The endangered whooping crane, *Grus americana* [AOU, 204].

6. It seems more likely that the "flees" are lice, since fleas do not attach themselves to hosts for any length of time. If lice, they would be human body lice, *Pediculus humanus*. Harwood & James, 129–41.

7. Two blank pages follow in the Elkskin-bound Journal.

8. Here follows in Codex H, p. 71, Clark's astronomical observation as probably copied from the Elkskin-bound Journal. As no significant differences were noted, it is not printed here.

[Clark] *October 27th ⟨Wednesday⟩ Sunday 1805*

a verry windy night and morning   wind from the West and hard,

⟨h   m   s⟩

⟨Took an altitude of the Suns upper Limb. At   8   34   50⟩ ⟨and 38° 57′ 0″⟩

Took time and distance of Suns and moons nearest Limbs ⟨moon⟩ Sun West

	Time			*distance*		
	h	m	S			
P M	3	20	37	61°	0′	0″
″		22	33	61	0	45
″		23	23	61	1	15
″		24	24	61	1	45
″		25	25	61	2	15
″		26	22	61	2	30
″		27	25	61	2	30
″		28	23	61	3	15
″		29	9	61	3	30
″		29	50	61	3	30

Send out hunters and they killed 4 deer 1 pheasent and a Squirel   the 2 Chiefs and party Continue with us, we treat them well give them to eate & Smoke, they were joined by Seven others, from below who Stayed about 3 hours and returned down the river in a pet, Soon after the Chiefs deturmined to go home   we had them put across the river   the wind verry high, we took a vocabelary of the Languages of the 2 nations, the one liveing at the Falls call themselves *E-nee-shur*[1]   The other resideing at the levels or narrows in a village on the Std. Side call themselves *E-chee-*

lute not withstanding those people live only 6 miles apart, but fiew words of each others language— the language of those above having great Similarity with those tribes of flat heads we have passed— all have the Clucking tone anexed which is predomint. above, all flatten the heads of their female children near the falls, and maney above follow the Same Custom[2] The language of the *Che-luc-it-te-quar*[3] a fiew miles below is different from both in a Small degree. The wind increased in the evening and blew verry hard from the Same point W. day fair and Cold— The Creek at which we are Encamped is Called by the natives—*Que-nett*— Some words with Shabono about his duty— ⟨Falls M⟩ The pinical of Falls mountain bears S 43° W. about 35 miles

[Clark] *October 27th Sunday 1805*

Wind hard from the west all the last night and this morning.[4] Some words with Shabono our interpreter about his duty. Sent out Several hunters who brought in *four Deer,* one *Grouse* & a *Squirel*. The two Chiefs & party was joined by Seven others from below in two canoes, we gave them to eate & Smoke Several of those from below returned down the river in a bad humer, haveing got into this pet by being prevented doeing as they wished with our articles which was then exposed to dry— we took a Vocabelary of the Languages of those two chiefs which are verry different notwithstanding they are Situated within Six miles of each other, Those at the *great falls* Call themselves *E-nee-shur* and are understood on the river above: Those at the Great Narrows Call themselves *E-che-lute* and is understood below, maney words of those people are the Same,[5] and Common to all the *flat head* Bands which we have passed on the river, all have the *clucking* tone anexed which is prodomonate above. all the Bands flatten the heads of the female Children, and maney of the male children also. Those two Chief leave us this evening and returned to their bands, the wind verry high & from the West, day proved fair and Cool.

The nativs Call this Creek near which we are encamped—*Que-nett.*

1. The three tribal names here may have been added to blank spaces.
2. As Clark notes, many tribes of the lower Columbia and the Northwest Coast de-

formed the soft skulls of their infants by applying pressure with a headband or a special attachment to a cradleboard. The result was a pointed skull that lasted through life, apparently without any bad physical or mental effects. This deformation was a mark of status; slaves were not allowed to deform the skulls of their children. For Clark's sketches of the process and some of the results, see figs. in vol. 6.

3. Investigators place the Wishram—the easternmost Chinookan tribe—in this area. They report that the Wishram occupied the north shore and the closely allied Wasco tribe occupied the south shore of the Columbia River, and plot villages of these peoples essentially between Mosier, Wasco County, Oregon, and Wishram, Klickitat County, Washington. Spier & Sapir; Lewis (TCV), 179–204; Spier, 20–24. The "Che-luc-it-te-quar" name may represent Upper Chinookan *č-i-l-ktí-gʷa-x*, "he is pointing at him." Perhaps when Lewis or Clark pointed at someone and asked his tribe, they got this answer. Curtis, 180 n. 1.

4. Here follows Clark's astronomical observation in Codex H, p. 74; being a repeat of the other entry, it is not printed here.

5. Whether the Chinook trade jargon had come into existence by the time of Lewis and Clark is still a debated issue among linguists; it may be that all these Indians were using it, based on the Chinook language which was widespread in the northwest. It served the same function as the sign language on the Great Plains. This would account for the captains' noting similar words used by people of different language families. Hodge, 1:274–75.

[Clark]   *October 28th Monday 1805*[1]

a windey morning   loaded our Canoes and Set out at 9 oClock a m   3 Canoes Came ⟨up⟩ down from the Village above & 2 from that below   in one of those Canoes a Indian wore his hair cued, and had on a round hat. Wind from West

Course distanc

N. 50° W.   2   miles   Cove in a Lard. bend   Clift of rocks on each Side of 90 feet high, fiew pine

N. 10° W.   2/4   miles to an Indian village of the *Chee-luck-it-te-quar* nation of 8 houses in the form of those above, passed the mouth of a Small Creek

Those Indians have a musket a Sword, and Several Brass *Tea* kittles which they appear to be verry fond of   we purchased of those people five Small dogs, and Some Dried beries & white bread of roots, the wind rose and we were obliged to ⟨ly⟩ lie by about 1 mile below on the Lard. Side

North 1 mile to a rock Island on the Stard. Side.   we had not landed long eer an Indian Canoe Came from below with 3 Indians in it, those Indians make verry nice Canoes of Pine. Thin with aporns & Carve on the head imitation of animals & other heads; The Indians above Sacrafise the property of the Deceased to wit horses Canoes, bolds [bowls] Basquets of which they make great use to hold water boil their meet &c. &c.   great many Indians came down from the uppr Village & Sat with us, Smoked, rained all the evenig & blew hard from the West   encamped on the Lard Side opsd. an Rock in a verry Bad place[2]

[Clark]   *October 28th Monday 1805*

A cool windey morning   we loaded our Canoes and Set out at 9 oClock, a. m.   as we were about to Set out 3 canoes from above and 2 from below came to view us   in one of those Canoes I observed an Indian with round hat Jacket & wore his hair cued [*NB: he Said he got them from Indians below the great rapid who bought them from the whites*]   we proceeded on river inclosed on each Side in high Clifts of about 90 feet of loose dark coloured rocks[3]   at four miles we landed at a village of 8 houses on the Stard. Side under Some rugid rocks, Those people call themselves *Chil-luckit-te-quaw,*[4] live in houses Similar to those described, Speake Somewhat different language with maney words the Same & understand those in their neighbourhood   Cap Lewis took a vocabilary of this Language   I entered one of the houses in which I Saw a British musket, a cutlash [cutlass] and Several brass Tea kittles of which they appeared verry fond   Saw them boiling fish in baskets with Stones, I also Saw [*NB: badly executed*] figures of animals & men Cut & painted on boards in one Side of the house which they appeared to prize, but for what purpose I will not venter to Say,—.   here we purchased five Small Dogs, Some dried buries, & white bread made of roots, the wind rose and we were obliged to lie by all day at 1 mile below on the Lard. Side.   we had not been long on Shore before a Canoe came up with a man woman & 2 children, who had a fiew roots to Sell, Soon after maney others joined them from above, The wind which is the cause of our delay, does not retard the motions of those people at all, as their canoes are calculated to ride the highest waves, they are built of white cedar or Pine verry light wide in the middle and tapers at each end, with aperns, and heads of animals carved on the bow, which is generally raised.[5] Those people make great use of Canoes, both for transpotation and fishing, they also use of bowls & baskets made of Grass & [*NB: bark*] Splits[6] to hold water and boil their fish & meat. Maney of the nativs of the last Village Came down Set and Smoke with us, wind blew hard accompanied with rain all the evening, our Situation not a verry good one for an encampment, but Such as it is we are obliged to put up with, the harbor is a Safe one, we encamped on the Sand wet and disagreeable   one Deer killed this evening, and another wounded near our Camp.

1. Clark now has the days of the week correct in his Elkskin-bound Journal. It may have been at this date that he went back to make corrections.

2. In Wasco County, Oregon, a few miles below The Dalles, in the vicinity of Crates Point, and above Rowena. *Atlas* map 78. It is near the archaeological site of Bad Place (after Lewis and Clark), an area occupied primarily after 1400 A.D. Cole. Clark has the number "5" at the end of this line showing the day's mileage accumulation.

3. These cliffs are composed of the middle Miocene Frenchman Springs Member of the Wanapum Basalt. The rocks here have been broken and fractured by a thrust fault that has moved these rocks some distance to the south.

4. For the Chil-luckit-tequaws see notes at the previous day's entry. The village referred to here may be *nayakxa'tcix* village, meaning "tooth" or "row of pointed rocks." Spier & Sapir, 166.

5. For a more complete description and drawings of the canoes of the lower Columbia, see below, February 1, 1806.

6. The bark splits are probably from the roots of western redcedar, which was used extensively in Indian basketry. Gunther, 19–20.

[Clark]   *October 29th Tuesday 1805*

a Cloudy morning   wind Still from th West not hard, we Set out at day light   proceeded on about 5 miles and Came too at a Lodge of a Chief which we made at the upper village at th *falls*   about his house there is Six others[1]   This chief gave us to eate Sackacommis burries Hasel nuts[2] fish Pounded, and a kind of Bread made of roots—   we gave to the Women pices of ribon, which they appeared pleased with—   those houses are large 25 feet Sqr and contain abt. 8 men, Say 30 inhabitents—

Course

N. 55° W.	4	miles to a Lard. point, pasd a run on Lard Side
West	8	miles to Rock Island near the middle of River passed 7
	12	Houses of Indians about 50 men at 1 mile on the Stard Side. Brakfast Those people fish at the last narrows, & have but little pounded fish, Som dried and buries

Those people are friendly   gave us to eate fish Beries, nuts bread of roots & Drid beries and we Call this the friendly Village   We purchased 12 dogs of them & 4 Sacks of Pounded fish, and Some fiew Dried Berries and proceeded on   at 4 miles further we landed to Smoke a pipe with the people of a village of 11 houses[3]   we found those people also friendly Their Village is Situated imediately below the mouth of a River[4] of 60 yards water which falls in on the Stard. Side and heads in the mountains to the N. & N, E, the Indians inform us that this river is long ⟨but⟩ and full of falls   no Salmon pass up it. They also inform that 10 nations lives on this river by hunting and on buries &c. The Countrey begin to be thinly timbered with Pine & low white oake verry rocky and hilley—   We purchased at this vilg 4 dogs—   at the end of this Course is 3 rocks, in the river and a rock point from the Lard.   the middle rock is large and has a number of graves on it   we call it the Sepulchar Island.[5] The last River we call Caterack River from the number of falls which the Indians inform is on it   The Indians are afraid to hunt or be on th Lard Side of this Columbia river for fear of the Snake Ind. who reside on a fork of this river which falls in above the falls   a good[6] Situation for winter quarters if game can be had is just below Sepulchar rock on the Lard Side, high & pine and oake timber   the rocks ruged above, good hunting Countrey back, as it appears from the river   Indian village opsd. of 2 Lodgs[7] river ½ mile wide at rocks

	12	miles brought foward
S. 60° W.	5	miles to a point of rocks Island in a Lard bend, passed 2 rocks in the river— passed 2 Houses at 1 mile on the Stard Side and 2 at 4 miles on the Stard. Side Countrey on the Lard. Side has more timber than common and looks well for huntg. high and ruged.—[8]

S. 80° W.   6   ⟨to a point⟩ miles to 4 Houses in a point of a timbered bottom on the Lard. Side at a large creek or River 40 yr.   passed a bottom on the Stard Side the distance in which there is 14 Indian houses— The falls mountain covered with Snow is South

S. 70° W.   6   miles to a high Clift of rocks Std bend   passed a large creek at 1 mile on the Stard. Side in which the Indians catch fish, a large Sand bar from the Lard. Side for 4 miles, at which place a small stream of water falls over a rock of 100 feet on the Lard Side   passed 4 Indian Houses at 5 miles in a bottom on the Lard Side

The robes of those Indians are, of wolf deer Elk, wild cats, Some fox, & Deer   I saw one of the mountain Sheep, th wool thick and long Corse hair on the back, resembling bristles— those animals live among the rocks in those mountains below, orter is much valued by those people they Cew their hair on each Side with it and ware it about the necks with the tail in front

S. 56° W.   6   miles to a point of timbr. bottom on the Lard. Side, passd. a Stard. point at 2 miles   Here the mountains are high on each Side, the high points of those to the Lard. has Snow

                 29

                  6

ms.   35

Came too at 3 miles on this Course at 3 Houses of flatheads and Encamped on the Stard. Side,[9] a Pond lies back of those people in which we Saw great numbers of the Small Swan.[10]   we Purchased of those people 3 Dogs they gave us   High bush cramburies,[11] bread of roots and roots, they were pleased with musick of th violin.

[Clark]   *October 29th Tuesday 1805*

A cloudy morning wind from the West but not hard, we Set out at day light, and proceeded on about *five* miles   Came too on the Stard. Side at a village of 7 houses built in the Same form and materials of those above, here we found the Chief we had Seen at the long narrows named [*blank*] we entered his lodge and he gave us to eate Pounded fish, bread made of roots, Filberts nuts, & the berries of Sackecomme [*NB: Sac de Commis*]. we gave to each woman of the lodge a brace of Ribon of which they were much pleased.   each of those houses may be calculated to contain 8 men and 30 Soles, they are hospitable and good humered Speak the Same language of the inhabitants of the last village, we call this the friendly village. I observed in the lodge of the Chief Sundery articles which must have been precured from the white people, Such a Scarlet & blue Cloth Sword Jacket & hat. I also observed two wide Split boards with images on them Cut and painted in emitation of a man; I pointed to this image and asked ⟨The⟩ a man to what use he put them to, he Said Something the only word I understood was "good," and then Steped to the image and took out his Bow & quiver to Show me, and Some other of his war emplemints, from behind it.

The Chief then directed his wife to hand him his medison bag which he opened and Showed us 14 fingers [*NB: different fingers not little or middle fingers*] which he Said was the fingers of his enemies which he had taken in war, and pointed to S. E. from which direction I concluded they were Snake Indians; this is the first Instance I ever knew of the Indians takeing any other trofea of their exploits off the dead bodies of their Enimies except the Scalp.—   The Chief painted those fingers with Several other articles which was in his bag red and Securely put them back, haveing first mad a Short harrang which I Suppose was bragging of what he had done in war.   we purchased 12 Dogs and 4 Sacks of fish, & Some fiew ascid berries, after brackfast we proceeded on, the mountains are high on each Side, containing Scattering pine white oake & under groth, hill Sides Steep and rockey; at 4 miles lower we observed a Small river falling in with great rapidity on the Stard. Side below which is a village of 11 houses, here we landed to Smoke a pipe with the nativs and examine the mouth of the river, which I found to be 60 yards wide rapid and deep, The inhabitants of the village are friendly and Chearfull; those people inform us also those at the last village that this little river is long and full of falls, no Salmon pass up it, it runs from N. N. E.   that *ten* nations live on this river and its waters, on buries, and what game they Can kill with their Bow & arrows we purchased 4 dogs and Set out— (this village is the of the Same nation of the one we last passed) and proceeded on The Countrey on each side begin to be thicker timbered with Pine and low white Oake; verry rockey and broken. passed three large rocks in The river the middle rock is large long and has Several Squar vaults on it. we call this rockey Island the Sepulchar— The last river we passed we Shall Call the *Cataract* River from the number of falls which the Indians say is on it— passed 2 Lodges of Indians a Short distance below the Sepulchar Island on the Stard. Side river wide, at 4 mile passed 2 houses on the Stard. Side, Six miles lower passed 4 houses above the mouth of a Small river 40 yards wide on the Lard. Side[12] a thick timbered bottom above & back of those houses; those are the first houses which we have Seen on the South Side of the Columbia River, (and the axess to those dificuelt) for fear of the approach of their common enemies the Snake Indians, passed 14 houses on the Std. Side Scattered on the bank— from the mouth of this little river which we shall Call Labeasche River, the *falls mountain* [NB: Mount Hood] is South and the top is covered with Snow. one mile below pass the mouth of a large rapid Stream on the Stard. Side,[13] opposit to a large Sand bar, in this creek the Indians above take their fish, here we Saw Several canoes, which induced us to call this Canoe Creek it is 28 yards wide, about 4 miles lower and below the Sand bar is a butifull cascade falling over a rock of about 100 feet [NB: high], a Short distance lower passed 4 Indian houses on the Lard. Side in a timbered bottom, a fiew miles further we came too at 3 houses on Stard. Side, back of which is a pond in which I Saw Great numbers of Small Swan, Capt. Lewis and [I] went into the houses of those people who appeared Somewhat Surprised at first Their houses are built on the Same Construction of those above, Speak the Same language and Dress in the Same way, robes of the Skins of wolves Deer, Elk, wild cat, or Loucirvia[14] & fox, also Saw a mountain Sheap Skin the wool of which is long, thick, & corse with long corse hare on the top of the neck and back Something resembling bristles of a goat, the skin was of white hare, those animals these people inform me by Signs live in the mountains among the rocks, their horns are Small and Streight, Orter Skins are highly prised among those people as well as those on the river above, They Cue their hare which is divided on each Sholder, and also ware Small Strips about their necks with the tale hanging down in front.— Those people gave us, *High bush cram berries,* [*NB: described hereafter not H. B. Crs*] bread made of roots, and roots; we purchased three dogs for the party to eate; we Smoked with the men, all muche pleased with the violin—. Here the mountains are high on each Side, those to the Lard. Side has Some Snow on them at this time, more timber than above and of greater variety.

1. Shown as a seven-house village of Chilluckittequaws on *Atlas* maps 78, 86; it was in Klickitat County, Washington, a little above present Lyle. It may be the Friendly Village site (after Clark's designation) which was occupied about 1780 A.D. Cole.

2. See above, October 22, 1805, where the nuts are called "Philburts" as in Clark's notebook entry for this day. Saccacommis is bearberry or kinnikinnick, *Arctostaphylos uva-ursi* (L.) Spreng. It is the same plant which Lewis and Clark collected at Fort Mandan (see part 3 of Chapter 10, vol. 3). The plant is relatively abundant in the Cascade Range. Hitchcock et al., 4:7.

3. In Klickitat County, just below Klickitat River. *Atlas* map 78. Lyle site is in this general area and a permanent village named *xla'tixat* ("klikitat") was occupied by Klickitat peoples here. Cole; Ray (NVCB), 148.

4. "Cataract River" on *Atlas* map 78; present Klickitat River.

5. The later Memaloose Ilahee or Memaloose Island, in Wasco County, Oregon, a few miles above Mosier, Wasco County. Here begins a new page of the Elkskin-bound Journal, on which and under the text, is a sketch map (fig. 10) showing the Kooskooskee (Clearwater) and Kimooenem (Snake) rivers with some tributaries and their junction, with circular symbols presumably representing Indian habitations. At the bottom of the preceding page is the notation, "S. 60 W 5," the first course listed next in this entry. *Atlas* map 78. Examples of these graves are shown in Strong (SACR) and in Seaman. Some of these were apparently excavated in 1934 but have never been reported and described in detail. Memaloose Ilahee is derived from Chinook jargon words for "land of the dead." Either the Wishram or the Dalles Indians used Memaloose Island as a burial ground. Strong (SACR), 80–83; Seaman, 114–15; Phebus, 141–45; Spier & Sapir, 271.

6. There is an asterisk here, but it is unclear how or if it relates to other such marks in the text.

7. In Klickitat County. *Atlas* map 78.

8. There is an asterisk here, but it is unclear how or if it relates to other such marks in the text.

9. In Skamania County, Washington, a little above the mouth of Little White Salmon River, "Little lake C" on *Atlas* map 78. Investigators report two villages in this area on the

north shore of the Columbia occupied by White Salmon and Klickitat peoples. Spier & Sapir, 167.

10. Probably the tundra (Lewis and Clark's whistling) swan, *Cygnus columbianus* [AOU, 180]; see the description on March 9, 1806.

11. Contrary to the interlineation in the second entry this probably is the American cranberrybush, *Viburnum trilobum* Marsh. (also known as high-bush cranberry, *V. opulus* L.). It is rare in Washington and restricted to the Columbia gorge. The species is more common in the northeastern United States which explains Lewis's familiarity with the name. However, the squashberry, *V. edule* (Michx.) Raf., also has edible fruits which can be dried and may have been the item in question. Little (MWH), 200; Hitchcock et al., 4:468–70.

12. "River Labiche" on *Atlas* map 78 and named for expedition member François Labiche, now Hood River, meeting the Columbia at present Hood River, Hood River County, Oregon.

13. White Salmon River, "Canoe Creek" on *Atlas* map 78, the present boundary between Skamania and Klickitat counties.

14. Lynx, *Lynx canadensis.* Burroughs, 92.

[Clark]   *October 30th Wednesday 1805*

A Cloudy morning. Some little rain all night, after eating a Slight brackfast of venison we Set out.

The rocks project into the river in maney places and have the appearance of haveing fallen from the highe hills   those projected rocks is common & Small Bays below & nitches in the rocks   passed 4 Cascades or Small Streams falling from the mountains on Lard.[1]

S. 70° W.   3   miles to a point of rocks on the Stard. Side, passed a number of Stumps at Some distance in the Water,

This part of the river resembles a pond partly dreaned leaving many Stumps bare both in & out of the water, current about 1 mil pr. Hour

S. 74° W   2   miles to a point of a timbered bottom on Stard. Side   halted to Dine, killed a Deer & 3 ducks & a Squirel of the Mountains[2] we can plainly hear the roreing of the grand Shutes below, saw the large Buzard white head and part of the wings white

West   4   miles to the mouth of a river on th Stard. Side of about 60 yards wide   passed Std. point & many large rocks promiscuissly in the river both above and below this river a large Sand bar on the Lard Side

The bottom above the river is about ¾ of a mile wide and rich, Some deer & bear Sign— rained moderately all day we are wet and cold. Saw Several Specis of wood which I never Saw before, Some resembling Beech & others Poplar.— Day dark and disagreeable

S. 45° W.	2	miles to a large rock in the river, passed Several rocks and a large Sand bar on the Lard. Sid verry large rock near the Stard. Side High Mounts. on each Side, ruged and covd. with a variety of timber Such as Pine Spruce Seder Cotton wood Oake
S. 30 W.	4 15	miles to a Island, at the Commencement of the grand Shute and the Stard. Side where we Campd. passed maney large rocks in the river [neither?] in th, a large Creek on the Std. Side at 2 miles, with an Island in the mouth. passed 3 Islands on the Stard. one on the Lard above 2 Small Islands opsd. to us on which there growes 6 large Pine, 4 rock Islands which almost Chokes up the river— a deep bay to th Stard. on which the Indians live in 8 large worm Houses 2 ponds back of this on the Stard 1 above the Islands, one on the Lard. side. Several Small rocks—in dift. pts.

I with 2 men proceeded down the river 2 miles on an old Indian parth to view the rapids, which I found impassable for our canoes without a portage, the roade bad   at 1 mile I saw a Town of Houses laterly abandoned[3] on an elevated Situation opsd. a 2d Shute, returned at dark. Capt. Lewis and 5 men went to the Town found them kind[4]   they gave Beries & nuts, but he cd. get nothin from them in the way of Information, the greater part of those people out collecting roots below, rained all the evining   Those people have one gun & maney articles which they have purchased of the white people their food is principally fish

[Clark]   *October 30th Wednesday 1805*

A cool morning, a moderate rain all the last night, after eating a partial brackfast of venison we Set out   passed Several places where the rocks projected into the river & have the appearance of haveing Seperated from the mountains and fallen promiscuisly into the river, Small nitches are formed in the banks below those projecting rocks which is comon in this part of the river, Saw 4 Cascades caused by Small Streams falling from the mountains on the Lard. Side, a remarkable circumstance in this part of the river is, the Stumps of pine trees are in maney places are at Some distance in the river, and gives every appearance of the rivers being damed up below from Some cause which I am not at this time acquainted with, the Current of the river is also verry jentle not exceeding 1 ½ mile pr. hour and about ¾ of a mile in width. Some rain, we landed above the mouth of a Small river on the Stard. Side[5] and Dined   J. Shields Killed a Buck & Labiech 3 Ducks, here the river widens to about one mile large Sand bar in the middle, a Great [rock] both in and out of the water, large ⟨round⟩ Stones, or rocks are also permiscuisly Scattered about in the river, this day we Saw Some fiew of the large Buzzard[6]   Capt. Lewis Shot at one, those Buzzards are much larger than any other of ther Spece or the largest Eagle white under part of their wings &c. The bottoms above the mouth of this little river ⟨which we Call⟩ is rich covered with grass & firn & is about ¾ of a mile wide rich and rises gradually, below the river (which is 60 yards wide above its mouth) the Countery rises with Steep assent.   we call this little river ⟨fr Ash⟩ New Timbered river from a Speces of Ash[7] ⟨that wood⟩ which grows on its banks of a verry large and different from any we had before Seen, and a timber resembling the beech[8] in bark ⟨& groth⟩ but different in its leaf which is Smaller and the tree smaller.   passed maney large rocks in the river and a large creek on the Stard. Side in the mouth of which is an Island,[9] passed on the right of 3 Islands ⟨on⟩ near the Stard. Side, and landed on an Island close under the Stard. Side at the head of the great Shute,[10] and a little below a village of 8 large houses on a Deep bend on the Stard. Side, and opposit 2 Small Islands imediately in the head of the Shute, which Islands are covered with Pine, maney large rocks also, in the head of the Shute. Ponds back of the houses, and Countrey low for a Short distance. The day proved Cloudy dark and disagreeable with Some rain all day which kept us wet. The Countary a high mountain on each Side thickly Covered with timber, Such as Spruc, Pine, Cedar, Oake Cotton &c. &c.[11] I took two men and walked down three miles to examine the Shute and river below proceeded along an old Indian path, passd. an old village at 1 mile on an ellevated Situation of   this village contained verry large houses built in a different form from any I had Seen, and laterly abandoned, and the most of the boads put into a pond of water near the village, as I conceived to drown the flees, which was emencely noumerous about the houses—. I found by examonation that we must make a portage of the greater per-potion of our Stores 2½ miles, and the Canoes we Could haul over the rocks, I returned at Dark   Capt Lewis and 5 men had just returned from the village, Cap L. informed me that he found the nativs kind, they gave him berries, nuts & fish to eate; but he could get nothing from them in the way of information. The greater part of the inhabitants of this village being absent down the river Some distance Colecting roots   Capt. L. Saw one gun and Several articles which must have been precured from the white people.   a wet disagreeable evening, the only wood we could get to burn on this little Island on which we have encamped is the newly discov-ered *Ash,* which makes a tolerable fire.   we made fifteen miles to daye.

1. Shown nameless on *Atlas* map 78. There are a number of creeks near Viento, Hood River County, Oregon, in the right location, including Viento, Starvation, Cabin, Warren, Lindsey, and Summit creeks.

2. Probably the western gray squirrel. By mountains Clark does not mean the Rocky Mountains, but rather the hills along the Columbia River. See Lewis's entry of February 25, 1806.

3. This is the area below the Cascades in Skamania County, Washington. Clark's texts and maps of the terrain and of Indian settlements in this region cannot be matched with precision to twentieth-century archaeological work. This site appears on figs. 28 and 29 as "old village" and "a village of large wood houses" and is shown on *Atlas* maps 78 and 79 as "an old village of very large houses." It is the "old village . . . on an ellevated Situation" in the codex entry. Investigators have called it *wała'la* and Wahlala ("their lake"). Spier & Sapir, 167; Beckham, 17–19, 27. It appears to have sat very near the Bridge of the Gods.

4. Identified on *Atlas* map 79 as the Yehuh, a Chinookan-language group of whom little is known. The town is variously noted as having eight houses. Investigators have re-ported it as the Y-eh-huh village. Minor, Toepel, & Beckham, 41–51; Beckham, 17–19, 24–26. It was located downstream from Stevenson and near the Bridge of the Gods.

5. "New Timbered River" in this entry, but "Crusats River" after Pierre Cruzatte of the party on *Atlas* map 78 and in the combined course table at November 1. An earlier name has been scratched out on the map. It is the present Wind River, in Skamania County.

6. The California condor, *Gymnogyps californianus* [AOU, 324], now nearly extinct. The last wild condor was captured for care in southern California in April 1987. Correctly described by Lewis and Clark as the largest North American bird, it was already known to science, but they were the first to note its presence on the Columbia. See below, February

16, 1806, for a lengthy description, and weather remarks for October 28 and 29, 1805. Burroughs, 201–3; Cutright (LCPN), 241.

7. Oregon ash, *Fraxinus latifolia* Benth. This large tree is the only native species of ash in the Pacific Northwest. It is interesting that the Oregon ash and the red, or Oregon, alder, *Alnus rubra* Bong., are mentioned together, since the flora of the Columbia gorge here is an extension of the flora of the western Cascade lowlands, which the explorers were encountering for the first time. The red alder and Oregon ash reach their eastern-most distributional limits in southern Skamania and western Klickitat counties. Other species such as Sitka spruce, Oregon white oak, hazelnut, and western redcedar are all part of this lowland flora which extends eastward up the Columbia gorge. Hitchcock et al., 4:57; Little (CIH), 127-W.

8. The red alder, then new to science. The comparison of this tree with the American beech, *Fagus grandifolia* Ehrh., which is commonly found in the eastern United States is appropriate. The bark of the red alder is thin, gray, and smooth, just like the beech and the growth form is somewhat similar. The leaves of the red alder are similar in terms of the toothed margin and shape, but smaller than the beech, which confirms the red alder identification. Little (CIH), 104-W, 125-E; Hitchcock et al., 2:74; Cutright (LCPN), 261 n. 19, 274.

9. Nameless on *Atlas* map 79; present Rock Creek, below Stevenson in Skamania County.

10. Nearly opposite present Cascade Locks, Hood River County, where they camped until November 1, 1805, on an island in Skamania County. They were just above the Cascades of the Columbia (the "Great Shute"), now inundated by Bonneville Dam. *Atlas* maps 78, 79.

11. The spruce is Sitka spruce, *Picea sitchensis* (Bong.) Carr., at its eastern distributional limit along the Columbia River. Little (CIH), 42-W. The cottonwood is black cottonwood, the pine is ponderosa pine, and the oak is Oregon white oak.

[Clark]   *October 31st Thursday 1805*

a cloudey raney morning   I proceed down the river to view it more at leasure, I took Jos. Fields & Peter Crusat and proceeded on down, Send Crusat back at 2 ms. to examine the rapid near the shore & I proceeded on down about 10 miles to a very high rock[1] in a bottom on the Stard. opsd. 2 Islands covered with timber on which I saw Inds. at a distance; found the river rocky for 6 miles, after which the Current became uni-form— at 1 mile I passed an old deserted village on a Pond on a high Situation of 8 Houses— at 3½ miles one house the only remt. of an antient Village[2] ½ a mile lower I saw 8 Vaults for the Dead which was nearly Square 8 feet Closely Covered with broad boads Curiously engraved, the bones in Some of those vaults wer 4 feet thick, in others the Dead was yet layed Side of each other nearly East & west, raped up & bound Securley in robes, great numbers of trinkets Brass Kittle, Sea Shells, Iron, Pan Hare &c. &c. was hung about the vaults and great many wooden gods, or Images of men Cut in wood, Set up round the vaults, Some of those So old and worn by time that they were nearly worn out of Shape, and Some of those vaults So old that they were roted entirely to the ground— not withstanding they wood is of Pine & [*one word illegible*] or Seder as also the wooden gods

I can not learn certainly if those people worship those woden emiges, they have them in conspicuous parts of their houses at 5 miles I passed 4 large houses[3] on the Stard Side a little above the last rapid and opposit a large Island[4] which is Situated near the Lard. Side— The enhabitents of those houses had left them closely Shut up, they appeared to Contn. a great deel of property and Provisions Such as those people use, I did not disturb any thing about those houses, but proceed on down below the rapid which I found to be the last, a large village has at Some period been on the Stard. Side below this rapid The bottom is high Stoney and about 2 miles wide covered with grass, here C[overed?] is the head of a large Island in high water,[5] at this time no water passes on the Stard. Side I walked thro this Island which I found to be verry rich, open & covered with Strawberry vines,[6] and has greatly the appearance of having at Some period been Cultivated, The natives has dug roots in Some parts of this Isld. which is about 3 miles long & 1 Wide, a Small Island covered with timber opposit the lower point no water runs on the Stard. Side. of it. below and in the middle of the river is a large Island Covered with tall trees opposit the Strawberry Island on its Stard. Side a creek falls in which has no running water at present, it has the appearanc of throwing out emense torents— I saw 5 Indians in a canoe below— Jo. killed a Sand hill Crane & we returned by the same rout to camp at the grand Shute where I found Several Indians, I Smoked. Two canoes loaded with fish for the Trade below Came down & unloaded the after noon fare

S. 30° E[7] 1 mile to a Lard Bend passing the grand Shute which is ¼ of a mile and the Wate Confined within about 150 yards, passing with Tremendious force, great number of rocks on the upper pt. of this Shute, a low pine Mountain on the Stad. Side high one on the Lard Side—

S. 30° W.   1   mile to a Lard. bend   passd. Several rocks in the river & a rapid at ¾ of a mile th water being Confined between large rocks, maney of which is under water. an old village of 8 houses on the Stard. Side on the hill opposit

S. 45° W.   2   miles to a high rock above the upper point of a large Isld. on the Lard Side, passed many rocks in different directions, a house on the Stard. at 1 mile just below is 8 Indian *vaults* in which is great number of dead raped up their trinkets, & wooden Gods are placed around the vaults, they lie East & west

S. 60° W[8]   2   miles to a large black rock in a Stard. bend at the Comencement of a rapid opsd. a Lower point of an Island passed a rapid at ½ Ms. Ld not bad. Several large rocks in the river permiscusly, 4 large Ind. houses without inhabitants on the Stard. Side at 1½ mile a Island on the Lard Side extensive high Stoney bottoms on the Stard Side

South[9]   2   miles to a Creek under a Bluff in a Lard bend passed the rapid ¼ of a mile long— the upper point of a large Island on the Stard. Side no water running on the Stard. Side of it at present this Island is high rich and open Covered with Strawbery vines a narrow open bottom on the Lard. Side

Those Indians Cut off the hands of those they kill & proserve the fingers.

[Clark]   *October 31st Thursday 1805*

A Cloudy rainey disagreeable morning I proceeded down the river to view with more attention [*NB: the rapids*] we had to pass on the river below, the two men with me Jo. Fields & Peter Crusat proceeded down to examine the rapids the Great Shute which commenced at the Island on which we encamped Continud with great rapidity and force thro a narrow chanel much compressd. and interspersed with large rocks for ½ a mile, at a mile lower is a verry Considerable rapid at which place the waves are remarkably high, and proceeded on in a old Indian parth 2½ miles by land thro a thick wood & hill Side, to the river where the Indians make a portage, from this place I dispatched Peter Crusat (our principal waterman) back to follow the river and examine the practibility of the Canoes passing, as the rapids appeared to continue down below as far as I could See, I with Jo. Fields proceeded on, at ½ a mile below the end of the portage passed a house where there had been an old town for ages past as this house was old Decayed and a plac of flees I did not enter it, about ½ a mile below this house in a verry thick part of the woods is 8 vaults which appeared Closely Covered and highly deckerated with orniments. Those vaults are all nearly the Same Sise and form 8 feet Square, 5 feet high, Sloped a little So as to convey off the rain made of Pine or Cedar boards Closely Connected & Scurely Covered with wide boards, with a Dore left in The East Side which is partially Stoped with wide boards curiously engraved. In Several of those vaults the dead bodies wre raped up verry Securely in Skins tied around with cords of grass & bark, laid on a mat, all east & west and Some of those vaults had as maney as 4 bodies laying on the Side of each other. the other Vaults Containing bones only, Some contained bones for the debth of 4 feet. on the tops and on poles attached to those vaults hung Brass kittles & frying pans pearced thro their bottoms, baskets, bowls of wood, Sea Shels, Skins, bits of Cloth, Hair, bags of Trinkets & Small peices of bone &c and independant of the [*NB: Hieroglyphics, figures of men & animals*] curious ingraveing and Paintings on the boards which formed the vaults I observed Several wooden Images, cut in the figure of men and Set up on the ⟨South⟩ Sides of the vaults all round. Some of those So old and worn by time, that they were nearly out of Shape, I also observed the remains of Vaults rotted entirely into the ground and covered with moss. This must bee the burrying place for maney ages for the inhabitants of those rapids, the vaults are of the most lasting timber Pine & Cedar— I cannot Say certainly that those nativs worship those wooden idols as I have every reason to believe they do not; as they are Set up in the most conspicious parts of their houses, and treated more like orniments than objects of aderation. at 2 miles lower & 5 below our Camp I passed a village of 4 large houses abandend by the nativs, with their dores bared up, I looked into those houses and observed as much property as is usial in the houses of those people which induced me to conclude that they wre at no great distance, either hunting or Colecting roots, to add to their winter Subsistance. from a Short distance below the vaults the mountain which is but low on the Stard. Side leave the river, and a leavel Stoney open bottom Suckceeds on the Said Std. Side for a great Distance down, the mountains high and rugid on the Lard Side this open bottom is about 2 miles a Short distance below this village is a bad Stoney rapid and appears to be the last in view I observed at this lower rapid the remains of a large and antient Village which I could plainly trace by the Sinks in which they had formed their houses, as also those in which they had buried their fish— from this rapid to the lower end of the portage the river is Crouded with rocks of various Sizes between which the water passes with great velociety createing in maney places large Waves, an Island which is Situated near the Lard. Side occupies about half the distance the lower point of which is at this rapid. immediately below this rapid the high water passes through a narrow Chanel through the Stard. Bottom forming an Island of 3 miles ⟨wide⟩ Long & one wide, I walked through this Island which I found to be verry rich land, and had every appearance of haveing been at Some distant period Cultivated. at this time it is Covered with grass intersperced with Strawberry vines.[10] I observed Several places on this Island where the nativs had dug for roots and from its lower point I observed 5 Indians in a Canoe below the upper point of an Island near the middle of the river Covered with tall timber, which indued me to believe that a village was at no great distanc below, I could not See any rapids below ⟨for⟩ in the extent of my view which was for a long distance down the river, which from the last rapids widened and had everry appearance of being effected by the tide,— [NB: This was in fact the first tide water] I deturmind to return to Camp 10 miles distant, a remarkable high detached rock Stands in a bottom on the Stard Side near the lower point of this Island on the Stard. Side about 800 feet high and 400 paces around, we call the Beaten [NB: Beacon] rock. a Brook falls into the narrow Chanel which forms [NB: what we call] the Strawberry Island, which at this time has no running water, but has every appearance of dischargeing emence torrents &c. &c. Jo. Fields Shot a Sand hill Crane. I returned by the Same rout on an Indian parth passing up on the N W. Side of the river to our Camp at the Great Shute. found Several Indians from the village, I Smoked with them; Soon after my return two Canoes loaded with fish & Bear grass for the trade below, came down from the village at the mouth of the Catterack River, they unloaded and turned their Canoes up Side down on the beech, & camped under a Shelveing rock below our Camp

one of the men Shot a goose above this Great Shute, which was floating into the Shute when an Indian observed it, plunged into the water & Swam to the Goose and brought in on Shore, at the head of the Suck, [*NB: great danger, rapids bad, a descent close by him (150 feet off) of all Columbia river, current dashed among rocks if he had got in the Suck—lost*] as this Indian richly earned the goose I Suffered him to keep it which he about half picked and Spited it up with the guts in it to roste.

This Great Shute or falls is about ½ a mile with the water of this great river Compressed within the Space of 150 paces in which there is great numbers of both large and Small rocks, water passing with great velocity forming & boiling in a most horriable manner, with a fall of about 20 feet, below it widens to about 200 paces and current gentle for a Short distance.   a Short distance above is three Small rockey Islands, and at the head of those falls, three Small rockey Islands are Situated Crosswise the river, Several rocks above in the river & 4 large rocks in the head of the Shute; those obstructions together with the high Stones which are continually brakeing loose from the mountain on the Stard Side and roleing down into the Shute aded to those which brake loose from those Islands above and lodge in the Shute, must be the Cause of the rivers daming up to Such a distance above, ⟨and Show⟩ where it Shows Such evidant marks of the Common current of the river being much lower than at the present day

1. Beacon Rock is an eroded volcanic pipe or plug composed of middle to lower Miocene olivine basalt. It is in Skamania County, Washington, just above Skamania in Beacon Rock State Park. It was called Castle Rock for many years, but Clark's name (given in the codex entry) was restored in 1916. Clark's estimate of its height is remarkably correct. Biddle (BR); Appleman (LC), 189; *Atlas* maps 79, 88.

2. This is the "old village" on *Atlas* map 79, in Skamania County between the Bridge of the Gods and Bradford Island. It is noted as having only one house. Investigators have named it *sk!Ema'niak* or Skamanyak ("obstructed"). Spier & Sapir, 167; Beckham, 17–19, 28; Minor.

3. Investigators disagree on the relation of this village to the next site ("a large village has at Some period been"). Some view the two as a part of one complex, while others see them as separate entities. Beckham, 17–18, 31–34; Minor, Toepel, & Beckham, 41–51; Dunnell & Whitlam, 5–7; Dunnell; Phebus, 127–30. Only the first site is shown on *Atlas* map 79; both are represented on figs. 28 and 29. They are in Skamania County opposite present Bradford and Hamilton islands.

4. Present Bradford Island, in Hood River County, Oregon, now crossed by Bonneville Dam; "Brant I." on figs. 28 and 29. *Atlas* map 79.

5. Lewis and Clark's "Strawberry Island" is now Hamilton Island in Skamania County. *Atlas* map 79. Archaeological work on the island is discussed by Dunnell & Campbell.

6. The woodland strawberry, *Fragaria vesca* L. var. *crinita* (Rydb.) C. L. Hitchc. Booth & Wright, 112; Hitchcock et al., 3 : 108.

7. In the Codex H compendium of courses these courses are given under the date of November 1, 1805.

8. In Codex H this distance is given as three miles.

9. In Codex H this course appears under the date of November 2, 1805, with the distance given as one mile.

10. A vertical line through this passage from "from this rapid" to about this point was probably penned by Biddle, but not in his usual red ink.

[Lewis and Clark]   [*Weather, October 1805*][1]

Day of the month	Wind	State of the Weather
[October] 1st	E	f
2d	N	f
3rd	E	f
4th	E	f
5th	E	f
6th	E	f
7th	E	f
8th	E	f
9th	S W	c
10th	N W	f
11th	E & S W	c
12th	E & S W	f
13th	S W.	f. a. r
14th	S. W.	f
15th	S W	f
16th	S W	f
17th	S E	f

18th	S E	f
19th	S E	f
20th	S W	f
21st	S W	f
22nd	S W	f
23rd	S W	f
24th	W	f
25th	W	f
26th	W.	f
27th	W.	f
28th	N W.	r a f
29th	W.	f. a. r
30th	S E.	r. a r
31st	S W	f. a r

Note from the 1st to 7th of October we were at the mouth of Chopunnuish river makeing Canoes to Decend the Kooskooske.

Note from the 7th to the 16th octr. we were decending Kooskooske & Lewises river, the 17th 18 at the mouth of Lewis River.

Note from the 18th to the 22d of octr. descending the Great Columbia to the falls.

Note from the 22d to the 29th about the Great Falls of the Columbia river.

note from the 29th of Octr. to the 3d of Novr. in passing through the western mountains below falls.

Note the balance of Novr. and December between the Mountains & Pacific Ocean.

[*Remarks*][2]

October 3d	The easterly winds which blow imediately off the mountains are very cool untill 10 a m. when the day becomes verry worm and the winds Shift about[3]
13th	rained moderately from 4 to 11 a M. to day.
28th	a Violent wind a moderate rain commenced at 4 oClock P. M. and continued untill 8 P. M.
29th	rained moderately all day. Saw the first large Buzzard or Voultur of the Columbia.[4]
30th	rained moderately all day. arrived at the Grand rapids. Saw a different Species of ash[5]
31st	Some rain last night and this morning.

1. Lewis has no weather data for this month. Clark wrote a combined weather table for October, November, and December in Codex I, which we have separated by month. In the margin of the combined table were notes on their travels and weather remarks which we have placed after the October table.

2. Clark's remarks are in Codex I and Voorhis No. 4; the former is followed here.

3. In Voorhis No. 4 substantially the same remark appears under October 8.

4. In Voorhis No. 4 Clark writes, "first Vulture of the Columbia Seen to day," under October 28. This is the California condor. For October 29 he says, "I shot at a vulture"; the daily journals date the shooting of the first condor on October 30.

5. In Voorhis No. 4 Clark here adds "to any I have ever seen."

[Clark]   *November 1st Friday 1805*

a verry cold morning wind from N. E and hard

Took equal altitudes of Sun

	h	m	s		h	m	s
A. M.	9	22	51	P M	3	12	21
	"	25	6		"	14	38
	"	27	24		"	16	47

altitude produced 36° 22′ 15″

Set all hands packing the loading over th portage which is below the Grand Shutes and is 940 yards of bad way over rocks & on Slipery hill Sides   The Indians who came down in 2 Canoes last night packed their fish over a portage of 2½ miles to avoid a 2d *Shute*.   four of them took their canoes over the 1st portage and run the 2d Shute, Great numbers of Sea otters,[1] they are So Cautious that I with deficuelty got a Shute at one to day, which I must have killed but Could not get him as he Sunk

Lattitude: 45° 44′ 3″ North—
Cronomiter is 3 m 27 s too slow m. Time

                                                        1st Novr. P M
Observed time and distance of the moons western Limb from *Antares* ★ West—

		Time			*Distance*	
	h	m	s			
P. M.	7	5	33	91°	50′	45″
	"	8	25	"	51	15

"	10	53	"	52	00
"	17	1	"	52	30
"	18	59	"	52	30

The mountains is so high that no further observations can be made with this ★ observed time and distance of Moon's Western Limb from α *Arietis* ★ East

		Time			*distance*	
	h	m	s			
P M.	7	29	34	58°	4'	30"
	"	33	12	"	4	
	"	35	21	"	3	15
	"	37	16	"	2	
	"	39	2	"	1	
	"	40	35	"	0	15

We got all our Canoes and baggage below the Great Shute[2] 3 of the canoes being Leakey from injures recved in hauling them over the rocks, obliged us to delay to have them repaired   a bad rapid just below us three Indian canoes loaded with pounded fish for the &c. trade down the river arrived at the upper end of the portage this evening. I Can't lern whether those Indians trade with white people or Inds. below for the Beeds & copper, which they are So fond of—   They are nearly necked, prefuring beeds to anything—   Those Beeds they trafick with Indians Still higher up this river for Skins robes &c. &c. The Indians on those waters do not appear to be Sickly, Sore eyes are Common and maney have lost their eyes, Some one and, maney both, they have bad teeth, and the greater perpotion of them have worn their teeth down, maney into the gums, They are rather Small high Cheeks, women Small and homely, maney of them had Sweled legs, large about the knees,—owing to the position in which they Set on their hams, They are nearly necked only a piece of leather tied about their breech and a Small robe which generally comes to a little below their wastes and Scercely Sufficely large to cover arround them when confined—[3]   they are all fond of Clothes but more So of Beeds perticularly blue & white beeds. They are durty in the extreme both in their Coockery and in their houses.

Those at the last Village raise the beads [beds] about five feet from the earth—under which they Store their Provisions—   Their houses is about

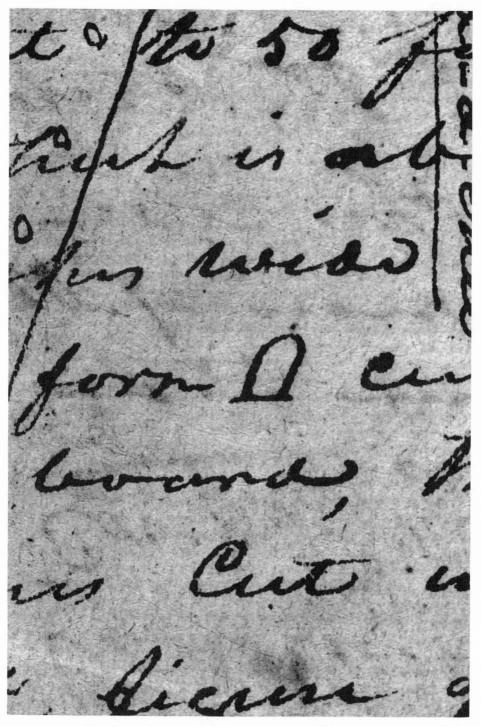

27. Shape of a Hut Door, November 1, 1805, Elkskin-bound Journal

33 feet to 50 feet Square, the dore of which is about 30 Inc. high and 16
Inches wide in this form[4] cut in a wide pine board   they have maney im-
eges Cut in wood, generally, in the figure of a man—   Those people are
high with what they have to Sell, and Say the white people below Give
them great Prices for what they Sell to them. Their nose are all Pierced,
and the wear a white Shell maney of which are 2 Inch long pushed thro
the nose—   all the women ⟨are⟩ have flat heads pressed to almost a point
at top   The press the female childrens heads between 2 bords when
young—untill they form the Skul as they wish it which is generally verry
flat. This amongst those people is considered as a great mark of buty—
and is practised in all the tribes we have passed on this river more or
less.   men take more of the drugery off the women than is common with
Indians—

Names of Tribes[5]
E-neé-Shur   at the falls
E-chee-lute   at the lower whorl
Che-luck-it-te-guar   below
Chim-ná-pum   Nation above
qua-Ca-ha—   near

[Clark]   *November 1st Friday 1805*

A verry Cool morning wind hard from the N. E. The Indians who arrived last evining took their Canoes on ther Sholders and Carried them
below the Great Shute, we Set about takeing our Small Canoe and all the
baggage by land 940 yards of bad Slippery and rockey way   The Indians
we discoverd took ther loading the whole length of the portage 2½ miles,
to avoid a Second Shute which appears verry bad to pass, and thro' which
they passed with their empty canoes. Great numbers of Sea Otters, they
are So cautious that I with dificuelty got a Shot at one to day, which I must
have killed, but could not get him as he Sunk

we got all our baggage over the Portage of 940 yards, after which we
got the 4 large Canoes over by Slipping them over the rocks on poles
placed across from one rock to another, and at Some places along partial

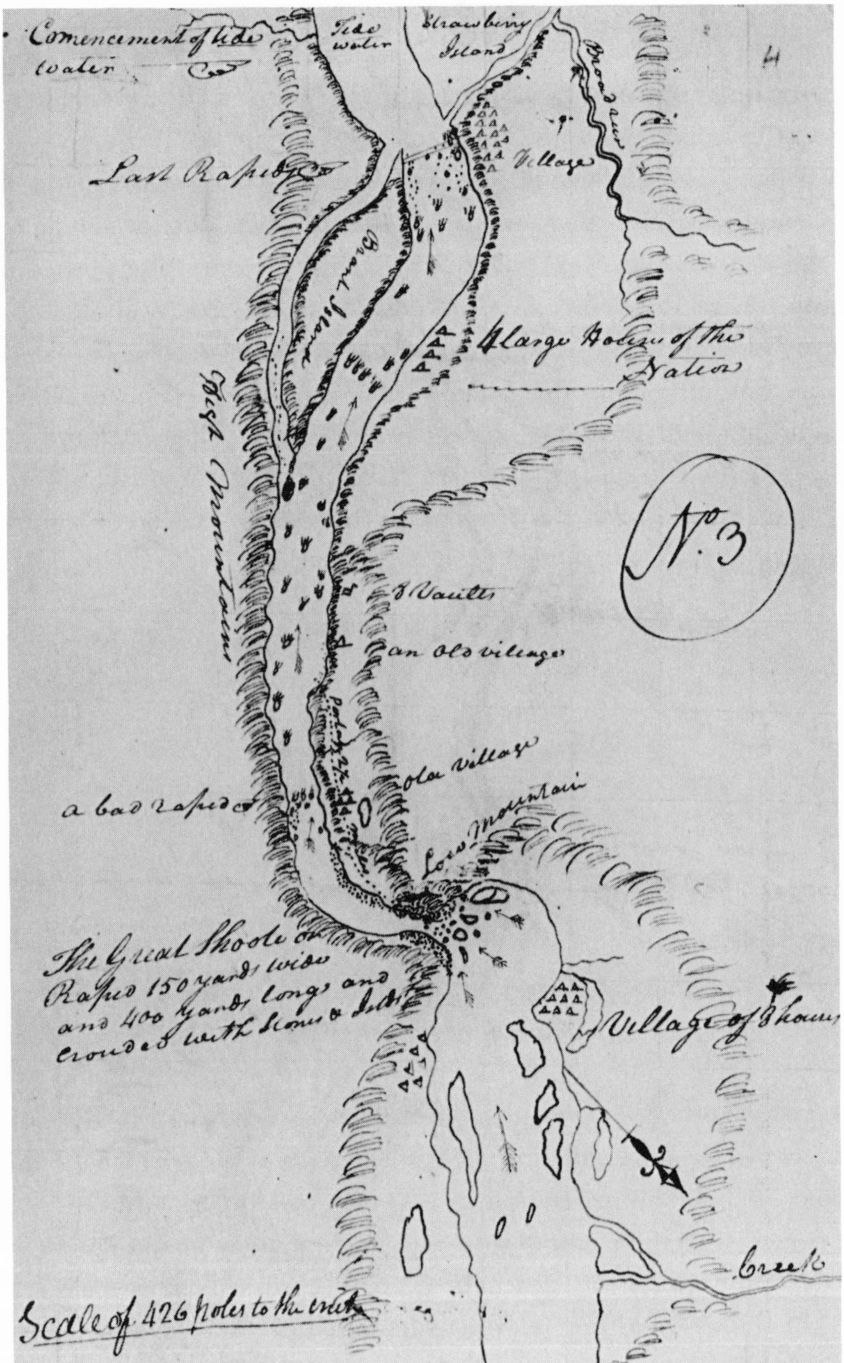
Comencement of tide water
Tide water
Strawberry Island
4
Last Rapids
Village
A large Houses of the Nation
No. 3
8 Vaults
an old village
old village
a bad rapid
Low mountain
The Great Shoote or Rapid 150 yards wide and 400 yards long and crouded with Stones & Isds
Creek
Scale of 426 poles to the creek

28. Great Rapids (Cascades) of the Columbia River, Washington and Oregon, October 30–November 2, 1805, Codex H, p. 4

Streams of the river. in passing those canoes over the rocks &c. three of them recived injuries which obliged us to delay to have them repared.

Several Indian Canoes arrived at the head of the portage, Some of the men accompanied by those from the village came down to Smoke with us, they appear to Speak the Same language with a little different axcent[6]

I visited the Indian ⟨Lodge⟩ *Village* found that the Construction of the houses Similar to those abov described, with this difference only that they are larger Say from 35 to 50 feet by 30 feet, raised about 5 feet above the earth, and nearly as much below The Dores in the Same form and Size cut in the wide post which Supports one end of the ridge pole and which is carved and painted with different figures & Hieroglyphics Those people gave me to eate nuts berries & a little dried fish, and Sold me a hat of ther own taste without a brim, and baskets in which they hold their water— Their beads are raised about 4½ feet, under which they Store away their dried fish, between the part on which they lie and the back wall they Store away their roots burries nuts and valuable articles on mats, which are Spread also around the fire place which is Sunk about one foot lower than the bottom flore of the house, this fire place is about 8 feet long and Six feet wide Secured with a fraim those houses are calculated for 4, 5 & 6 families, each familey haveing a nice painted ladder to assend up to their beads. I Saw in those houses Several wooden *Images* all cut in imitation of men, but differently fasioned and placed in the most conspicious parts of the houses, probably as an orniment I cannot lern certainly as to the traffick those Inds. carry on below, if white people or the indians who trade with the Whites who are either Settled or visit the mouth of this river. I believe mostly with the latter as their knowledge of the white people appears to be verry imperfect, and the articles which they appear to trade mostly i e' Pounded fish, Beargrass, and roots; cannot be an object of comerce with furin merchants— however they git in return for those articles Blue and white *beeds* copper Tea Kittles, brass arm bands, some Scarlet and blue robes and a fiew articles of old clothes, they prefer beeds to any thing and will part with the last mouthfull or articles of clothing they have for a fiew of those beeds, those beeds the trafick with Indians Still higher up this river for roabs, Skins, cha-pel-el bread,[7] bear-

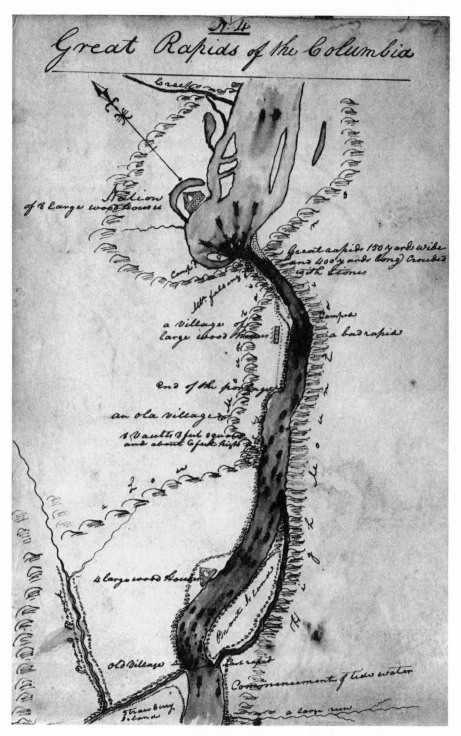

29. Great Rapids (Cascades) of the Columbia River, Washington
and Oregon, October 30–November 2, 1805, Voorhis No. 4

372

grass &c. who in their turn trafick with those under the rockey mountains for Beargrass, ⟨*guarmash*⟩ *Pashico* roots & robes &c.

The nativs of the waters of the Columbia appear helthy, Some have tumers on different parts of their bodies, and Sore and weak Eyes are common, maney have lost their Sight entirely great numbers with one eye out and frequently the other verry weak; This misfortune I must again asscribe to the water &c. They have bad teeth, which is not common with indians, maney have worn their teeth down and Some quite into their gums, this I cannot Satisfactorily account for it, do ascribe it in some measure to their method of eateing, their food, roots pertiularly, which they make use of as they are taken out of the earth frequently nearly covered with Sand, I have not Seen any of their long roots offered for Sale clear of Sand.[8] They are rether below the Common Size high cheeks womin Small and homely, and have Swelled legs and thighs, and their knees remarkably large which I ascribe to the method in which they Sit on their hams—go nearly necked wareing only a piece of leather tied about their breast which falls down nearly as low as the waste, a Small roabe about 3 feet Square, and a piece of leather tied about their breach, They [X: *womin*] have all flat heads in this quarter ⟨both men and women,⟩ They are tirty in the extream, both in their person and cooking, ware their hare loose hanging in every direction. They asc high prices for what they Sell and Say that the white people below give great prices for every thing &c.

The noses are all pierced and when they are dressed they have a long tapered piece of white shell or wampum ⟨pushed⟩ put through the nose, Those Shells are about 2 inches in length. I observed in maney of the villeages which I have passed, the heads of the female children in the press for the purpose of compressing their heads in their infancy into a certain form, between two boards[9]

Course Distance & Remarks Decending the Columbia River
from the Lewis's River in Latd. *46° 15′ 13⁹⁄₁₀″* N.
to the Great Pacific Ocian—estimated[10]

	miles	
		18th October 1805.
S 55° E	12	To a bend on the Lard side opposite a verry bad rapid opposit to a lower point of a large Island on the Stard.

Side & Several Small Islds. in the river. passed a Island in the mouth of the *Ki moo e nim.* one in the middle of the river 3 miles long at 8 miles; and one a little below on which was 9 mat Lodges of Indians drying fish 2 Lodges on Std. at the rapid.

S 20° E   2½   Miles to 2 Lodges of Indians on a Small Island near the Stard. point.

S 45° E   1½   Miles to the mouth of a Brook under a high hill on the Lard. Side, here the river enters a high range of hills about 200 feet rugid black rocks makeing out into the river from each Side.

S. 12° W.[11]   4   Miles to a point of rocks in a Lard. Bend passed 2 Small Islands one on each side and one in the middle at 2 miles at the uppr. point 2 Lodges of Indians drying fish opsd. a rapid, passed 9 Lodges of Indians drying fish on an Island Close under the Stard. Side, one mile lower 5 Lodges of Indians drying fish on the Same Island. ⟨no bottom⟩ Encamped on the Lard Side

19th of October 1805.

S. 45° W.   14   Miles to a rock on the Lard. Shore resembling a hat at a rapid at the lower point of an Island in the middle of the river on which there is 7 Lodges of nativs drying fish, and opposit the head of an Isld. near the Std. side on which is 5 Lodges of nativs drying fish at 8 miles passed an Island close to the Lard Shore 6 miles long opposit the Lower point of this long Island is a Smal Island on which is 5 Lodies deserted at present. passed a Stard point at 4 miles.

S 80° W.   7   miles to a point of rocks in a Stard. Bend passed the Island near the Stard. Side at 1 mile (passed a verry bad rapid) above the Expiration of the Course passed rapid 2 miles long with Sevl. Small Islands in it low lands on Lard Side, See 2 mountains S W. & W. Covered with Snow. This rapid has large banks of Muscle Shells.

S 70° W.   12   Miles to a Small Island on the Lard Side at some willows passed 20 Lodges of Indians drying fish Scattered on the Stard. Bank in a vally. haveing passed the high

Countrey on the Stard. at ½ a mile. passed a Small rapid at 11 miles.

S. 45° W.   3
             56

Miles to Some willow trees below an Island close under the Lard. Side, opposit to 24 Lodges of nativs drying fish on the Stard. Side and on a Small Island in the middle of the river. Countrey low on each Side. This nation above was much allarmed at our approach. we encamped on the Lard. Side.

20th October 1805

West   6

Miles to a Stard. bend at the head of a rapid   passed 3 Indian Lodges on Lard. deserted.

S. 20° W.   10

Miles to a Lard. bend opposit a large Island on the Stard. Side   passed rocky bad rapid with a chain of rocks from the Stard Side, & Several Small Islands near the Lard. side   Great number of Pelicans at this rapid and black comerant 4 Lodges of Indians fishing on an Island close to the Stard. Side.

S 60° W.   8

Miles to the Comencement of a high land on the Stard. Side.   passed 3 Islands nearly opposit to each other 2 on the Stard. large one on the Lard Small 17 Lodges of Indians fishing on those 3 Islands, a vault at the upper point of the 1st. Island.   passed a bad rapid at the lower point of a Small Island at 7½ miles on which 4 Lodges of nativs drying fish.

S. 45° W.   18
             42

Miles to a point of highland in the Std. bend   passed a large Island in the middle of the river at 8 miles below which we passed a Lard. point 5 Small Islands on the lard. and 5 on the Stard. Sides, and one Small one in the middle of the river at 16 miles.   passed a Small rapid.

21st October 1805

South   3

Miles to a Larboard bend of high land.

S. 55° W.   17

Miles to a Lard Bend below a rapid and high ruged rocks.   passed a Small Island at 2½ miles; one at 4 miles in the middle of the river below Some Swift water 8 Lodges of Indians on the Stard Side drying fish.   (we Brackfast &c.)   passed a rapid at 10 miles below a Stard pt. 2 Lodges on Std.   passed 5 Lodges of nativs drying fish on the Stard Side above the lower rapid, opsd. Som rocks out in the river from both sides.

N. 45° W.   4   Miles to a Stard. Bend passing the lower point of an Is-land at 1 mile 2 Lodges of nativs on the Stard Shore dry-ing fish.   the rocks on the Lard. appear to have Sliped into the river from the Clifts—   at 2 miles passed a very bad rockey rapid dificuelt and Crooked, eminc rocks in it 2 Lodges of nativs below on the Stard. Side. Some fiew low pine on the tops of the hills.

S 60° W.   5   Miles to be the Stard. Bend   passed many rugid black rocks in different parts of the river.   a bad rapid at 2 miles, the river narrow at the expiration of this course

river ☞   a river falls in on the Lard Side R de page 40 yards wide. Islands of rocks in every direction

S. 52° W.   13   Miles to the upper point of a rock Isld. 80 feet high at a rapid passed the little river rapid and through narrow Chanels between hugh large rocks.   4 Lodges of Inds. on Stard. Side opposit (Encamped at) 5 Lodges of In-dians below a Small Island four miles below the little river [12]   at 10 miles passed rapid large rocks nearly across the river.   6 Lodges of Indians drying fish on the Std. Side   at 12 miles passed a bad rapid.   5 Lodges of nativs on Std. 20 Stacks of fish and Inds. gigging

22nd October 1805

S. 30° W.   3   Miles to the Mouth of *To war ne hi ooks*[13] River in a Lard Bend 200 yards wide and very rapid and contains a great qty of water rapid ¼ of a mile up this river which is three long 3 Sand Islands in the mouth of this river

144   Miles From *Lewis's river*[14]

West   4   Miles to a bend on the Stard Side   passed the rock Is-land at 2 miles 8 Lodges on its Lower point, at 3 miles 10 Lodges on the Stard. Main Shore   at the end of this course is 6 Lodges of nativs opposit is the lower point of a large Island near the Lard Side from the mouth of [*blank*]

S. 45° W.   2   Miles to a point of Sand on the Stard. side opposit to the center of the great Falls   passed 17 Lodges scattered on

The Stard Bank (Portage of 1200 yards on the Stard Side over rock & sand)

Falls	6	Miles from *Clarks River*

24th October 1805

West   2   Miles passing a Lard. Point of Sand, and a Stard. point. 3 lodges above a Deep bend to the Stard. to a point of high rocks at the enterance of a narrow Chanel. Lodges on the Stard Side at the foot of the rock

S. 70° W.   2   Miles to a rock Island in the middle of the river at a bad rapid, passed through the little narrows ¼ of a mile long & 45 yards wide, bad whorly boils & Sucks. a Lodge below where the river widens to about 200 yds

S. 50° W.   2   Miles to a high rugid rock at the mouth of the Great narrows a Deep bend to the Stard. Side on which is a village of 21 worm comfortable houes Passed a large rock in the middle of the river

Grt. Narrows   6   Miles from the Great *Falls*

25th October 1805

S. 34° W.   3   Miles through a Narrow Swift bad Chanel from 50 to 100 yards in width, one verry bad place in this Chanel at ½ mile maney bad whorls and Sucks, a rock which Seperates The Chanel at 2½ miles the Current running aginst the upper point, to the enterance of a Deep bend to the Stard. Side (made a portage of ½ a mile below the 1st bad place in the Chanel) one of the Canoes filled, and afterwards run against a rock in the Chanel.

S. 20° W.   2   Miles to a high rock on the Lard Side passed through a narrow Chanel on The Stard. of a large rock which divides the Chanel at 1 mile. (Saw a Chief)

N. 60° W.   1   Mile to a high rock in a Stard. Bend passed a Deep bason on the Lard Side and between rugid rocks. Still water

S. 60° W.   4
              10   Miles to the mouth of a large Creek in the Lard Bend, a high point of rocks (on which we Camped) and near Some Timbered bottom of white oake and pine river ½ a mile wide and Current jintle.

N. 50° W.	2	Miles to a nitch in the Lard. Bend a Clift of rocks on each Side about 90 feet high on which there is Some fiew pine.
N. 10° W.	2	Miles to the *Chel-luck-it-te-quar* Village of Eight houes on the Stard Side under Some high rocks, a Small Creek falls in on the Lard Side.
North	1	Mile to a rock island on the Stard Side opposit to which the wind obliged us to come to the Lard. side is a nitch above a point of high rocks where we Stayed all night. rained &c. &c.

N. 55° W.	4	Miles to a Lard point passed a Brook on Lard.
West	8	Miles to a rock Island near the middle of the river at 1 mile is a friendly Village of 7 houses of the *Chil luck it te quar* Nation and the residance of their great Chief— at
Cataract river ☞		5 miles passed the mouth of a River which we call Cataract river 60 yards wide on the Std. side below the mouth of which is a Village of 11 houses of the *Chil luck it te quar* nation
S. 60° W.	5	Miles to a rock Island in a Lard Bend, passd. 2 rocks in the river passed 2 houses on the Std. side at 1 mile; and 2 houses at 4 miles on the Stard. Side.
S. 80° W. river ☞	6	Miles to 4 houses in a point of Timber bottom on the lard. Side above the enterance of a ⟨large⟩ river 40 yard wide we call river La biache a bottom on the Stard. Side in which there is scattered on the bank 14 Houses of Indians (The falls mountain covered with Snow is South)
S. 70° W.	6	Miles to a high clift of rocks in a in Stard. bend passing a large Sand bar from the Lard. for 4 miles. a large Creek 28 yards wide at 1 mile I call Canoe Creek, a butifull Spring below. A Small Stream fall over rocks of 100 feet Lard Side. at 5 miles passed 4 Indian Houses in a bottom on the Lard Side.
S. 56° W.	6	Miles to a point of a timbered bottom on the lard. Side.

passed a Stard. point at 2 miles, here the mountains are high and those on the Lard. has Snow on them.   at 3 miles is 3 houses of Indians on the Star Side (where we Encamped)

30th of October 1805

S 70° W.	3	Miles to a point of rocks on the Stard. Side passed a number of Stumps at Some distance in the water current Still 1 mile pr. hour
S. 74° W.	2	Miles to a point of a timbered bottom on the Stard. Side. Stumps & rocks out in the water
West	4	Mile to the mouth of a river on the Std. side about 60 yards wide maney large rocks promiscuisly in the river both above and below a large Sand bar in the middle of
river ☞		the river. This river we Call Cruzats River.[15]
S. 45° W.	2	Miles to a large rock in the river passed Several rocks and a large Sand bar out in the river. High mountains on each side rough and covered with a very thick groth of Pine Cedar Cotton & Oake
S. 30° W.	4	Miles to a Small Island in the head of the grand Shoote near the Stard. Side (on which we Encamped) passed maney large rocks in the river at 2½ miles passed a large Creek on the Stard. Side with a Small Island in the mouth passed on the inner side of 3 Islands near the Stard. Side a little below the Creek. one Island on the Lard Side above. at 3¾ miles is 8 large worm houses on the Stard Side back of which is houses of [*blank*] Nation

Gt. Shoots 65 Miles

1st November 1805

S. 30d E	1	Mile to a Lard Bend passed the Grand Shoote which is ¼ of a mile long the water confined with in 150 yds. passing over imince Stones with tremendious force & low mountain Slipping in on the Stard Side high on the Lard Side great numbers of Sea otters.
S 30° W.	1	Mile to a Lard Bend passing Several rocks in the river. a verry bad rapid at ¾ of a mile the water being confined between large rocks maney of which is just under

379

water, opposit to this rapid on an ellivated Situation Stard. near a pond in an Old Village of 8 large houses partly taken down and avacuated.

S. 45° W. 2   Miles to a high rock the upper point of a large Island near the Lard Shore passed many large rocks against which the water passed with great force at 1 miles passed a house on the Stard. Side a little below the end of the portage a Short distance. below this house is 8 *vaults* also on the Stard. Side.

S 68d W. <u>3</u>   Miles to a large black rock in a Std. Bend at the foot of a sast rapid opposit the lower end of the Island on the Lard. Side, passing a village of 4 large houses at 1 ½ miles an extensive Stoney bottom on the Stard. Side, the mounts. on the Lard Side high and ruged. passing maney large rocks against which the water beats with great force.

Last rapid <u>7</u>   Miles from the *Grand Shute*.

1. Again, probably a seal rather than a sea otter; see above, October 23, 1805.

2. Camp was in Skamania County, Washington, above Bonneville Dam and near the present communities of Fort Rains and North Bonneville. The area of the "Great Rapids" is shown on Clark's detailed sketch map (fig. 28) in Codex H, p. 4, and on a nearly identical version (fig. 29) in Voorhis No. 4. *Atlas* maps 79, 88.

3. On this page and part of the preceding page in the Elkskin-bound Journal is a sketch map (fig. 14 above). The text was apparently added later as the words are worked in around the map to some degree. See note at entry of October 18, 1805.

4. Fig. 27, showing the door shape, appears at this point in the text of the Elkskin-bound Journal.

5. This list is inserted at the top and bottom of the page in the Elkskin-bound Journal, upside down to the rest of the text. The heading is written over "S. 55° W."

6. Clark's astronomical table inserted here in Codex H, p. 93, was probably copied from the Elkskin-bound Journal; no significant differences are apparent and it is not printed here.

7. "Cha-pel-el" is the Chinookan term *a-sáblal*, "bread" (etymology obscure); the term in Chinook jargon is *saplíl*. It is cous, *Lomatium cous* (Wats.) Coult. & Rose, then new to science. It was an important foodstuff in this region and eastward. On the return trip in 1806 cous would also become a useful food source for the party. Cutright (LCPN), 283–84, 288–89, 370, 373; Hitchcock et al., 3 : 548–49.

8. A vertical line is drawn through this passage about the roots, perhaps by Biddle, but not in his usual red ink.

9. Three-quarters of the page in Codex H, p. 97, is blank following this entry.

10. See note at October 18, 1805. The words "Lewis's River" appear to have been substituted for some erased words.

11. The numeral "20″" to the side of this course represents the mileage accumulation for October 18.

12. Coues underlined the words "Encamped at" above and he has marked off the passage at this point and labeled it "Oct. 22d." He also has written, "only 4 miles of this course on Oct. 21, making 33 miles altogether." All the writing was done in pencil. Coues is correct; see n. 1 at entry of October 21, 1805. The number "140″" to the side of this course is an accumulative figure to this point.

13. The name appears to have been added to a blank space as does the term "*Clarks*" below. They are both the same stream, today's Deschutes River. See above, October 22.

14. The total of "144" is incorrect based on calculating Clark's figures as given here. The word "Lewis's" appears to have been substituted for some erased words.

15. "Cruzats" appears to have been substituted for some erased words.

Volume 5

Sources Cited

Alexander Alexander, James M., III. "Archaeological Test Excavations at 45BN184, Plymouth Park, Benton County, Washington." Washington State University, Washington Archaeological Research Center, Project Report No. 26. Pullman, 1976.

Allen (PG) Allen, John L. *Passage Through the Garden: Lewis and Clark and the Image of the American Northwest.* Urbana: University of Illinois Press, 1975.

Ames Ames, Kenneth M. "A Prehistory of the Clearwater Drainage and Adjacent Portions of the Columbia Plateau." Idaho State Historical Society, Boise, 1980.

Ames & Marshall Ames, Kenneth M., and Alan G. Marshall. "Villages, Demography, and Subsistence Intensification on the Southern Columbia Plateau." *North American Archaeologist* 2 (1980): 25–52.

Aoki Aoki, Haruo. "What Does 'Chopunnish' Mean?" *Idaho Yesterdays* 10 (Winter 1966–67): 10–11.

AOU American Ornithologists' Union. *Check-list of North American Birds.* 6th ed. Baltimore, Md.: American Ornithologists' Union, 1983. [AOU] in brackets with numbers refers to a species item-number in the book.

Appleman (LC) Appleman, Roy E. *Lewis and Clark: Historic Places Associated with Their Transcontinental Exploration (1804–06).* Washington, D.C.: United States Department of the Interior, National Park Service, 1975.

Atlas Moulton, Gary E., ed. *Atlas of the Lewis and Clark Expedition*. Lincoln: University of Nebraska Press, 1983.

Bailey Bailey, L. H. *Manual of Cultivated Plants*. Rev. ed. New York: Macmillan, 1949.

Bakeless (LCPD) Bakeless, John. *Lewis and Clark, Partners in Discovery*. New York: William Morrow, 1947.

Beckham Beckham, Stephen Dow. "'This Place is Romantic and Wild': An Historical Overview of the Cascades Area, Fort Cascades, and the Cascades Townsite, Washington Territory." Report to Portland District U.S. Army Corps of Engineers, Heritage Research Associates Report No. 27. Eugene, 1984.

Benson (HLCE) Benson, Keith R. "Herpetology on the Lewis and Clark Expedition: 1804–1806." *Herpetological Review* 3 (1978): 87–91.

Benson (CUSC) Benson, Lyman. *The Cacti of the United States and Canada*. Stanford, Calif.: Stanford University Press, 1982.

Biddle (BR) Biddle, Henry J. "Beacon Rock on the Columbia: Legends and Traditions of a Famous Landmark." *WPO Publication* No. 3 (July 1978).

Booth & Wright Booth, W. E., and J. C. Wright. *Flora of Montana, Part II*. Bozeman: Montana State University, 1959.

Borror, Delong, & Triplehorn Borror, D. J., D. M. Delong, and C. A. Triplehorn. *An Introduction to the Study of Insects*. 4th ed. New York: Holt, Rinehart, and Winston, 1976.

Brauner Brauner, David Ray. "Alpowai: The Culture History of the Alpowa Locality." Ph.D. diss., Washington State University, 1976.

Burroughs Burroughs, Raymond Darwin. *The Natural History of the Lewis and Clark Expedition*. East Lansing: Michigan State University Press, 1961.

Butler (ALCV) Butler, B. Robert. "Art of the Lower Columbia Valley." *Archaeology* 10 (September 1957): 158–65.

Butler (WM)	———. "The Physical Stratigraphy of Wakemap Mound: A New Interpretation." M.A. thesis, University of Washington, 1960.
Caldwell	Caldwell, Warren W. "The Archaeology of Wakemap Mound: A Stratified Site near The Dalles on the Columbia River." Ph.D. diss., University of Washington, 1956.
Chamberlain	Chamberlain, Alexander F. "Algonkian Words in American English: A Study in the Contact of the White Man and the Indian." *Journal of American Folk-Lore* 15 (October-December 1902): 240–67.
Chance & Chance	Chance, David H., and Jennifer V. Chance. "Archaeology at Spaulding, 1978 and 1979." University of Idaho, Anthropological Report No. 85. Moscow, 1985.
Chatters (LCEM)	Chatters, Roy M. "The Discovery of a Lewis and Clark Expedition Medal: A Personal Recollection." *Bunchgrass Historian* 10 (Summer 1982): 3.
Chuinard (OOMD)	Chuinard, Eldon G. *Only One Man Died: The Medical Aspects of the Lewis and Clark Expedition.* Glendale, Calif.: Arthur H. Clark, 1979
Clark	Clark, William P. *The Indian Sign Language.* 1885. Reprint. Lincoln: University of Nebraska Press, 1982.
Clemens & Wilby	Clemens, W. A., and G. V. Wilby. *Fishes of the Pacific Coast of Canada.* Bulletin 68 (rev.). Ottawa: Fisheries Research Board of Canada, 1949.
Cleveland et al.	Cleveland, Gregory, Bruce Cochran, Judith Giniger, and Hallett Hammatt. "Archaeological Reconnaissance on the Mid Columbia and Lower Snake River Reservoirs for the Walla Walla District Army Corps of Engineers." Washington State University, Washington Archaeological Research Center, Project Report No. 27. Pullman, 1976.
Cole	Cole, David L. "Archaeological Research in the Bonneville Dam Pool." University of Oregon

	Museum of Natural History, Report to the National Park Service. Eugene, 1974.
Coues (HLC)	Coues, Elliott, ed. *History of the Expedition under the Command of Lewis and Clark. . . .* 1893. Reprint. 3 vols. New York: Dover Publications, 1965.
Cressman et al.	Cressman, Luther S., David L. Cole, Wilbur A. Davis, Thomas M. Newman, and Daniel J. Scheans. "Cultural Sequences at The Dalles, Oregon: A Contribution to the Pacific Northwest Prehistory." *Transactions of the American Philosophical Society*, n.s., 50, pt. 10 (December 1960): 1–108.
Criswell	Criswell, Elijah Harry. *Lewis and Clark: Linguistic Pioneers*. University of Missouri Studies, vol. 15, no. 2. Columbia: University of Missouri Press, 1940.
Crosby	Crosby, Alfred W. *The Columbian Exchange: Biological and Cultural Consequences of 1492*. Westport, Conn.: Greenwood Publishing, 1972.
Curtis	Curtis, Edward S. *The North American Indian*. Edited by Frederick W. Hodge. 20 vols. Cambridge: The University Press (vols. 1–5); Norwood, Mass.: Plimpton Press (vols. 6–20), 1907–30.
Cutright (HLCJ)	Cutright, Paul Russell. *A History of the Lewis and Clark Journals*. Norman: University of Oklahoma Press, 1976.
Cutright (LCIPM)	———. "Lewis and Clark Indian Peace Medals." *Bulletin of the Missouri Historical Society* 24 (January 1968): 160–67.
Cutright (LCPN)	———. *Lewis and Clark: Pioneering Naturalists*. Urbana: University of Illinois Press, 1969.
Cutright (LCPP)	———. "Lewis and Clark: Portraits and Portraitists." *Montana, the Magazine of Western History* 19 (Spring 1969): 37–53.
Daubenmire	Daubenmire, Rexford. "Forest Vegetation of Northern Idaho and Adjacent Washington, and its Bearing on Concepts of Vegetation Classification." *Ecological Monographs* 22 (October 1952): 301–30.

Daugherty   Daugherty, Richard D. "Excavations in the Ice Harbor Reservoir, 1957–1960: A Preliminary Report." Washington State University Laboratory of Anthropology, Report of Investigations No. 10. Pullman, 1961.

Dumond & Minor   Dumond, Don E., and Rick Minor. "Archaeology in the John Day Reservoir, The Wildcat Canyon Site, 35-GM-9." University of Oregon Anthropological Papers No. 30. Eugene, 1983.

Duncan   Duncan, Mary Ann. "Archaeological Assessment of the Proposed Horsethief Lake Interpretive Facility." University of Washington, Office of Public Archaeology, Institute for Environmental Studies, Reconnaissance Report No. 25. Seattle, 1979.

Dunnell   Dunnell, Robert C. "A Note on Archaeological Sites Mentioned by Lewis and Clark in the North Bonneville Area, Washington." *Northwest Anthropological Research Notes* 13 (Fall 1979): 201–7.

Dunnell & Campbell   Dunnell, Robert C., and Sarah K. Campbell. "History of Aboriginal Occupation of Hamilton Island, Washington." University of Washington, Department of Anthropology, Reports in Archaeology No. 4. Seattle, 1977.

Dunnell & Whitlam   Dunnell, Robert C., and Robert G. Whitlam. "Test Excavations and Mitigation Plan for 45-SA-11, Skamania County, Washington." Report of the Department of Anthropology, University of Washington, to the National Park Service. Seattle, 1977.

Ewers (ILUM)   Ewers, John C. *Indian Life on the Upper Missouri.* Norman: University of Oklahoma Press, 1968.

Fahey   Fahey, John. *The Flathead Indians.* Norman: University of Oklahoma Press, 1974.

Fryxell & Daugherty   Fryxell, Roald, and Richard D. Daugherty. "Interim Report: Archaeological Salvage in the Lower Monumental Reservoir, Washington, 1962." Washington State University Laboratory of Archaeology and Geo-chronology, Report of Investigations No. 21. Pullman, 1962.

Galm et al.   Galm, Jerry R., Glenn D. Hartmann, Ruth A. Masten, and Garry Owen Stephenson. "A Cultural Resources Overview of Bonneville Power Administration's Mid-Columbia Project, Central Washington." Eastern Washington University Reports in Archaeology and History, Archaeological and Historical Services, Report No. 100–16. Cheney, 1981.

Garth   Garth, Thomas R. "The Middle Columbia Cremation Complex." *American Antiquity* 18 (July 1952): 40–56.

Gilmore (UPI)   Gilmore, Melvin R. *Uses of Plants by the Indians of the Missouri River Region.* 1919. Reprint. Lincoln: University of Nebraska Press, 1977.

Glover   Glover, Richard, ed. *David Thompson's Narrative, 1784–1812.* Toronto: Champlain Society, 1962.

Goodspeed   Goodspeed, Thomas H. *The Genus Nicotiana: Origins, Relationships, and Evolution of its Species in Light of their Distribution, Morphology, and Cytogenetics.* Waltham, Mass.: Chronica Botanica, 1954.

Gunther   Gunther, Erna. *Ethnobotany of Western Washington: The Knowledge and Use of Indigenous Plants by Native Americans.* Rev. ed. Seattle: University of Washington Press, 1973.

Hahn   Hahn, Barton E. *Flora of Montana: Conifers and Monocots.* Bozeman: Montana State University, 1977.

Hanson (PB)   Hanson, Charles E. "The Point Blanket." *The Museum of the Fur Trade Quarterly* 12 (Spring 1976): 5–10.

Harris   Harris, Burton. *John Colter: His Years in the Rockies.* New York: Charles Scribner's Sons, 1952.

Harwood & James   Harwood, Robert F., and Maurice T. James. *Entomology in Human and Animal Health.* 7th ed. New York: Macmillan, 1976.

Hitchcock et al.   Hitchcock, C. Leo, Arthur Cronquist, Marion Ownbey, and J. W. Thompson. *Vascular Plants*

	of the Pacific Northwest. 5 vols. Seattle: University of Washington Press, 1955–69.
Hodge	Hodge, Frederick Webb, ed. *Handbook of American Indians North of Mexico.* 1912. Reprint. 2 vols. St. Clair Shores, Mich.: Scholarly Press, 1968.
Holmgren	Holmgren, Virginia C. "A Glossary of Bird Names Cited by Lewis and Clark." *We Proceeded On* 10 (May 1984): 28–34.
Hyde (IHP)	Hyde, George E. *Indians of the High Plains: From the Prehistoric Period to the Coming of the Europeans.* Norman: University of Oklahoma Press, 1959.
Jackson (LLC)	Jackson, Donald, ed. *Letters of the Lewis and Clark Expedition with Related Documents, 1783–1854.* 2d ed. 2 vols. Urbana: University of Illinois Press, 1978.
James	James, Thomas. *Three Years Among the Indians and Mexicans.* Edited by Milo M. Quaife. New York: Citadel Press, 1967.
Jefferson	Jefferson, Thomas. *Notes on the State of Virginia.* Edited by William Peden. Chapel Hill: University of North Carolina Press, 1955.
Jones et al.	Jones, J. Knox, Jr., David H. Armstrong, Robert S. Hoffmann, and Clyde Jones. *Mammals of the Northern Great Plains.* Lincoln: University of Nebraska Press, 1983.
Josephy (NNP)	Josephy, Alvin M., Jr. "The Naming of the Nez Perces." *Montana, the Magazine of Western History* 5 (Autumn 1955): 1–18.
Josephy (NP)	———. *The Nez Perce Indians and the Opening of the Northwest.* New Haven: Yale University Press, 1965.
Kartesz & Kartesz	Kartesz, John T., and Rosemarie Kartesz. *A Synonymized Checklist of the Vascular Flora of the United States, Canada, and Greenland.* Chapel Hill: University of North Carolina Press, 1980.
Küchler	Küchler, A. W. *Potential Natural Vegetation of the Conterminous United States.* New York: American Geographical Society, 1964.

Lee et al.   Lee, David S., Carter R. Gilbert, Charles H. Hocutt, Robert E. Jenkins, Don E. McAllister, and Jay R. Stauffer, Jr. *Atlas of North American Freshwater Fishes*. Raleigh: North Carolina State Museum of Natural History, 1980.

Lewis (TCV)   Lewis, Albert Buell. "Tribes of the Columbia Valley and the Coast of Washington and Oregon." *Memoirs of the American Anthropological Association* 1 (1906): 147–209.

Little (CIH)   Little, Elbert L., Jr. *Atlas of United States Trees*. Vol. 1, *Conifers and Important Hardwoods*. Washington, D.C.: United States Department of Agriculture, Forest Service, 1971.

Little (MWH)   ———. *Atlas of United States Trees*. Vol. 3, *Minor Western Hardwoods*. Washington, D.C.: United States Department of Agriculture, Forest Service, 1976.

Lowie (IP)   Lowie, Robert H. *Indians of the Plains*. 1954. Reprint. Lincoln: University of Nebraska Press, 1982.

Lowie (NS)   ———. *The Northern Shoshone*. Anthropological Papers of the American Museum of Natural History, vol. 2, part 2. New York: American Museum of Natural History, 1909.

Madsen   Madsen, Brigham D. *The Bannock of Idaho*. Caldwell, Idaho: Caxton Printers, 1958.

Majors (LCRM)   Majors, Harry M. "Lewis and Clark Enter the Rocky Mountains." *Northwest Discovery* 7 (April and May 1986): 4–120.

Marshall   Marshall, Alan G. "Nez Perce Social Groups, an Ecological Interpretation." Ph.D. diss., Washington State University, 1977.

Mattson   Mattson, Daniel M. "Cultural Resource Investigations of the Dworshak Reservoir Project, North Fork Clearwater River, Northern Idaho." University of Idaho, Anthropological Research Manuscript Series No. 81. Moscow, 1983.

Meinig   Meinig, Donald W. *The Great Columbian Plain: A Historical Geography, 1805–1910*. Seattle: University of Washington Press, 1968.

Minor | Minor, Rick. "Archaeological Testing at 45SA16, Skamania County, Washington." Report to Portland District U.S. Army Corps of Engineers, Heritage Research Associates Report No. 33. Eugene, 1984.

Minor, Toepel, & Beckham | Minor, Rick, Kathryn Anne Toepel, and Stephen Dow Beckham. "An Overview of Investigations at 45SA11: Archaeology in the Columbia River Gorge." Report to Portland District U.S. Army Corps of Engineers, Heritage Research Associates Report No. 39. Eugene, 1986.

Mueggler & Stewart | Mueggler, Walter F., and William L. Stewart. "Grassland and Shrubland of Western Montana." United States Department of Agriculture, Forest Service, General Technical Report INT-66. Ogden, Utah, 1980.

Murdock | Murdock, George Peter. "Notes on the Tenino, Molala, and Paiute of Oregon." *American Anthropologist*, n.s., 40 (July-September 1938): 395–402.

Nance | Nance, Charles R. "45WT2: An Archaeological Site on the Lower Snake River." M.A. thesis, Washington State University, 1966.

Nelson (LMLG) | Nelson, Charles M. "Archaeological Reconnaissance in the Lower Monumental and Little Goose Dam Reservoir Areas, 1964." Washington State University Laboratory of Anthropology, Report of Investigations No. 34. Pullman, 1965.

Oglesby | Oglesby, Richard Edward. *Manuel Lisa and the Opening of the Missouri Fur Trade*. Norman: University of Oklahoma Press, 1963.

Osborne | Osborne, Douglas. *Excavations in the McNary Reservoir Basin near Umatilla, Oregon*. Bureau of American Ethnology, Bulletin 166. Washington, D.C.: Government Printing Office, 1957.

Osborne, Bryan, & Crabtree | Osborne, Douglas, Alan Bryan, and Robert H. Crabtree. "The Sheep Island Site and the Mid-Columbia Valley." Bureau of American Ethnology, Bulletin 179, River Basin Surveys

	Papers No. 24, 267–306. Washington, D.C.: Government Printing Office, 1961.
Osborne & Crabtree	Osborne, Douglas, and Robert H. Crabtree. "Two Sites in the Upper McNary Reservoir." *Tebiwa* 4 (Fall 1961): 19–36.
Peebles (LT)	Peebles, John J. "On the Lolo Trail: Route and Campsites of Lewis and Clark." *Idaho Yesterdays* 9 (Winter 1965–66): 2–15.
Peebles (RW)	———. "Rugged Waters: Trails and Campsites of Lewis and Clark in the Salmon River Country." *Idaho Yesterdays* 8 (Summer 1964): 2–17.
Pennak	Pennak, Robert W. *Fresh-water Invertebrates of the United States.* New York: Ronald Press, 1953.
Pfister et al.	Pfister, Robert D., Bernard L. Kovalchik, Stephan F. Arno, and Richard C. Presby. "Forest Habitat Types of Montana." United States Department of Agriculture, Forest Service, General Technical Report INT-34. Ogden, Utah, 1977.
Phebus	Phebus, George E. "The Smithsonian Institution 1934 Bonneville Reservoir Salvage Archaeology Project." *Northwest Anthropological Research Notes* 12 (Fall 1978): 113–77.
Prucha (IPM)	Prucha, Francis Paul. *Indian Peace Medals in American History.* Lincoln: University of Nebraska Press, 1971.
Ray (CI)	Ray, Verne F. "The Chinook Indians in the Early 1800s." In *The Western Shore: Oregon Country Essays Honoring the American Revolution,* edited by Thomas Vaughan, 121–50. Portland, Oreg.: American Revolution Bicentennial Commission of Oregon, 1975.
Ray (NVCB)	———. "Native Villages and Groupings of the Columbia Basin." *Pacific Northwest Quarterly* 27 (April 1936): 99–152.
Ray & Lurie	Ray, Verne F., and Nancy Oestreich Lurie. "The Contributions of Lewis and Clark to Ethnography." *Journal of the Washington Academy of Sciences* 44 (November 1954): 358–70.
Rees	Rees, John E. "The Shoshoni Contribution to

Lewis and Clark." *Idaho Yesterdays* 2 (Summer 1958): 2–13.

Rhodes   Rhodes, Richard A. *Eastern Ojibwa-Chippewa-Ottawa Dictionary.* Berlin: Mouton, 1985.

Rice (CSWC)   Rice, Harvey S. "The Cultural Sequence at Windust Caves." M.A. thesis, Washington State University, 1965.

Rice (NAD)   ———. "Native American Dwellings and Attendant Structures of the Southern Plateau." Eastern Washington University Reports in Archaeology and History, Archaeological and Historical Services, Report No. 100–44. Cheney, 1985.

Rodeffer   Rodeffer, Michael J. "A Classification of Burials in the Lower Snake River Region." *Northwest Anthropological Research Notes* 7 (Spring 1973): 101–31.

Ronda (LCAI)   Ronda, James P. *Lewis and Clark among the Indians.* Lincoln: University of Nebraska Press, 1984.

Ross   Ross, Alexander. *Adventures of the First Settlers on the Oregon or Columbia River.* Edited by Milo Milton Quaife. Chicago: R. R. Donnelly and Sons, 1923.

Ruby & Brown (CIIT)   Ruby, Robert H., and John A. Brown. *The Cayuse Indians: Imperial Tribesmen of Old Oregon.* Norman: University of Oklahoma Press, 1972.

Ruby & Brown (CITC)   ———. *The Chinook Indians: Traders of the Lower Columbia River.* Norman: University of Oklahoma Press, 1976.

Russell (GEF)   Russell, Carl P. *Guns on the Early Frontiers: A History of Firearms from Colonial Times through the Years of the Western Fur Trade.* Berkeley: University of California Press, 1962.

Sapir   Sapir, Edward. "Preliminary Report on the Language and Mythology of the Upper Chinook." *American Anthropologist,* n.s., 9 (July-September 1907): 533–44.

Schalk   Schalk, Randall F., ed. "Cultural Resource Investigations for the Lyons Ferry Fish Hatchery

Project, near Lyons Ferry, Washington." Washington State University Laboratory of Archaeology and History, Project Report No. 8. Pullman, 1983.

Schwede   Schwede, Madge L. "An Ecological Study of Nez Perce Settlement Patterns." M.A. thesis, Washington State University, 1966.

Seaman   Seaman, Norma G. *Indian Relics of the Pacific Northwest*. Portland, Oreg.: Binfords and Mort, 1967.

Secoy   Secoy, Frank Raymond. *Changing Military Patterns on the Great Plains (17th Century through Early 19th Century)*. Monographs of the American Ethnological Society, no. 21. Locust Valley, N.Y.: J. J. Augustin, 1953.

Shiner   Shiner, Joel L. "The McNary Reservoir: A Study in Plateau Archaeology." Bureau of American Ethnology, Bulletin 179, River Basin Surveys Papers No. 23, 149–266. Washington, D.C.: Government Printing Office, 1961.

Space   Space, Ralph S. *The Lolo Trail: A History of Events Connected with the Lolo Trail Since Lewis and Clark*. Lewiston, Idaho: Printcraft Printing, 1970.

Spier   Spier, Leslie. "Tribal Distribution in Washington." General Series in Anthropology, No. 3. Menasha, Wis.: George Banta, 1936.

Spier & Sapir   Spier, Leslie, and Edward Sapir. "Wishram Ethnology." University of Washington Publications in Anthropology, Vol. 3, No. 3, 151–300. Seattle: University of Washington Press, 1930.

Spinden   Spinden, Herbert Joseph. "The Nez Percé Indians." *Memoirs of the American Anthropological Association* 2 (1908): 165–274.

Sprague (ABP)   Sprague, Roderick. "Aboriginal Burial Practices in the Plateau Region of North America." Ph.D. diss., University of Arizona, 1967.

Sprague (PBS)   ———. "The Descriptive Archaeology of the

Palus Burial Site, Lyons Ferry, Washington." Washington State University Laboratory of Anthropology, Report of Investigations No. 32. Pullman, 1965.

Sprague & Birkby   Sprague, Roderick, and Walter H. Birkby. "Miscellaneous Columbia Plateau Burials." *Tebiwa* 13 (Spring 1970): 1–32.

Strong (SACR)   Strong, Emory. *Stone Age on the Columbia River*. Portland, Oreg.: Binfords and Mort, 1959.

Strong, Schenck, & Steward   Strong, William Duncan, W. Egbert Schenck, and Julian H. Steward. "Archaeology of The Dalles-Deschutes Region." University of California Publications in American Archaeology and Ethnology, Vol. 29, No. 1, 1–154. Berkeley, 1930.

Swanson   Swanson, Earl H., ed. *Languages and Cultures of Western North America: Essays in Honor of Sven S. Liljeblad*. Caldwell, Idaho: Caxton Printers, 1970.

Terrell   Terrell, John U. *Traders of the Western Morning: Aboriginal Commerce in Precolumbian North America*. Los Angeles: Southwest Museum, 1967.

Thompson (WC)   Thompson, Robert S. "Paleoenvironmental Investigations at Seed Cave (Windust Cave H-45FR46), Franklin County, Washington." Eastern Washington University Reports in Archaeology and History, Archaeological and Historical Services, Report No. 100–41. Cheney, 1985.

Thwaites (LC)   Thwaites, Reuben, Gold, ed. *Original Journals of the Lewis and Clark Expedition, 1804–1806*. 8 vols. New York: Dodd, Mead, 1904–5.

Toups   Toups, Polly A. "The Early Prehistory of the Clearwater Valley, North-Central Idaho." Ph.D. diss., Tulane University, 1969.

Trafzer & Scheuerman   Trafzer, Clifford E., and Richard D. Scheuerman. *Renegade Tribe: The Palouse Indians and the Invasion of the Inland Pacific Northwest*. Pullman: Washington State University Press, 1986.

Trenholm & Carley — Trenholm, Virginia C., and Maurine Carley. *The Shoshonis: Sentinels of the Rockies*. Norman: University of Oklahoma Press, 1964.

USGS — United States Geological Survey, 30′ × 60′ quadrangle, 1 : 100,000 planimetric maps.

Walker (NPA) — Walker, Deward E., Jr. *Conflict and Schism in Nez Perce Acculturation: A Study in Religion and Politics*. Pullman: Washington State University Press, 1968.

Wallace — Wallace, W. Stewart, ed. *Documents Relating to the North West Company*. Toronto: Champlain Society, 1934.

Wheeler — Wheeler, Olin D. *The Trail of Lewis and Clark, 1804–1806*. 2 vols. New York: G. P. Putnam's Sons, 1904.

Wilke et al. — Wilke, Steve, Rinita Dalan, James O. Wilde, Karen James, Robert M. Weaver, and David Harvey. "Cultural Resource Overview and Survey of Select parcels in the Dalles Reservoir, Oregon and Washington." Report to the Portland District U.S. Army Corps of Engineers, Geo-Recon International. Seattle, 1983.

Wolf — Wolf, James R. "Lewis and Clark: Pioneers on the Continental Divide Trail." *Dividends* 8 (July 1987): unpaged.

Index

Celilo (Great) Falls (*continued*)
365; maps of, 326n; navi-
gational problems, 331,
333; mentioned, 227,
228n, 230, 250, 318,
340n, 343, 345, 377
Celtis douglasii, 263n. *See also*
Hackberry, netleaf
Celtis reticulata, 263n. *See also*
Hackberry, netleaf
Centrocercus urophasianus, 76n.
See also Grouse, sage
Ceryle alcyon, 13n. *See also*
Kingfisher, belted
Chalcedony, 147n
Challis Volcanics, 141n, 148n
Charbonneau, Toussaint: returns, 17, 109, 143; in-
jured, 18; duties of, 24,
158; illness of, 42, 44; dis-
cipline, 93, 256, 345; in-
terpreter, 111, 122, 163;
information of, 165; men-
tioned, 14, 45, 52, 85n,
100, 113–14, 116n, 118,
120, 129, 131, 268, 304,
306
Chemise. *See* Clothes
Cherries, 261
Cherry, choke: as food, 81,
130, 137, 139, 156, 163;
and Indians, 142; ob-
served, 218, 241; men-
tioned, 86n, 224n
Chert, 147n
Chicken (dunghill fowl), 74,
76n, 129, 131
Chief Joseph Pass, 186n
Chimnapam Indians. *See* Yakima Indians
China Island, 233n
Chinookan Indians, 328n. *See
also* Languages, Indian,
Chinookan
Chinook trade jargon, 346n,
353n, 380n
Chippewa Indians, 122
Chopunnish Indians. *See* Nez
Perce Indians
Chronometer, 56, 237, 366
Chrysops sp., 58n. *See also* Fly,
deer
Cinchona, 14n. *See also* Medi-
cine, barks
Cirsium foliosum, 21n

Cirsium undulatum, 21n
Clark, William: journal-keep-
ing methods, 21–22n,
52n, 94n, 95n, 102n,
117n, 132n, 157n, 179n,
182n, 196n, 199n, 205n,
210n, 214n, 215n, 217n,
228n, 231n, 234n, 240n,
243n, 250n, 259n, 260n,
283n, 284n, 290–91n,
300n, 307n, 313n, 319n,
325n, 326n, 336n, 340n,
343n, 344n, 345n, 346n,
348n, 353n, 364n, 380n,
381n; injured, 162–63
Clark Fork (East Fork Clark's)
River: characteristics of,
192, 194, 196, 198n, 199,
230, 231n; mentioned,
185, 195n, 237
Clay, 10n, 18, 45, 52n, 63n,
78, 85n, 196n
Clearwater Mountains, 94n
Clearwater (Flathead, Kooskooskee) River: arrive at,
3, 228n; characteristics of,
4, 248, 256; conditions of,
233; name of, 248n; navi-
gational problems, 249–
51; mentioned, 131n, 197,
198n, 205n, 233–34n,
237, 240, 250n, 252n,
259–60n, 278, 287, 289,
319, 353n
Climate. *See* Weather conditions; Weather obser-
vations
Cloth, 89, 134, 226, 351, 361
Cloth, wiping, 230, 231n
Clothes: leggings, 8, 112,
117–19, 122, 127, 134,
139, 158, 259, 339; moccasins, 8–9, 78–80, 94n,
119, 122, 126, 133–34,
174, 198, 209, 259, 339;
making, 9, 11, 121; dressing skins for, 13, 121, 143,
288; hat, 68, 104, 346–47,
351, 371; shirt, 104, 112,
117–18, 122, 126–27,
139, 158, 187, 189, 231–
32, 259, 278, 286, 289,
309; coat, 112, 117–18;
shoes, 114; skins, 231,
272; collars, 122, 128,

134–35; chemise, 122,
134, 261; waistcoat, 123–
24; girdle, 126–27, 134;
breechcloth, 127; garter,
134; buttons, 149; belt,
189; jacket, 309, 317, 339,
347, 351; cap, 339; In-
dian, 122, 149, 319n,
341–42, 346–47, 351,
367, 371, 373; snowshoes,
259; as presents, 371;
mentioned, 115, 218, 243,
272, 313n. *See also* Beads;
Robes; Shells
Clouds. *See* Weather conditions
Clover, 58, 98, 116. *See also*
Thermopsis, mountain
Clover, longstalk, 60n
Coal Gulch, 186n
Coat. *See* Clothes
Cobbles, 17n, 86n
Cock, mountain. *See* Grouse,
sage
Cock, plains, or prairie. *See*
Grouse, sage
Codex journals: Codex Fa begins, 24; discussed, 29n,
51n, 86n, 102n, 117n,
141n, 146n, 147n, 157n,
174n, 195n, 196n, 198n,
199n, 210n, 214n, 231n,
240n, 245n, 248n, 260n,
263n, 290–91n, 300n,
307n, 325n, 326n, 328n,
336n, 340n, 344n, 346n,
364n, 380n, 381n; Codex
Fa ends, 44; Codex F
ends, 145; Codex Fb be-
gins, 148; Codex Fb ends,
173; Codex Fc begins,
191; Codex Fc ends, 197;
Codex Fd begins, 211;
Codex Fd ends, 229; Co-
dex G ends, 259; Codex
H begins, 261. *See also*
Voorhis journals
Colaptes auratus, 223n. *See also*
Flicker, northern
Colic. *See* Medical problems
Collars. *See* Clothes
Collins, John, 116n, 137–39,
141n, 224n, 235, 318
Colorado River, 90, 95n
Colter, John: duties of, 116n,